CW00705276

Edited and designed
by David Dew

Contributors

Richard Birch
Mark Boylan
James Burn
Dave Edwards
Richard Forristal

Dylan Hill
James Hill
Callum Jamieson
Paul Kealy
Andrew King

Steve Mason
Kevin Morley
Dave Orton
Brian Sheerin
Nick Watts

Cover artwork by Jay Vincent
Inside artwork by Nigel Jones and Stefan Searle

Published in 2017 by Racing Post Books, Raceform, 27 Kingfisher Court, Hambridge Road, Newbury, RG14 5SJ

ISBN: 978-1910497135

LOWDOWN FROM THE TRAINERS

RACING POST EXPERTS

THE LOWDOWN GORDON ELLIOTT

You ain't seen nothing yet – Elliott readying 'strongest ever' squad

CANADIAN rock group **Bachman-Turner Overdrive enjoyed a hit single in the mid-70s with You Ain't Seen Nothing Yet, a mantra that might also be suitable for Gordon Elliott's new and improved title challenge for the season ahead.**

Elliott feels that the calibre of weaponry in his arsenal is deadly and describes his current bunch of horses at Cullentra House Stables as his strongest ever.

"We're dealing with the strongest bunch of horses that we've ever had," he says. "I check them every evening and there's times where you just stand back and appreciate the amount of quality we have here.

"I love it. But if I'm being completely honest, I want more horses because I'm hungry and I want to be champion trainer."

The 39-year-old targeted some of the most valuable handicap chases last season with a sniper-like precision that enabled him to throw down the gauntlet to Willie Mullins in the championship race.

Ultimately denied the title, he still enjoyed his best season with 193 domestic winners and €4,380,705 in prize-money.

His headline horses, spearheaded by Apple's Jade, Labaik and Fayonagh, landed memorable victories at the Cheltenham Festival, where Elliott was crowned top trainer for the first time having struck with six winners.

However, Elliott plays down his achievements, and admits he was left "completely heartbroken" after Mullins wrestled back his crown on the final two days of the Punchestown festival.

"I genuinely didn't think I had any chance of winning the championship from the start but then when it started happening for us I threw everything at it," he reflects.

"I was gutted we got beat but at the same time I was proud of myself and all of the staff. We had lots of winners at Punchestown but I left there absolutely heartbroken on the Saturday evening when I should have been delighted.

"If anything it's made us stronger and we have some serious horses here for the season ahead."

Apple's Jade was the most successful of Elliott's string last season, winning three Grade 1s and, along with Cheltenham and Punchestown Champion Bumper winner Fayonagh, the trainer believes he has the two

....

Elliott's raids at Perth are well known and his runners at the Scottish venue continue to be a source of profit (66-236, 28%, +£6.40) but his highest level-stake returns in Britain come at Cheltenham (12-102, 12%, +£16.13)

'There's times where you just stand back and appreciate the amount of quality we have here'

In Ireland Elliott's hurdlers are best backed at Roscommon (12-53, 23%, +£13.17). His chasers return the best figures at Clonmel (6-25, 24%, +£23.70)

best mares in Britain or Ireland.

"Fayonagh and Apple's Jade go out in the same lot together most mornings and it was only recently that I can remember looking at both of them and thinking how lucky I am to have two mares of their quality in the yard at the same time," he says. "Are they the best two mares in Ireland or Britain right now? You'd have to say that they probably are on what they achieved last season.

'Fantastic schooling'

Fayonagh's schooling has been fantastic at home. She really does jump well and she's already favourite for the mares' novice hurdle at Cheltenham and that will be her long-term target.

"She'll start off in a mares' maiden hurdle at one of my favourite tracks, either Navan or Down Royal, and we'll take it from there."

Of **Apple's Jade**, one of around 20 Gigginstown Stud-owned horses who joined Elliott from Mullins's last year, he says: "She was a star for us last season and she must be some mare to already have five Grade 1s in the bank as a five-year-old.

"I shouldn't have run her at Down Royal last year. I didn't have her that long but, in fairness to her, she showed she takes her racing well throughout the season."

Apple's Jade destroyed her rivals by 14 lengths in the Mares' Champion Hurdle at Punchestown, a performance that marked her down as a Stayers' Hurdle candidate.

Mares route likely for Jade

Nonetheless, Elliott believes a repeat bid in the mares' hurdle at Cheltenham looks the most likely long-term target. "I'm a firm believer in campaigning horses in races they can win and, right now, she looks like she'd take the beating in the mares' hurdle at Cheltenham again," he explains.

"While I wouldn't rule out the Stayers, the race in my head is the mares' hurdle."

Others high on Elliott's shortlist for mares to follow this season are Missy Tata, Shattered Love, Dinaria Des Obeaux and Three Swallowsnick.

He says: "**Missy Tata** did a suspensory last year but she's back going well again and we're looking forward to sending her over a fence.

"**Shattered Love** has had a wind operation and I think she'll make up into a good staying mare over fences.

"**Dinaria Des Obeaux** has also had a wind operation and I wouldn't be surprised if she turned out to be all right this season. She goes chasing.

"**Three Swallowsnick** is also back. She broke her pelvis at Navan last December but she's cantering away. That might not do her any harm at all because she's still a maiden for this season and you'd imagine there will be plenty to look forward to with her."

GORDON ELLIOT
LONGWOOD, COUNTY MEATH, IRELAND

	Races Run	1st	2nd	3rd	Unpl	Per cent	£1 Level Stake
Non-hcp Hdles	1928	282	293	220	1133	14.6	-711.61
Hcp Hdles	1238	120	118	102	898	9.7	-416.02
Non-hcp Chses	794	146	152	120	376	18.4	-174.35
Hcp Chses	521	49	35	50	387	9.4	-225.52
Hunter Chses	22	4	2	0	16	18.2	-0.13
N.H. Flat	496	115	92	58	231	23.2	+14.64
Totals	**4999**	**716**	**692**	**550**	**3041**	**14.3**	**-1512.99**

BY MONTH

	W-R	Strike-rate (%)	£1 level stake
January	45-379	11.9	-178.68
February	56-348	16.1	-118.89
March	53-335	15.8	-114.16
April	44-428	10.3	-127.24
May	74-516	14.3	-121.12
June	60-387	15.5	-52.51
July	54-470	11.5	-256.15
August	62-498	12.4	-171.00
September	30-234	12.8	-78.61
October	81-379	21.4	-54.14
November	80-487	16.4	-118.41
December	77-538	14.3	-122.08

FAVOURITES

	W-R	Strike-rate (%)	£1 Level Stake
Non-hcp Hdles	144-351	41.0	-32.14
Hcp Hdles	48-217	22.1	-51.60
Non-hcp Chses	78-176	44.3	-7.85
Hcp Chses	26-84	31.0	+7.90
N.H. Flat	69-146	47.3	+12.42

Runners in Ireland for current and last four seasons

Apple's Jade: will probably be aimed at Mares' Hurdle repeat

'Samcro could be anything'

Elliott won 42 bumpers in Ireland last season and is visibly excited about those who will be jumping hurdles this season, most notably **Samcro**, who he says "could be anything".

"The turn of foot he showed with Lisa O'Neill in his bumper at Fairyhouse was unreal – you'd swear he just jumped in and joined the race with a furlong left to run," he says of the unbeaten Gigginstown youngster.

"He came from Colin Bowe's so he's very well schooled and I can't wait to get him over hurdles this year. He'll start off at Down Royal in November as long as the ground is soft enough and I think two and a half miles will be his trip this season."

Poli Roi, Minellafordollars, Last Minute Man, Rapid Escape and Empire Burleque are all previous bumper winners who Elliott believes will be worth following over flights.

Poli will be different horse now

Elliott adds: "We like **Poli Roi** a lot. He'll be one who'll need a trip and I don't think he ran his true race in the Champion Bumper at Punchestown when he was third behind Fayonagh. He'll be a better horse this season.

"**Minellafordollars** looked very good when he won his bumper at Navan. We're lucky with some of the owners we have here because they're buying lovely, big staying chasers and this fella looks like he has a nice future.

"I put forward **Last Minute Man** in most of my stable tours last season as a bumper

horse worth following but he ended up getting big and backward and I didn't get to run him until January, when he won a bumper at Down Royal. He's growing again and he's absolutely massive now. He'll make a nice staying novice hurdler this year but he'll be better when he goes over fences."

Rapid well regarded

"We didn't hide how much we liked **Rapid Escape** before he ran in the Land Rover bumper at Punchestown and, even though he was beaten, we still think a lot of him. We'll probably start him in a bumper at Down Royal and take it from there.

"I was very impressed with **Empire Burleque** when he won his bumper at Fairyhouse. It was a bit of a cat and mouse race that day and he got a bit light on us after that so we didn't run him again. He's back cantering away now and he looks great."

Blow By Blow, the 2016 Punchestown Champion Bumper winner, and the unbeaten **Lucky Pass** have yet to run for Elliott since joining him from Mullins, but are expected to go novice hurdling this season.

'Brilliant' Duty going chasing

Last season **Death Duty** was billed as an Irish banker in the Albert Bartlett Novices' Hurdle at Cheltenham but was beaten when unshipping Bryan Cooper at the last hurdle. Elliott reckons he found a genuine excuse for that lacklustre display, saying: "He came home sick after Cheltenham – he was half colicky. He twisted something inside over there and he ended up running no race in the Albert Bartlett.

"Some people were saying the race beat him but he was beaten at the top of the hill, so it was nothing to do with the race, more so the fact he was sick. I knew something wasn't right with him because he looked terrible in himself. In hindsight, I shouldn't have run him."

"He's back looking brilliant again. I think he's a very good horse and I've been looking forward to getting him over fences since his bumper days."

DID YOU KNOW?

Gordon Elliott used to be a jockey and rode a winner over jumps for Martin Pipe at Cheltenham. However, you could also be mistaken for thinking he's a British Australian journalist, producer, radio and television personality. However he's not to be confused with the face of Good Morning Australia or the television talk show The Chew.

Excitement over Storyteller

With news of some of his other bright hopes this season, Elliott adds: "**The Storyteller** was one of my naps of Cheltenham but he went lame a few days before the Martin Pipe Handicap Hurdle and it took us about a month to get him right. He had a nice break and remains exciting."

"**Sutton Place** is a bit of a monster. I thought the worst when he pulled up in the Stayers' Hurdle at Punchestown but he just gave himself a knock and he was fine afterwards.

"We gave him a thorough examination but nothing came up. Maybe he just touched a nerve or something but he has been perfect ever since.

"The only reason why he didn't go chasing last year was that he had a wind operation and, by the time he was ready to run, it was probably best to keep his novice status for this season.

"He's going chasing and I've always felt he was going to be a stayer but Barry [Geraghty] thinks he has enough class for two miles.

"**Tombstone** has the potential to be a nice two-mile novice chaser as well."

Outlander operation

Last season's Lexus Chase winner **Outlander** was disappointing subsequently, and Elliott says he was operated on for a kissing spine at the end of the term. The JNwine.com Champion Chase at Down Royal in November will be the nine-year-old's first target.

Sutton Place: described by Elliott as a monster, he will be running over fences this season

The Chris Jones-owned **Mega Fortune** is expected to stay over hurdles, while **Campeador** wears the unfortunate title of being one of the most unlucky horses in training after he fell at the last in two valuable handicap hurdles at Cheltenham and Fairyhouse, respectively.

"I think he has a very big engine and hopefully his luck will change," Elliott says of the JP McManus-owned grey.

"He'll stay hurdling – he just needs a bit of luck to show what he's capable of."

Elliott continues: "**Brelade** goes chasing but something like the Wessex Youth Trust Handicap Hurdle at Ascot could suit him before that day comes.

"**Mick Jazz** was lame on the morning of the County Hurdle and we couldn't run him, which was very disappointing as I thought he would run a big race.

"It ended up that he had a fracture in a hind joint so we put a screw in it, but he missed the best part of the season as a result. Hopefully he'll win a big handicap hurdle this year and make up for that."

Highlight of last season

Elliott labels the success of **Cause Of Causes** in last year's cross-country race as one of the highlights of his season and a similar path awaits this term.

"Cause Of Causes is a hero of a horse and I'd have to say him winning the cross-country at Cheltenham was one of my highlights from last season.

"He's won at the past three Cheltenham Festivals and, if he is to make it a fourth straight win there, I think his best chance would be in the cross-country again. He was electric there last season before finishing second in the Aintree National. That looks a good plan for him again."

Of his youngsters, Elliott nominates a handful to watch.

"I think **Cracking Smart** could be a dark horse this year. He was beaten in a maiden hurdle on his debut for us at Naas at the beginning of the year before bolting up in a bumper at Fairyhouse and we're looking forward to sending him over hurdles.

"**Battle Over Doyen** and **Gun Digger** are two young horses who have joined us since running in their point-to-points and I think they're capable of doing a bit of damage this season.

Best of bumper bunch

"I think the pick of our bumper horses could be **Dinons**, who finished second behind Noel Meade's Red Jack in a valuable bumper at Fairyhouse.

"I'd also keep an eye on an unraced gelding we have called **Ocean Crest**. Both are going very well and should be up to winning their bumper before going on to better things hopefully."

Interview by Brian Sheerin

SUPER STATS

Elliott's numbers have gradually been on the rise over the past few seasons and he recorded personal-best figures in Britain last term (30-170, 18%, -£16.17) and wasn't far short of the £1 million prize-money barrier in a campaign which saw him crowned leading trainer at the Cheltenham Festival

Last season, any hurdlers sent to Cartmel were worth looking out for (4-12, 33%, +£1.88)

Hurdlers sent to Britain who run in Graded races provide the best level-stakes return (6-49, 12%, +£28.50) but his strike-rate is much higher in novice contests (32-97, 33%, +£2.45) and sellers (6-16, 38%, +£3.36)

Elliott's record with hurdlers in Britain is best over the shorter trips ranging from 2m-2m1f (38-138, 28%, +£12.52), but his chasers do better over longer distances at 2m7f-plus (15-100, 15%, +£13.75)

Richard Johnson rides the majority of Elliott's successful British raiders but to a level-stake loss and last year it was the records of Henry Brooke (3-10, 30%, +£1.75) and amateur Lisa O'Neill (2-3, 67%, +£19.50) that were more eyecatching

In Ireland, Thurles is easily the best track to follow Elliott's string for a profitable level-stakes return (20-82, 24%, +£17.40), especially in bumpers (4-9, 44%, +£22.50)

Super Stats figures throughout the guide relate to the current season and the previous four seasons

Ladbrokes

WATCH ALL UK & IRISH

RACING LIVE
IN-SHOP

THE LOWDOWN NICKY HENDERSON

3,000 winners in sight and vast array of talent headed by mighty Bite

NICKY Henderson last season claimed a second trainers' title in five years – his fourth in all – in a season that had its sad points as well as joyous highlights.

It was a grey November weekend last year when the master of Seven Barrows was forced to retire superstar Sprinter Sacre and saw Simonsig fatally injured at Cheltenham, but he bounced back in spectacular fashion with 154 winners – his best since 2011-12 – and prize-money of just under £2.9 million.

It is likely Henderson will break the 3,000 career-winner mark this season as he prepares a squad he describes as very exciting.

There might be a million good reasons for **Might Bite** to run at Haydock in the Betfair Chase, but Henderson is open-minded where one of the stars of the last jumps season begins a campaign that has the 32Red King George VI Chase inked in as a major target.

The eight-year-old, who was in the process of producing a blistering performance in the Kauto Star Novices' Chase at Kempton last Christmas, but fell at the final fence before nearly throwing away victory in the RSA Chase at the festival when hanging dramatically right to allow stablemate Whisper a whiff of victory, only to rally for a memorable success.

He was much more professional in Aintree's Mildmay Novices' Chase and is vying for favouritism with Thistlecrack for the King George and is a general 10-1 for the Timico Cheltenham Gold Cup – the last two legs in Jockey Club Racecourses' Chase Triple Crown, which starts with the Betfair Chase.

Connections of any horse to land all three will pocket a £1 million bonus, and Henderson says: "The King George is going to be his first main objective and that's on the grounds of what he was going to do in the Kauto Star had he not fallen at the last – it would've been a mighty performance.

"The £1 million bonus is very commendable and the point of it being there is to attract the King George horses – you can't win it if you don't win the first leg, so everyone is going to want to turn up at Haydock and we could, as the Betfair Chase has its attractions, but I'm not convinced it's the best place for him to start.

"This horse might just be better suited to having, if possible, an easier preparation race for the King George, than what is likely to be a very tough race at Haydock.

••

Henderson's highest level-stake profit came at Ludlow last season (9-21, 43%, +£9.21) but over the last five seasons, Doncaster has been his most profitable track (34-84, 40%, +£48.85)

'It would've been a mighty performance had he not fallen at the last in the Kauto Star'

"He does have his idiosyncrasies and maybe it's not the right road if we can find an easier introduction, but it's a possibility – he looks unbelievable and Toby [Lawes, assistant] says he feels great."

The big guns

Might Bite summered at Hillwood Stud with **Altior**, who emulated his flawless hurdling career by going unbeaten over fences last term, winning the Arkle and Sandown's Grade 1 Celebration Chase on his final two starts of the season.

Comparisons with Henderson's former star two-mile chaser Sprinter Sacre, who was retired last year, were inevitable but the trainer cautions: "He has a long way to go to fill Sprinter's shoes, but only because they were very big shoes."

His intended starting point is the Tingle Creek Chase at Sandown in December and all roads lead to the Champion Chase, for which he is 6-4 favourite.

Henderson, who is likely to resist the temptation to step up the athletic son of High Chaparral in trip for the King George, adds: "In between the Tingle Creek and Cheltenham there's the Desert Orchid, Clarence House and Game Spirit, but we'll take one step at a time. He and [second-favourite] Douvan have never met, so that would be the big clash and you'd rather like it to be in the Champion Chase and not before. The one thing you might do is look at the Melling Chase at Aintree if you were ever going to try Altior over two and a half miles."

DID YOU KNOW?

The master of Seven Barrows has a Twitter account and it's quite informative too with plenty of interesting content – have a look @sevenbarrows. Away from racing, Henderson's loves include salmon fishing in Scotland. His annual vaunts up to Spey are very popular in the training community and he is joined by the likes of fellow trainer Kim Bailey.

Henderson also has the ace in the Champion Hurdle pack in **Buveur D'Air**, who gave the trainer an outright record sixth success in hurdling's most prestigious prize in March.

His early season options include Newcastle's Fighting Fifth Hurdle and the International Hurdle at Cheltenham, although owner JP McManus's hurdling riches include stablemate **My Tent Or Yours**, who chased Buveur D'Air home in the Champion and Aintree Hurdle and was also second in the Punchestown Champion Hurdle, and Philip Hobbs's Triumph Hurdle winner Defi Du Seuil.

"It was a top-class performance from Buveur at Cheltenham and he's right up there with our other Champion Hurdle winners," reflects Henderson.

L'Ami Serge, who provided Henderson with his 100th Grade 1 winner in the French Champion Hurdle during the summer, will be treated as a Stayers' Hurdle contender, giving the stable significant players in each of Cheltenham's championship events.

Targeting the National

There is one notable omission among Henderson's four trainers' titles, 58 Cheltenham Festival triumphs and countless other big-race wins – success in the Grand National.

Zongalero and The Tsarevich came closest to providing Henderson with victory in the world's most famous jumps race when finishing second in 1979 and 1987 and **Vyta Du Roc**, runner-up in the bet365 Gold Cup, has been identified as one contender for the Aintree marathon.

"We've got to try to find a National horse and it's becoming a bit of a bugbear," says Henderson. "Vyta Du Roc is perhaps the most likely and it was a hell of a run when he finished second at Sandown, so he could be one, but there are others.

"I think **Beware The Bear** will be a National horse at some stage, but this could be a year too early, and I suppose you could think about **Whisper**, who had a great time

Buveur D'Air: gave Henderson a record sixth win in the Champion Hurdle

last season and will go for the Ladbrokes Trophy at Newbury first. O O Seven, who ran a great race when fourth over the National fences in the Topham, is another. For a novice, he jumped like a stag and flew home, while Gold Present may also come into that.

"He ran a very good race when second in the novice handicap chase at the festival and although I'm not sure he wants four miles, he was going the right way all year."

The National is unlikely to ever be on old favourite Top Notch's agenda, but Henderson was delighted with his "amazing" campaign, which included victory in the Grade 1 Scilly Isles Novices' Chase. A defence of his Betfred Peterborough Chase crown could be the starting point for Josses Hill, whose owner Alan Spence saw Kilcrea Vale develop into a useful sort over fences last term, winning twice and finishing fifth in Cheltenham's JLT Novices' Chase.

Power leads novice chase team

In Arkle hero Altior and RSA winner Might Bite, Nicky Henderson boasted two of the best novice chasers around last season and while it might be asking too much for a repeat of their fantastic achievements, the trainer has a typically strong squad to fire over fences this term.

Among the chief hopes are Brain Power, who won classy handicaps at Sandown and Ascot before finishing eighth in the Champion Hurdle, and River Wylde, Henderson's Dovecote winner and a fine third in the Supreme Novices' Hurdle. They are around 20-1 for the Racing Post Arkle.

"We schooled Brain Power over fences this time last year and nearly went chasing, but I just thought he didn't know enough," the trainer says. "He's quite a timid horse and running in those big handicaps over hurdles did him good.

"I think River Wylde could also be very good, but there's a pretty long list of horses we hope could be as well."

River Wylde's owners Mike Grech and Stuart Parkin also have Stowaway Magic to look forward to along with Lough Derg Farmer and Constantine Bay, who Henderson thinks would have bettered his fourth in the Albert Bartlett Novices' Hurdle with more luck.

One for the four-miler

That pair are expected to take high rank in the staying novice division, while Henderson is hopeful the mud-loving Lessons In Milan is one for the National Hunt Chase.

French Listed winner Fixe Le Kap, who was also second in the Imperial Cup, and Protek Des Flos are five-year-olds with futures over fences, which also applies to the well-regarded William Henry, who won two of his four appearances last term, and Rather Be, a Grade 3 winner over hurdles at Aintree's Grand National meeting who "could also be quite good".

Burbank, fourth in a commonly hot Neptune Investment Management Novices' Hurdle at Cheltenham, is another whom connections have high hopes for, while Beat That, who has some first-class novice hurdle form from a few seasons ago, is "getting there".

On the gallops at Seven Barrows, where Nicky Henderson has a crack team ready for action

NICKY HENDERSON
UPPER LAMBOURN, BERKS

	No. of Hrs	Races Run	1st	2nd	3rd	Unpl	Per cent	£1 Level Stake
NH Flat	43	75	22	10	9	34	29.3	+3.42
Hurdles	117	362	87	60	38	175	24.0	-62.48
Chases	47	177	44	27	23	83	24.9	-53.94
Totals	**173**	**614**	**153**	**97**	**70**	**292**	**24.9**	**-113.00**
15-16	152	421	84	55	50	232	20.0	-94.71
14-15	157	505	129	92	62	222	25.5	-54.00

BY MONTH

NH Flat	W-R	Per cent	£1 Level Stake	Hurdles	W-R	Per cent	£1 Level Stake
May	6-14	42.9	+4.73	May	8-32	25.0	-2.28
June	1-3	33.3	+4.00	June	5-14	35.7	+9.85
July	0-1	0.0	-1.00	July	2-11	18.2	-4.00
August	0-0	0.0	0.00	August	1-6	16.7	-2.75
September	0-1	0.0	-1.00	September	2-6	33.3	+1.88
October	0-3	0.0	-3.00	October	4-17	23.5	-5.13
November	3-8	37.5	+2.75	November	8-36	22.2	-12.10
December	2-9	22.2	-4.63	December	12-61	19.7	-18.76
January	1-5	20.0	-3.47	January	13-34	38.2	+11.28
February	1-6	16.7	-3.13	February	10-36	27.8	-11.82
March	4-14	28.6	+3.00	March	7-44	15.9	-21.56
April	4-11	36.4	+5.15	April	15-65	23.1	-7.08

Chases	W-R	Per cent	£1 Level Stake	Totals	W-R	Per cent	£1 Level Stake
May	4-12	33.3	-2.27	May	18-58	31.0	+0.18
June	0-3	0.0	-3.00	June	6-20	30.0	+10.85
July	0-3	0.0	-3.00	July	2-15	13.3	-8.00
August	1-3	33.3	-0.90	August	2-9	22.2	-3.65
September	0-1	0.0	-1.00	September	2-8	25.0	-0.12
October	0-9	0.0	-9.00	October	4-29	13.8	-17.13
November	9-24	37.5	+11.79	November	20-68	29.4	+2.44
December	11-34	32.4	-8.97	December	25-104	24.0	-32.36
January	5-12	41.7	+2.33	January	19-51	37.3	+10.14
February	5-18	27.8	-4.40	February	16-60	26.7	-19.35
March	4-26	15.4	-14.11	March	15-84	17.9	-32.67
April	5-32	15.6	-21.42	April	24-108	22.2	-23.35

DISTANCE

Hurdles	W-R	Per cent	£1 Level Stake	Chases	W-R	Per cent	£1 Level Stake
2m-2m3f	38-123	30.9	-2.34	2m-2m3f	15-35	42.9	-1.68
2m4f-2m7f	20-130	15.4	-49.57	2m4f-2m7f	12-58	20.7	-17.73
3m+	1-17	5.9	-12.00	3m+	6-45	13.3	-20.64

TYPE OF RACE

Non-Handicaps	W-R	Per cent	£1 Level Stake	Handicaps	W-R	Per cent	£1 Level Stake
Nov Hrdls	37-129	28.7	-32.51	Nov Hrdls	0-8	0.0	-8.00
Hrdls	32-89	36.0	+13.15	Hrdls	18-136	13.2	-35.13
Nov Chs	30-68	44.1	+1.21	Nov Chs	1-14	7.1	-12.17
Chases	6-20	30.0	-8.98	Chases	2-56	3.6	-46.50
Sell/Claim	0-0	0.0	0.00	Sell/Claim	0-0	0.0	0.00

RACE CLASS

	W-R	Per cent	£1 Level Stake
Class 1	23-141	16.3	-54.07
Class 2	15-78	19.2	-26.58
Class 3	28-126	22.2	-20.91
Class 4	67-197	34.0	-10.12
Class 5	11-36	30.6	+4.65
Class 6	9-36	25.0	-5.98

FIRST TIME OUT

	W-R	Per cent	£1 Level Stake
Bumpers	16-43	37.2	+9.79
Hurdles	23-94	24.5	-13.16
Chases	11-36	30.6	-0.95
Totals	50-173	28.9	-4.32

Statistics relate to all runners in Britain from May 1, 2016 to April 30, 2017

Noel Fehily generally has a solid record for the yard and his rides over the past five seasons have returned a healthy level-stake profit (17-54, 31%, +£13.31)

Henderson's runners in Listed chases have returned a profit over the last five seasons (5-22, 23%, +£1.50)

He runs in the Brain Power colours of Michael Buckley, whose two-time hurdles winner **Reigning Supreme** also looks set to be a force in his new discipline.

Baden, **Cultivator** and **Divine Spear** are others in the mix, along with lightly raced Sullivan Bloodstock Limited-owned pair **Charming Zen**, who was impressive over hurdles at Doncaster in February, and **Cosmos Des Obeaux** – "a nice, big horse".

"That's quite a good team to start with among others and I'm hopeful they could be up to scratch," Henderson adds.

Duo could yet reach the top

Do not give up on Jenkins and Charli Parcs, says Nicky Henderson, who believes the pair are still capable of showing the form that made some speculate they could join the elite at Seven Barrows.

Jenkins won two of his three outings, but hopes of him making the Supreme Novices' Hurdle, which he was favourite for at one point, were never realised.

"I do hope he's back and I have an inkling we're getting there because that was a disaster of a year," says Henderson, left baffled by the handicapper's assessment of the Azamour gelding's form.

"How he got rated 137 is beyond me. He's only rated that high because he was being hyped as a Supreme horse.

Altior: last season's Arkle winner is set to start out in the Tingle Creek

"He has no more performed to 137 than flown to the moon. He won two shocking races and 117 would have been more like it.

"There's nothing to tell you he's 137 on what he's achieved, but I'm hopeful we can get him back because I do think he's a good horse, even if he wasn't one last year. There are little buds appearing – we've schooled him a few times and he's been completely different."

Charli Parcs was talked up as a Triumph Hurdle player after bolting up at Kempton, but he fell on his subsequent start and finished sixth at the festival.

"I always thought Charli Parcs was going be a top-class horse and he is, and he will be," adds Henderson, who is thrilled with how Fred Winter second **Divin Bere**, who pushed Triumph winner Defi Du Seuil all the way in Aintree's Anniversary 4-Y-O Juvenile Hurdle, has summered, noting: "He's done very well and looks fantastic."

His problem, the trainer concedes, is defying a lofty mark as a four-year-old hurdler stepping into open company, something facing **Call Me Lord**, who made his only start for the Lambourn maestro a winning one at Sandown on the final day of last term.

He says: "They've batted themselves into the 140s and we know what the second season is like for the juvenile hurdlers."

Lough Derg Spirit's mark of 137, in part down to smooth wins at Kempton and Musselburgh, is "maybe more workable" and there could be a decent handicap hurdle in him, although a switch to chasing is an option as his schooling over fences as been high class.

Supreme sixth **Beyond Conceit**, who relished stepping up to 3m½f for the Sefton Novices' Hurdle, in which he was second, will be aimed at staying hurdle prizes, while **Thomas Campbell** is "going the right way" and **Tales Of The Tweed** "progressed enormously" last term.

New names on the roster

The conveyor belt of young talent at Seven Barrows rarely stops turning and this autumn is no different with a clutch of bumper horses and new arrivals whetting the appetite that they might be the next Sprinter Sacre or Altior.

Having finished third in the Champion Bumper, **Claimantakinforgan** is "probably the best of the bumper horses from last season" according to Henderson, who rates dual winner **Captain Woodie** as "very promising".

The trainer was also impressed with how **Royal Ruby** and **Storm Of Intrigue** won their bumpers and there should be more to come from **Doux Pretender**, who was green on his debut for the stable, while **Take To Heart**, **Monbeg Legend** and **Follow The Bear** are already winners over hurdles, but remain novices for the season.

The summer signings are also well thought of, but there is one area Henderson is lacking in. The champion trainer says: "**On The Blindside** is a five-year-old who won from a big field in a point-to-point that has produced some winners, while **Burrows Edge** and **Cracking Destiny** look likeable, sharp types.

"**Mr Whipped** and **Pacific De Baune** are also coming along nicely and **Settie Hill** is an interesting sort who won a bumper at Market Rasen before joining us. He's a half-brother to Toast Of New York, whom Michael [Buckley] had such fun with on the Flat. He looks the part, while **The Bottom Bar**, **Indian Hawk**, who won a British point, and **Turtle Wars** are others to note.

"We are, however, drastically short on three-year-olds and have only **We Have A Dream**, a likeable, little horse who won in France, and the gorgeous **Apple's Shakira**, but we need some three-year-old ammo otherwise we're not going to win the Triumph."

'Amazing bunch of mares'

Henderson has traditionally been a force with mares and expect that to remain the case in the 2017-18 campaign as the trainer has what he describes as an "amazing bunch".

Of the senior names in that division, he reckons we did not see the best of high-class

French import **Kotkikova** last term, but "she seems in particularly good form" and is pencilled in for a brace of mares' chases in November, while **Casablanca Mix** will also go over fences.

Kayf Grace, winner of the Grade 2 bumper for mares at Aintree last year, and the smart Verdana Blue, who was fourth in the mares' novices' hurdle at the festival, are others Henderson is relishing seeing in action.

"**Kayf Grace** won her first start over hurdles at Bangor very easily and I thought she was made for the festival race, but she was lame behind and didn't make it," he says. "She's back and looks great, but the annoying thing is she won her only start over hurdles, so is a once-raced, non-novice. That makes life very difficult, but she's a very talented mare, as is **Verdana Blue**, who could start at Wetherby on Charlie Hall day. I like her a lot and she loves decent ground."

The new distaff arrivals also have Henderson drooling.

'Most gorgeous I've seen in ages'

"I've got a batch I think are absolutely staggering and if we can't find something good, I won't be doing my job very well," he adds. "I have to start with three of JP's [McManus] who are three of the most gorgeous mares I've seen in ages.

"**Dame De Compagnie** is a four-year-old who was second at Auteuil last October and is beautiful. I love her, as I do **Countister**, who isn't the biggest, but won a Flat race and four AQPS races in France.

"To go with them is **Melangerie**, who won two bumpers including a decent race at Cheltenham, and I hope the Queen has a nice filly in **Sunshade**, who won her only bumper and could be exciting.

"**Tell It To Me** also won a bumper in good style and **The Vocalist** will be our Million In Mind horse, while **Monbeg Zena**, **Loveherandleaveher** and **Kupatana** are point-to-point winners from Ireland we rather like – they're lovely types and that's a fierce bunch of girls."

Interview by James Burn

SUPER STATS

Aside from the exploits of Sprinter Sacre and Altior, the 2015-16 campaign was disappointing on the numbers front. But Henderson hit back last term with 154 winners on the board and securing nearly £2.9 million in prize-money and landing his fourth trainers' championship

His raids at Plumpton (7-18, 39%, +£2.67) are always worth looking out for, while his runners at Worcester (24-72, 33%, +£14.60) provide a regular source of success

Henderson has a fine strike-rate with his hurdlers at Towcester (8-16, 50%, +£5.57) while his chasers have always fared well at Kempton (18-59, 31%, +£6.74)

His bumper horses are best followed at Southwell (9-16, 56%, +£8.13) and on Kempton's Polytrack (6-11, 55%, +£11.45)

December is usually a fruitful period for the yard and that was the case again last term. The 25 winners during the month was more than any other although they returned a level-stake loss. Henderson's most profitable period last term came in January (20-52, 38%, +£12.65)

Nico de Boinville rode the majority of the yard's winners last term but to a level-stake loss. The most eyecatching figures were those posted by Davy Russell (5-11, 45%, +£2.45) and Freddie Mitchell (3-5, 60%, +£3.40), a conditional to keep a close eye on

Champion Hurdle the plan for last season's brilliant juvenile Defi

LAST season was the fourth in a row that saw Somerset trainer Philip Hobbs smash through the 100-winner mark during a campaign in which he amassed in excess of £1.5 million in prize-money, helped in no small terms by latest stable star Defi Du Seuil.

Last season's dual festival winner is set to return to Cheltenham at the end of next month as Hobbs plots a campaign centred around a tilt at the Stan James Champion Hurdle.

Defi Du Seuil landed the Triumph Hurdle at the Cheltenham Festival last March and Hobbs is set to unleash the four-year-old at the track's Showcase meeting in October, and says: "He arrived back in the yard in August after his summer break at owner JP McManus's Martinstown Stud and looks absolutely fantastic. We were obviously delighted with him last season as he was unbeaten in seven races.

"It's a long time since I trained a horse to win seven races on the trot and he's an exciting prospect. With that in mind, he's very likely to return to action at Cheltenham at the end of October, and we'll take the rest of the season from there.

"If he's going to develop into a Champion Hurdle hopeful he'll have to run well in the Cheltenham race, where he'll also have to shoulder an 8lb penalty for his Grade 1 successes in the Triumph and at Aintree, but he was the best horse of his age last season so in theory should be up to it."

Looking further ahead for Defi Du Seuil, who is currently second favourite for the Champion Hurdle, Hobbs adds: "As long as Cheltenham goes to plan the next stop will be either the Fighting Fifth at Newcastle or International Hurdle back at Prestbury Park in December – he doesn't get a penalty in the Fighting Fifth so that might be the right option."

Hobbs certainly knows what it takes to win a Champion Hurdle as he saddled Rooster Booster to take the hurdling crown in 2003. However, he stressed the pair are very different types, saying: "It's not really possible to make any comparison between them as Rooster Booster didn't see a racecourse until he was five and Defi Du Seuil is a much more forward type, being French-bred."

Elsewhere, Hobbs is pinning many of his hopes for the autumn and winter months on a number of youngsters and novice chasers as he fears many of the older and proven

Hobbs often has a strong finish to the season and that was the case again last term with his runners in April posting a level-stake profit (14-62, 23%, +£7.01)

'He arrived back in the yard in August after his summer break and looks fantastic'

performers might struggle with their handicap marks after a successful 2016-17 season.

He says: "We've got a number of potentially decent younger horses among the team and they're important as far as the future is concerned.

"I hope the ex-French pair of Demopolis and Dostal Phil, who won on their only starts in their native country, can pay their way.

"**Demopolis** won over hurdles at Auteuil in May and arrived last month – he looks a lovely prospect for the juvenile hurdle division and will run in a couple of months or so.

"**Dostal Phil** came to us via the Arqana Sale after winning an AQPS Flat race at Deauville and the hope is he can develop into a nice novice hurdle type.

"We've also always liked **Who's My Jockey**, who made a winning debut in a Market Rasen bumper last April. He's well-bred, being a half-brother to dual Champion Hurdle winner Hurricane Fly, and will now go hurdling. He's very likely to start off over a stiff two miles.

"One we bought at the Cheltenham December Sale was **Robbin'Hannon**. He won his only start in an Irish point-to-point and was a ready winner on his first start for us over hurdles at Warwick in March. With a mark of 142 he remains a novice until the end of October, so we're aiming him at the Grade 2 Persian War Novices' Hurdle at Chepstow first."

Sandhill Stables has plenty of recruits who have run only in bumpers so far and, as such, are packed with potential. One of those is **Awake At Midnight**, who has run twice with some promise and is closely related to Grade 1 winner Planet Of Sound. "He's a big, strong chasing type who has the potential to improve," says Hobbs.

Ballygown Bay is another in a similar mould, having run in a pair of Warwick bumpers at the start of the year. Hobbs says: "He's grown during the summer and, in all

Defi Du Seuil (5): Triumph Hurdle winner scored seven wins in a row last season

likelihood, he'll go straight over hurdles, probably starting at 2m4f."

Costly Dream sports the colours of Trevor Hemmings and is expected to improve on what we've seen from him so far: "He's a big, strong horse who disappointed us on his debut in a bumper at Haydock last November. However, the ground was atrocious and we've done some work on his wind since, which will hopefully make a difference. I'd expect him to go straight over hurdles.

Crack amateur rider Derek O'Connor rode **Musical Slave** in a bumper at the Punchestown festival and was impressed with what he saw as his mount finished sixth on his debut. Hobbs also speaks highly of the four-year-old, saying: "We like him very much – he's a big, strong stayer in the making. He'll hopefully do well in 2m4f novice hurdles this season and is one to look forward to."

Smart squad for novice chases

On the novice chase front, Hobbs is keen on the likes of War Sound, Wait For Me, Sternrubin, Sneaky Feeling and Strong Pursuit as the quintet are considered capable of surpassing what they did over hurdles.

The trainer says: "**War Sound** aggravated a joint problem last year and had to miss the whole of last season as a result, but he won the Swinton Hurdle in 2015 and is rated 148 over hurdles. He'll be going novice chasing."

"**Wait For Me** made a successful debut over fences at Worcester in the middle of September, staying on well over 2m4f. I think chasing will really suit him.

"**Sneaky Feeling** and Strong Pursuit were always going to be better suited by fences. Sneaky Feeling gave the impression he was still quite green last season and chasing will be his game, but we might give him one run over hurdles beforehand.

"**Strong Pursuit** has come back from his summer break a much stronger horse and will be going straight over fences."

Sternrubin is likely to try to emulate his former stablemates Detroit City and Big Easy in bidding to win the Betfred Cesarewitch at Newmarket in October, before switching back to jumping to try his hand novice chasing.

Hobbs says: "His future over jumps for the

PHILIP HOBBS

WITHYCOMBE, SOMERSET

	No. of Hrs	Races Run	1st	2nd	3rd	Unpl	Per cent	£1 Level Stake
NH Flat	30	42	3	5	5	29	7.1	-33.75
Hurdles	106	347	76	54	38	179	21.9	-12.11
Chases	61	204	32	34	24	114	15.7	-46.17
Totals	**158**	**593**	**111**	**93**	**67**	**322**	**18.7**	**-92.03**
15-16	146	534	118	83	83	250	22.1	-47.85
14-15	137	557	103	93	78	283	18.5	-82.31

BY MONTH

NH Flat	W-R	Per cent	£1 Level Stake	Hurdles	W-R	Per cent	£1 Level Stake
May	0-2	0.0	-2.00	May	1-21	4.8	-16.50
June	0-1	0.0	-1.00	June	1-7	14.3	-1.00
July	0-0	0.0	0.00	July	0-11	0.0	-11.00
August	0-0	0.0	0.00	August	5-10	50.0	+16.25
September	0-0	0.0	0.00	September	1-5	20.0	-3.47
October	0-5	0.0	-5.00	October	11-45	24.4	+1.38
November	1-9	11.1	-6.63	November	9-51	17.6	-17.47
December	0-6	0.0	-6.00	December	7-49	14.3	-1.87
January	0-3	0.0	-3.00	January	9-37	24.3	+7.93
February	0-4	0.0	-4.00	February	10-30	33.3	-2.26
March	1-7	14.3	-3.75	March	10-43	23.3	-8.97
April	1-5	20.0	-2.38	April	12-38	31.6	+24.88

Chases	W-R	Per £1 cent	Level Stake	Totals	W-R	Per cent	£1 Level Stake
May	8-21	38.1	+21.38	May	9-44	20.5	+2.88
June	2-12	16.7	-4.25	June	3-20	15.0	-6.25
July	2-12	16.7	+4.00	July	2-23	8.7	-7.00
August	0-5	0.0	-5.00	August	5-15	33.3	+11.25
September	0-3	0.0	-3.00	September	1-8	12.5	-6.47
October	1-16	6.3	-9.00	October	12-66	18.2	-12.62
November	4-25	16.0	-4.67	November	14-85	16.5	-28.77
December	4-24	16.7	-0.50	December	11-79	13.9	-8.37
January	1-20	5.0	-17.50	January	10-60	16.7	-12.57
February	3-22	13.6	-13.59	February	13-56	23.2	-19.85
March	4-22	18.2	-1.67	March	15-72	20.8	-14.39
April	3-22	13.6	-12.38	April	16-65	24.6	+10.12

DISTANCE

Hurdles	W-R	Per £1 cent	Level Stake	Chases	W-R	Per cent	£1 Level Stake
2m-2m3f	33-138	23.9	-16.43	2m-2m3f	11-46	23.9	+9.37
2m4f-2m7f	22-97	22.7	+30.86	2m4f-2m7f	10-69	14.5	-10.25
3m+	0-25	0.0	-25.00	3m+	5-54	9.3	-34.67

TYPE OF RACE

Non-Handicaps	W-R	Per cent	£1 Level Stake	Handicaps	W-R	Per cent	£1 Level Stake
Nov Hrdls	30-98	30.6	+21.01	Nov Hrdls	2-14	14.3	-2.00
Hrdls	20-78	25.6	-25.86	Hrdls	24-157	15.3	-5.25
Nov Chs	4-20	20.0	-4.59	Nov Chs	1-20	5.0	-9.00
Chases	6-16	37.5	+9.58	Chases	20-129	15.5	-28.17
Sell/Claim	0-0	0.0	0.00	Sell/Claim	0-0	0.0	0.00

RACE CLASS

	W-R	Per cent	£1 Level Stake
Class 1	9-66	13.6	-18.64
Class 2	15-90	16.7	-15.00
Class 3	26-147	17.7	-18.84
Class 4	48-228	21.1	-33.34
Class 5	10-37	27.0	+10.53
Class 6	3-25	12.0	-16.75

FIRST TIME OUT

	W-R	Per cent	£1 Level Stake
Bumpers	3-30	10.0	-21.75
Hurdles	16-85	18.8	-31.79
Chases	9-43	20.9	-4.67
Totals	28-158	17.7	-58.21

DID YOU KNOW?

Philip Hobbs has had over 2,000 winners and he and his wife Sarah have bought most of them. Hobbs was an accomplished rider and rode the likes of 1986 Grand National winner West Tip. Sarah is the daughter of Olympic gold medallist Bertie Hill, who was successful in the 1956 games in Stockholm.

Statistics relate to all runners in Britain from May 1, 2016 to April 30, 2017

rest of the autumn lies in novice chases as he's just the type who can make his presence felt in that division.

Fences also beckon for **Jerrysback**, who is unbeaten in two runs over hurdles for Hobbs. However, he might be staying over hurdles for a little while, as the trainer points out: "He's a big, strong horse whose future lies over fences, but we could have a look at something like the Silver Trophy before going chasing. He has a lovely attitude, is potentially very decent and held in high regard by Wilson Dennison in Ireland, for whom he won one of his four point-to-points before joining us."

County Hurdle third **Ozzie The Oscar** could also make his mark in novice chases.

Hobbs says: "We're hoping he'll develop into a decent two-mile novice chaser. He produced a career-best in the County but disappointed in the Scottish Champion Hurdle. He's had a good break and has plenty of ability."

Balthazar King was a huge people's favourite having twice won over the Cheltenham cross-country course at the festival and finished second in the Grand National. He was retired last April, but his brother **For Good Measure** has plenty of his attributes in that he is tough and genuine – and Hobbs is eyeing a switch to fences this term after some promising runs over hurdles last season. He says: "He ran some very good races in defeat last season and hopefully the switch to novice chases will bring about further improvement."

It's a hive of activity at Philip Hobbs's Somerset yard as his string heads to the gallops as the season starts to step up a gear

Old stagers back for more

Hobbs has news of some of the names we might be more familiar with, starting with a two-time winner at Cheltenham in **Village Vic**.

The trainer says: "He ran some very good races during the first half of last season, getting placed three times at Cheltenham, including when finishing runner-up in the BetVictor Gold Cup. His form tailed off and he isn't easy to place off a mark of 158, but I imagine he'll be going back to Cheltenham.

"**Royal Regatta** was a Grade 2 winner at Ascot last November but his form tended to be in and out. Two and a half miles is his trip and the obvious starting point is the Old Roan at Aintree.

"**Rock The Kasbah** looked very good on occasions over fences last season, winning twice at Chepstow and finishing sixth in the bet365 Gold Cup at Sandown on his final start. In between he lost his confidence on occasions and ballooned his fences.

"I'm hoping he's an improver and we'll be looking at races like the Badger Ales at Wincanton and the race we all know as the Hennessy."

One of the horses Hobbs might have difficulty in placing this season is 12-time winner **Garde La Victoire**, who goes particularly well at Cheltenham and has three wins at the track on his CV.

Hobbs says: "He's a lovely horse who's done very well for us over the years, but he was unhealthy in the spring after beating only two home in the Champion Chase and isn't the easiest to place off his mark. We may aim him at a conditions race at Auteuil in October."

Gumball a dark horse

Asked to name a horse from his team that readers should keep on the right side, Hobbs says: "I'm quite keen on **Gumball**, who finished third on his only start in the French provinces at Dieppe in the spring. The form might not look that special but he's a very interesting recruit."

Interview by Andrew King

SUPER STATS

Hobbs enjoyed another solid campaign last term returning figures in keeping with the three previous seasons. He sent out 111 winners and earned over £1.5 million in prize-money

He posts his highest level-stake figures at Newbury (21-11, 19%, +£53.47) and Stratford (19-71, 27%, +£34.98)

His runners in Wales are always worth a look. Last season he was 6-13 at Ffos Las (46%, +£10.08) and 11-41 at Chepstow (27%, +£6.38)

Hurdlers are best followed at Sandown (7-25, 28%, +£19.85) while his record over hurdles at Cheltenham also reads well (13-92, 14%, +£14.87)

Hobbs has a fine strike-rate with his chasers at Worcester (9-37, 24%, +£4.05) while he also returns a decent level-stake profit over fences at Aintree (5-40, 13%, +£13.50)

He has sent out most of his bumper winners at Warwick (6-21, 29%, -£0.85) but Hobbs's runners in such races are best followed at Uttoxeter (3-8, 38%, +£16.38) and Huntingdon (3-7, 43%, +£1.04)

Chasers also fare well in Listed affairs (8-39, 21%, +£9.87) while he was 2-2 in Graduation chases last term (+£4.33)

His partnership with Richard Johnson rewards punters well (287-1228, 23%, +£10.07) although last year the eyecatching figures were returned by Liam Heard (4-11, 36%, +£6.00) and Tom O'Brien (16-95, 17%, +£5.65)

RETURN OF THE JUMPS

YORKSHIRE'S PREMIER JUMP RACETRACK

OVER £140,000 PRIZE FUND

FESTIVE JUMPERS RACEDAY
SATURDAY 16 DECEMBER
Featuring the Sheffield Greyhound Stadium Mare's Steeple Chase

FRI 1 DECEMBER   **SAT 2** DECEMBER   **FRI 15** DECEMBER   **SAT 16** DECEMBER   **FRI 29** DECEMBER

doncaster racing & events

doncaster-racecourse.co.uk

THE LOWDOWN ALAN KING

Yanworth flying the flag with young talent ready to shine through

LAST season was a pretty good one for Alan King. The master of Barbury Castle amassed over a century of winners with nearly £1.4 million in prize-money, his best figures since 2008-09. There were no Cheltenham Festival victories, but plenty of young talent shone throughout the winter, leaving him with lots of ammo to fire over the coming months.

In particular, King looks to have a strong team of horses who are set to tackle fences this term – none stronger than his stable star **Yanworth**, who went off favourite for last season's Champion Hurdle. He disappointed there, but made amends when winning over three miles at Aintree the following month – his second Grade 1 victory of the season – leaving plenty of options as to what distance he goes over as a novice chaser this term, with a trip to Exeter looking a likely starting point.

"There's a beginners' chase for him in October there or we could go for a novice event in November," says King. "Most likely we'll be going two and a half miles-plus with him but we'll wait and see."

Another of King's who took part in the Champion Hurdle was **Sceau Royal**. He ran with great credit to finish sixth in that event and fences now beckon for the promising five-year-old.

"He'll go the chasing route over two miles and we're looking forward to it," he says. "He's always been a good jumper of hurdles and if he takes to fences anything like as well then he could be very exciting."

Sceau Royal also took part in the Scottish Champion Hurdle, as did **Winter Escape**. JP McManus's six-year-old has had very little racing with just six career starts, but he has always looked to have potential and ran with great credit when fifth in the County Hurdle off the back of an absence.

"We're going the chasing route with Winter Escape and I'd imagine he'll be going over two miles," says King.

"**The Unit** was another one of ours who was very progressive last season. He'll also be going over fences now and we'll be looking to try two and a half miles with him."

One of the highest money earners for King over the last 12 months has been **Who Dares Wins**. He has been performing well on the Flat and over hurdles and ran a cracker

....

Wayne Hutchinson rides the vast majority of the yard's winners but to a hefty level-stake loss. However, his mounts on King's chasers posted a profit last year (10-55, 18%, +£13.07)

'He's always been a good jumper of hurdles and if he takes to fences anything like as well then he could be very exciting'

King's hurdlers did particularly well in December last year (15-52, 29%, +£10.78) to finish third in last term's Coral Cup. He looks likely to have a crack at the Cesarewitch before returning to jumps with his career set to be continuing over the smaller obstacles rather than fences.

"We'll probably stick to handicap hurdles with him," says King. "That will also be the same route for **Elgin**, who did well for us in novice hurdles last season. He's done really well over the summer and strengthened up."

King had 23 winners in handicap hurdles last season, with a useful strike-rate of 18 per cent, and success in that sphere looks likely to continue with another strong team. As well as Who Dares Wins and Elgin, King also has the promising McManus pair of River Frost and Midnight Maestro.

"**Midnight Maestro** will probably start back hurdling. He's a fine physical specimen so we'll see where we end up going with him. We'll start the season continuing over hurdles with **River Frost** as well.

"**Azzerti** remains over hurdles too. He acts well on soft ground but I don't necessarily think he needs it. The key with him is we need to get him switched off – he was quite buzzy in his racing last term."

Azzerti was one of King's more lightly raced novice hurdlers in 2016-17. He looks promising as does **Sir Antony Browne**, although his trainer is concerned his current mark will make life tough for him.

"He got put up a lot following his third at Ayr in April and I fear a mark of 141 might be too high, but he'll continue over hurdles as well."

Sadly one hurdler of King's whom we won't be seeing this season is Messire Des Obeaux. Third in last season's Neptune, he has since suffered a tendon injury and is on the easy

River Frost: the JP McManus-owned runner is among the pack before striking at Plumpton last season

list. So too is Master Blueyes, King's top juvenile hurdler from last season. However, there are other four-year-olds in the squad who look likely to boost the trainer's firepower over hurdles during the winter.

Velvet set for handicaps

One of last term's juveniles who could be well handicapped is **Dino Velvet**. He had little luck in running when finishing eighth in last season's Fred Winter and could be a fair bit better than that effort.

"We're likely to start him off in what used to be the Free Handicap Hurdle at Chepstow's first big meeting of the season in October. He'll go there and that's also likely to be the first target for another one of our top four-year-olds **Fidux**.

"We could end up racing over a bit further with Dino Velvet later in the season, but we'll see how he gets on at Chepstow first."

King is not so bullish about his hopes for another two of his four-year-olds. "We had a good time with **Coeur De Lion** last term, but his mark is now pretty high. He'll probably want two and a half miles, but I fear he's going to find life tough over hurdles this season.

"We ran **Rainbow Dreamer** on the Flat at the Royal meeting where he put up a great performance to finish fourth in the Ascot Stakes. However, he came back very jarred

up so is having a bit of a break now. It could be a while before we next see him."

Two areas where King's success has always been perhaps a little underrated is in the mares' events and on the Flat.

He always tends to have a strong team of mares, while on the Flat his performances continue to improve, and he is already closing in on 20 winners this season, not a mile off his personal best for the calendar year.

Some of King's best performers on the Flat have gone on to prove a success over hurdles, including **Cosmeapolitan**, who got off the mark on his sole start over the smaller obstacles at Newbury in December.

"We'll go hurdling again with him," says King. "He's already won a race over jumps so we'll probably look at some of those introductory handicaps over two miles to start with.

"We also have Cosmeapolitan's half-sister **Sula Island**. There could be a chance she'll go over hurdles – I'm just not sure whether she'd be strong enough for jumps yet."

Legend ready to tackles fences

King has no such doubts about his super-consistent mare **Dusky Legend**, who again finished placed in the Dawn Run Mares' Novices' Hurdle at last season's festival. Fences now beckon for her.

"She's very good," says King. "We'll be

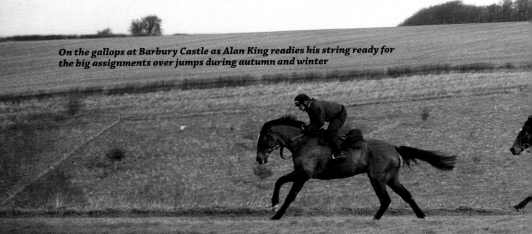

On the gallops at Barbury Castle as Alan King readies his string ready for the big assignments over jumps during autumn and winter

ALAN KING
BARBURY CASTLE, WILTS

	No. of Hrs	Races Run	1st	2nd	3rd	Unpl	Per cent	£1 Level Stake
NH Flat	29	51	6	12	9	24	11.8	-9.25
Hurdles	90	337	82	65	56	134	24.3	-57.04
Chases	26	100	15	13	14	58	15.0	-3.97
Totals	**128**	**488**	**103**	**90**	**79**	**216**	**21.1**	**-70.26**
15-16	122	403	68	59	54	222	16.9	-120.54
14-15	122	455	77	78	45	254	16.9	-132.51

BY MONTH

NH Flat	W-R	Per cent	£1 Level Stake	Hurdles	W-R	Per cent	£1 Level Stake
May	1-2	50.0	+0.75	May	9-25	36.0	+3.45
June	0-1	0.0	-1.00	June	2-5	40.0	+6.50
July	1-1	100.0	+2.00	July	3-12	25.0	-3.25
August	0-2	0.0	-2.00	August	2-5	40.0	-0.25
September	1-1	100.0	+6.00	September	1-5	20.0	+1.00
October	0-4	0.0	-4.00	October	7-28	25.0	-4.25
November	1-10	10.0	+4.00	November	16-54	29.6	-13.77
December	1-8	12.5	-1.00	December	15-52	28.8	+10.78
January	1-4	25.0	+4.00	January	10-31	32.3	+13.54
February	0-6	0.0	-6.00	February	7-42	16.7	-16.95
March	0-6	0.0	-6.00	March	5-46	10.9	-36.83
April	0-6	0.0	-6.00	April	5-32	15.6	-17.00

Chases	W-R	Per cent	£1 Level Stake	Totals	W-R	Per cent	£1 Level Stake
May	3-11	27.3	+5.00	May	13-38	34.2	+9.20
June	1-6	16.7	-3.63	June	3-12	25.0	+1.87
July	1-5	20.0	-0.50	July	5-18	27.8	-1.75
August	1-3	33.3	-1.39	August	3-10	30.0	-3.64
September	0-1	0.0	-1.00	September	2-7	28.6	+6.00
October	1-7	14.3	-3.00	October	8-39	20.5	-11.25
November	1-13	7.7	-11.17	November	18-77	23.4	-20.94
December	1-14	7.1	-9.00	December	17-74	23.0	+0.78
January	1-11	9.1	0.00	January	12-46	26.1	+17.54
February	3-9	33.3	+3.71	February	10-57	17.5	-19.24
March	0-8	0.0	-8.00	March	5-60	8.3	-50.83
April	2-12	16.7	+25.00	April	7-50	14.0	+2.00

DISTANCE

Hurdles	W-R	Per cent	£1 Level Stake	Chases	W-R	Per cent	£1 Level Stake
2m-2m3f	37-154	24.0	-11.11	2m-2m3f	4-24	16.7	-9.92
2m4f-2m7f	14-73	19.2	-14.87	2m4f-2m7f	3-25	12.0	-14.38
3m+	6-22	27.3	-1.81	3m+	4-35	11.4	+13.38

TYPE OF RACE

Non-Handicaps	W-R	Per cent	£1 Level Stake	Handicaps	W-R	Per cent	£1 Level Stake
Nov Hrdls	28-94	29.8	-8.67	Nov Hrdls	1-7	14.3	+2.00
Hrdls	31-112	27.7	-25.48	Hrdls	22-124	17.7	-24.88
Nov Chs	4-20	20.0	-12.84	Nov Chs	1-4	25.0	+7.00
Chases	0-7	0.0	-7.00	Chases	8-60	13.3	+11.50
Sell/Claim	0-0	0.0	0.00	Sell/Claim	0-0	0.0	0.00

RACE CLASS

	W-R	Per cent	£1 Level Stake
Class 1	12-91	13.2	-31.30
Class 2	8-62	12.9	-0.40
Class 3	20-95	21.1	-14.30
Class 4	50-179	27.9	-8.40
Class 5	10-31	32.3	-6.85
Class 6	3-30	10.0	-8.00

FIRST TIME OUT

	W-R	Per cent	£1 Level Stake
Bumpers	6-29	20.7	+12.75
Hurdles	20-77	26.0	-15.67
Chases	4-22	18.2	-4.17
Totals	30-128	23.4	-7.09

DID YOU KNOW?

Alan King is a big darts fan, although the Alan King Darts Memorial, which is held in New Zealand, is not named after him! King comes from Scotland and started his career under the guidance of John Wilson at Cree Lodge Stables in Ayr. Having joined David Nicholson in 1985, he was promoted to assistant trainer the following year.

Statistics relate to all runners in Britain from May 1, 2016 to April 30, 2017

going novice chasing with her. Another one of our mares who was very progressive last season was **Midnight Tour**, who put up some particularly good performances at Cheltenham, winning there in April. We'll continue down the hurdling route with her.

"**Tara View** will probably start off over hurdles too, although we could try chasing with her later on. We could also look at going over three miles."

Jump racing fans simply love their star veterans and there is no more popular horse in King's yard than his evergreen grey **Smad Place**.

There were no victories for the ten-year-old last season, but his third place in the Aintree Bowl in April showed he is indeed no back-number just yet, and his trainer has the Charlie Hall Chase down as his first target.

"Smad had a good summer and is back in work. He's in decent form and we'll look to start him off at Wetherby.

"His mark is probably a little high now for the big handicaps so we'll have to duck and dive a bit this season, but we're happy with him."

Another of King's established stars is **Uxizandre**. However, the former Ryanair Chase winner isn't back in work yet and hopes for another big chase prize before Christmas could rest with **Label Des Obeaux**, who looks set to be aimed at what used to be the Hennessy, now the Ladbrokes Trophy.

"Label Des Obeaux is well and he'll probably be targeted at Newbury," says King. "We'll look to get one run into him beforehand. He did well last season although I'm a bit fearful he might not be in love with Cheltenham too much."

King's love for Cheltenham and the jumps remain as strong as ever and we can expect his powerful team to continue to be a major force at the showcase meetings as he bids to hit the 100-winner mark for the second year on the spin.

Interview by James Hill

SUPER STATS

Last season was a good one on the numbers front for King. His tally of 104 winners and prize-money in excess of £1.3 million were his best figures since the 2008-09 campaign

King is best followed at Doncaster (22-85, 26%, +£43.87). At the smaller tracks his best returns are posted at Bangor (16-51, 31%, +£25.19) and Stratford (15-48, 31%, +£16.98)

During recent seasons his hurdlers have done best at Doncaster and Stratford but King's runners over timber did particularly well at Kempton last season (8-26, 31%, +£7.67)

Over fences King has high strike-rates at Huntingdon (6-17, 35%, +£9.06), Exeter (8-25, 32%, +£5.74) and Plumpton (4-9, 44%, +£2.58)

King does particularly well with runners in bumpers and most of his winners in that sphere come at Towcester (4-8, 50%, +£6.08), Newbury (5-24, 21%, +£1.85) and Huntingdon (5-20, 25%, +£0.13)

King posts positive level-stake returns in Listed (5-20, 25%, +£17.00) and novice chases (45-166, 27% +£0.15), while his handicappers over fences last term also returned a profit (11-73, 15%, +£15.87)

January is often a good month for the yard and that was the case again last season with the first month of the calendar year being his most profitable during the 2016-17 campaign (12-46, 26%, +£17.54)

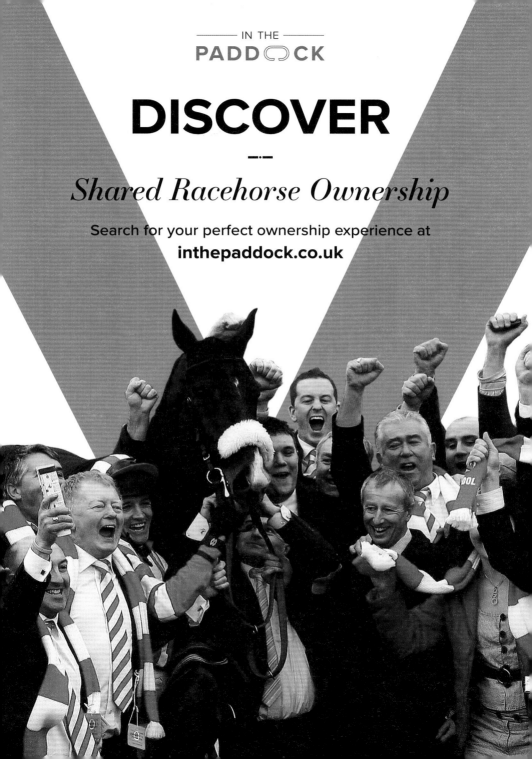

THE LOWDOWN WILLIE MULLINS

Faugheen to return as master trainer looks for season without setback

ALTHOUGH **Willie Mullins will have relished each of his 11 trainers' titles, the 2016-17 season that saw him collect a tenth championship in a row after a titanic tussle with Gordon Elliott will surely go down as one of his finest.**

In a campaign defined by excelling in the face of adversity, the Closutton genius bounced back from Gigginstown House Stud's decision to remove around 60 horses from his care by masterminding an array of star performances.

Mullins didn't simply lose run-of-the-mill performers either. Apple's Jade, Outlander, Don Poli and A Toi Phil were quality performers. Crucially, there were also valuable prize-money contributors among the 20 departees switched to Gordon Elliott's title-chasing camp. They were now fighting for a different corner.

Although the top-level performers weren't replaceable, the fact Mullins was able to fill the empty boxes within a matter of weeks is testimony to his training talents.

Furthermore, a freak accident cost gifted chaser Vautour his life; Faugheen and Annie Power – winners of the previous two Champion Hurdles – endured season-stopping injuries, and Min had only two appearances before meeting with a setback in February, all of which meant the quality of the Closutton army was depleted. Still, Mullins would not be defeated.

Punchestown proved to be his playground. He unleashed all of his firepower at the Kildare venue's finale, taking the title lead for the first time with just 12 races of the season to go, thanks to son Patrick's heroics in riding a Grade 1 double and four winners in all on the last two days of the festival. Mullins went on to settle the argument with Elliott by a margin of €199,495.

It was a sweet success, but attentions are now turned to the upcoming campaign. "I'm looking forward to this season and once again we have a nice team this year," Mullins says. "I'm just hoping that we don't have as many setbacks as last year."

The champion trainer has issued positive reports regarding plenty of his flagbearers, including **Faugheen**, who has been stifled by injury since January 2016 and that emphatic Irish Champion Hurdle success.

"I've been delighted with him," enthuses Mullins. "He's back in full training and had been doing fast work before he went to grass.

"We had nothing to run him in at the time

....

Mullins has long had a high strike-rate in bumpers and those runners in Ireland return a decent profit to a high strike-rate (166-442, 38%, +£17.98)

'I've been delighted with Faugheen – he's back in full training and had been doing fast work before he went out to grass'

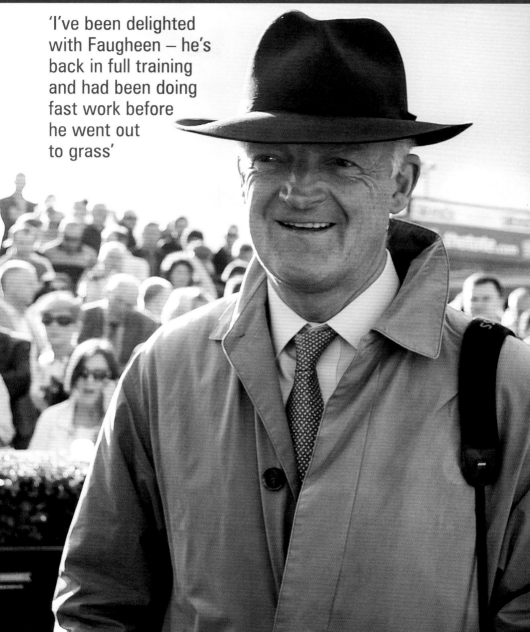

WILLIE MULLINS
BAGENALSTOWN, COUNTY CARLOW

	Races Run	1st	2nd	3rd	Unpl	Per cent	£1 Level Stake
Non-hcp Hdles	2400	778	477	288	857	32.4	-198.79
Hcp Hdles	702	96	55	52	499	13.7	-99.15
Non-hcp Chses	1112	356	178	135	443	32.0	-78.95
Hcp Chses	422	44	37	29	312	10.4	-104.14
Hunter Chses	32	6	3	2	21	18.7	-8.20
N.H. Flat	1072	359	210	116	387	33.5	+10.93
Totals	**5740**	**1639**	**960**	**622**	**2519**	**28.6**	**-478.30**

BY MONTH

	W-R	Strike-rate (%)	£1 level stake
January	207-639	32.4	-27.14
February	184-580	31.7	+27.30
March	102-379	26.9	-39.27
April	179-793	22.6	+89.51
May	116-491	23.6	-127.87
June	46-183	25.1	-8.55
July	116-376	30.9	-12.79
August	108-386	28.0	-109.49
September	74-294	25.2	-42.26
October	69-265	26.0	-27.59
November	195-577	33.8	-43.41
December	243-777	31.3	-156.74

FAVOURITES

	W-R	Strike-rate (%)	£1 Level Stake
Non-hcp Hdles	588-1160	50.7	-31.11
Hcp Hdles	52-164	31.7	+32.85
Non-hcp Chses	257-522	49.2	+4.32
Hcp Chses	15-84	17.9	-18.14
N.H. Flat	277-638	43.4	-33.97

Runners in Ireland for current and last four seasons

and we didn't want to take him to France, but he's in good shape and the Morgiana Hurdle or Hatton's Grace look the likeliest starting points."

Superstar in great shape

Douvan had shaped like a chaser from another galaxy until suffering a small stress fracture to his pelvis which resulted in an underwhelming effort in last season's Champion Chase. Mullins now reports the flying French-bred to be in good heart.

"Douvan has been in with us for ages, cantering away, and I'm very happy with him," he says.

Of the prospect of stepping up in trip from the minimum, over which he has been generally campaigned, Mullins adds: "It's all about getting him back and no decision has been made as to what road he'll go down. We want to get him and **Min** back to their best before making a call on where next."

The latter, who also sports the pink and green of Rich and Susannah Ricci, had looked

scintillating in a pair of chase starts towards the end of 2016. After a setback ruled him out of the Cheltenham and Punchestown festivals, he was given an extended break with a view to 2m senior chasing.

"He met with a setback last year but since he's been back in, all has been great – hopefully we don't have any repeats," says the 61-year-old handler.

Yorkhill's plan undecided

Few could argue that one of the most talented thoroughbreds in training isn't **Yorkhill**, but the seven-year-old has shown a tendency to jump out to his left, most noticeably in the Ryanair Gold Cup at Fairyhouse on his latest start.

With Ruby Walsh having gushed that the horse had "Gold Cup written all over him and always had" after success in the JLT Novices' Chase at Cheltenham, Mullins then sent out mixed signals after Fairyhouse, saying that he could be a Champion Hurdle sort.

"We haven't decided whether he'll be starting over hurdles or fences at this stage," he says now. "He obviously favours going left-handed, but when races present themselves going the opposite direction, you have to go for them – it's not a hard and fast rule with him."

He adds: "It's looking like he's more manageable in that regard over hurdles. There are a few things I want to try out with him, that might help a bit, and gaining more experience should bring his jumping on."

Speaking of the Gold Cup, **Djakadam**

Yorkhill: long-range targets this season have still to be decided

could well be returning to the Cotswolds for a fourth attempt at the blue riband of jump racing, with Mullins reporting the eight-year-old to have "summered very well".

He adds: "I imagine he'll keep to the staying chasing route again this season."

Un De Sceaux produced one of the most visually exciting performances in recent Cheltenham memory when leaping his way to victory in the Ryanair Chase.

Sights are set on a similar campaign to last season, which saw him win a hat-trick of Grade 1s.

"He's been fantastic," exudes Mullins. "He'll stick to the same sort of races as last season and he's probably best suited with a bit of ease in the ground."

Vroum Vroum back from injury

The OLBG Mares' Hurdle in March came to a thrilling conclusion, with Apple's Jade getting the better of former stablemates Vroum Vroum Mag and Limini, but the versatile eight-year-old runner-up disappointed on her final start last season at Punchestown.

"**Vroum Vroum Mag** picked up an injury at the start in the Punchestown Champion Hurdle on her last start and took a while to recover," he says of the classy mare. "She's back now and we'll mix it over hurdles and fences this season."

The third-placed finisher on that occasion, **Limini**, hasn't been seen since. "She's in great shape and is another who summered very well," Mullins reports. "She definitely looks like one for the Mares' Hurdle."

Of his staying hurdling star **Nichols Canyon**, Mullins adds: "He'll be returning for a campaign towards the Stayers' Hurdle at Cheltenham alongside **Penhill**, who should be back in later this season, potentially starting off around Christmas."

Another versatile sort for the Closutton team has been **Wicklow Brave**, an Irish Leger winner on the Flat and Punchestown Champion Hurdle winner under National Hunt rules.

"Nick Peacock's eight-year-old has been a great servant and proved to be a very important horse last season, pushing us in front for the first time in the trainers' title race at Punchestown," Mullins says. "He's been busy on the Flat but he'll return to hurdles this season."

Another performer who proved vital in pushing Mullins over the line at Punchestown is the exhilarating **Great Field**, unbeaten over fences in four starts, and one who could be an exciting force once more this term.

"Great Field has a big engine and Jody McGarvey gets on great with him," says Mullins. "Being a novice last year, he's going to have to improve and we don't have any targets for him just yet."

The champion trainer also notes: "**Bellshill** has returned to us and is fine. He probably hasn't shown us his true potential yet. **Black Hercules** is in good shape and we'll develop a plan as time goes on. **Killultagh Vic** is at Colin McBratney's place and I hear he's in great shape too."

Melon maturing

In the midst of the excitement of the Cheltenham Festival, perhaps it could be argued that the achievements of **Melon** were rather overlooked, as he performed to an extraordinarily high standard behind the enigmatic Labaik, on only his second hurdles start.

"I think it was a fantastic run in the Supreme Novices' considering it was only his fourth lifetime start and second try over hurdles," Mullins agrees. "When you bear in mind what he encountered in terms of more experienced horses, I think there's huge scope for improvement."

With regard to his likely path for the 2017-18 season, Mullins admits that although the five-year-old is physically capable for fences, there could be experience to be gained over hurdles first.

He says: "He's a fine horse and has matured even more now after coming back. I think from chatting to his owners that we might go down the hurdle route because he's so

Vroum Vroum Mag: set to mix it up with runs over hurdles and fences this season

inexperienced – he could do with another season hurdling."

The future of Melon's Punchestown conqueror **Cilaos Emery** has yet to be decided, while Mullins believes there could be more to come from **Battleford** than he produced over hurdles when he embarks on a campaign over fences this season.

C'est Jersey will join him in the novice chasing department, with staying distances potentially his domain.

Let's Dance must be one of the most popular mares in the yard, having secured the €50,000 stable staff

bonus when landing the mares' novices' hurdle at Cheltenham after winning at Leopardstown in January. She was perhaps coming to the end of a busy and productive season when beaten on her final starts.

"I'd imagine around 2m4f would be her ideal distance and we'll likely target mares' races this season, without any particular starting point in mind," says Mullins.

He adds: "**Augusta Kate** will take the same route and she has matured quite a lot over the summer – it surprised me how well she developed. She's physically much

Augusta Kate: reported to have matured over the summer

stronger too and I'm looking forward to seeing her out this term."

While the Supreme Racing Club has recently seen one of their main flagbearers retire in the shape of Pique Sous, and with Airlie Beach due to head to the breeding sheds in the near future, **Bunk Off Early** could be one who can bring more success to the syndicate.

"He looked very promising at Christmas but didn't maintain that promise as the season progressed," Mullins says of him. "We'll get him back in now and see what he can do, but I haven't made any decision as to which direction he's going to go."

Bacardys set to go chasing

The Shanakiel Racing Syndicate's **Bacardys** surely must be one of Patrick Mullins' favourite horses in training, having won a Grade 2 Aintree bumper on the gelding in 2016 before partnering him to a pair of Grade 1 wins over hurdles last term in

Bacardys: dual Grade 1 winner over hurdles

the Deloitte at Leopardstown and Champion Novice Hurdle at Punchestown.

The trainer says of the horse who claimed the scalps of Finian's Oscar and Death Duty in April: "Bacardys is a consistent, good horse and I imagine he'll go chasing this season.

"**Saturnas** is also a Grade 1 winner but he didn't run after the Deloitte, when he picked up a little injury, but that's all behind him."

Crack Mome was a name on plenty of racegoers' lips ahead of Cheltenham last spring. He had won nicely at Clonmel before taking second at long odds-on in the Moscow Flyer Novice Hurdle (Grade 2), and connections believe there could be more to come.

"He could probably go down as a little disappointing towards the end of last season [only beating one home in the Supreme Novices' Hurdle] but I think he was immature," Mullins suggests.

"I think he's come back stronger for his break and a decision is yet to be made on whether he'll stick to hurdles or try chasing."

Getabird could be Supreme flyer

While it's early to be discussing bumper horses and novice hurdling types, **Lac Kivu** was one who got plenty of tongues wagging at Punchestown when annihilating the opposition in a May maiden hurdle.

However, he was bitterly disappointing next time at the Galway festival. "We're not happy with him at all since Galway and he won't be out in the near future," Mullins relays. "It looks like he might have to miss the season."

On a more positive note, last season's Champion Bumper fancy **Getabird**, who missed the Cheltenham Festival through injury after impressing in a pair of bumpers, looks set to be campaigned at a decent level this term.

"Getabird is in cantering away and will go novice hurdling," Mullins says.

"We'll let him tell us where he wants to go in terms of distance, but he could easily be a Supreme Novices' Hurdle horse, with what he showed in bumpers."

Interview by Mark Boylan

DID YOU KNOW?

The master of Closutton has a fancy new website – wpmullins.com. We are introduced to the team and there's merchandise available. Check out the WP Mullins collection of breeches, softshell jackets and sleeveless warmers. Special offers include a racing trousersuit for €200.

7BETS4FREE.COM
FIXED BRUSH HURDLE SERIES FINAL

WORTH £25,000
WEDNESDAY 25 OCTOBER

FOR TICKETS VIST
WORCESTER-RACECOURSE.CO.UK

Looking to future with yard full of exciting and unexposed youngsters

TEN-TIME champion trainer Paul Nicholls had to give best to Nicky Henderson last season for the second time in the last five years and, without a Kauto Star, Denman, Master Minded or Silviniaco Conti on the team, he is already pretty much resigned to coming up short once again.

Surprise packages such as Cliffs Of Dover, Frodon and San Benedeto kept him in the title race last season, but Nicholls accepts it is the Grade 1 winners who win titles, and he would be hard-pressed to nominate a single serious candidate for championship races.

However, you would be mistaken if you thought the mood at Manor Farm Stables was anything but upbeat. For Nicholls has a stable brimming with potential – literally dozens and dozens of youngsters who could be anything.

He says: "We've got as strong a team as we had last season, and we'll have a good season again, but we don't have so many at the Graded end, so we'll need a miracle to win the trainers' championship.

"I'm not going to lose sleep over it though. We had 171 winners last season, which was more than we'd ever had before, and if we could get near that and top £2 million in prize-money again we'll be happy.

"I think Nicky will be champion again and the biggest danger to him might be Dan [Skelton, his former assistant] rather than Colin [Tizzard], although Dan won't be champion by winning all those races around the smaller tracks."

One can sense the anticipation as Nicholls casts his eye down the 130-plus names on his most up-to-date list. For underneath an outwardly more relaxed demeanour the ambition still burns bright, and he is clearly loving his job as much as ever, his enthusiasm invigorated by getting back in the saddle to ride out regularly for the first time in years.

He says: "You can't buy those Kauto Stars and Neptune Collonges any more – horses who have already won three or four and you know they are Graded horses. You might have to buy them after they've won a maiden, or just been placed in one, and then try to make them into Graded winners, and that's a brave man's route.

"But we've got some lovely young horses and we've got to be patient and not rush

....

Nicholls churns out winners all season and has been profitable to follow in periods when the races come thick and fast – he has returned a level-stake profit in October (29-72, 40%, +£19.88), November (24-93, 26%, +£9.95) and March (15-73, 21%, +£12.52)

'We've got as strong a team as we had last season but we'll need a miracle to win the trainers' championship'

them, as they are our future. There's so much to look forward to."

He describes this season's team as "an awesome bunch", and nominates Modus, Movewiththetimes, El Bandit and Capitaine as among the more likely to make it to the top.

Novice chasing for Modus

"**Modus** could be a really good novice chaser," Nicholls says. "Having won the Lanzarote last season he's rated 156 over hurdles and we like to think hurdlers like him often end up 10lb or 20lb higher when they go over fences if they can jump, which makes him really interesting. He's schooled really well.

"**Movewiththetimes** won a bumper and two novice hurdles and was then only just beaten by Ballyandy in the Betfair Hurdle, running very well. He had a minor setback afterwards, which is why he didn't run at Cheltenham. Whether we give him a run over hurdles to see where we are with him will be up to connections, but ultimately he's going to be a very smart chaser.

"**El Bandit** won six over hurdles, including the Persian War at Chepstow, and he started this season well when absolutely bolting up in a valuable novice chase at Warwick in May. He wants three miles-plus and will be a grand novice chaser. I don't think I have a Hennessy horse this year – although **Le Mercurey** and **Present Man** will probably get entries – but if I did have one it might be a novice like El Bandit. It's a long shot, but Strong Flow won the race as a novice."

And of **Capitaine**, Nicholls says: "He won a Grade 2 over hurdles at Ascot last season and had his first run over fences at Newton Abbot in May, when he won well. He's a really exciting novice chaser."

Discussing some of his brighter hopes, Nicholls can't stop himself from adding **Dolos**, **Topofthegame**, **Copain De Classe** and more into the mix, concluding that he has an awful lot of horses who are going to win novice chases.

"Dolos is a 135-rated hurdler who goes novice chasing now," he says. "He's tough and professional and is one of those who might end up being a Frodon or a San Benedeto.

"Topofthegame is a giant of a horse who has chaser written all over him. He won his only point-to-point and then in three runs over hurdles he won at Ascot first time, when he surprised us a little, and ended up only just beaten there on his last start. He might not go to the top as a novice, but he'll go on improving for a season or two and will be a serious horse one day.

"Copain De Classe is a massive horse who won two novice hurdles last season and just needed time. He's built like a chaser and is one I'm really looking forward to. He's a work in progress but worth waiting for."

Stars of the future

The list of potential novice hurdle and bumper stars is even longer. Among them is **Captain Cattistock**, **Casko D'Airy**, **Cereal Killer**, **Dan McGrue**, **Dynamite Dollars**, **Get Out The Gate**, **If You Say Run**, **Kapcorse**, **Mont Des Avaloirs**, **Posh Trish**, **Stradivarius Davis**, **The Dellercheckout**, **Western Honour** and **Worthy Farm**.

Nicholls points out: "You just don't know what you might have with these novice hurdlers and bumper horses. If we'd been doing this years ago you'd never have known at the same stage what Denman might be. He'd won an Irish point-to-point, like a lot of these, but he showed nothing at home. It's only when you get going with them on the track that you really find out."

Going into detail about some of the new names on the roster at the master trainer's stables this season, Nicholls reveals: "**Binge Drinker** is new to us and is a really interesting one, as he beat Might Bite at Ffos Las on his only start over fences.

"I've got it in mind that he might be a Welsh National horse, and he could run first in the three-mile trial they have there early in December. Ultimately I see him as a Grand National horse, but he'd need five or

PAUL NICHOLLS
DITCHEAT, SOMERSET

	No. of Hrs	Races Run	1st	2nd	3rd	Unpl	Per cent	£1 Level Stake
NH Flat	20	24	7	3	3	11	29.2	-2.06
Hurdles	100	332	92	39	40	161	27.7	-39.89
Chases	77	317	72	50	37	158	22.7	-36.44
Totals	**161**	**673**	**171**	**92**	**80**	**330**	**25.4**	**-78.39**
15-16	165	581	123	106	77	275	21.2	-71.23
14-15	141	531	128	89	82	232	24.1	+52.54

BY MONTH

NH Flat	W-R	Per cent	£1 Level Stake
May	1-3	33.3	+2.00
June	0-0	0.0	0.00
July	1-1	100.0	+1.75
August	0-0	0.0	0.00
September	0-0	0.0	0.00
October	3-5	60.0	+5.25
November	0-5	0.0	-5.00
December	0-1	0.0	-1.00
January	0-1	0.0	-1.00
February	0-1	0.0	-1.00
March	0-1	0.0	-1.00
April	2-6	33.3	-2.06

Hurdles	W-R	Per cent	£1 Level Stake
May	5-19	26.3	-8.60
June	3-6	50.0	-1.89
July	2-7	28.6	-2.45
August	3-5	60.0	+2.79
September	1-4	25.0	-2.20
October	18-42	42.9	+9.84
November	13-47	27.7	+5.57
December	9-41	22.0	-9.76
January	6-28	21.4	-4.21
February	7-43	16.3	-9.25
March	6-35	17.1	-11.70
April	19-55	34.5	-8.03

Chases	W-R	Per cent	£1 Level Stake
May	5-23	21.7	-13.11
June	2-11	18.2	-5.55
July	0-8	0.0	0.00
August	0-6	0.0	-6.00
September	4-4	100.0	+3.74
October	8-25	32.0	+4.78
November	11-41	26.8	+9.38
December	11-45	24.4	+13.07
January	2-30	6.7	-27.04
February	10-31	32.3	-12.81
March	9-37	24.3	+25.22
April	10-56	17.9	-20.12

Totals	W-R	Per cent	£1 Level Stake
May	11-45	24.4	-19.71
June	5-17	29.4	-7.44
July	3-16	18.8	-8.70
August	3-11	27.3	-3.21
September	5-8	62.5	+1.54
October	29-72	40.3	+19.87
November	24-93	25.8	+9.95
December	20-87	23.0	+2.31
January	8-59	13.6	-32.25
February	17-75	22.7	-23.06
March	15-73	20.5	+12.52
April	31-117	26.5	-30.215

Statistics relate to all runners in Britain from May 1, 2016 to April 30, 2017

DISTANCE

Hurdles	W-R	Per cent	£1 Level Stake	Chases	W-R	Per cent	£1 Level Stake
2m-2m3f	37-131	28.2	-15.94	2m-2m3f	18-62	29.0	-7.27
2m4f-2m7f	34-106	32.1	-9.27	2m4f-2m7f	26-121	21.5	-36.53
3m+	4-21	19.0	+7.00	3m+	12-80	15.0	+3.38

TYPE OF RACE

Non-Handicaps	W-R	Per cent	£1 Level Stake	Handicaps	W-R	Per cent	£1 Level Stake
Nov Hrdls	46-122	37.7	-11.89	Nov Hrdls	2-8	25.0	-1.00
Hrdls	23-83	27.7	-12.86	Hrdls	21-118	17.8	-13.13
Nov Chs	34-86	39.5	+3.43	Nov Chs	3-24	12.5	-8.25
Chases	10-47	21.3	-11.00	Chases	18-135	13.3	-17.32
Sell/Claim	2-3	66.7	+0.37	Sell/Claim	0-0	0.0	0.00

RACE CLASS

	W-R	Per cent	£1 Level Stake
Class 1	22-196	11.2	-78.05
Class 2	24-124	19.4	+12.04
Class 3	43-140	30.7	+2.33
Class 4	69-175	39.4	-10.10
Class 5	8-22	36.4	+0.11
Class 6	5-16	31.3	-4.72

FIRST TIME OUT

	W-R	Per cent	£1 Level Stake
Bumpers	7-20	35.0	+1.94
Hurdles	22-83	26.5	-15.41
Chases	14-58	24.1	-9.09
Totals	43-161	26.7	-22.56

Bright young thing: Paul Nicholls has high hopes for Modus

six runs before then. He's exciting.

"**Darling Maltaix** is one I like. He won his only bumper in France and may have one more bumper run here in the autumn before going novice hurdling. We've given him plenty of time and he's benefited from it."

'He's a model chaser'

"**Give Me A Copper** is a really exciting horse who has won a bumper and a point-to-point in Ireland and two novice hurdles. He's been beaten only once and was wrong that day. He's a model chaser who stays very well and has a great attitude. He could be a Hennessy type next season.

"**Secret Investor** won his only point-to-point in Ireland and then ran very well to be second to Kimberlite Candy at Ascot in November on his only start over hurdles. We've given him lots of time and he's a ready-made winner.

"**Some Man** won his only point-to-point in Ireland, fairly bolting up, and his dam was a sister to Denman, so he's one to look forward to in novice hurdles.

And then there are the juveniles. Nicholls makes mention of **Grand Sancy**, **Risk And Roll** and **Chief Craftsman**, a former Luca Cumani maiden from the Flat.

Going into more detail, the trainer says:

DID YOU KNOW?

Paul Nicholls began his training operation at Manor Farm, Ditcheat, by replying to an advert in the Sporting Life. Previously he'd been assistant trainer to David Barons and played a key role in training Seagram to win the 1991 Grand National. Nicholls had also been a jockey with Barons, winning back-to-back Hennessys with Broadheath and Playschool. Nicholls initially started out with just eight horses with his first winner holding a licence being named after the village in which he was raised, Olveston.

"**Malaya** is a lovely three-year-old and could be as good as anything we've got. She had decent Flat form in France and very quickly translated it to hurdles, winning two of her three races there and maybe should have won all three. She's a very exciting filly.

'Elegant and going nicely'

"**Sao** is another very nice juvenile who won at Compiegne in May for Guillaume Macaire, who also had his half-brother Frodon at the same stage. He's an elegant-looking horse and goes nicely.

"**Tommy Hallinan** showed a nice level of form on the Flat in Ireland and we bought him and gelded him after he won at Cork in May. He'll be a nice juvenile."

Many of the horses we know from past campaigns are also on the way back to action, with some returning from injury.

Starting with **Politologue**, Nicholls says: "He won three novices last season and was desperately unlucky not to win the Grade 1 Maghull Novices' Chase at Aintree, where he came down at the last and left San Benedeto to benefit from it. We'd been riding him patiently to get home over two and a half miles, but Aintree showed me he can make a top-class two-miler this season. He's going for the Haldon Gold Cup first and we'll get plenty of graft into him before that. After that we'll know if he's good enough to go the Graded route or else stays handicapping.

'Life is going to be tough for him'

Frodon was a revelation last season and won the Caspian Caviar Gold Cup when still a four-year-old. Nicholls says: He's a joy to train but life is going to be tough for him now off 152, although he did win six last season and is still only five, and so he could go on improving a little. He'll probably go for some of those conditions races, but he'll definitely have an entry in some of the better handicaps."

Another five-year-old giving Nicholls reason for a decent campaign is **Clan Des Obeaux**.

"He was very impressive in the Berkshire Chase and was then an excellent second to

THE JOCKEY CLUB
Since 1750

—— 2017 ——
FIXTURE LIST

MIDWEEK GO RACING RACEDAY
Thursday 5th October

MIDWEEK GO RACING RACEDAY
Tuesday 17th October

**THE BRIAN MARTIN PALLETS
ANNUAL BEER FESTIVAL RACEDAY**
Sunday 5th November

**MICHAELMAS HURDLE
GO RACING RACEDAY**
Tuesday 14th November

WINTER LADIES DAY*
Saturday 25th November

THE PETERBOROUGH CHASE DAY*
Sunday 10th December

BOXING DAY RACING*
Tuesday 26th December

*FEATURE DAYS

BOOK TICKETS NOW
01480 453 373

RACE O

HUNTINGDON.THEJOCKEYCLUB.CO.UK

HUNTINGDON
A Jockey Club Racecourse

Whisper at Cheltenham. He started off brilliantly but lost his bottle a bit and became a bit disappointing, developing a tendency to jump right. He had a little breathing issue, which was a factor, so he had a little wind op in the summer. He's only five and I think there's a lot of improvement in him. There's a good race in him, and he might start with a prep over hurdles in something like the Tote Silver Trophy at Chepstow."

Vicente to go for Ayr hat-trick

Two seasons ago Vicente landed the Scottish National to assure Nicholls a late victory in the trainers' championship. And last year, although the title could not be won, Vicente won the Ayr marathon for the second year running, and the plan this time is to attempt a third victory in the race.

Nicholls says: "He just seems to blossom in the spring and he'll have a lightish campaign geared towards a bid to win the Scottish National for the third year in a row. He'll have an entry in the National, but I don't honestly think his jumping is good enough. It was probably a blessing he fell at the first there in April, as it meant he didn't have a race and was fresh for Ayr two weeks later.

Irving leads hurdles team

For a trainer perhaps better known for his expertise with chasers, there are plenty of established hurdlers at Manor Farm who leap off the page, kicking off with **Irving**, who will again be bidding to make a winning start to his latest campaign.

"He has problems with his joints and is difficult to train, but he always wins first time out and last season it was the Fighting Fifth, which he also won in 2014. After Christmas it can be a waste of time, but if he can win a Grade 1 again first time out everyone will be happy. He'll go straight to Newcastle.

Cliffs Of Dover was a revelation last season and has Nicholls eyeing victory in a decent handicap: "What he did last season as a juvenile was amazing. He couldn't win a race on the Flat and came here rated 64, so I wasn't expecting him to win six races over hurdles, including the Grade 2 at Doncaster.

"He jarred a tendon and, although it was only minor, he'd also had a fair bit of stick on the Flat and so we left him alone in the second half of the season.

"He'll have a steady preparation for his return, and he might have one run on the Flat, as he's obviously well handicapped. I'm aiming to have him ready for something nice around Christmas. If he doesn't win another Graded race he'll definitely win a big handicap.

Zarkandar back for more

At the other end of the age scale is ten-year-old **Zarkandar**, winner of ten races for the stable, all of them Graded races and four of them Grade 1.

Nicholls says: "We were thinking of retiring him, but he's too young for that. He'll probably have just four races and we'll keep him below the very top level in small-field

Sam Twiston-Davies is the one most likely to be on board the yard's bumper winners. Last season, he was 3-9 for the yard in such races (33%, +£1.25), but look out for the occasions when Stan Sheppard is utilised in this sphere. The conditional rider was 2-7 for the yard in NH Flat races last term and 1-2 the season before

....

Nicholls made good use of conditional riders last term. Over hurdles, Harry Cobden had a fantastic record for the yard (24-54, 44%, +£16.92) while over fences, those ridden by Jack Sherwood fared best from a level-stake perspective (6-17, 35%, +£14.75)

....

Nicholls has a successful knack of placing his hurdlers in Listed races. His runners in this area return a level-stake profit (15-54, 28%, +£5.27)

Clan Des Obeaux (5): had a breathing operation during the summer

conditions races, possibly in France or Ireland. The race at Aintree in November that he would have won last year is an obvious target again."

A five-year-old who can be expected to win races over hurdles this season is **Zubayr**. "Things didn't quite fall into place for him last season, but he was only just touched off in the Scottish Champion Hurdle and would have won if he had jumped the last," says Nicholls.

"There's a good handicap in him on the Flat one day, but in the short term he could be one for the Elite Hurdle at Wincanton."

Ptit Zig didn't manage to score in Britain after winning the French Champion Hurdle

in June 2016, but Nicholls is considering a switch back to fences for him: "He ran some honest races in defeat and picked up plenty of place money. He could go for the Wetherby Grade 2 that Silsol won last year, and it wouldn't surprise me if we had another go over fences with him one day."

Ready to return to action

And there is news of **Silsol**: "He had a minor injury but he's back again and will be running in the good staying hurdles. He'll be ready for Wetherby again, but he'd want cut in the ground to be running there.

Emerging Talent is another on the comeback trail after some time on the

sidelines. Nicholls reports: "He's a good horse who won three of his last four over hurdles two seasons ago and was second to Native River the season before. He got a leg and has had 18 months off, but he's come back in good shape and I've been riding him myself, so he'll be fit, that's for sure."

The 2016 Fred Winter Hurdle winner **Diego Du Charmil** is another set to switch to chasing this season, with Nicholls saying: "He's got to the top of his mark over hurdles now and is going over fences. He's a lovely big horse and is going to be a really nice novice chaser. He'll start at two miles."

Another festival winner in the stable is **Ibis Du Rheu**, who landed the Martin Pipe Hurdle in 2016, only to struggle subsequently. Nicholls says: "It was hard to find races for him last season, so he ended up carrying top weight in a couple of races and running okay. He needed to mature and we've not seen the best of him by a long way."

Old Guard has two big wins to his name having landed Cheltenham's Greatwood and International Hurdles during a profitable spell at the end of 2015. Nicholls reports: "He's had a wind op and will probably mix and match hurdling and chasing. He's won only one chase and didn't jump well, but if I can get him jumping well he'll probably go for a graduation chase."

'I'm sure he's well handicapped'

One who had been aimed at the Cheltenham Festival last season was **Romain De Senam**, only to miss the cut for the novice handicap chase by one.

Nicholls says: "I'm convinced he wants a

Emerging Talent (left): Nicholls has been riding him out and reports him to be in good shape

strongly run two and a half miles, and I'm sure he's well handicapped off 133, so he'll be going straight for the BetVictor Chase at Cheltenham off a light weight."

San Benedeto ran in the top 2m handicaps last season and kept on improving, winning six, including the Grade 1 at Aintree in which Politologue fell at the last. Nicholls reports: "He'll probably start off in the Haldon Gold Cup and then go for the £100,000 handicap at Ascot at the end of November."

Nicholls also has an early target in mind for his **Present Man**, who rattled off a four-timer over fences last season and rose up the handicap by 17lb: "He loves going right-handed and attacking his fences. We're aiming him first at the Badger Ales Chase at Wincanton in November."

Fences are expected to bring the best out of **Adrien Du Pont**, and Nicholls says: "He's always been a chaser in the making and he'll leave his mark of 143 well behind when he goes over fences."

As De Mee is a superb jumper who enjoyed his finest hour when he won the Grand Sefton at Aintree. Nicholls has that race in mind again and is also considering an entry in the Grand National.

"**Le Prezien** was a good novice chaser last season. He's very solid, so he'll be going for some of those better handicaps.

"**Tommy Silver** is a 146-rated hurdler who won at Taunton and Plumpton last season and loves decent ground. He's going over fences and will be a nice two-mile or two-and-a-half-mile novice chaser.

"I've always liked **Antartica De Thaix** a lot and she found her niche last season, winning three in a row including a Listed chase for mares at Huntingdon. She'll be running in all of those mares' Listed races and should do well again.

"It was only a four-runner race when **Diamond Guy** won his bumper at Wincanton last season, but he won by half the track and he's a horse we like. He jumps well and has a bright future."

Interview by Graham Dench

SUPER STATS

Just over £2.5 million in prize-money wasn't enough to earn Nicholls the trainers' title last season – an honour he has conceded just twice in the last 12 years – but his tally of 171 winners for last season was a personal best

His hurdlers are best followed at a couple of tracks close to his base in Ditcheat. Nicholls has sent out plenty of winners over timber at Taunton (34-101, 34%, +£8.91) and Wincanton (50-123, 41%, +£9.97) with high strike-rates and solid level-stake returns

Anything Nicholls sends north is always worth a look. Decent figures are posted at Ayr (11-39, 28%, +£36.00), Perth (5-11, 45%, +£7.66), Carlisle (4-6, 67%, +£5.95) and Musselburgh (6-18, 33%, +£4.11)

A strike-rate of 11% at Cheltenham is respectable given how competitive the racing is at Prestbury Park, and some of his winners oblige at decent prices as a level-stake profit of £2.63 at the track demonstrates

Chasers can be backed with confidence at Haydock (10-26, 38%, +£5.73) and Fontwell (18-39, 46%, +£11.09). At the latter venue, Nicholls was 7-14 over fences last term (50%, +£13.28) and 4-5 the season before that (80%, +£2.98)

Success in bumpers is most frequent at Wincanton. Nicholls is 7-22 in that sphere at the Somerset venue (7-22, 32%, +£6.44)

TOTEPOOL
JUMP
SEASON
OPENER

THE WINTER SEASON STARTS AT CHEPSTOW

OKTOBERFEST SATURDAY
14TH OCTOBER
**£50, 000 Grade 3 Totepool
Silver Trophy Handicap Hurdle**

FAMILY SUNDAY
15TH OCTOBER
**£35,000 Grade 2 Totepool
Persian War Novices' Hurdle**

TOP RUNNERS AT CHEPSTOW'S JUMP SEASON OPENER FROM 2011 - 2016

CUE CARD 2011
The most popular jumper of recent years. Top class performer. Won his first novice chase here. Looked set to win the 2016 Cheltenham Gold Cup when coming down three out.

BLAKLION 2014
Tough staying type. Since graduating to fences he won the 2016 RSA Chase at Cheltenham and finished fifth in the Hennessy. Made favourite for the 2017 Grand National, he came in fourth.

SIRE DE GRUGY 2013
Won a handicap here easily before going on to take the Tingle Creek, Desert Orchid, Clarence House, Champion Chase and Celebration Chase, all in that season. The winner of 17 races altogether.

SHELFORD 2014
A game winner of two hurdles here and 8 in all, including twice in France. Novice chasing now and a good second in the valuable Uttoxeter Summer Cup in July.

ALTIOR 2015
The 34 length winner of a novice hurdle here has won all his ten races since, including the Arkle at Cheltenham. He is generally considered to be the top two mile chaser in Britain and Ireland.

VICENTE 2014
Second to Blaklion here when the going was soft. Much better on fast ground and has won the last two runnings of the Scottish Grand National.

BOOK NOW!

WHAT STARS WILL WE SEE IN 2017?

chepstow-racecourse.co.uk | 01291 622260

THE LOWDOWN DAVID PIPE

Cheltenham ace Temps leads way as big aim is to increase winner tally

I N his own words, David Pipe recalls last season as tough. Yet a Cheltenham Festival winner always helps to distract from some of the unfortunate setbacks suffered along the way.

Only twice in 11 years has Pipe arrived back from Cheltenham at his Pond House stable empty-handed, a terrific record many trainers can only aspire to.

For the second year running Un Temps Pour Tout was victorious in the Ultima Handicap Chase and landed the all-important prize for the stable when fighting off favourite Singlefarmpayment in one of the finishes of the festival.

All roads will lead back to the festival this year for many of his string as Pipe begins mapping out plans for his squad. "It's still early days and we'll form more solid plans for our stronger horses over the next few weeks," he says in the middle of September. "The string is mostly back in but the majority are only steadily cantering and haven't done any serious work as of yet.

"We don't do anything too intense until around November when the proper soft ground tends to turn up as most of mine like that."

A third win in the Ultima is Pipe's aim for **Un Temps Pour Tout** as well as a potential shot at the Grand National.

The trainer says: "He'll start later on this year, probably in the new year as he races a lot better towards the end of the season. We'll aim for another Cheltenham win and he'll get an entry in the National too."

The Pond House team last season seemed to carry momentum into Aintree and had four runners in the National. Vieux Lion Rouge, Ballynagour, La Vaticane and Doctor Harper all returned safe and sound, although it is likely the race was the last hurrah for stable veterans Ballynagour and La Vaticane, with the latter likely to head off to stud and the former as a Cheltenham Festival winner in 2014.

Vieux Lion Rouge had been tipped up in many circles for the big one after winning over the national fences in the Becher Chase last December and following up impressively

DID YOU KNOW?

David Pipe learned his training trade with stints around the world. Before he took over the reins from his father at Pond House he spent time with Michael Dickinson in the States, Criquette Head-Maarek in France and Joey Ramsden in South Africa. Pipe was also a hugely successful point-to-point trainer, amassing no fewer than 164 winners.

'He'll be aimed at the National again. He had a good summer and his season will certainly be based around Aintree'

DAVID PIPE RACING

in the National Trial at Haydock. He ran well to finish sixth at Aintree and Pipe is now looking forward to another shot at the prize.

He says: "He'll be aimed at the National again. He had a good summer – it's early days and he's only back in light cantering but his season will certainly be based around Aintree."

Pipe alludes to the tough campaign he endured last season, with the team picking up 59 winners, compared to 80 a year earlier.

Yet his stayers performed well towards the end of the season and brought in plenty of welcome prize-money.

Doctor Harper will return for another season and will be on the lookout for the usual prizes again for the Johnson family. Pipe says: "He'll be targeted at plenty of long-distance chases but is always in the grip of the handicapper so we'll take it step by step and find the best opportunities."

Vieux Lion Rouge: season will be based at the Grand National, in which he finished sixth last season

RACING POST

The Racing Post app.
Home to racing's top information.
Home to racing's top bookies.

Why continually flit between apps when racing's best information and top bookies are sitting side by side in one app? Better yet, you can remain logged in to all four bookies at once and simply switch account to bet with the best odds. Home sweet home, as they say.

When You Bet on Racing,
You Can Bet on Racing Post.

Racer's return will be delayed

Pipe reports the 2015 Champion Bumper winner **Moon Racer** suffered some colic over the summer and will be out until the new year. He says: "He had some problems in the summer and we're not going to see him out until the new year in all likelihood. He'll be aimed at some valuable handicaps rather than following a similar route to last season, especially at first."

Moon Racer was sent off at just 10-1 for the Champion Hurdle on the back of a Grade 2 strike at the track last November but was ultimately pulled up at the festival. He was also a little disappointing at Aintree, but a handicap mark of 142 looks ripe for exposing if he can recapture his best form.

The versatile **Starchitect** is one horse Pipe can look forward to running, and the trainer believes with some aid from the assessor it could be a fruitful campaign.

"The handicapper was harsh enough with him last year and he didn't get the best of luck at Cheltenham and perhaps didn't stay at Aintree, where he still finished third. Anything around two and a half miles will suit this season and we'll look at all the big handicap chases with him."

More to come from Champers

Champers On Ice showed plenty of ability as a novice chaser last season and certainly has a prize in him this year. Unlike a lot of

Moon Racer (right): could exploit a decent handicap mark when returning to action in the new year

Pipe's horses he seemed to do his best work early in the season and could be one to watch early on.

Pipe says: "In hindsight Champers On Ice's run behind American at Warwick in a Listed novice chase in January now looks very good after the winner bolted up again at Uttoxeter. On top of that, I'm not certain he quite did himself justice last season and I'm sure there's more to come."

Second in his point-to-point to Finian's Oscar in October last year, Mr Clarkson entered last season with a big reputation. He duly delivered with four wins over hurdles but will miss this term with a tendon injury he suffered at Cheltenham.

Mr Big Shot will be back in action, however, and it's easy to see why he comes with a decent reputation. Although he was

Pipe's hurdlers are best followed over longer distances as those running over trips ranging from 2m7f-3m2f return a handsome profit (48-321, 15%, +£18.89). However, his chasers tend to fare better over shorter distances with those running over trips ranging from 2m1f-2m3f posting the best figures (11-35, 31%, +£9.20)

kept to lesser company last year, he more than impressed on his two starts over hurdles and is unbeaten having also won a bumper on his racecourse debut in March last year.

Plans are still to be laid out for the exciting six-year-old but Pipe says: "He's always shown a lot at home and has improved every time he's gone on the racecourse. He's still very big and backwards and that's why we've been quiet with him so far. We'll probably start him off over hurdles and see what happens after that."

Rose to fly over long distances

Rathlin Rose helped Guy Disney record a historic double last season as the amputee teamed up with the nine-year-old to win the Royal Artillery Gold Cup and Grand Military Gold Cup in a story that gained much media attention.

Pipe believes there may still be more to come from the horse, saying: "Last season was fantastic for more than one reason, but he's a decent long-distance chaser and like a lot of ours relishes the mud. He'll be campaigned with that in mind."

Bidourey's unfinished business

One who made an immediate impact when joining the Pipe stable in 2014 was **Bidourey**. He won his first four starts, before picking up an injury when stepped up in grade for the Ladbroke Hurdle at Ascot in December 2015 and hasn't raced since.

Pipe retains the utmost faith in the six-year-old, however, and things are slowly beginning to look up after a frustrating layoff.

He says: "Bidourey has been an unlucky horse. He won't be out until possibly the new year after picking up another small problem at the end of last year. He's got age on his side, though, so I'm sure we'll get him back soon and there's certainly some unfinished business."

King's Socks is another name for the notebook. He is yet to run for Pipe, again due to injuries, but there is plenty of excitement surrounding his long-awaited return to the track.

The French import did well across the Channel with a Listed hurdle win as a four-year-old, followed by two finishes behind Willie Mullins' Footpad. He was bought for €210,000 at the Arqana July sales in 2016 and Pipe will be hoping he can become a flagship horse for the team.

He says: "He picked up an injury last season and still hasn't been able to run for us. We'll hopefully have him on the racecourse around Christmas. He's got some very good form and will be aimed at the festivals."

Orchard pleasing in his work

Another horse yet to make his debut for Pipe is **Orchard Thieves**. He was purchased for £115,000 at the Cheltenham Festival sales in 2016 after finishing second in an Irish point-to-point.

The trainer says: "He hasn't run for us since coming over from Ireland but we're pleased with what he's been showing at home in his work. Whether he starts over hurdles or just

Rathlin Rose: helped Guy Disney to achieve a memorable feat last season and is expected to do well this time, especially when the ground is riding soft

DAVID PIPE

NICHOLASHAYNE, DEVON

	No. of Hrs	Races Run	1st	2nd	3rd	Unpl	Per cent	£1 Level Stake
NH Flat	16	22	3	2	5	12	13.6	-6.00
Hurdles	83	259	32	25	20	182	12.4	-116.10
Chases	52	206	24	20	17	145	11.7	-71.99
Totals	**116**	**487**	**59**	**47**	**42**	**339**	**12.1**	**-194.09**
15-16	126	575	80	77	68	350	13.9	-115.92
14-15	136	582	116	72	66	328	19.9	-50.46

BY MONTH

NH Flat	W-R	Per cent	£1 Level Stake	Hurdles	W-R	Per cent	£1 Level Stake
May	0-3	0.0	-3.00	May	3-18	16.7	-2.88
June	0-2	0.0	-2.00	June	1-11	9.1	-4.50
July	0-0	0.0	0.00	July	1-10	10.0	-3.00
August	1-1	100.0	+4.50	August	2-13	15.4	-2.00
September	1-1	100.0	+4.00	September	3-17	17.6	-0.67
October	0-0	0.0	0.00	October	3-19	15.8	-8.38
November	0-0	0.0	0.00	November	5-32	15.6	-11.13
December	0-2	0.0	-2.00	December	6-35	17.1	-11.26
January	1-4	25.0	+1.50	January	3-32	9.4	-24.68
February	0-3	0.0	-3.00	February	1-23	4.3	-21.00
March	0-5	0.0	-5.00	March	2-28	7.1	-18.75
April	0-1	0.0	-1.00	April	2-21	9.5	-7.88

Chases	W-R	Per cent	£1 Level Stake	Totals	W-R	Per cent	£1 Level Stake
May	2-21	9.5	-9.00	May	5-42	11.9	-14.88
June	3-15	20.0	-2.38	June	4-28	14.3	-8.88
July	2-14	14.3	-9.79	July	3-24	12.5	-12.79
August	2-14	14.3	0.00	August	5-28	17.9	+2.50
September	1-7	14.3	+3.00	September	5-25	20.0	+6.33
October	1-15	6.7	-9.50	October	4-34	11.8	-17.88
November	1-19	5.3	-10.00	November	6-51	11.8	-21.13
December	4-23	17.4	-1.30	December	10-60	16.7	-14.56
January	1-23	4.3	-20.90	January	5-59	8.5	-44.08
February	3-15	20.0	+1.13	February	4-41	9.8	-22.87
March	3-21	14.3	-2.75	March	5-54	9.3	-26.50
April	1-19	5.3	-10.50	April	3-41	7.3	-19.38

DISTANCE

Hurdles	W-R	Per£1 cent	Level Stake	Chases	W-R	Per cent	£1 Level Stake
2m-2m3f	13-102	12.7	-63.43	2m-2m3f	4-20	20.0	-6.79
2m4f-2m7f	10-76	13.2	-26.55	2m4f-2m7f	3-64	4.7	-44.00
3m+	3-21	14.3	-5.13	3m+	12-99	12.1	-20.42

TYPE OF RACE

Non-Handicaps	W-R	Per cent	£1 Level Stake	Handicaps	W-R	Per cent	£1 Level Stake
Nov Hrdls	8-53	15.1	-27.59	Nov Hrdls	0-9	0.0	-9.00
Hrdls	4-30	13.3	-19.71	Hrdls	17-159	10.7	-60.55
Nov Chs	5-17	29.4	-5.49	Nov Chs	2-16	12.5	-6.38
Chases	2-5	40.0	+0.38	Chases	14-152	9.2	-50.50
Sell/Claim	3-7	42.9	+1.75	Sell/Claim	0-1	0.0	-1.00

RACE CLASS / FIRST TIME OUT

RACE CLASS	W-R	Per cent	£1 Level Stake	FIRST TIME OUT	W-R	Per cent	£1 Level Stake
Class 1	4-48	8.3	-16.75	Bumpers	3-16	18.8	0.00
Class 2	7-59	11.9	-15.63	Hurdles	9-66	13.6	-32.80
Class 3	19-141	13.5	-38.30	Chases	7-34	20.6	+7.08
Class 4	21-184	11.4	-97.96				
Class 5	5-37	13.5	-23.46	Totals	19-116	16.4	-25.72
Class 6	3-18	16.7	-2.00				

Statistics relate to all runners in Britain from May 1, 2016 to April 30, 2017

in a bumper, we're undecided as of yet and will take our time."

Eur Gone West is another Irish import, purchased in June after finishing third on his first point-to-point.

The four-year-old is settling into life at Pond House but Pipe is quietly optimistic about his future, saying: "We don't know too much about him yet, but he looks a good stamp of a horse and should prove useful."

It's Obvious was bought for £85,000 at the Aintree sales in 2016 after two runs in Irish point-to-points, finishing runner-up on the second occasion in a race in which the front two pulled 30 lengths clear. He is another to have suffered a setback but is expected to make his debut for Pipe soon.

The trainer says: "He'll start out in a bumper. It will just be nice to get him back on the track this year and he should be competitive."

Buster Edwards made his debut under rules early in September and showed plenty of promise when second at Worcester in a maiden hurdle. Pipe believes he will improve with time and will need a step up in trip to reach his potential.

Pipe says: "He ran a solid race at Worcester on his debut against more experienced rivals and looks to be improving. Hopefully he can go one better soon and anything from two and a half miles up to three miles will eventually see him at his best."

One for the Ces

Pipe also has a likely runner for October's valuable Cesarewitch Handicap at Newmarket in **Friday Night Light**. Another recent French import, he showed plenty of ability on the Flat as a three-year-old for Elie Lellouche.

He is likely to need a run beforehand – to get into the race and to freshen him up – but looks completely unexposed and should get his preferred ground at this time of year.

Pipe says: "He might have a hurdle run before the Cesarewitch just to keep him going. He's got form over shorter distances on the Flat but he gives us the impression he should stay the trip.

Interview by Callum Jamieson

SUPER STATS

Pipe endured a disappointing season last term on the numbers front. A total of 59 winners was his lowest since taking the helm at Nicholashayne in 2006 while the prize-money earned was just shy of £800,000 – only the third time he has failed to break the £1 million barrier

Pipe returns his highest level-stake profit with runners at Haydock (12-67, 18%, +£49.00)

His most impressive strike-rates come at Perth (13-24, 54%, +£23.11) and Leicester (11-24, 46%, +£15.06) where he also returns a healthy level-stake profit

Pipe's chasers tend to do well at Wincanton (8-27, 30%, +£13.13)

He sent out plenty of winners last season at Worcester (7-37, 19%, +£0.38), Market Rasen (5-14, 36%, +£6.70) and Uttoxeter (5-30, 17%, +£3.70)

Pipe's bumper runners at Cheltenham are always worth a look (3-9, 33%, +£4.75)

Pipe is at his best in bumpers when the focus is on stamina. National Hunt Flat races run in excess of 2m1f see his followers return a profit (4-10, 40%, +£12.13)

Tom Scudamore rides most of the yard's winners to a level-stake loss, but there are profits with chasers (86-440, 20%, +£8.77) and those running in bumpers (24-102, 24%, +£7.43)

—2017/18—

FIXTURE LIST

Wednesday 1st November

Thursday 16th November

Thursday 30th November

Thursday 14th December ~ FESTIVE FIXTURE

Saturday 30th December ~ CHRISTMAS RACEDAY

Tuesday 9th January ~ 2 FOR 1 OFFER*

Saturday 20th January

Sunday 4th February

Tuesday 20th February

Thursday 1st March

Monday 12th March ~ FREE RACEDAY

Monday 26th March ~ FAMILY RACEDAY

Thursday 12th April ~ LADIES DAY

Wednesday 25th April ~ EVENING RACEDAY

*Conditions apply

TAUNTONRACECOURSE.CO.UK

TAUNTON RACECOURSE
& conference centre

THE LOWDOWN LUCINDA RUSSELL

Riding the crest of a wave with high hopes Arthur can do it again

FOLLOWING a quiet couple of years Lucinda Russell shot back into the limelight with One For Arthur's superb success in last season's Grand National and is quite rightly upbeat about the new campaign.

"It's exciting for us to keep the momentum. We're very lucky to have such a brilliant team and some fantastic jockeys, including the amateurs. Everyone's enthusiasm is shining through and it's a fantastic time to be in the yard," Russell says.

And the trainer is delighted some key alterations made during last season came good in no uncertain terms: "We made some radical changes in October and November and they definitely worked," says Russell.

"It was a fantastic season. We started off slowly and after the changes it began to improve.

"We were confident heading into the spring – the horses began to run to a different level. It was great the momentum continued, and to see the improvement in horses was unbelievable."

One For Arthur bounded his way into Aintree contention with an impressive win in Warwick's Classic Chase, ending his four-race season rated 156, having started the year with a mark of 127.

It is not often the Grand National winner is said to have won with a bit in hand, but in One For Arthur's case that might just be true.

Unsurprisingly all roads will lead back to Aintree and One For Arthur will be targeted at a National repeat, but Russell knows the expectations will be higher this time.

"It will be tougher this year up the weights but ultimately I have it at the back of my mind that his best trip is four miles-plus, and his favourite track is the National course at Aintree. While it may not be so easy to win races in the build-up, our aim is to win the race again and that's what we'll set out to do.

"Every trainer will tell you, whichever horse you train – you just want to get them to that end goal. You race them and you want them to keep progressing. We're so lucky to have a horse like Arthur."

Last season's preparation came to fruition on Merseyside and Russell sees no reason to get distracted and be too clever this time.

"We'll look to take in the same races beforehand. Our plan is to go to Kelso for the race he won there last year, then the Becher Chase, then Warwick and once again the National – it's the right thing to do. The simple thing is always the best thing for the horse."

....

Hexham is where Russell sends out most of her winners and it's also where she provides her highest level-stake returns (38-218, 17%, +£50.22)

WINNERS IN LAST FIVE SEASONS 43, 48, 47, 66, 59

'Everyone's enthusiasm
is shining through and
it's a fantastic time to
be in the yard'

The Grand National factor has helped oversee what some are calling a resurgence in Scottish racing, but Russell does not think their National win is the only reason for her team's growth and Scottish racing in general.

"Last season we were working with 60 to 65 horses and this season we'll be around 80 or 85," Russell says. "The Grand National has helped in that sense, but I think the forward momentum in Scottish racing is mostly driven by the racecourses, and we're really starting to take steps forward."

River ready to flow over fences

Big River was another big improver for the yard last season. The seven-year-old began with a rating of 115 and after a convincing win at Kelso in March finished his campaign rated 144 over hurdles. He will go novice chasing this season.

"We've been schooling him over fences and he's jumped really well," the trainer says. "He had a heart issue a couple of years back that set him back slightly but he's over that and I'd like to think he'll be better over fences after progressing plenty last year. We'll look at some novice chases, hopefully the one at Kempton over Christmas."

One for the Scottish National

Another novice chaser Russell thinks highly of is **Sammy B**, a three-time winner over hurdles last season. "He's definitely a stayer and I really think he could be a Scottish National horse," says Russell.

"He's been jumping fences well at home and if he takes to them properly he could certainly be a National horse. Like Big River, we'll start him over fences soon."

With chances for the Scottish and Aintree nationals laid out, **Newtown Lad** may be the stable's hope for the Welsh National. He thrived in the mud last season during his first year over the fences and won at Uttoxeter and Ayr.

"He loves soft ground and won brilliantly at Uttoxeter last season," says Russell. "He's done well over the summer and once the soft

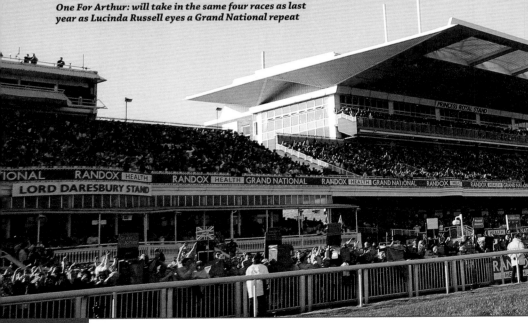

One For Arthur: will take in the same four races as last year as Lucinda Russell eyes a Grand National repeat

LUCINDA RUSSELL
ARLARY, PERTH & KINROSS

	No. of Hrs	Races Run	1st	2nd	3rd	Unpl	Per cent	£1 Level Stake
NH Flat	13	17	1	1	1	14	5.9	-2.00
Hurdles	61	222	22	24	27	149	9.9	-30.96
Chases	46	172	20	16	25	111	11.6	-40.29
Totals	**89**	**411**	**43**	**41**	**53**	**274**	**10.5**	**-73.25**
15-16	93	380	48	48	65	219	12.6	-48.21
14-15	112	512	47	64	60	341	9.2	-218.40

BY MONTH

NH Flat	W-R	Per cent	£1 Level Stake	Hurdles	W-R	Per cent	£1 Level Stake
May	0-0	0.0	0.00	May	2-24	8.3	-2.00
June	0-1	0.0	-1.00	June	0-18	0.0	-18.00
July	0-1	0.0	-1.00	July	2-13	15.4	+1.00
August	0-0	0.0	0.00	August	0-4	0.0	-4.00
September	0-1	0.0	-1.00	September	1-14	7.1	-1.00
October	1-2	50.0	+13.00	October	0-20	0.0	-20.00
November	0-3	0.0	-3.00	November	2-21	9.5	-12.00
December	0-3	0.0	-3.00	December	2-26	7.7	-7.17
January	0-3	0.0	-3.00	January	4-21	19.0	+35.50
February	0-0	0.0	0.00	February	1-12	8.3	-4.50
March	0-2	0.0	-2.00	March	6-26	23.1	+9.71
April	0-1	0.0	-1.00	April	2-23	8.7	-8.50

Chases	W-R	Per £1 cent	Level Stake	Totals	W-R	Per cent	£1 Level Stake
May	1-8	12.5	-3.50	May	3-32	9.4	-5.50
June	2-12	16.7	+3.50	June	2-31	6.5	-15.50

*Statistics relate to all runners in Britain
from May 1, 2016 to April 30, 2017*

DISTANCE

Hurdles	W-R	Per £1 cent	Level Stake	Chases	W-R	Per £1 cent	Level Stake
2m-2m3f	5-88	5.7	-49.50	2m-2m3f	4-31	12.9	-11.29
2m4f-2m7f	9-76	11.8	-6.79	2m4f-2m7f	8-56	14.3	+2.25
3m+	2-17	11.8	-2.67	3m+	7-46	15.2	+4.25

TYPE OF RACE

Non-Handicaps	W-R	Per cent	£1 Level Stake	Handicaps	W-R	Per cent	£1 Level Stake
Nov Hrdls	0-26	0.0	-26.00	Nov Hrdls	0-13	0.0	-13.00
Hrdls	1-26	3.8	-24.00	Hrdls	21-155	13.5	+34.04
Nov Chs	1-3	33.3	+4.00	Nov Chs	2-17	11.8	-9.75
Chases	0-3	0.0	-3.00	Chases	16-137	11.7	-23.04
Sell/Claim	0-1	0.0	-1.00	Sell/Claim	0-1	0.0	-1.00

RACE CLASS

	W-R	Per cent	£1 Level Stake
Class 1	2-7	28.6	+23.00
Class 2	1-19	5.3	-14.67
Class 3	5-71	7.0	-46.83
Class 4	26-216	12.0	-14.25
Class 5	8-84	9.5	-21.50
Class 6	1-14	7.1	+1.00

FIRST TIME OUT

	W-R	Per cent	£1 Level Stake
Bumpers	1-13	7.7	+2.00
Hurdles	2-45	4.4	-23.00
Chases	2-31	6.5	-20.50
Totals	5-89	5.6	-41.50

ground comes he'll be entered in some staying chases and could be a Welsh National type." says Russell.

Topham recovery mission

Imjoeking will turn 11 at the turn of the year, but Russell believes his form does the talking and there's no suggestion of beginning to ease him down, with another crack at the Topham Chase the big target.

"He's another who impressed everyone last year and we'll definitely take him back to Aintree for the Topham if we can," she says. "He was giving Derek [Fox] a terrific ride around there until he fell last April.

"He'll go in the usual handicap chases beforehand but did hurt himself a bit when he fell at Aintree so will have a bit longer off, but it won't be long before he's cantering again."

Another likely to be seen around Aintree regularly is **Tantamount**, a favourite at the yard, who signed off a busy season with a convincing win at Ayr.

Russell says: "He's been a fine horse but

DID YOU KNOW?

Lucinda Russell's partner and assistant trainer is eight-time champion jumps jockey Peter Scudamore. Russell, who became only the fourth woman to win the Grand National when successful at Aintree in April with One For Arthur, has been training since 1995 having previously evented, showjumped, trained point-to-pointers and been awarded a BSc Hons in Psychology at St Andrews University.

has a few issues now and again. He loves it around Aintree so we'll be on the lookout for races there.

"He's a very tenacious horse, but quite straightforward and very genuine. He used to hang badly at the end of his races but he's got much better with that now. We've found our formula with him now so there's no point changing that – he'll go over two and a half, up to three miles on good to soft ground," says Russell.

Vertigo hinted at some ability as a four-year-old last year and Russell thinks there are plenty of races out there for the youngster this season. "He'll stay over hurdles and should be one of our better staying hurdlers," she says.

"There's a niche out there for these horses and he's got such a great attitude."

'One of our most intelligent'

Another relative newcomer to the yard is **Deepsand**. "He's one of the most intelligent horses we have and we have to train him very differently because of that," Russell reveals.

"You can't do the same thing with him every day, so he spends a lot of time on the farm and jumping from field to field. He

On the schooling ground at Arlary House Stables

needs soft ground, and his run at Haydock last year was very impressive."

Forest Des Aigles has had five starts for the yard since arriving from Guillaume Macaire in France and Russell feels they have not got to the bottom of him yet: "He's a super horse and better than his handicap ratings. His aim will be the Northern Lights Series, a great initiative for us and the owners in this part of the world."

Russell has always been a huge fan of her stable jockey Derek Fox and is thankful to his talents for getting the best out of one of the stable's trickier customers.

"**Itstimeforapint** will be sent after further success in long-distance chases. Derek is brilliant on him as he's not the most

Forest Des Aigles (right): expected to show improved form this season

natural over the fences. I'd love to take him back to the four-mile chase at Musselburgh where he ended last season."

'She's been magic so far'

One of the new additions at the yard is **Simone**, who has been working well and has Russell looking ahead with excitement: "The owner is very keen to get some black type from this one. She's been magic so far in front of the hurdles and can dance in front of them. We'll start off small with her and are very hopeful she'll be useful with time."

Mighty Thunder won a bumper at Perth in June and is another youngster Russell sees capable of progressing plenty.

"He's exciting," she says. "He won his bumper well at Perth and has grown stronger over the summer. He'll be out in October or November and is a lovely horse with a great attitude.

"We're quietly hopeful for him and he should see some decent races over two and a half miles at some point. It was a very pleasing win for everyone at the yard when he scored first time out."

Boy's On Tour won an Irish point-to-point in April and finished a promising fourth

at Perth in September on his bumper debut for Russell. "He's a very handy little horse and we were pleased with his first run," she says. "He learned plenty that day and on good ground he could be a real Musselburgh or Kelso type in time. He could definitely be one to follow."

Younger pair on the up

There appears to be plenty of depth to Russell's team of younger horses, and **Blaydon** and **Emissaire** are two Russell speaks about enthusiastically.

Of Blaydon, Russell says: "He's bred very well and a solid horse to look forward to. He was in training last season but didn't get on the track, but will be racing soon, likely in a

bumper at Ayr towards the end of October. He's still quite green, very kind, but still quite naive. He tries hard and in the long term I'm hopeful he'll be one of our better chasers.

"**Emissaire** is really exciting. We bought him in France as a two-year-old and although he trained last year we didn't run him, but he's ready for some juvenile bumpers. He's a very strong youngster and a horse we all really like."

'A bit mad but super-talented'

An import from Ireland Russell is extremely excited about is **Saint Sreule**, a horse bought privately after a point-to-point: "We think he's talented. He's not big, but he was walking around the paddock with his head

up and it didn't bother him that it was pouring with rain.

"He went from the front and just as the horses came to him he went away again. He's a bit mad but is super-talented and we haven't managed to get him tired on the gallops yet."

Another recent acquisition from the point-to-point world in Ireland is the well-named **Champagnendiamonds**. "He's by Milan and we saw him at the sales a while back. He was third in a point-to-point and after that we had to buy him. He'll definitely be out as a novice hurdler soon and should be a good chaser eventually," says Russell.

Dino's Choice is another fresh face in the yard and was recently bought from Irish trainer Gavin Cromwell. "He's a very nice horse. He won a bumper for Gavin at Perth and Tom [Scudamore] said to us that we should buy him as he was one of the best bumper horses he's ridden. So we did and he should be an ideal type to go straight over hurdles with, likely at Kelso towards the end of October," says Russell.

There are a few older horses at Arlary who Russell believes should step up from their previous efforts last season. One of those potential improvers is **Moorstown**.

"I know he's low in the ratings but he's been improving over the summer. In soft ground over three miles I can definitely see him being rated well over 100 by the end of the season," says Russell.

Well Above Par has got a workable mark now according to the trainer and will be taken over fences, and the same can be said for **Haul Us In**. "She's a well-handicapped mare on her hurdles form and she'll be better with chasing in handicaps this season," says Russell.

Russell is also hopeful the yard's change in strategy can see **Island Heights** build on his promise displayed in chases, saying: "He had a bit of a stop-start season last year but he's got potential.

"He's the sort you'll see around Haydock as he loves the heavy ground. He doesn't get tired and just keeps galloping."

Interview by Callum Jamieson

SUPER STATS

A total of 43 winners last term was an average return compared to the standards Russell has set in recent years, but a prize-money tally just shy of the £1 million mark was easily a personal best, thanks largely to One For Arthur's Grand National success

Hurdlers do best at Haydock (5-30, 17%, +£36.00) while chasers are profitable to follow at Bangor (4-10, 40%, +£11.50)

Nearly all Russell's bumper winners are sent out close to her Scottish base with Musselburgh (2-12, 17%, +£2.00) and Newcastle (2-9, 22%, +£5.50) the most likely venues for success in National Hunt Flat races

Her runners in Graded chases shouldn't be underestimated (3-25, 12%, +£14.00). The strike-rate may not be high but winners at such a level usually return at a decent price

Russell's string is at its best when stamina is at a premium, especially over fences with chasers running over 3m3f-plus posting a handsome level-stake profit (10-44, 23%, +£38.63)

March has been a decent month for the yard for the past two seasons. She was 10-41 during that period last year (24%, +£12.08) and 6-37 the season before (16%, +£9.25)

Derek Fox is most likely to be on board the stable's winners, but conditional Stephen Mulqueen provided the best level-stakes return in chases for the yard last term (3-18, 17%, +£5.50)

THE LOWDOWN COLIN TIZZARD

Chasing powerhouses ready to go for another season to remember

LABELLING Colin Tizzard's last season as breakthrough would be hugely unfair, but the Dorset trainer has steadily amassed a serious team of horses and is extremely excited about getting the ball rolling ahead of what could potentially be an even greater campaign if the cards fall right.

"We were delighted with how last season went," he says. "We had 57 winners, which is our best ever, plus three more in Ireland and over two million in prize-money."

For part of last season Tizzard looked as if he may mount a serious challenge for the British trainers' championship. Ultimately, lack of numbers made it an almost impossible task with a couple of high-profile setbacks not aiding the cause.

Things are beginning to change, however, and the number of horses Tizzard has at his disposal continues to grow at Venn Farm.

"We had around 80 last season and that looks to have grown to about 110 for the upcoming campaign," says Tizzard.

"We have an awful lot of horses no one knows about yet and there will be a star or two among them. We've got only two horses in the yard who have run on the Flat, which is incredibly rare. This is what we do though – it's always been a long-term project."

An ever-present at the stable, and one you can't help but love is **Cue Card**. He showed glimpses of brilliance again last year and Tizzard isn't ready to give up with him yet.

"He's 11 and a senior horse now, but I don't see him deteriorating at all. We've had him back early this year and he's ready to go to Wetherby for the Charlie Hall Chase.

"We may have been a bit easy on him last year, but that's not the case this time and he's in lovely form. We'll likely go on to Haydock for the Betfair Chase and then to Kempton at Christmas."

Tizzard is likely to have a strong hand in the King George, no more so than with **Thistlecrack**, who is reportedly in good shape and over the injury that saw his season come to an end in January after suffering his first defeat over fences when going down to a mighty performance from Many Clouds.

"He's definitely on track. He'll have a prep run before the King George, possibly over hurdles and then we'll definitely be going for everything after that," says a determined Tizzard.

....

Tizzard tends to accelerate in October and had his strongest month in November during the 2016-17 campaign (16-58, 28%, +£44.49), while April was also a profitable month last season (6-39, 15%, +£51.63)

'We had around 80 horses last season and that looks to have grown to about 110 for the upcoming campaign'

DID YOU KNOW?

Colin Tizzard used to play cricket at school with Ian Botham. He proudly tells the story of when he had a trial for Somerset under-15s and got Botham out in the trial. They then went on to play together for Yeovil with Beefy as captain and Tizzard as vice-captain, and ironically it was Tizzard who was the all-rounder. In fact Tizzard has always remained a bit of an all-rounder – as well as continuing to grow his hugely successful training operation, he also has a 500-acre dairy farm.

Another of the Tizzard stable stars we could see in the King George is **Fox Norton**, although he is in the same ownership as Gold Cup winner Sizing John and might therefore miss out at Kempton.

"The owners have Sizing John so we'll have to stay at two miles, maybe two and a half when the time is right. He's a beautiful horse and was beaten only a nose in the Champion Chase.

"He was top-notch at Punchestown and Aintree and is ready if needed. He'll be there waiting for the King George if anything

happens to Sizing John," says Tizzard on his more-than-able deputy.

One of the unexpected stars of last season came in the shape of **Native River**, who has always threatened to break through into the big leagues and finally did. He is a rare horse with a combination of class and bravery, together with an almighty gallop.

After a long season last year, Tizzard will take his time with the seven-year-old but will be aiming just as high. He says: "He shook himself up a bit after a tough campaign so we won't see him until Christmas. We're back riding him now and we'll give him as much time as he needs.

"He's always been better after a prep run, second time out, so we'll look at something like Newbury in February and then head straight to the Gold Cup," says Tizzard.

Another going for gold

Tizzard has always believed in Topham Chase winner **Ultragold** and was less surprised than most when he won last

Native River (noseband): not expected to return to action until the end of the year and will head back to Cheltenham for another crack at the Gold Cup

season's Aintree prize at odds of 50-1.

"If you go back to when we bought him, he was running over three miles but I could never win with him until he went down to two miles. He was staying on in the Topham so we'll have to try him again up in trip.

"When we bought him it was for the Grand National. After a wind op last year he really picked up, staying on in his races. He'll be aimed at the Gold Cup and then we'll head to Aintree if we can," says Tizzard.

One of the most exciting younger horses throughout last season was **Finian's Oscar**. Although he missed Cheltenham, he won impressively at Aintree in the Grade 1 Mersey Novices' Hurdle and went unbeaten into Punchestown where he found only Bacardys too good.

"He'll go novice chasing this season. As a point-to-point winner he's got some experience and is a beautiful young horse. He's already shown he's got plenty of ability and we'll see how he goes," says Tizzard.

New names coming through

Tizzard's team has a deeper look to it this time, with talent spread across novice company – hurdlers and chasers. Much attention was given to the staying chasers last year, but this season could see some new stars break through.

Another novice chaser Tizzard will unleash is **Elegant Escape**. The five-year-old found only subsequent three-time bumper winner Samcro too good in his point-to-point in April 2016 and raced in many of the big novice hurdles towards the backend of last season.

"We've been schooling him over fences – he's a lovely horse. He won at Chepstow and Ascot last year before we threw him in deeper. He was fifth in the Neptune and was right there until a mistake two out. I think he'll be a better horse this year, and we'll go novice chasing with him, probably over two and a half miles to begin with," says the trainer.

Adding to the already strong-looking novice chasing team is **West Approach**, who shot up the ratings last season and ran third behind Unowhatimeanharry in the Cleeve Hurdle.

"We had big plans for him last year. He ended up rated 157 as a novice hurdler

Finian's Oscar: a Grade 1 winner over hurdles last season, he is expected to take high rank as a novice chaser this time

despite winning only one race at Newton Abbot in the spring.

"We tried to make him Thistlecrack number two which would have been nice. He's been schooling over fences and we're looking forward to taking him novice chasing," says Tizzard.

A horse many assumed would be going over fences for the first time is Grade 1 winner **Pingshou**. But Tizzard has different ideas for now.

"The plan is to keep him over hurdles for now – he may be good enough for a go at the Champion Hurdle. He's rated 150 so will have some improvement to find first.

"Last year was only his first full year racing, and he got better and better as it went on. We'll start off at Wincanton early on in the season and then there's the Fighting Fifth at Newcastle, and that'll tell us just how good he is. If it comes to it we can go novice chasing – it's nice to have the options," says Tizzard.

Four for Newbury showpiece

Another of the big races Tizzard picked up last season was the Hennessy – now Ladbrokes Trophy – at Newbury with Native River. He looks to be assembling a strong team again and could have a number of runners.

Royal Vacation had a disappointing end to his last campaign with two pulled-up efforts, but had won well twice beforehand.

"He's had a wind operation," reveals Tizzard. "And we've also had a look at his shins. He'll be campaigned to try and win the Hennessy with a run beforehand.

"He's a Grade 1 winner, albeit when Might Bite fell, and his last two runs were a bit of a miss. He seems in strong form and we'll get him back racing with the Hennessy at the front of our minds."

Alary came into last season with a big reputation and as a Gold Cup fancy for many. He had a tricky start to life in Britain, but Tizzard is sure he is past that and will aim him at the Newbury race as well.

"He arrived at our yard when things weren't going so well so was disappointing for the most part," says the trainer.

"But he's a classy horse and didn't run badly in the Ryanair. If you see him on the gallops he's a machine and we'll give him one run over hurdles before taking him to Newbury," says Tizzard.

Sizing Codelco could have the same early season target. He rounded off his last campaign with valuable wins at Aintree and Punchestown and is now rated 160 over fences.

"It's likely we'll give him a prep run and then look at the Hennessy once we know where we are with him," says the trainer. "He's won off 154 so there isn't heaps more to find," says the Dorset trainer.

The Hennessy team could be completed by **Theatre Guide**. "He was beaten only half a length at Sandown at the end of last year and we've done his wind too. He was making a big noise in last year's Hennessy and still went very well that day. He'll have another crack this year," adds Tizzard.

Big reputations to go on the line

Venn Farm has also had an influx of exciting younger talent, none more so than **Slate House**. He comes from Ireland with a big reputation and a €260,000 price tag.

"He's a beautiful-looking horse. He's got the point-to-point form, he's got the breeding and everyone who rides him thinks the world of him. He should be out at the bigger tracks over two and a half miles and we'll go from there," says an excited Tizzard.

Another name to add to the mix is €270,000 purchase **Vision Des Flos**, and Tizzard knows he's lucky to be getting horses like this. "He comes with a big reputation. He's already working like a beautiful horse. Some of his relations have won well over the summer and I'm definitely a fan of his. He's the right size and won a £100,000 bumper at the Punchestown festival on his only start so we're lucky to have him. We'll go straight over hurdles with him."

Storm Home was brought over for last season but was never seen under the Tizzard banner due to a setback. "We didn't get him on the track as he wasn't right after his fall in

COLIN TIZZARD
MILBORNE PORT, DORSET

	No. of Hrs	Races Run	1st	2nd	3rd	Unpl	Per cent	£1 Level Stake
NH Flat	16	26	1	3	4	18	3.8	-23.00
Hurdles	45	161	19	25	26	91	11.8	-41.86
Chases	49	220	37	36	26	121	16.8	+71.61
Totals	**86**	**407**	**57**	**64**	**56**	**230**	**14.0**	**+6.75**
15-16	58	325	51	39	53	182	15.7	-45.75
14-15	61	294	38	34	41	181	12.9	-78.21

BY MONTH

NH Flat	W-R	Per cent	£1 Level Stake	Hurdles	W-R	Per cent	£1 Level Stake
May	0-2	0.0	-2.00	May	1-10	10.0	-7.38
June	0-0	0.0	0.00	June	2-3	66.7	+6.00
July	1-1	100.0	+2.00	July	0-5	0.0	-5.00
August	0-0	0.0	0.00	August	0-1	0.0	-1.00
September	0-0	0.0	0.00	September	0-2	0.0	-2.00
October	0-4	0.0	-4.00	October	2-18	11.1	-4.00
November	0-1	0.0	-1.00	November	6-25	24.0	+14.60
December	0-4	0.0	-4.00	December	2-23	8.7	-4.25
January	0-5	0.0	-5.00	January	2-17	11.8	-11.90
February	0-3	0.0	-3.00	February	1-19	5.3	-17.94
March	0-3	0.0	-3.00	March	1-20	5.0	-12.00
April	0-3	0.0	-3.00	April	2-18	11.1	+3.00

Chases	W-R	Per cent	£1 Level Stake	Totals	W-R	Per cent	£1 Level Stake
May	2-6	33.3	+12.75	May	3-18	16.7	+3.37
June	0-2	0.0	-2.00	June	2-5	40.0	+4.00
July	0-1	0.0	-1.00	July	1-7	14.3	-4.00
August	1-5	20.0	+7.00	August	1-6	16.7	+6.00
September	0-4	0.0	-4.00	September	0-6	0.0	-6.00
October	5-27	18.5	-1.33	October	7-49	14.3	-9.33
November	10-32	31.3	+30.89	November	16-58	27.6	+44.49
December	6-41	14.6	+15.73	December	8-68	11.8	+7.48
January	5-34	14.7	-2.59	January	7-56	12.5	-19.49
February	4-20	20.0	-5.46	February	5-42	11.9	-26.40
March	0-30	0.0	-30.00	March	1-53	1.9	-45.00
April	4-18	22.2	+51.63	April	6-39	15.4	+51.63

DISTANCE

Hurdles	W-R	Per cent	£1 Level Stake	Chases	W-R	Per cent	£1 Level Stake
2m-2m3f	10-52	19.2	+28.69	2m-2m3f	6-36	16.7	-2.97
2m4f-2m7f	7-51	13.7	-22.65	2m4f-2m7f	10-58	17.2	+39.17
3m+	0-19	0.0	-19.00	3m+	15-86	17.4	+40.74

TYPE OF RACE

Non-Handicaps	W-R	Per cent	£1 Level Stake	Handicaps	W-R	Per cent	£1 Level Stake
Nov Hrdls	9-47	19.1	+13.04	Nov Hrdls	0-7	0.0	-7.00
Hrdls	3-25	12.0	+2.00	Hrdls	7-82	8.5	-49.90
Nov Chs	7-25	28.0	+28.97	Nov Chs	1-13	7.7	0.00
Chases	7-26	26.9	-4.98	Chases	21-143	14.7	+51.63
Sell/Claim	0-0	0.0	0.00	Sell/Claim	0-0	0.0	0.00

RACE CLASS

	W-R	Per cent	£1 Level Stake
Class 1	21-94	22.3	+107.06
Class 2	8-64	12.5	-20.01
Class 3	10-94	10.6	-24.92
Class 4	14-108	13.0	-21.88
Class 5	2-27	7.4	-20.50
Class 6	2-20	10.0	-13.00

FIRST TIME OUT

	W-R	Per cent	£1 Level Stake
Bumpers	1-16	6.3	-13.00
Hurdles	5-32	15.6	+3.88
Chases	9-38	23.7	+37.92
Totals	15-86	17.4	+28.80

Statistics relate to all runners in Britain from May 1, 2016 to April 30, 2017

Sizing Codelco (left): could be part of a strong challenge for the Ladbrokes Trophy at Newbury

a point-to-point. The winner [Getabird] was favourite for the Champion Bumper before he also got injured," says Tizzard.

"He seems fine now. We'll get him into a bumper and then straight over hurdles."

The Alan Potts-owned **New To This Town** is another acquisition for the Tizzard stable, but one the trainer will be taking his time with: "We've done his wind. He was making noises on the gallops so we had to act. He's only just cantering and we'll have to take our time with him."

Quite By Chance and Third Intention are another two horses Tizzard is hopeful of securing further prize-money with. "**Quite By Chance** is higher in the handicap now but is a great jumper and a big, strong horse. We won't be frightened of running him over the big fences too – he could handle Aintree very well."

On **Third Intention**, Tizzard is less expectant: "He won the Old Roan Chase at Aintree first time out last season and we're going back for this year. It's a good race and we've run him over every trip with all sorts of changes so we'll see how he goes again.

"We've done his wind again. As he gets into the veteran stage he needs all the help he can get. He only needs to drop a few pounds to get in the veteran series so that would be his second chance if needed."

Sizing Granite had a challenging season last winter, but sprang to life at the Punchestown festival, and Tizzard is keen to talk up the nine-year-old: "He was going nowhere last season and then at Punchestown he absolutely bolted up. I know he's going to be ten but I hope that we can nab a few big ones with him."

Tempestatefloresco was pulled up in the Kerry National during September, but Tizzard is hopeful a switch of strategy can help rebuild his confidence: "He didn't run very well at Listowel – he was up to his knees in mud and didn't like it.

"He's rated 145 over fences and that'll be his limit. As he's still a novice hurdler we've got that option."

Interview by Callum Jamieson

SUPER STATS

Numbers are on the up at the Colin Tizzard yard. Last year saw the Dorset trainer send out a record 58 winners, who amassed just over £2 million in prize-money. Tizzard's runners returned a level-stake profit of £8.75 throughout the 2016-17 campaign

Tizzard doesn't send many runners north but he has a fine strike-rate when he does, with his records at Newcastle (4-7, 57%, +£30.00) and Wetherby (4-12, 33%, +£11.98) standing out

While he cannot match the volume of Nicholls or Henderson, Tizzard can compete on quality with his records at Aintree (10-35, 29%, +£94.99) and Ascot (8-48, 17%, +£11.28) testament to that

Tizzard returned his best figures at Aintree last term (6-16, 38%, +£78.00) but he also had solid records at Newton Abbot (6-25, 24%, +£16.88) and Newbury (5-19, 26%, +£4.23)

The majority of his winners come over fences and his runners post decent figures at Wincanton (11-62, 18%, +£6.33), Kempton (6-35, 17%, +£23.85) and Haydock (4-15, 27%, +£4.96) in this area

Another pointer to the quality in Tizzard's yard is the fact he has returned a level-stake profit in Graded and Listed races over fences (Graded: 22-125, 18%, +£68.59; Listed: 5-26, 19%, +£23.00) and hurdles (Graded: 9-53, 17%, +£8.68; Listed: 3-12, 25%, +£1.56)

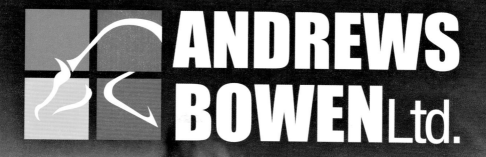

Raiders continue to raise bar with more and more impressive feats

A YEAR ago, we mused in these pages how a final haul of 15 Cheltenham Festival winners felt something like peak Irish domination on the jumps scene.

Having witnessed Don Cossack and Annie Power complete the Gold Cup-Champion Hurdle double and Rule The World prevail in the Grand National, it was hard to envisage how such comprehensive prolificacy might be topped.

We should have known better. Notwithstanding that it is also symptomatic of a new reality that makes for a greater gap between the haves and have-nots, those operating in the upper echelons once again carried all before them in the 2016-17 campaign.

Despite Douvan's capitulation, the Champion Chase, Ryanair Chase, Gold Cup treble was won by Irish-based horses for a first time, with Special Tiara, Un De Sceaux and Sizing John all soaring majestically in the Cotswolds. The cross-channel raiders departed with 19 of the 28 Cheltenham Festival races, a sensational record that still seems scarcely credible.

The heavyweight clash between Willie Mullins and Gordon Elliott – who shaded the leading trainer award at Cheltenham – was an enthralling sub-plot that continued throughout the season. Elliott's omnipotence in the €100,000 Grade A handicaps nearly got him over the line in front of the perennial title-holder in the domestic title race, but in the end Mullins eked past him on the penultimate day of the season.

It was an epic encounter that ultimately saw Mullins prevail by €199,495, and there is every chance a similar joust will ensue this time.

Joseph O'Brien also continues to make inroads at the top of the table, but in many ways last term was all about the second coming of Jessica Harrington.

With the glorious Moscow Flyer era well gone and Jezki struggling to hold his own against the big guns, the arrival of Alan Potts' horses injected fresh life into Harrington's Moone stable. The most successful female trainer in festival history after three Prestbury Park wins took her running tally there to 11, Harrington's exploits with Sizing John were an achievement to savour.

She also produced a second exceptional staying chasing prospect in the runaway Irish Grand National hero Our Duke, so there is every chance that her fingerprints will again be all over the division this time around.

SENIOR CHASERS

One of the themes of last season was the manner in which sentiment clouded objective judgement. That is all fine and dandy if it is

Special Tiara: will be mixing it with the best over two miles again this season

merely punters and bookmakers making markets on the basis of such emotionally involved methodology, but it is less so when it comes to the official handicapping of horses.

On any rational analysis of form and performance in the sport's definitive championship events, **Sizing John** was the outstanding staying chaser.

However, in the official end-of-term classifications, it was Many Clouds, a horse who never came within a country mile of winning a Grade 1 during a five-year career, who inexplicably topped the pile on 171.

It was an injustice for Sizing John (169), who had comprehensively proven himself in every facet of what is the most gruelling discipline.

Our Duke's Fairyhouse rout in the Irish Grand National confirmed him a deeply exciting novice. After a campaign that saw other smart turns from **Yorkhill**, **Disko**, **Coney Island**, **Road To Respect** and

even **Acapella Bourgeois**, there seems to be real depth to the Irish staying chasing ranks.

The prospect of Yorkhill reverting to hurdles is surely slim. He is an unpolished diamond, but he could develop into a serious Gold Cup candidate if he grows up a little.

A similar comment applies to **Great Field**. He has a frantic and erratic way of doing things, but he will make them all go over two miles if he can keep it together. While **Min** remains an unknown quantity, he is another with obvious potential.

Champion Chase winner **Special Tiara** will continue to mix it with the best over two miles on good ground or faster, but both he and the brilliant Ryanair victor **Un De Sceaux** will have their mettle tested by **Douvan** and rising British stars Altior and Fox Norton.

If Douvan returns to the peak of his strength this season, it will be fascinating to see what route they elect to go with him. He

Min (right): something of an unknown quantity but has clear potential over fences

may be an out-and-out two-miler, but he may be even more special than that as well, so it's not beyond the realm of possibility he could vie to end Willie Mullins' frustrating Gold Cup hoodoo.

Djakadam has repeatedly fallen just short in that quest. He has never made the breakthrough at elite level over three miles-plus, and the suspicion remains that he is best suited to bullying the opposition over intermediate distances.

It is a long time since he ran a bad race and he is still only eight, so he will doubtless continue as a classy and willing bruiser, but one who lacks the knockout punch.

SENIOR HURDLERS

With Faugheen and Annie Power absent last season, the Irish-based hurdlers fell a little short at the highest level. Encouraging reports continue to surface in relation to **Faugheen**'s seemingly imminent return.

A near two years off the track will not be easily overcome given the level at which he has competed, and it might not be out of the question that the nine-year-old will end up being tried over longer trips. That said, he could still be up there with the best of them over two miles in deep ground at home in the winter months.

The dogged **Nichols Canyon** was certainly revitalised by three miles last term, and he will continue to be a force in that realm. It will be interesting to see what connections opt to do with **Apple's Jade** as she emerged as a proper prospect last term.

She still has something to prove against the best geldings, but has the scope to mix it at the highest level over a trip. While **Melon** could mature into a fair type, **Labaik** has physical as well as psychological issues to overcome if he is to make an impact this term.

NOVICES

As ever there is a considerable element of second-guessing at play here, but a few stand out. **Petit Mouchoir** bloomed over hurdles last year and might be an ideal type to go down the Arkle route, while **Supasundae** could make an impact over further as a chaser.

Sutton Place is the sort who could go either way, while **Getabird** and **Fayonagh** are two of the more exciting bumper performers due to go novice hurdling.

ANTE-POST ANALYSIS NICK WATTS

Back Defi to make leap from Triumph winner to becoming Champion

CHAMPION HURDLE

Yorkhill is single figures in certain places for the Champion Hurdle and it would be folly to count him out in a race in which last year's winner and market leader Buveur D'Air is solid but not as yet spectacular.

He is owned by JP McManus, who also has **Defi Du Seuil** to consider, and I really hope he makes the grade and can put himself in the reckoning for this.

It isn't easy to make the leap from Triumph Hurdle to the Champion Hurdle, but not many win the juvenile race as easily as he did.

He started his career at Ffos Las and won at Chepstow on soft ground over Christmas, so it was understandable many were keen to oppose him in the Triumph – running on ground quicker than he was used to.

His jumping hadn't always been the most fluent either, but none of this had the slightest effect on him and he had the race sewn up before turning in.

He was slightly more workmanlike when following up at Aintree but that was entirely understandable bearing in mind it was his eighth race of the campaign – and he surely merits a crack at the championship race rather than being shunted out over fences.

If you wanted a real speculator, however, you could do worse than consider the Willie Mullins-trained **Let's Dance**.

Forget her late-season defeats at Fairyhouse and Punchestown – there was a trainers' title being fought and she was very probably over the top.

Before that, however, she was exceptional at distances ranging from two to two and a half miles and didn't look slow when winning the Grade 2 mares' novice hurdle at the festival in March.

Ruby Walsh gave her plenty to do that day, but she did it very easily and was strong all the way to the line.

The drawback is that connections could take the soft option and keep her to mares events, but they also have Limini and Vroum Vroum Mag in that bracket. If Let's Dance could hit the ground running early on then she could force her way into the reckoning – particularly if Faugheen becomes a declining force.

CHAMPION CHASE

One race Mullins has never got right at Cheltenham is the Champion Chase, and his curse showed no signs of diminishing last season when Douvan put in an injury-induced below-par run.

Where he goes next is anyone's guess as he could possibly go up in trip at some stage, but Mullins and the Riccis do have ample back-up with **Min**, who looks very interesting.

Likely to stay at the minimum trip, he looked awesome last season in two chase starts, including when taking a Grade 1 at Leopardstown's Christmas meeting with ease.

His jumping was a joy to behold, but before we could get too excited about a clash with Altior in the Arkle, he was ruled out of the remainder of the campaign through injury.

Expected to be back this season, he could easily mop up Graded chases in Ireland before the festival and 12-1 for the Champion Chase looks a decent price.

STAYERS' HURDLE

This is a race Mullins won for the first time last season with **Nichols Canyon**.

Even Annie Power managed to get beaten in it before that but, having got the taste for it, Mullins might well do it again this year and with the same horse.

At certain stages previously Nichols Canyon had looked a horse without a trip – one who was good enough to win domestic Grade 1s over two miles but not a Champion Hurdle, and one who, up until last March, had not been properly tested over an extreme trip.

However, he showed at Cheltenham that a staying trip is exactly what he requires, putting in a dour performance to see off Lil Rockerfeller and Unowhatimeanharry. The latter got revenge on him at Punchestown, but if they clash again next year, we can expect Nichols Canyon to come out on top again.

With Apple's Jade possibly staying among the mares, and with Yanworth going chasing, a price of 7-1 doesn't look unreasonable for Nichols Canyon to retain his crown.

CHELTENHAM GOLD CUP

Jumps fans will be used to the running plans of Mullins being as clear as mud, but as far as **Yorkhill** is concerned his reticence in nominating targets is justified.

Judged solely on his JLT win last season he could easily be fancied for the Gold Cup, with his sure-footed jumping, ability to travel easily, his class and his liking for Cheltenham all hugely positive attributes.

However, his horror show at Punchestown when throwing away a Grade 1 chase seemed to deflate Mullins to the point that he actually mooted the possibility of him returning to hurdles and pursuing a Champion Hurdle campaign.

His wayward antics on his final start of the season were extraordinary, and something rarely seen at the top level. He jumped persistently out to his left, violently at times, but would still have beaten Road To Respect save for almost coming to a complete halt at the last fence.

Bemused, probably shell-shocked, Mullins was at a loss to know what to do next or how to explain it. But, surely the most simple suggestion would be to stick to left-handed tracks?

It's not like he didn't take to chasing. He had form figures 1112, and it's worth noting that he was also beaten at Punchestown the previous season and put in a below-par display at Aintree before scraping to victory.

Therefore, the probability is that he doesn't take a huge amount of racing and that his trips to Cheltenham take a lot out of him.

Mullins shouldn't panic and should aim him at the Cheltenham Gold Cup but whether he does or not who knows. At 8-1 he would be my idea of the winner, but if he swerved the gig then **Our Duke** would be a worthy alternative.

He was nothing amazing as a hurdler but was transformed by chasing last season and saved his best for last with a stunning display in the Irish Grand National.

He ran away with that devilishly difficult handicap, showing stamina, class and a sound jumping technique. He has all the attributes you look for in a Gold Cup winner and, while he may not have Yorkhill's brilliance, he doesn't share his quirks.

RPRS AND TOPSPEED STEVE MASON AND DAVE EDWARDS

Our time and ratings experts with five to back all season long

ON THE FIGURES

Buveur D'Air More than justified the decision to abandon a novice chase campaign when landing the top hurdling prizes at Cheltenham and Aintree. Has had only seven starts over hurdles and still has the potential to improve on his current Racing Post rating of 171.

Captain Forez Still a maiden over hurdles but earned a RPR of 150 when splitting smart novices Finian's Oscar and Messire Des Obeaux in a Grade 1 at Aintree on National day. Should make his mark at the highest level in novice company.

Champagne Classic Landed the Martin Pipe at Cheltenham en route to taking the notable scalp of the Albert Bartlett winner Penhill in Grade 1 company at Punchestown. Can develop into a leading staying novice chaser.

Fountains Windfall Made tremendous progress in the spring, completing a hat-trick with a wide-margin win in a valuable staying handicap hurdle at Aintree. Could switch to chasing, but an official hurdle rating of 146 looks worth exploiting in the short term.

Fox Norton Stepped up significantly in his second season over fences, landing Grade 1s at Aintree and Punchestown. Not quite in the same class as Altior and Douvan, but could prove the one to beat at interim trips and the Ryanair looks a logical target.

ON THE CLOCK

Behind Time Disappointed twice after making a winning return over hurdles at Cheltenham in November but is lightly raced and it may pay to keep faith in Harry Fry's six-year-old.

Might Bite Took a crashing fall at the last when well clear at Kempton on Boxing Day and almost threw away the RSA when veering off a true line at Cheltenham. Nicky Henderson's trail-blazer has an engine and the King George is on the agenda.

River Wylde Made steady progress last term winning three times over hurdles and earned his time stripes when third in the Supreme. Below par at Aintree, the six-year-old could go over fences or stay hurdling but there are more races to be won in either sphere.

Road To Respect Clocked a quicker time than Ryanair winner Un De Sceaux when scoring over course and distance on the same day at the Cheltenham Festival and followed up at Fairyhouse. Decent ground suits Noel Meade's progressive six-year-old between two and a half and three miles.

Shantou Village Recorded four wins from five over fences last term and Neil Mulholland's seven-year-old fell in the other. Signed off with a Sandown success in April and on good ground he could pick up some decent prizes this term.

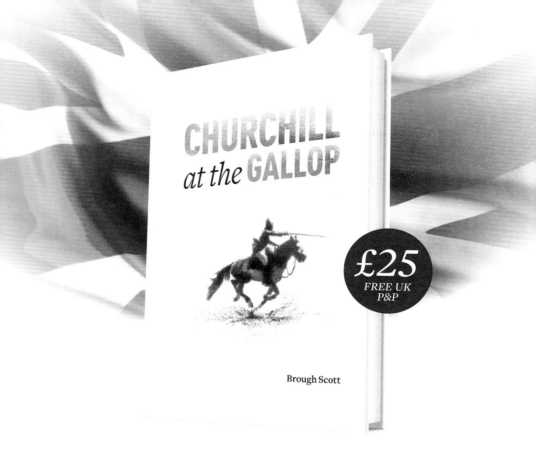

Future champions – Bowen and Might Bite set to fly this season

WHO are going to be the new stars of the 2017-18 campaign? That's the million-dollar question all jumps enthusiasts will ask themselves before the season proper kicks off at Chepstow in mid-October.

Those who kept their eye on the action over the summer will have one name firmly on their lips in terms of jockeys – James Bowen. And it was no surprise when towards the end of September it was announced he will join the all-conquering yard of champion trainer Nicky Henderson this season as the conditional rider at Seven Barrows.

The son of West Wales trainer Peter and younger brother of jockey Sean, he hails from a good racing family and possesses the natural ability to be a star.

Teenager Bowen, who in May set a new record for a novice rider during his first season in point-to-points, has already created a stir around the minor jumps tracks, with victories aboard the likes of Strumble Head and Dotties Dilema earning plenty of plaudits.

However, it was his handling of Get Home Now in a Fontwell handicap hurdle in August which made the biggest impression and marked him down as a youngster with limitless potential.

It was clear Bowen wanted to set the fractions on his father's nine-year-old, but dual champion Richard Johnson was having none of that and swept past him aboard Bobble Emerald after the opening hurdle.

If Bowen's game-plan had been to make all, it was now in ruins after just ten seconds. Lesser riders would have panicked and driven their mount upsides Johnson in a bid to regain the lead. Not Bowen, who sat in second place, several lengths behind Bobble

Might Bite: last season's RSA Chase winner could develop into a mighty performer

Emerald, and focused on getting his mount nicely switched off and into a good jumping rhythm.

He also showed tremendous self-confidence and judgement when Johnson upped the tempo before the third-last, giving Get Home Now plenty of time to move into a higher gear before sweeping past the long-time leader rounding the final turn and powering away to score by 18 lengths from a staying-on Ramore Will.

Bowen's composure and body language throughout the race – and particularly over the final two flights – reminded me of a young Aidan Coleman, and it wouldn't be any surprise to find him among jump racing's elite riders in three years' time. Make the most of any claim he might retain this season because it represents punting gold dust and won't be available for long.

HORSES TO WATCH

Thistlecrack, Sizing John, Native River, Djakadam and Coneygree will all have their army of supporters for the Cheltenham Gold Cup, but there are three young guns who could really explode next March.

Might Bite obviously possesses his share of quirks, but he is also blessed with a Rolls-Royce engine and, with very few miles on the clock for an eight-year-old, could develop into an awesome performer this season.

His last-gasp RSA Chase triumph may have provided sheer drama, but it also exuded sheer class.

He has the right man behind him in champion trainer Nicky Henderson, and there is every reason to believe he could go right to the very top.

So too could **Yorkhill**, a horse containing a priceless combination of speed and stamina, and it will be fascinating to see which big-race avenue Willie Mullins takes him down.

His pace, which was in evidence when he landed the Grade 1 Tolworth Hurdle at Sandown over two miles in January 2016, could conceivably see him challenge for the Champion Chase.

However, it is his stamina – which appears to be consistently underrated in some quarters – that may eventually prove the asset which enables him to become a true giant of the sport.

A point-to-point winner over three miles, Yorkhill gives every indication he will stay the Gold Cup trip and, if that proves to be the

case, could prove tough to beat.

Of all the winners at the 2017 festival, I thought Yorkhill was the most impressive when securing the Grade 1 JLT Novices' Chase with a performance which oozed class.

He jumped beautifully, travelled with supreme ease, and then showed a turn of foot to seal the deal.

His record of nine wins from just 11 starts under rules says plenty about him and, aged just seven, it is realistic to expect even better to come from him in 2017-18.

Gold Cups are rarely run in attritional conditions these days but, if the ground did make bottomless stamina the premium requirement, it is unlikely **Our Duke** would be inconvenienced.

He created a fantastic impression when romping home in the Irish Grand National by 14 lengths from Bless The Wings at Fairyhouse in April and he rates another tremendously exciting young talent.

Even less exposed than Might Bite and Yorkhill, the Jessica Harrington-trained seven-year-old could be a diner at racing's top table for many years to come and his progress this season is awaited with excitement.

I wouldn't put anyone off backing any – or all – of that trio for Gold Cup glory, but the horse on whom I'm planning potentially my biggest bet is likely to be tackling a Class 5 handicap hurdle off a mark of just 87 at one of the minor southern tracks.

Ali Stronge's **Camakasi** produced a career-best performance on the Flat in late August to land a Bath handicap over a mile and a quarter in hugely impressive fashion by eight lengths from Silver Dixie.

Once George Wood pressed the button over two furlongs out, the six-year-old lengthened his stride and pulverised his rivals.

That victory resulted in the handicapper raising his Flat turf mark to 77, so it doesn't take a genius to see there is ample scope to exploit a low hurdle rating.

There is no real evidence to suggest Camakasi won't prove any less capable over hurdles than on the Flat.

He jumped proficiently during his last spin over obstacles at Exeter last October, and clearly wasn't himself that day, finishing in rear behind Karl Marx.

If Camakasi gets his act together over jumps, his connections and backers alike are going to have an enormous amount of fun with him.

Our Duke (4): Irish National winner looks an immense talent over fences

DARK HORSES DAVE ORTON

A dozen names away from the top table who could soon be winning

CARLOS DU FRUITIER Ben Pauling

While his impressive bumper success at Warwick last season came on deep terrain, trainer Ben Pauling has always thought of Carlos Du Fruitier as a top-of-the-ground performer and sent him to Aintree's Grand National meeting for his final outing in that division. He had excuses when dropping away that day and is very much expected to make his mark for the stable over hurdles this term for his burgeoning stable. Stepping up in distance certainly won't hurt.

COOL MIX Iain Jardine

This twice-raced five-year-old created a fine impression when running a big race and finding only the exciting Pym too strong in a bumper last term at Ayr's Scottish Grand National meeting. He cruised off the home bend that day, looking in control, and time will surely tell he bumped into a smart winner. Iain Jardine's grey son of Fair Mix should win a bumper before heading over hurdles and ought to win his share of races when faced with a stiffer test in that sphere.

HOKE COLBURN Harry Whittington

We didn't see the best of this one over hurdles last season. He left many disappointed, but trainer Harry Whittington endured a frustrating campaign overall and the bonus is that this talented five-year-old starts afresh this term with an attractive opening handicap mark of 115. It'll be a big surprise if he doesn't show his true colours and take full advantage of that figure.

HOUSESOFPARLIAMENT Joseph O'Brien

It may seem amiss to suggest this former smart Flat performer (2016 St Leger third) as a dark jumper to follow. However, due to a sluggish start after joining trainer Joseph O'Brien he'll no doubt always be regarded as being below the initial high expectations. His win at the Galway festival was a fine effort considering the minimum trip there was really too sharp, though, and it confirmed he's got his act together again. He should be well up to landing a decent pot when upped in trip.

ITS ALL GUESSWORK Gordon Elliott

Its All Guesswork came good when fitted with a tongue tie last season, winning easily when upped to three miles on good ground at Bellewstown, and rates a work in progress for this season. He's a dour stayer and trainer Gordon Elliott will have a plan in place through the winter. Chasing will be his game but there's a big prize in him before making that switch.

JURY DUTY Gordon Elliott

Third in the Pertemps Final at the Cheltenham Festival last season, Jury Duty has it in him to step up to the Stayers' Hurdle division should connections opt to remain over hurdles. However, he is built to jump fences and would be a real force to be reckoned with in the staying novice division. Targets such as the RSA or the four-mile National Hunt Chase in March should be within reach.

KINGS RYDE Nicky Henderson

A huge eyecatcher on his bumper debut at Worcester in June, Kings Ryde could hardly have done the job any easier when making all first time up over hurdles at Southwell in September. He relished stepping up to two and a half miles there and bounced off the sound surface. Although a chaser in the making, he ought to progress into a decent hurdler for Nicky Henderson this term.

MON LINO Paul Nolan

A late-maturing sort, when Mon Lino moved up from the minimum distance it all began to click into place and he won in the style of a very well-handicapped horse when gaining a second hurdle success at Killarney in May. Paul Nolan gave him the summer off to grow and he should be more than capable of adding a few more staying handicaps to his tally through the winter. Chasing is also an exciting prospect and he ought to go on to even better things once tackling a fence.

QAVIY CASH Dan Skelton

Snapped up for 85,000gns by Dan Skelton after opening his Flat account on his handicap debut at Hamilton Park for Hugo Palmer in July, Qaviy Cash could make up into a very useful juvenile hurdler. He stays well, which dictates that ultimately trips beyond two miles will be his game and connections are eyeing some decent spring targets.

PYM Nicky Henderson

An exciting prospect for novice hurdling. He created a deep impression when winning a traditionally strong bumper on his debut at Ayr's Scottish Grand National meeting last term, overcoming inexperience to score with a lot left in the tank, and seemed right at home on the good to soft going. He runs in the same colours as Altior and the vibes are strong ahead of his impending switch to jumps.

TOKARAMORE Iain Jardine

Given plenty of time since a tough race on bottomless ground in Listed company at Cheltenham's 2016 November meeting, this dual bumper winner is one to side with when setting sail over hurdles in the mares' novice hurdle division. Iain Jardine rates her highly and is sure to map out a profitable campaign north of the border prior to dipping her toes back down south later on. She'll have no issue getting two and a half miles.

ZAROCCO Iain Jardine

Might have initially been assumed to have run below expectations when beaten 17 lengths on her bumper debut at Carlisle in April. However, she came up against two useful mares that day, both with more experience, and there was definite promise in her display. She's been given time to mature by trainer Iain Jardine and is well up to winning early in the campaign. Her sire Shirocco is making a name for himself in the jumps sphere and his progeny have little issue with winter ground.

 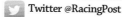

The horses sure to be big players this season at the key meetings

AMERICAN Harry Fry

Made rapid strides in a short space of time last season and looks a natural for the Welsh National and might be up to taking on the top company when the going is deep. The winner of his only point-to-point, he won just one of his three hurdles starts and was well beaten in Grade 2 company at Fairyhouse on his final outing in that sphere, but fences and soft ground have clearly been the making of him.

American went three starts unbeaten last season, making the most of racing up with the leaders each time and he closed with a powerful jumping and galloping display to thump Rock The Kasbah by eight lengths at Warwick in January.

The runner-up was beaten little more than two lengths in the bet365 Gold Cup on his next start, so the form looks solid and, with time on his side, American has the potential to still rate a fair bit higher than his current mark of 157. The one proviso, of course, is the ground, as he must have it very soft – he missed all the spring festivals – and is considered very fragile. But when he gets his conditions it will take a good one to beat him.

CAPTAIN FOREZ Dan Skelton

Sometimes a horse catches your eye the first time you see him – and that was very much the case for me when Captain Forez made his British debut for Dan Skelton in November, running a six-length third to Jenkins. It was

hard not to be impressed with the way he galloped from the front at Newbury and, while he got tired approaching the second-last, that was a big effort from a four-year-old having only his second outing. The winner hasn't really made the grade yet as he can't jump, but fourth-placed Pingshou won a Grade 1 at Aintree and overall the form was strong.

Captain Forez showed the benefit of that outing when giving the much more battle-hardened Capitaine a race in a Grade 2 at Ascot next time and, four months later, he returned to run an excellent second to Finian's Oscar at Aintree in the Grade 1 Mersey Novice Hurdle, seeing out the two-and-a-half-mile trip well.

Although he looks a surefire top-class chaser of the future, Skelton is keen not to rush him, so it's apparently hurdles again this year and he'll doubtless be long odds-on when he wins his maiden before being upped in class again. Likely to take high rank among the novices, but whatever he does this season, stardom will hopefully await when he faces fences.

CLAN DES OBEAUX Paul Nicholls

This Paul Nicholls-trained gelding has long been highly regarded but, while he has won four of his ten starts, he has also been beaten at short prices on several occasions.

There is a chance connections' opinion of

American: tough to beat in staying chases when the mud is flying

Irish Saint: without a win since 2015 – but that can all change this season

him was a little high to begin with and I'll admit to being of the opinion he could be a bit soft. However, we would do well to remember he is still only a five-year-old and if you replace 'soft' for 'weak' there is every reason to believe he has the potential to develop into a top-class chaser.

He certainly looked the part when galloping his rivals into the ground on his second start over fences at Newbury, jumping and moving effortlessly and, while he was beaten half a length by Whisper when odds-on at Cheltenham's New Year meeting, the runner-up was beaten only a nose by stablemate Might Bite in the RSA and has always been high class.

The Racing Post rating of 154 Clan Des Obeaux earned there has been bettered in the last ten years only by Master Minded and Bristol De Mai in the January of their five-year-old careers, so he's in good company. His British wins have come by margins of 21, ten and 11 lengths, and he has yet to face a big field over fences, but he almost certainly will do this season and if he can handle the hustle and bustle, a mark of 148 is unlikely to prove beyond him.

IRISH SAINT Paul Nicholls

It is arguably a bit strange putting in a horse to follow who hasn't won since February 2015, but Irish Saint missed all of the 2015-16 season due to injury and was bafflingly kept at the wrong trip for all four starts last season.

Having travelled really well over hurdles on his return from the absence in November, he was sent back over fences at Ascot the following month and, having made a promising move just before the home bend, was clearly out on his legs approaching the last. Still the experiment with three miles continued and Irish Saint again travelled

well only to empty out at Sandown in February and finished tired, after which he was made favourite for the BetBright Chase at Kempton. That hard race at Sandown may have taken its toll as he didn't travel with as much fluency as before – although was still there entering the straight – and finished well beaten.

On the plus side, that campaign has done no harm at all to Irish Saint's handicap mark and he could do some serious damage if dropped back to around two and a half miles off a mark of 144 this season. The last time he ran over that trip he was fourth, albeit beaten a fair way, to Vautour in the JLT Novices' Chase in March 2015.

Connections seem to have the idea he must go right-handed, but on RPRs there is no difference between his best chase and hurdles form either way round and I'd be gunning for something like the BetVictor Gold Cup.

ITS'AFREEBEE Dan Skelton

This could be one of the best-handicapped second-season chasers around.

Having beaten Le Prezien in a Grade 2 novice hurdle and then run third to Yorkhill and Yanworth in the Neptune two seasons ago, Its'afreebee was switched to fences for the next campaign, but not all went to plan.

He started well enough at Fakenham and, after a rather tame effort at Cheltenham, then slammed former World Hurdle winner Cole Harden at Wetherby, after which he was given a handicap mark of 144. Unfortunately that was where things started to go wrong as he was beaten a long way when third to the very useful Waiting Patiently at Haydock in January and was then thumped even further when odds-on for a little race at Southwell.

Those runs were not him and he was fairly well supported for the Close Brothers' Novice Handicap Chase at the festival only for his saddle to slip little past halfway.

He has something to prove now, but the handicapper has been quick enough to relent and a mark of 137 is well below the level he has already shown and there's every chance he'll leave it behind again this season.

LET'S DANCE Willie Mullins

The idea of putting up a dozen horses in this book is not to be too obvious, but I'll have to admit if Let's Dance sticks to her own sex you're not going to get rich backing her.

Having remained a maiden as a juvenile over hurdles for Willie Mullins, she was able to race in novice company again last season and won four on the spin before lining up for the first running of the mares' novice hurdle at the Cheltenham Festival, which she won with a fair bit in hand at odds of just 11-8.

Although beaten on her next two starts at the Fairyhouse and Punchestown festivals, running at three big meetings in the spring is never easy and there is no doubt she was ready to do the business at Cheltenham. I actually think she was a bit below her best on her final two starts, but have no doubt she has plenty more improvement in her.

She might not have the potential to be the next Annie Power, but she'll hold her own in Graded company in Ireland and should be a big contender for the mares' hurdle back at Cheltenham in March as that will be over a more suitable trip.

NO HASSLE HOFF Dan Skelton

Another of Skelton's string who could prove extremely well handicapped when getting his right conditions.

Having fallen when well clear at the last at odds of 1-7 on his hurdles debut at Fontwell in November, he made no mistake next time at Hereford. That wasn't much of a race, but it confirmed No Hassle Hoff was well suited to the mud and he improved again when a solid third to the ultra game Wholestone and Ami Desbois in a Grade 2 at Cheltenham, before going down by only a head to Nicky Henderson's Constantine Bay (now rated 144) at Doncaster.

No Hassle Hoff also went to Aintree, where he was well backed to win a 22-runner handicap but could manage no better than fourth to the enterprisingly ridden Fountains Windfall, who slipped well clear with four to jump and stayed there. He is better than that and perhaps soft ground could be the key to him improving again this term. If it is, the Fixed Brush Hurdle at Haydock in November could be an ideal early season target.

OUR DUKE Jessica Harrington

Jessica Harrington won the Cheltenham Gold Cup in March with Sizing John and time might tell that the biggest danger to her stable star is housed in the same yard.

Having achieved a top RPR of just 138 in three starts over hurdles, Our Duke's rise over fences was little short of stratospheric. He was a Grade 1 winner on his second start when scoring at Leopardstown in December, his first attempt at three miles, and after finding a drop back in trip against him in the Flogas next time (second) he turned the Irish National into a procession at Fairyhouse. He did so by racing up with the pace all the way and galloping his rivals into submission. An RPR of 172 for that success was stunning for one so inexperienced and puts him in good company.

In the past ten years the only other chasers to have nudged 170 having not had more than three previous chase starts have been Diamond Harry, Sprinter Sacre, Un De Sceaux, Vautour, Douvan, Coneygree and Altior. If all goes well, he is going to be a major player at the top level this year.

SAMCRO Gordon Elliott

This might come as a surprise to some, but according to RPRs, Champion Bumper winner Fayonagh didn't even make the top ten of bumper performers in Britain and Ireland last season. Top of the pile was Gordon Elliott's Samcro, a stablemate of Fayonagh, but owned by Gigginstown House Stud and therefore kept well away from the big spring bumpers.

The winner of his sole point-to-point, he raced only three times for Elliott last season, but won them all, two of them by wide margins. The closest he came to defeat was a half-length win at Navan in December, but they crawled throughout and a sprint finish was not in his favour, although Jamie Codd

did not need to be hard on him to win anyway.

He closed his campaign with a 17-length win at Fairyhouse in April and, while you can't get massively excited about those he beat, there is no doubt he has a serious engine.

We can expect him to take high order among the novice hurdlers this term. As usual, he's been priced up for all the major Cheltenham novice contests, but I'd imagine he'll want further than two miles.

TRUCKERS LODGE Tom George

The Worlds End won a Chepstow bumper at the end of the 2015-16 campaign for Tom George, who last season took both divisions of the same race with Truckers Lodge and Forgot To Ask. Both won by wide margins (nine lengths and 11 respectively), but the cheaply bought Truckers Lodge did so in a considerably faster time from a well-backed horse of Paul Nicholls and that looks the slightly stronger form.

Either way, both are probably well worth following and may slip under the radar given connections. Bred to want a good deal further than two miles over jumps, he could well be up to tackling Graded company this season.

WILLIE BOY Venetia Williams

Still has a fair bit to learn about jumping, but is potentially very well handicapped despite being put up 15lb for winning at Uttoxeter on Midlands National day.

A point-to-point winner on his second start in that sphere, Willie Boy joined Venetia Williams in November and after only three moderately promising hurdles runs before Christmas, was put away for three months before returning in a novice handicap chase at Sandown, where he was well backed but got no further than the first.

It took us only seven days to find out why he'd been so well supported, though, as he returned under 12st at Uttoxeter to make all and win with his head in his chest despite making a terrible mistake two out.

He could make big strides and, like a lot of Williams' better horses, he seems to go very well on soft ground.

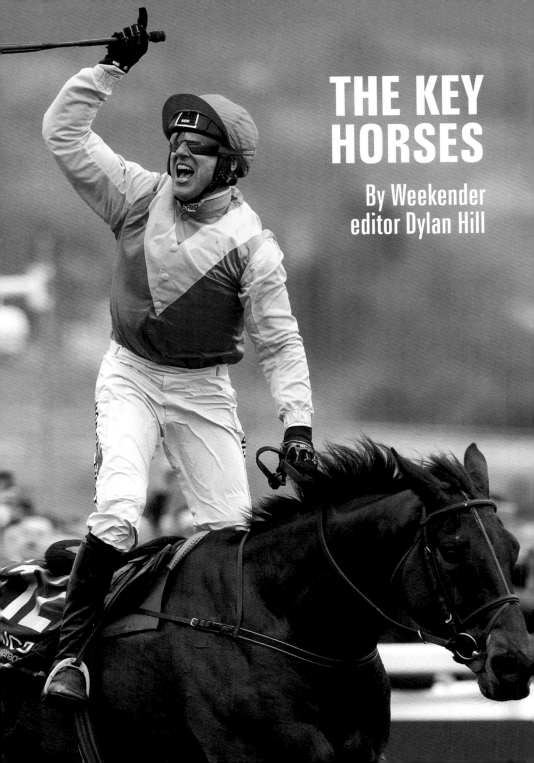

THE KEY HORSES

By Weekender editor Dylan Hill

A Genie In Abottle (Ire)

6 b g Beneficial - Erkindale Miss (Supreme Leader)

Noel Meade (Ir)   Gigginstown House Stud

PLACINGS: 1311/6321253-   RPR **147c**

Starts	1st	2nd	3rd	4th	Win & Pl
10	3	2	3	-	£37,140

12/16	Fair	3m Ch sft-hvy	£4,974
3/16	Naas	3m Mdn Hdl sft-hvy	£5,426
2/16	Naas	2m3f NHF 5-7yo soft	£4,522

Ran well in several good staying novice chases last season, although slightly disappointing when only fifth in the National Hunt Chase at Cheltenham (was 4-1 favourite); may have found the ground too quick and worth another chance over longer trips.

A Toi Phil (Fr)

7 b g Day Flight - Lucidrile (Beyssac)

Gordon Elliott (Ir)   Gigginstown House Stud

PLACINGS: 2/0117/P116515124-4   RPR **152+c**

Starts	1st	2nd	3rd	4th	Win & Pl
16	6	2	-	2	£154,096

3/17	Navn	2m4f Gd2 Ch heavy	£21,432
143 1/17	Leop	2m5f 126-154 Ch Hcap good	£50,427
11/16	Punc	2m6½f Nov Gd2 Ch soft	£18,438
11/16	DRoy	2m3½f Ch good	£5,653
1/16	Navn	2m4f Nov Gd2 Hdl soft	£18,529
12/15	Leop	2m2f Mdn Hdl heavy	£6,953

Won four times during a busy novice chasing campaign last season, gaining his biggest success in a valuable 2m5f handicap at Leopardstown; came up short against the very best novices but fourth in the Galway Plate and should continue to do well in handicaps.

Abolitionist (Ire)

9 b g Flemensfirth - All The Roses (Roselier)

Ellmarie Holden (Ir)   Mrs Catherine Holden

PLACINGS: 46164/9121622/2213-0   RPR **150c**

Starts	1st	2nd	3rd	4th	Win & Pl
45	7	8	5	9	£167,466

137 3/17	Naas	3m 118-146 Ch Hcap sft-hvy	£50,427
7/15	Limk	3m Ch good	£9,360
111 5/15	Kbgn	3m1f 102-122 Ch Hcap gd-yld	£9,360
115 12/14	Fair	2m7f 100-115 Hdl Hcap soft	£5,750
98 7/14	Bell	3m 95-109 Hdl Hcap gd-fm	£6,038
93 5/14	Punc	3m 85-102 Hdl Hcap good	£4,888
90 7/13	Slig	2m4f 80-95 Hdl Hcap good	£3,528

Better than ever last season on his return from more than a year out, winning the Leinster National in between fine placed efforts in the

Troytown and the Irish National; has shot up the weights but should continue to run well in big staying handicaps.

Acapella Bourgeois (Fr)

7 ch g Network - Jasmine (Valanjou I)

Sandra Hughes (Ir)   Slaneyville Syndicate

PLACINGS: 70/1/31211/4F341165-   RPR **157+c**

Starts	1st	2nd	3rd	4th	Win & Pl
16	6	1	2	2	£93,140

2/17	Navn	3m Nov Gd2 Ch sft-hvy	£21,432
1/17	Navn	2m4f Ch soft	£6,833
3/16	Fair	2m4f Nov Gd2 Hdl yield	£19,522
2/16	Thur	2m4f Nov Gd2 Hdl soft	£19,522
12/15	Leop	2m4f Mdn Hdl heavy	£6,953
10/14	Rcpp	1m4f NHF 4-5yo gd-sft	£4,167

Won twice over fences last season and particularly impressive when making all in a Grade 2 novice chase at Navan (beat Grade 1 winner Road To Respect by 32 lengths); less effective on quicker ground in the spring but fascinating to see him back on soft or heavy.

Agrapart (Fr)

6 b/br g Martaline - Afragha (Darshaan)

Nick Williams   The Gascoigne Brookes Partnership III

PLACINGS: 521316/74139-   RPR **158h**

Starts	1st	2nd	3rd	4th	Win & Pl
11	3	2	1	1	£142,853

1/17	Chel	2m4½f Cls1 Gd2 Hdl soft	£22,887
137 2/16	Newb	2m1½f Cls1 Gd3 128-153 Hdl Hcap heavy	£88,273
12/15	Aint	2m1f Cls3 Nov Hdl soft	£6,279

Claimed some big scalps when landing last season's Relkeel Hurdle at Cheltenham; suspicion that was largely due to testing conditions (has gained all four wins on ground from soft to heavy) and outclassed when ninth in the Stayers' Hurdle.

Air Horse One

6 gr g Mountain High - Whisky Rose (Old Vic)

Harry Fry   The Dons

PLACINGS: 1272U3/6411140-   RPR **143h**

Starts	1st	2nd	3rd	4th	Win & Pl
13	4	2	1	2	£47,184

132 2/17	Asct	2m3½f Cls2 119-142 Hdl Hcap soft	£28,152
1/17	Tntn	2m3f Cls4 Nov Hdl 4-7yo good	£4,549
1/17	Extr	2m1f Cls4 Mdn Hdl soft	£3,249
5/15	Extr	2m1f Cls6 NHF 4-6yo good	£1,625

Needed seven runs to get off the mark over

hurdles but proved highly progressive in the new year, completing a hat-trick in a valuable handicap at Ascot and finishing a close fourth in the County Hurdle at Cheltenham; didn't run his race at Punchestown last time.

Al Boum Photo (Fr)

5 b g Buck's Boum - Al Gane (Dom Alco)

Willie Mullins (Ir)   Mrs J Donnelly

PLACINGS: F/3115-   RPR **145+h**

Starts	1st	2nd	3rd	4th	Win & Pl
5	2	-	1	-	£29,059
	4/17 Fair	2m4f Nov Gd2 Hdl sft-hvy			£21,432
	1/17 Thur	2m Mdn Hdl 4-5yo yld-sft			£5,256

Yet another smart French recruit for Willie Mullins; won twice in four races last season, most notably in a Grade 2 novice hurdle at Fairyhouse; raced too freely when stepped up to 3m at Punchestown, finishing only fifth behind Champagne Classic.

Alary (Fr)

7 ch g Dream Well - Cate Bleue (Katowice)

Colin Tizzard   Alan Potts

PLACINGS: 44F1/231F6/23632PF6-   RPR **158c**

Starts	1st	2nd	3rd	4th	Win & Pl
23	2	4	3	3	£295,098
0	9/15 Autl	2m6f List Ch Hcap v soft			£38,372
	4/15 Autl	2m6f Ch 5yo v soft			£20,465

Talked up by connections as a Gold Cup horse following purchase from France last season but disappointing in three runs, although not running badly when he fell three out in a graduation chase at Exeter behind Tea For Two; probably needs mark to come down.

Alcala (Fr)

7 gr g Turgeon - Pail Mel (Sleeping Car)

Paul Nicholls   Owners Group 016

PLACINGS: 1446132/63F313-11111   RPR **159+c**

Starts	1st	2nd	3rd	4th	Win & Pl
22	9	2	4	3	£111,015
	8/17 NAbb	2m5f Cls3 Nov Ch good			£7,280
	8/17 NAbb	3m2f Cls3 Nov Ch good			£6,498
147	7/17 MRas	2m5½f Cls1 List 126-152 Ch Hcap good			£28,475
142	6/17 NAbb	2m5f Cls2 129-155 Ch Hcap gd-fm			£14,128
135	6/17 NAbb	2m5f Cls3 Nov 133-135 Ch Hcap gd-sft			£6,393
130	4/17 Ludl	3m Cls3 Nov 111-130 Ch Hcap good			£6,657
	2/16 Font	2m1½f Cls4 Nov Hdl 4-7yo heavy			£3,899
	10/15 Worc	2m4f Cls4 Mdn Hdl gd-sft			£3,249
	8/13 Vitt	1m4f NHF 3yo gd-sft			£4,878

Has taken a long time to fulfil his potential (sent off 7-2 for the Adonis on his British debut in 2015) but flourished this summer, completing a hat-trick in the Summer Plate and winning again twice subsequently; stays further and handles cut in the ground (has won on heavy).

Alisier D'Irlande (Fr)

7 br g Kapgarde - Isati'S (Chamberlin)

Henry de Bromhead (Ir)   R S Brookhouse

PLACINGS: 1/361/F115/3U5617-   RPR **155+c**

Starts	1st	2nd	3rd	4th	Win & Pl
13	4	-	2	-	£53,211
	2/17 Naas	2m Gd3 Ch heavy			£23,953
	2/16 Leop	2m1f Nov Ch soft			£9,496
	2/16 Naas	2m Ch soft			£6,331
	3/15 Thur	2m Mdn Hdl yld-sft			£5,349

Exciting front-running chaser who revels in testing conditions, winning his last three races on soft or heavy going, although he got his ground only once last season; much less effective on quicker surface but ran well enough when seventh in the Red Rum at Aintree.

Alpha Des Obeaux (Fr)

7 b g Saddler Maker - Omega Des Obeaux (Saint Preuil)

Mouse Morris (Ir)   Gigginstown House Stud

PLACINGS: 22F/22212/35113P486-   RPR **147c**

Starts	1st	2nd	3rd	4th	Win & Pl
19	4	7	2	1	£193,876

11/16	Cork	2m4f Nov Gd3 Ch good	£17,353
10/16	Thur	2m6f Ch good	£4,974
1/16	Gowr	3m Gd2 Hdl heavy	£18,750
11/14	Punc	2m4f Mdn Hdl 4yo yield	£5,750

Brilliant second in the 2016 World Hurdle (beaten only by Thistlecrack and 22 lengths clear of the third) but plagued by physical problems since, breaking blood vessels for the second time when fourth in the RSA Chase last season; still a big talent.

Altior: superstar chaser cruised to success in last season's Arkle

ON THE FIGURES

ALTIOR Unbeaten over hurdles and fences, he gained the sixth success of another scintillating season when slamming the Champion Chase winner Special Tiara at Sandown. That earned him a RPR of 177 and he looks capable of posting figures well in excess of 180.
[Steve Mason, Racing Post Ratings]

Altior (Ire)

7 b g High Chaparral - Monte Solaro (Key Of Luck)

Nicky Henderson   Mrs Patricia Pugh

PLACINGS: 13/611111/111111-   RPR **177+c**

Starts	1st	2nd	3rd	4th	Win & Pl
14	12	-	1	-	£365,735

4/17	Sand	1m7½f Cls1 Gd1 Ch good	£71,188
3/17	Chel	2m Cls1 Nov Gd1 Ch gd-sft	£99,663
2/17	Newb	2m½f Cls1 Gd2 Ch soft	£28,475
12/16	Kemp	2m Cls1 Nov Gd2 Ch good	£22,780
12/16	Sand	1m7½f Cls1 Nov Gd1 Ch gd-sft	£25,628
11/16	Kemp	2m2f Cls4 Nov Ch soft	£4,549
3/16	Chel	2m½f Cls1 Nov Gd1 Hdl gd-sft	£68,340
12/15	Kemp	2m Cls2 Nov Hdl gd-sft	£11,696
11/15	Chel	2m½f Cls1 Nov Gd2 Hdl gd-sft	£17,286
10/15	Asct	1m7½f Cls3 Nov Hdl good	£7,798
10/15	Chep	2m Cls4 Nov Hdl good	£3,899
5/14	MRas	2m½f Cls6 NHF 4-6yo good	£1,560

Won six out of six over fences last season to make it 11 unbeaten over jumps, including victories in the Supreme Novices' Hurdle and Arkle Chase; also stepped out of novice company twice, thrashing Champion Chase winner Special Tiara at Sandown; sets the standard in the 2m chasing division and spent summer as the market leader in Champion Chase ante-post lists

American (Fr)

7 b g Malinas - Grande Sultane (Garde Royale)

Harry Fry					The Jago Family Partnership
PLACINGS: 1/316/111-				RPR **161 +c**	

Starts	1st	2nd	3rd	4th	Win & Pl
6	4	-	1	-	£56,173
148	3/17	Uttx	3m Cls2 Nov 122-148 Ch Hcap soft		£18,768
	1/17	Wwck	3m Cls1 Nov List Ch soft		£14,305
	11/16	Extr	3m Cls3 Nov Ch soft		£9,495
	11/15	Asct	2m5¹/₂f Cls2 Nov Ch gd-sft		£12,512

Won three out of three when sent chasing last season and particularly impressive when landing a novice handicap at Uttoxeter off 148; gained all three wins on soft and missed RSA Chase due to quicker ground so may be one for midwinter staying handicaps.

American Tom (Fr)

6 b g American Post - Kirkla (Bikala)

Willie Mullins (Ir)					Mrs S Ricci
PLACINGS: 3/1/1F-				RPR **140 +c**	

Starts	1st	2nd	3rd	4th	Win & Pl
4	2	-	1	-	£18,823
	12/16	Punc	2m Cls Ch yld-sft		£5,200
	11/15	Gowr	2m Nov Hdl 4yo soft		£8,023

Has won two out of three starts since moving to Willie Mullins and found to be coughing after his sole defeat at Naas (tailing off when fell four out); had looked very impressive previously and could still prove a big star, although needs to gain experience.

Ami Desbois (Fr)

7 b g Dream Well - Baroya (Garde Royale)

Graeme McPherson				EPDS Racing Partnership 12 & Partner	
PLACINGS: 45/42238/1123151-				RPR **145 +h**	

Starts	1st	2nd	3rd	4th	Win & Pl
14	4	3	2	2	£37,599
	4/17	Newc	2m4¹/₂f Cls4 Nov Hdl good		£3,249
137	2/17	Weth	3m Cls3 115-137 Hdl Hcap soft		£5,523
126	11/16	Hayd	2m7f Cls3 110-130 Hdl Hcap soft		£6,498
	5/16	Hexm	2m7¹/₂f Cls5 Mdn Hdl good		£2,464

Won four times last season, all at a relatively modest level, but also ran well in the face of other stiff tasks, including when fifth in the Albert

---

Bartlett at Cheltenham; probably best over that 3m trip but effective over 2m4f; set to go novice chasing.

Anibale Fly (Fr)

7 b g Assessor - Nouba Fly (Chamberlin)

Tony Martin (Ir)					John P McManus
PLACINGS: 211/1346/112P142-				RPR **148c**	

Starts	1st	2nd	3rd	4th	Win & Pl
14	6	3	1	2	£130,451
	1/17	Naas	3m Nov Gd3 Ch yld-sft		£22,692
	11/16	Navn	2m1f Ch yld-sft		£7,235
135	4/16	Punc	2m4f 125-149 Hdl Hcap yield		£43,382
	12/15	Navn	2m Mdn Hdl heavy		£7,488
	4/15	Fair	2m NHF 4-7yo soft		£7,221
	3/15	Navn	2m NHF 5-7yo heavy		£4,814

Not far off last season's best novice chasers, twice finishing second at Grade 1 level behind Coney Island and Disko; inconsistent otherwise (won three times but well below best on two other occasions); likely to find his level in good staying handicaps.

Antartica De Thaix (Fr)

7 gr m Dom Alco - Nouca De Thaix (Subotica)

Paul Nicholls				I Fogg, C Barber, D Macdonald & C Giles	
PLACINGS: 26/2U1232/22F1114-				RPR **151 +c**	

Starts	1st	2nd	3rd	4th	Win & Pl
15	4	6	1	1	£52,594
	3/17	Winc	2m4f Cls4 Nov Ch gd-sft		£4,660
	3/17	Hntg	2m4f Cls1 List Ch soft		£17,165
	2/17	Bang	2m4¹/₂f Cls4 Nov Ch soft		£5,326
	2/16	Tntn	2m3f Cls4 Nov Hdl heavy		£4,549

Proved herself a smart mare when winning three times over fences last season, most notably a Listed race at Huntingdon, having reportedly needed to learn to settle; stopped quickly when trying to make all in stronger company at Cheltenham.

Any Second Now (Ire)

5 b g Oscar - Pretty Neat (Topanoora)

Ted Walsh (Ir)					John P McManus
PLACINGS: 113U-				RPR **142h**	

Starts	1st	2nd	3rd	4th	Win & Pl
4	2	-	1	-	£31,443
	1/17	Punc	2m Nov Gd2 Hdl soft		£22,440
	12/16	Navn	2m Mdn Hdl 4yo yld-sft		£5,426

Big chasing type who won first two races over

ON THE CLOCK

AMERICAN Harry Fry's exciting seven-year-old is unbeaten in three starts over fences and clocked a standout time at Uttoxeter in March. A resolute galloper, soft ground is a pre-requisite and he could be a Welsh National candidate. [Dave Edwards, Topspeed]

90TH ANNIVERSARY

SEDGEFIELD RACECOURSE

BEAT THE BEST COMPETITION

In memory of legendary trainers Denys Smith and Arthur Stephenson.

Arthur Stephenson had a record breaking 260 number of wins here at Sedgefield and Denys Smith 145 wins.

The trainer who comes closest to both Arthur & Denys will win a fantastic prize in February 2018.

STABLE YARD COMPETITION

A competition introduced to reward loyal Stable Yards.

The Stable Yard who receives the most Best Turned Out Awards, will also receive a fantastic prize in February 2018.

Tel: 01740 621925

www.sedgefield-racecourse.co.uk

Sedgefield Racecourse, Racecourse Road, Sedgefield, Stockton-on-Tees, TS21 2HW

hurdles last season, including a Grade 2 at Punchestown; outpaced when third in a stronger race at that level but should do better beyond 2m (unseated rider early when stepped up in trip at Fairyhouse).

Apple's Jade (Fr)

5 b m Saddler Maker - Apple's For Ever (Nikos)

Gordon Elliott (Ir)   Gigginstown House Stud

PLACINGS: 1121/1221211-   RPR **157+h**

Starts	1st	2nd	3rd	4th	Win & Pl
11	7	4	-	-	£348,420
	4/17	Punc	2m4f Gd1 Hdl gd-yld		£50,427
	3/17	Chel	2m4f Cls1 Gd1 Hdl gd-sft		£61,897
	12/16	Fair	2m4f Gd1 Hdl gd-yld		£43,382
	4/16	Punc	2m Gd1 Hdl 4yo yield		£43,382
	4/16	Aint	2m1f Cls1 Gd1 Hdl 4yo soft		£56,437
	12/15	Leop	2m Gd2 Hdl 3yo heavy		£21,415
	5/15	Vich	2m1/2f Hdl 3yo good		£7,814

Outstanding four-time Grade 1 winner, with her last three successes achieved over 2m4f having twice been a beaten favourite over 2m; should again prove hard to beat in mares' company this season after winning at Cheltenham and Punchestown last term; tends to need a run to find her best.

Ar Mad (Fr)

7 b g Tiger Groom - Omelia (April Night)

Gary Moore   Ashley Head

PLACINGS: 4032541/61111/4-   RPR **169+c**

Starts	1st	2nd	3rd	4th	Win & Pl
13	5	1	1	1	£76,089
155	2/16	Plum	2m31/2f Cls3 Nov 136-155 Ch Hcap heavy		£6,498
	12/15	Kemp	2m Cls1 Nov Gd2 Ch gd-sft		£19,933
	12/15	Sand	1m71/2f Cls1 Nov Gd1 Ch gd-sft		£25,748
	11/15	Sand	1m71/2f Cls3 Ch gd-sft		£6,975
	4/15	Plum	2m41/2f Cls4 Nov Hdl good		£4,224

Exciting chaser whose progress has been badly held up by injuries, with just one run since a promising novice campaign two seasons ago ended prematurely; shaped well that day when a close fourth in the Tingle Creek despite several blunders; more to come.

Arbre De Vie (Fr)

7 b g Antarctique - Nouvelle Recrue (Ragmar)

Willie Mullins (Ir)   Mrs S Ricci

PLACINGS: /114/2203/022UB2-761   RPR **155+c**

Starts	1st	2nd	3rd	4th	Win & Pl
19	3	6	2	1	£78,786
	8/17	Gway	2m61/2f Ch soft		£13,141
	2/15	Wwck	2m5f Cls3 Nov Hdl soft		£6,498
	12/14	Fair	2m4f Mdn Hdl soft		£4,600

Largely disappointing since promising much with a close fourth in the 2015 Albert Bartlett Hurdle at Cheltenham, but had been slowly getting his act together over fences and won impressively

at Galway in August from Shaneshill; could be a leading novice chaser.

Arctic Fire (Ger)

8 b g Soldier Hollow - Adelma (Sternkoenig)

Willie Mullins (Ir)   Wicklow Bloodstock (Ireland)

PLACINGS: 42/123322F/21142/13-   RPR **163h**

Starts	1st	2nd	3rd	4th	Win & Pl
19	5	6	4	2	£348,463
158	3/17	Chel	2m1f Cls1 Gd3 134-158 Hdl Hcap good		£54,103
	11/15	Fair	2m4f Gd1 Hdl soft		£39,535
	11/15	Navn	2m4f Gd2 Hdl yld-sft		£20,155
	5/14	Punc	2m Nov Hdl gd-yld		£12,188
	10/13	Tipp	2m Mdn Hdl 4-5yo good		£4,207

Former Champion Hurdle runner-up who proved as good as ever despite a long absence last spring, winning the County Hurdle on his return under top weight; relished a strong gallop that day and may now be better over further in smaller fields.

Aso (Fr)

7 b/br g Goldneyev - Odyssee Du Cellier (Dear Doctor)

Venetia Williams   The Bellamy Partnership

PLACINGS: 00/22213561/4218434-   RPR **161c**

Starts	1st	2nd	3rd	4th	Win & Pl
24	7	5	4	3	£173,456
145	12/16	Chep	2m31/2f Cls2 127-149 Ch Hcap soft		£25,320
	4/16	NAbb	2m5f Cls3 Nov Ch soft		£7,280
	1/16	MRas	2m51/2f Ch soft		£12,777
	1/15	Hayd	2m Cls1 Nov Gd2 Hdl heavy		£15,661
	12/14	Tntn	2m3f Cls4 Nov Hdl soft		£3,574
	11/14	Wwck	2m Cls4 Nov Hdl soft		£3,899
	7/13	Gran	1m4f NHF 3yo gd-fm		£4,065

Slightly unlucky to manage only a single win last season having gone close in several big handicaps, including when fourth in the BetBright Chase on first run over 3m even after going up 7lb for Chepstow win; higher again now after Ryanair Chase third.

Astre De La Cour (Fr)

7 b/br g Khalkevi - Gracieuse Delacour (Port Etienne)

Robert Walford   The Front Runners Partnership

PLACINGS: F/41F/511/04/045122-   RPR **146+c**

Starts	1st	2nd	3rd	4th	Win & Pl
16	5	2	-	3	£59,529
125	12/16	Tntn	2m2f Cls3 125-132 Ch Hcap gd-fm		£8,862
135	4/15	Aint	2m11/2f Cls2 128-146 Cond Am Hdl Hcap good		£24,760
125	3/15	Strf	2m11/2f Cls3 110-125 Hdl Hcap gd-sft		£6,498
	1/14	Asct	1m71/2f Cls3 Hdl 4yo heavy		£5,630
	3/13	Pmnl	1m4f NHF 3yo heavy		£4,472

Won a big handicap hurdle at Aintree in 2015 and did well when tackling fences for the second time last season; second to subsequent Grand Annual runner-up last time and well clear of third; open to further progress after just four runs over fences.

Augusta Kate

6 b m Yeats - Feathard Lady (Accordion)

Willie Mullins (Ir)   The Masters Syndicate

PLACINGS: 1172/11F615-   RPR **143+h**

Starts	1st	2nd	3rd	4th	Win & Pl
10	5	1	-	-	£111,192

4/17	Fair	2m4f Nov Gd1 Hdl gd-yld	£50,427
11/16	Thur	2m7f Mdn Hdl yield	£4,974
4/16	Punc	2m List NHF 4-7yo yield	£17,353
11/15	Navn	2m List NHF 4-7yo soft	£20,155
9/15	List	2m NHF 4-7yo yld-sft	£6,419

Gutsy winner of a Grade 1 mares' novice hurdle at Fairyhouse last season, outstaying Let's Dance; seems sure to get 3m on that evidence and had excuses when below par in the Albert Bartlett.

Aux Ptits Soins (Fr)

7 gr g Saint Des Saints - Reflexion Faite (Turgeon)

Paul Nicholls   J Hales

PLACINGS: 1/311/5/21428-   RPR **149h**

Starts	1st	2nd	3rd	4th	Win & Pl
10	4	2	1	1	£115,191

	12/16	Kels	2m7¹/₂f Cls3 Nov Ch gd-sft	£10,128
139	3/15	Chel	2m5f Cls1 Gd3 138-158 Hdl Hcap good	£45,560
	9/14	Autl	2m1¹/₂f Hdl 4yo v soft	£19,200
	3/14	Autl	2m1¹/₂f Hdl 4yo heavy	£19,200

Won the Coral Cup on his British debut in 2015 but hasn't achieved much since, albeit not helped by a year absence after that win; reverted to hurdles with little success last term after some wretched jumping at Doncaster but had got off the mark over fences prior to that.

Bacardys (Fr)

6 b g Coastal Path - Oasice (Robin Des Champs)

Willie Mullins (Ir)   Shanakiel Racing Syndicate

PLACINGS: F1/131/3F11P1-   RPR **155+h**

Starts	1st	2nd	3rd	4th	Win & Pl
9	5	-	2	-	£144,107

4/17	Punc	2m4f Nov Gd1 Hdl gd-yld	£50,427
2/17	Leop	2m2f Nov Gd1 Hdl soft	£45,385
12/16	Leop	2m Mdn Hdl yield	£6,331
4/16	Aint	2m1f Cls1 Gd2 NHF 4-6yo soft	£22,508
12/15	Leop	2m NHF 4yo heavy	£5,349

Dual Grade 1 winner as a novice hurdler last season, doing best when beating Finian's Oscar by a short head over 2m4f at Punchestown; had lost all chance when badly hampered in the Neptune at Cheltenham; should stay further and could go chasing.

Bachasson (Fr)

6 gr g Voix Du Nord - Belledonne (Shafoun)

Willie Mullins (Ir)   Edward O'Connell

PLACINGS: 611/111128U/F21-   RPR **148+c**

Starts	1st	2nd	3rd	4th	Win & Pl
13	7	2	-	-	£71,650

2/17	Gowr	2m4f Ch heavy	£7,371
10/15	Tipp	2m Nov Gd3 Hdl good	£15,116
9/15	Gway	2m2f Nov Hdl good	£9,093
7/15	Gway	2m Nov Hdl 4yo yield	£10,078
7/15	Slig	2m Mdn Hdl 4yo good	£5,616
9/14	Stra	1m4f NHF 3yo v soft	£5,000
7/14	Vitt	1m4f NHF 3yo gd-sft	£4,583

Improved steadily in three runs over fences last season, winning a good beginners' chase at Gowran on his final run, only to miss potential Grade 1 targets in the spring; coped well with heavy ground that day but trainer expects him to improve on quicker.

Baie Des Iles (Fr)

6 gr m Barastraight - Malownia (Smadoun)

Ross O'Sullivan (Ir)   Mrs Z Wentworth

PLACINGS: 1121336F/71246/0513-   RPR **148c**

Starts	1st	2nd	3rd	4th	Win & Pl
20	6	2	4	1	£162,614

141	2/17	Punc	3m4f 126-154 Ch Hcap soft	£25,214
130	1/16	Punc	3m1f 106-130 Am Ch Hcap heavy	£8,625
	10/14	Autl	2m1¹/₂f Ch 3yo heavy	£34,000
	9/14	Autl	2m2f Hdl 3yo v soft	£26,000
	8/14	Roya	1m6¹/₂f NHF 3yo gd-sft	£4,167
	5/14	Vich	1m4f Hdl 3yo soft	£8,400

Chase winner as a three-year-old in France and quickly thrust into top staying handicaps having won again at Punchestown on Irish chasing debut; did well when fifth in last season's Welsh National and improved again with another victory at Punchestown.

ON THE FIGURES

APPLE'S JADE Didn't quite match the figure she achieved at Aintree as a juvenile, but still picked up three Grade 1s last season, including when seeing off the challenge of a couple of very smart rivals at Cheltenham. Looks set for another successful season. [Steve Mason, Racing Post Ratings]

Balko Des Flos (Fr)

6 ch g Balko - Royale Marie (Garde Royale)

Henry de Bromhead (Ir)   Gigginstown House Stud

PLACINGS: 1/10154/72133F3-1   RPR **155+c**

Starts	1st	2nd	3rd	4th	Win & Pl
14	5	1	3	1	£176,106
146	8/17	Gway	2m6¹/₂f 137-160 Ch Hcap good		£126,068
	1/17	Fair	2m5¹/₂f Ch soft		£5,879
	1/16	Punc	2m4f Mdn Hdl sft-hvy		£6,088
	5/15	Slig	2m2f NHF 4yo yield		£5,349
	1/15	Leop	2m NHF 4yo soft		£4,279

Impressive winner of the Galway Plate this summer; had won only once last season but ran several big races in defeat, including when third in a Grade 1 behind Disko, and still improving; best form at around 2m5f and yet to convince in three runs over 3m.

Ball D'Arc (Fr)

6 b g Network - Pretty Moon (Moon Madness)

Gordon Elliott (Ir)   Gigginstown House Stud

PLACINGS: 3117/62U21423111233-   RPR **162+c**

Starts	1st	2nd	3rd	4th	Win & Pl
24	8	5	4	1	£185,636
133	3/17	Naas	2m4f Nov Gd3 Ch sft-hvy		£17,083
	2/17	Navn	2m1f Nov Gd3 Ch sft-hvy		£21,432
	1/17	Fair	2m1f 127-142 Ch Hcap soft		£50,427
	10/16	Wxfd	2m Ch good		£5,200
	2/16	Naas	2m Nov Gd2 Hdl sft-hvy		£20,173
	1/16	Punc	2m Nov List Hdl sft-hvy		£14,338
	12/15	Limk	2m Mdn Hdl 4yo heavy		£6,686
	11/15	Thur	2m NHF 4-7yo yield		£4,814

Wonderfully progressive last season, completing a hat-trick with two wide-margin Grade 3 wins before running in-form Ballycasey to half a length at Fairyhouse; twice placed at Grade 1 level and perhaps not quite at his best as busy campaign took its toll.

Ballyandy

6 b g Kayf Tara - Megalex (Karinga Bay)

Nigel Twiston-Davies   Options O Syndicate

PLACINGS: 112114/23214-   RPR **151+h**

Starts	1st	2nd	3rd	4th	Win & Pl
11	5	3	1	2	£178,245
135	2/17	Newb	2m¹/₂f Cls1 Gd3 126-146 Hdl Hcap soft		£88,273
	3/16	Chel	2m¹/₂f Cls1 Gd1 NHF 4-6yo good		£39,865
	2/16	Newb	2m¹/₂f Cls1 List NHF 4-6yo heavy		£11,390
	11/15	Chel	2m¹/₂f Cls1 List NHF 4-6yo gd-sft		£11,390
	10/15	Worc	2m Cls6 NHF 3-5yo gd-sft		£1,560

Often unsuited by the slow tempo of novice hurdles last season but showed his true colours with a terrific Betfair Hurdle win; raised 12lb for that but new mark not beyond him and one to remember back at the Cheltenham Festival (won the 2016 Champion Bumper).

Ballybolley (Ire)

8 b g Kayf Tara - Gales Hill (Beau Sher)

Nigel Twiston-Davies   Simon Munir & Isaac Souede

PLACINGS: 7433314/2112P341-3F9   RPR **156+c**

Starts	1st	2nd	3rd	4th	Win & Pl
29	9	4	7	3	£134,507
133	4/17	Hayd	2m4f Cls2 115-140 Ch Hcap good		£30,970
	10/16	Hntg	2m4f Cls3 Nov Ch good		£6,498
	10/16	Weth	2m3¹/₂f Cls4 Nov Ch good		£3,994
129	3/16	Hayd	2m4f Cls2 110-136 Ch Hcap good		£30,970
	2/15	Kels	2m Cls4 Nov Hdl gd-sft		£3,249
	12/14	Aint	2m11f Cls3 Nov Hdl gd-sft		£7,507
	4/14	Aint	2m11f Cls1 Gd2 NHF 4-6yo gd-sft		£17,085
	3/14	Towc	2m Cls6 NHF 4-6yo gd-sft		£1,560
	12/13	Sthl	1m7¹/₂f Cls6 NHF 4-6yo good		£1,643

Has won the last two runnings of the Challenger Middle Distance Chase Final at Haydock, most impressively by 17 lengths in April; raised 10lb for that but could still have mileage in that mark (going well when fell three out in a valuable summer handicap at Uttoxeter).

Ballyandy: Champion Bumper winner also landed last season's Betfair Hurdle and remains one for the big occasion

Ballycasey (Ire)

10 gr g Presenting - Pink Mist (Montelimar)

Willie Mullins (Ir)				Mrs S Ricci

PLACINGS: /4935U6/F31513115-10   RPR **165+c**

Starts		1st	2nd	3rd	4th	Win & Pl
31		11	1	5	2	£263,336
	5/17	Klny	2m4¹/₂f Gd3 Ch soft			£20,171
	4/17	Fair	2m1f Gd2 Ch sft-hvy			£21,432
	2/17	Gowr	2m4f Gd2 Ch heavy			£22,692
	10/16	Gowr	2m4f Gd2 Ch yield			£19,522
150	8/16	Klny	2m4¹/₂f 122-150 Ch Hcap soft			£21,691
	11/14	Gowr	2m4f Ch heavy			£10,833
	2/14	Leop	2m5f Nov Gd1 Ch sft-hvy			£43,438
	11/13	Navn	2m1f Ch gd-yld			£8,415
	1/13	Thur	2m6f Nov Hdl heavy			£7,854
	12/12	Clon	2m4f Mdn Hdl heavy			£4,313
	12/11	Leop	2m4f NHF 4-7yo gd-yld			£5,948

Had largely struggled since a successful novice campaign three seasons ago (initially in Grade 1 company and later off a falling mark in handicaps) but found his level last term, winning three Grade 2s; should continue to do well in similar contests.

Ballyoptic (Ire)

7 b g Old Vic - Lambourne Lace (Un Desperado)

Nigel Twiston-Davies				Mills & Mason Partnership

PLACINGS: 31F/225111/1F2F4P5-   RPR **161+h**

Starts		1st	2nd	3rd	4th	Win & Pl
11		4	1	-	1	£112,271
148	10/16	Chep	2m3³/₄f Cls1 Gd3 131-148 Hdl Hcap good			£28,475
	4/16	Aint	3m³/₄f Cls1 Nov Gd1 Hdl soft			£56,270
	3/16	Uttx	2m4f Cls4 Nov Hdl soft			£5,064
	2/16	Ffos	2m4f Cls4 Nov Hdl 4-7yo heavy			£4,549

Not far off the best staying hurdlers last season and would have done better but for late falls when possibly coming to win the West Yorkshire Hurdle and likely to finish second to Unowhatimeanharry in the Long Walk; could go novice chasing.

Bapaume (Fr)

4 b g Turtle Bowl - Brouhaha (American Post)

Willie Mullins (Ir)				Mrs S Ricci

PLACINGS: 61/21231-2   RPR **144h**

Starts		1st	2nd	3rd	4th	Win & Pl
8		3	3	1	-	£158,684
	4/17	Punc	2m4f Hdl 4yo gd-yld			£50,427
	12/16	Leop	2m Gd2 Hdl 3yo yield			£19,522
	4/16	Fntb	1m7f Hdl 3yo v soft			£7,059

Very smart juvenile hurdler last season; enjoyed a steadily run race at Punchestown when deservedly landing a Grade 1 (placed in three others, including when third in the Triumph); turn of foot could be a potent weapon in top 2m hurdles.

Barney Dwan (Ire)

7 b g Vinnie Roe - Kapricia Speed (Vertical Speed)

Fergal O'Brien				Paul & Clare Rooney

PLACINGS: 52/5311413/2BU427-   RPR **150h**

Starts		1st	2nd	3rd	4th	Win & Pl
13		3	2	2	2	£68,171
129	3/16	Sand	2m4f Cls1 Nov Gd3 120-135 Hdl 4-7yo Hcap soft			£34,170
	12/15	Sedg	2m1f Cls4 Nov Hdl heavy			£3,769
	11/15	MRas	2m2¹/₂f Cls4 Nov Hdl gd-sft			£3,899

Failed to win last season but was a fine second in the Pertemps Final, building on three novice victories during the previous campaign; likely to revert to fences having looked unlucky when brought down three out on his second run last term.

Baron Alco (Fr)

6 ch g Dom Alco - Paula (Network)

Gary Moore				John Stone

PLACINGS: 134086/11120/312122-   RPR **156c**

Starts		1st	2nd	3rd	4th	Win & Pl
18		6	5	2	1	£99,830
	1/17	Plum	2m1f Cls3 Nov Ch soft			£7,988
	11/16	Plum	2m3¹/₂f Cls3 Nov Ch good			£6,657
127	12/15	Kemp	2m5f Cls3 118-135 Hdl Hcap gd-sft			£9,747
123	11/15	Font	2m1¹/₂f Cls3 110-124 Hdl Hcap soft			£6,330
116	10/15	Strf	2m2¹/₂f Cls3 107-129 Hdl Hcap good			£6,330
	11/14	Sand	2m Cls3 Hdl 3yo soft			£6,498

Very smart novice chaser last season; gained both wins at Plumpton and ran consistently well in stronger company, finishing second in a Grade 1 at Sandown and a red-hot Cheltenham Festival handicap; likely contender for more top handicaps.

Barters Hill (Ire)

7 b g Kalanisi - Circle The Wagons (Commanche Run)

Ben Pauling				Circle Of Friends

PLACINGS: 1111/1114/P-

Starts		1st	2nd	3rd	4th	Win & Pl
9		7	-		1	£81,630
	1/16	Donc	3m¹/₂f Cls1 Nov Gd2 Hdl good			£17,165
	12/15	Newb	2m4¹/₂f Cls1 Nov Gd1 Hdl soft			£22,780
	11/15	Hntg	2m3¹/₂f Cls4 Nov Hdl gd-sft			£3,899
	4/15	Aint	2m1f Cls1 Gd2 NHF 4-6yo gd-sft			£16,881
	2/15	Newb	2m¹/₂f Cls1 List NHF 4-6yo soft			£11,390
	12/14	Wwck	2m Cls6 NHF 4-6yo soft			£1,560
	11/14	Hntg	2m Cls6 NHF 4-6yo gd-sft			£1,560

Brilliant novice hurdler two seasons ago who took winning streak to seven (including the Challow Hurdle) before finishing fourth in the Albert Bartlett; suffered a tendon injury on chasing debut last season; trainer expects him to need at least 3m having lost a bit of speed.

'Very smart juvenile hurdler last season and his turn of foot could be a potent weapon in top 2m hurdles'

Barters Hill: class act expected to return to action this season after missing most of last term through injury

Battleford

6 b g Midnight Legend - Well Maid (Saddlers' Hall)

Willie Mullins (Ir)   Andrea & Graham Wylie

PLACINGS: **F/122/412282-**   RPR **142h**

Starts	1st	2nd	3rd	4th	Win & Pl
9	2	5	-	1	£46,799

12/16	Leop	2m4f Mdn Hdl yield	£5,879
1/16	Punc	2m NHF 5-7yo sft-hvy	£4,566

Second in the Cheltenham and Aintree bumpers in 2016 so slightly disappointing he didn't make more of a mark over hurdles, winning only a maiden; beaten favourite three times subsequently, including in the Martin Pipe at Cheltenham, but could do better over fences.

Baywing (Ire)

8 br g Winged Love - Cerise De Totes (Champ Libre)

Nicky Richards — David & Nicky Robinson

PLACINGS: 5065/1111P/414- RPR **148c**

Starts	1st	2nd	3rd	4th	Win & Pl
12	5	-	-	2	£37,075
	2/17	Weth	3m Cls1 Nov Gd2 Ch soft		£18,546
l25	1/16	Hayd	2m7f Cls3 124-137 Hdl Hcap heavy		£6,498
l12	12/15	Uttx	2m7¹/₂f Cls4 105-112 Hdl Hcap heavy		£3,509
l04	12/15	Uttx	2m4f Cls4 104-119 Hdl Hcap heavy		£3,509
89	11/15	Carl	2m4f Cls4 Nov 89-110 Hdl Hcap heavy		£3,249

Improved out of all recognition two seasons ago when winning four times, all on heavy ground, and won a Grade 2 novice chase at Wetherby last term; raised 15lb for that 33-1 success but should progress after just three runs over fences.

Beat That (Ire)

9 b g Milan - Knotted Midge (Presenting)

Nicky Henderson — Michael Buckley

PLACINGS: 26/121/16/6-2F RPR **145c**

Starts	1st	2nd	3rd	4th	Win & Pl
10	3	3	-	-	£117,856
	4/14	Punc	3m Nov Gd1 Hdl gd-yld		£46,500
	4/14	Aint	3m1¹/₂f Cls1 Nov Gd1 Hdl gd-sft		£56,270
	11/13	Asct	2m3¹/₂f Cls3 Mdn Hdl gd-sft		£5,630

Dual Grade 1 winner in 2014 but ran only once in virtually three years after those successes; finally back on track this spring/summer and showed enough in two beginners' chases (fell at the last when chasing Fagan at Perth) to suggest he could still win good races.

Bedrock

4 b g Fastnet Rock - Gemstone (Galileo)

Dan Skelton — The Risk Takers Partnership

PLACINGS: 53-1 RPR **143+h**

Starts	1st	2nd	3rd	4th	Win & Pl
3	1	-	1	-	£15,304
	5/17	Wwck	2m3f Cls4 Nov Hdl gd-sft		£3,899

Thrown in at the deep end in top juvenile hurdles with no experience last spring but emerged with huge credit, especially when third behind Defi Du Seuil at Aintree; off the mark at Warwick in May and will set a good standard in top novice hurdles.

Belami Des Pictons (Fr)

6 b g Khalkevi - Nina Des Pictons (Denham Red)

Venetia Williams — Hills Of Ledbury (aga)

PLACINGS: 533111/4111- RPR **155+c**

Starts	1st	2nd	3rd	4th	Win & Pl
10	6	-	2	1	£49,738
	2/17	Leic	2m6¹/₂f Cls3 Nov Ch soft		£9,495
	2/17	Wwck	3m Cls3 Nov Ch heavy		£9,419
l32	12/16	Newb	2m6¹/₂f Cls3 Nov 124-144 Ch Hcap gd-sft		£6,498
	3/16	Bang	2m3¹/₂f Cls4 Nov Hdl soft		£3,249
	3/16	Wwck	2m Cls4 Nov Hdl soft		£3,249
	10/15	Vich	2m2¹/₂f Hdl 4yo v soft		£8,186

Won three out of four as a novice chaser last season, although kept to a modest level with last victory coming at odds of 1-4 in a two-runner race; interesting to see how he fares in better company and trainer feels he'll be fine on better ground.

Bellshill (Ire)

7 b g King's Theatre - Fairy Native (Be My Native)

Willie Mullins (Ir) — Andrea & Graham Wylie

PLACINGS: /1202/1111302/111F3- RPR **155+c**

Starts	1st	2nd	3rd	4th	Win & Pl
16	8	3	2	-	£239,478
	12/16	Limk	2m3¹/₂f Nov Gd2 Ch heavy		£19,305
	11/16	Gowr	2m4f Ch yld-sft		£7,235
	4/16	Punc	3m Nov Gd1 Hdl gd-yld		£43,382
	1/16	Naas	2m4f Nov Gd1 Hdl heavy		£39,706
	12/15	Navn	2m4f Nov Gd2 Hdl heavy		£20,155
	11/15	Cork	2m Mdn Hdl heavy		£7,488
	4/15	Punc	2m Gd1 NHF 4-7yo gd-yld		£44,186
	11/14	Thur	2m NHF 4-7yo soft		£4,313

Dual Grade 1 winner as a novice hurdler two seasons ago and looked likely to scale similar heights as a chaser early last term until suffering jumping problems; got back on track when third in the RSA and looks a surefire improver as he gains confidence.

Benatar (Ire)

5 b g Beneficial - Carrigeen Lily (Supreme Leader)

Gary Moore — Ashley Head

PLACINGS: 11424- RPR **144h**

Starts	1st	2nd	3rd	4th	Win & Pl
4	1	1	-	2	£10,516
	1/17	Font	2m3f Cls5 Mdn Hdl soft		£2,274

Initially struggled to build on hurdles debut win last season but took a big leap forward when stepped up into Grade 1 company at Aintree, finishing fourth behind Finian's Oscar; should get 3m and looks a fine chasing prospect.

Benie Des Dieux (Fr)

6 b m Great Pretender - Cana (Robin Des Champs)

Willie Mullins (Ir)   Mrs S Ricci

PLACINGS: 141/633/1-   RPR **138+c**

Starts	1st	2nd	3rd	4th	Win & Pl
7	3	-	2	1	£74,889
12/16	Limk	2m3½f Ch sft-hvy			£6,105
4/15	Autl	2m2f Hdl 4-5yo v soft			£22,326
10/14	Autl	2m2f Hdl 3yo heavy			£22,000

Hugely exciting mare who made a spectacular chasing debut last season on her only run in Ireland, winning a beginners' chase by 30 lengths; hadn't been as good over hurdles in France, potentially limiting options, but could be anything over fences.

Beware The Bear (Ire)

7 b g Shantou - Native Bid (Be My Native)

Nicky Henderson   G B Barlow

PLACINGS: 22/2431/11174-   RPR **153+c**

Starts	1st	2nd	3rd	4th	Win & Pl
9	4	1	1	2	£24,299
136	12/16	Newb	2m7½f Cls3 Nov 116-136 Ch Hcap gd-sft	£6,498
130	11/16	Asct	3m Cls3 Nov 122-135 Ch Hcap gd-sft	£7,148
5/16	Sthl	3m Cls4 Nov Hdl good		£3,899
4/16	Bang	2m7f Cls5 Mdn Hdl heavy		£3,139

Firmly on the upgrade early last season, winning first two chases (four wins in a row overall); ran

much better than the bare form when seventh in the National Hunt Chase after badly losing his place early (rider lost irons) but slightly disappointing when only fourth at Ayr.

Beyond Conceit (Ire)

8 b g Galileo - Baraka (Danehill)

Nicky Henderson   Mrs Fitri Hay

PLACINGS: 1162-   RPR **148h**

Starts	1st	2nd	3rd	4th	Win & Pl
4	2	1	-	-	£42,984
2/17	Asct	2m3½f Cls2 Nov Hdl soft		£15,640
1/17	Newb	2m½f Cls4 Nov Hdl soft		£4,549

Has been plagued by injuries but put tendon and pelvis issues behind him when sent hurdling after more than three years out last season, winning twice and finishing second when stepped up to 3m in a Grade 1 at Aintree; totally unexposed as a stayer.

Big River (Ire)

7 b g Milan - Call Kate (Lord Americo)

Lucinda Russell   Two Black Labs

PLACINGS: 221/1/21521-   RPR **142+h**

Starts	1st	2nd	3rd	4th	Win & Pl
8	4	3	-	-	£31,774
132	3/17	Kels	3m2f Cls2 132-149 Hdl Hcap heavy	£14,621
115	12/16	Ayr	2m5½f Cls3 112-127 Hdl Hcap heavy	£7,148
10/15	Kels	2m Cls4 Mdn Hdl good		£3,249
3/15	Kels	2m Cls6 NHF 4-6yo gd-sft		£1,625

Progressive staying hurdler last season, winning

Beware The Bear: two-time winner over fences looked on the up last season

twice on heavy ground to add to maiden success in 2015 (missed following year through injury); beaten twice on quicker ground in between and seems most effective in very testing conditions.

Bigbadjohn (Ire)

8 br g Vinnie Roe - Celtic Serenade (Yashgan)

Rebecca Curtis				Nigel Morris

PLACINGS: 3041/1021/P312S1P-   RPR **148c**

Starts	1st	2nd	3rd	4th	Win & Pl
11	4	2	1	-	£50,716
	2/17	Asct	3m Cls1 Nov Gd2 Ch soft		£22,780
	11/16	Newb	2m6¹/₂f Cls3 Ch good		£7,148
	4/16	Newb	2m4¹/₂f Cls3 Nov Hdl gd-sft		£5,848
	6/15	List	2m4f NHF 4-7yo heavy		£5,349

Looked all about stamina when gaining his biggest win in last season's Reynoldstown; likely contender for good staying handicaps, although something to prove in bigger fields (pulled up in the National Hunt Chase and well held when slipped up in the Sky Bet Chase).

Binge Drinker (Ire)

8 b g Spadoun - Our Honey (Old Vic)

Paul Nicholls				Corsellis & Seyfried

PLACINGS: 231/111541/9/1-   RPR **151+c**

Starts	1st	2nd	3rd	4th	Win & Pl
11	6	1	1	1	£24,457
	11/16	Ffos	2m3¹/₂f Cls4 Nov Ch good		£5,198
133	3/15	Bang	2m7f Cls3 122-135 Ch Hcap gd-sft		£6,498
	12/14	Chep	2m7¹/₂f Cls4 Nov Hdl gd-sft		£3,119
	11/14	Ffos	3m Cls4 Nov Hdl soft		£3,119
	10/14	Worc	2m4f Cls5 Mdn Hdl gd-sft		£1,949
	2/14	Chep	2m Cls6 Am NHF 4-6yo heavy		£1,560

Fragile but clearly talented having beaten Might Bite on his chasing debut last season (runner-up made mistakes); has also won three times over hurdles but restricted to just that sole run since April 2015; has since left Rebecca Curtis.

Bishops Road (Ire)

9 b g Heron Island - Nice Resemblance (Shernazar)

Kerry Lee				Alan Halsall

PLACINGS: 153/86F30311UF/403P-   RPR **157c**

Starts	1st	2nd	3rd	4th	Win & Pl
21	5	1	4	1	£87,582
144	2/16	Hayd	3m4¹/₂f Cls1 Gd1 125-149 Ch Hcap heavy		£45,050
130	1/16	Sand	2m4f Cls3 116-130 Ch Hcap heavy		£9,384
123	1/15	Leop	2m5f 100-123 Ch Hcap yld-sft		£8,023
	10/13	Gowr	2m Mdn Hdl soft		£5,610
	5/13	Klny	2m1f NHF 5-7yo soft		£3,927

Won first two starts for Kerry Lee two seasons ago, most notably in the Grand National Trial

at Haydock; gained both those wins on heavy ground and yet to encounter those conditions again during winless run since; has also dropped to last winning mark.

Black Hercules (Ire)

8 b g Heron Island - Annalecky (Bob's Return)

Willie Mullins (Ir)				Andrea & Graham Wylie

PLACINGS: 1/114/0117/11F1/543-   RPR **158+c**

Starts	1st	2nd	3rd	4th	Win & Pl
14	7		1	2	£141,839
	3/16	Chel	2m4f Cls1 Nov Gd1 Ch good		£74,035
	1/16	Wwck	3m Cls1 Nov List Ch heavy		£13,253
	12/15	Navn	2m4f Ch heavy		£6,953
	12/14	Cork	3m Nov Gd3 Hdl heavy		£17,604
	11/14	Cork	2m Mdn Hdl heavy		£6,900
	1/14	Gowr	2m NHF 5-7yo soft		£7,475
	12/13	Punc	2m NHF 4yo gd-yld		£4,768

Won the JLT Novices' Chase in 2016 but came up short outside novice company last season when well beaten on all three starts, although finished a fair third behind Sizing John last time; may do better stepped back up to 3m (dual winner at the trip as a novice).

Black Op (Ire)

6 br g Sandmason - Afar Story (Desert Story)

Tom George				R S Brookhouse

PLACINGS: 1/19-   RPR **122+b**

Starts	1st	2nd	3rd	4th	Win & Pl
2	1	-	-	-	£1,949
	2/17	Donc	2m1¹/₂f Cls6 NHF 4-6yo good		£1,949

Bought for £210,000 after easy win in an Irish point-to-point and looked money well spent when winning first time out at Doncaster (beat Cheltenham third Claimantakinforgan); only ninth when favourite at Aintree next time but still a fine prospect.

Blaklion

8 b g Kayf Tara - Franciscaine (Legend Of France)

Nigel Twiston-Davies				S Such & CG Paletta

PLACINGS: 132P4/4F12113/45324-   RPR **162c**

Starts	1st	2nd	3rd	4th	Win & Pl
22	8	4	3	4	£283,599
	3/16	Chel	3m1¹/₂f Cls1 Gd1 Ch good		£85,425
	2/16	Weth	3m Cls1 Nov Gd2 Ch heavy		£19,221
	12/15	Chel	3m1¹/₂f Cls2 Nov Ch soft		£14,442
	12/14	Chel	3m Cls1 Nov Gd2 Hdl soft		£17,085
	10/14	Chep	2m3¹/₂f Cls1 Nov Gd2 Hdl soft		£17,085
	9/14	Prth	2m4f Cls4 Nov Hdl good		£3,119
	4/14	Hayd	1m7¹/₂f Cls5 NHF 4-6yo good		£1,949
	3/14	Ffos	2m Cls6 NHF 4-5yo soft		£1,625

Won the RSA Chase two seasons ago and ran

'Bought for £210,000 after easy win in an Irish point-to-point and looked money well spent when winning first time out at Doncaster'

a string of good races in defeat last season, especially after a midwinter breathing operation; finished fourth in the Grand National (went for home too soon) and second in the big trial at Haydock; can win a big handicap.

Blazer (Fr)
6 ch g Network - Juppelongue (Trebrook)

Willie Mullins (Ir)				John P McManus
PLACINGS: F1/391947/23-1				RPR **136+c**

Starts		1st	2nd	3rd	4th	Win & Pl
11		3	1	2	1	£38,429
	5/17	Punc	2m Ch good			£7,371
126	2/16	Leop	2m 109-133 Hdl Hcap heavy			£10,853
	2/15	Bord	2m2½f Hdl 4yo soft			£11,907

Proved miles better than opening mark of 126 over hurdles in Ireland when winning a 2m handicap on heavy despite subsequently showing he needs further and better ground; won a 2m beginners' chase in May and should again benefit from a step up in trip.

Bleu Berry (Fr)
6 b g Special Kaldoun - Somosierra (Blushing Flame)

Willie Mullins (Ir)				Luke McMahon
PLACINGS: 512/7F/1115-				RPR **144+h**

Starts		1st	2nd	3rd	4th	Win & Pl
9		4	1	-		£57,159
	4/17	Fair	2m Nov Gd2 Hdl sft-hvy			£22,692
	3/17	Naas	2m Nov List Hdl sft-hvy			£14,455
	2/17	Fair	2m Mdn Hdl sft-hvy			£6,844
	9/14	Clun	1m4f NHF 3yo v soft			£4,167

Missed nearly a year after falling on his hurdles debut in March 2016 but progressed rapidly at the end of last season, completing a hat-trick of

Bleu Et Rouge: talented performer but needs to get career over fences back on track

2m soft-ground wins in a Grade 2 at Fairyhouse; only fifth at Punchestown when upped in trip on quicker ground.

Bleu Et Rouge (Fr)
6 gr g Charming Groom - Lady Du Renom (Art Francais)

Willie Mullins (Ir)				John P McManus
PLACINGS: 22/141F5/1U4-				RPR **143+c**

Starts		1st	2nd	3rd	4th	Win & Pl
10		3	2	-	2	£63,504
	12/16	Leop	2m3f Ch yield			£6,331
	2/16	Leop	2m2f Nov Gd1 Hdl sft-hvy			£39,044
	11/15	Cork	2m Mdn Hdl 4yo heavy			£6,419

Grade 1-winning novice hurdler who made a smooth start over fences when beating Gangster at Leopardstown only for season to unravel; unseated early when favourite for the Irish Arkle and jumped poorly when well beaten next time.

Blood Crazed Tiger (Ire)
6 b g King's Theatre - Mardi Roberta (Bob Back)

Gordon Elliott (Ir)				Gigginstown House Stud
PLACINGS: P/0252/11113F4-				RPR **142h**

Starts		1st	2nd	3rd	4th	Win & Pl
11		4	2	1	1	£47,728
	11/16	Cork	3m Nov List Hdl good			£17,353
	10/16	Cork	3m Nov Hdl yield			£7,688
	10/16	Gowr	2m4f Mdn Hdl yield			£5,653
	5/16	Rosc	2m4f NHF 5-7yo good			£4,522

Won first three races over hurdles last season, the last two over 3m including a Listed contest at Cork; twice came up short in Grade 1 races subsequently, although perhaps unsuited by shorter trips; should make a better chaser.

Blow By Blow (Ire)

6 ch g Robin Des Champs - Shean Rose (Roselier)

Gordon Elliott (Ir)   Gigginstown House Stud

PLACINGS: 211/1-   RPR **136b**

Starts	1st	2nd	3rd	4th	Win & Pl
4	3	1	-	-	£54,509

4/16	Punc	2m Gd1 NHF 4-7yo gd-yld	£43,382
3/16	Fair	2m NHF 4-7yo yld-sft	£5,879
2/16	Navn	2m NHF 5-7yo heavy	£4,070

Won the Grade 1 bumper at Punchestown in 2016, claiming the notable scalp of Moon Racer having also beaten Death Duty at Fairyhouse; missed last season through injury but ready to get started in novice hurdles and could go to the top.

Bonny Kate (Ire)

7 ch m Beneficial - Peppardstown (Old Vic)

Noel Meade (Ir)   Mrs Patricia Hunt

PLACINGS: 1611P/U2111P/6333PP-   RPR **143c**

Starts	1st	2nd	3rd	4th	Win & Pl
19	6	2	3		£84,586

3/16	Limk	2m6f Nov Gd2 Ch heavy	£21,691
1/16	Punc	3m4f 120-148 Ch Hcap sft-hvy	£15,294
11/15	Fair	2m5¹/₂f Ch soft	£6,953
3/15	Limk	2m3f Hdl heavy	£8,023
3/15	Gowr	2m4f Mdn Hdl 4-5yo yld-sft	£6,686
12/14	Punc	2m2f NHF 4-7yo soft	£4,600

125 (left margin)

Knocking on the door in top staying handicap chases in Ireland last season, finishing third in the Troytown, Thyestes and Punchestown's Grand National Trial; has twice lost her way in the spring, including when twice pulled up in the Irish National (favourite in 2016).

Bouvreuil (Fr)

6 b g Saddler Maker - Madame Lys (Sheyrann)

Paul Nicholls   John P McManus

PLACINGS: 9213427/051524/5630-   RPR **151c**

Starts	1st	2nd	3rd	4th	Win & Pl
21	2	3	5	2	£92,893

1/16	Donc	2m3f Cls4 Nov Ch soft	£3,899
11/14	Engh	2m1¹/₂f Hdl 3yo heavy	£19,200

Twice second at the Cheltenham Festival and then third in a red-hot Plate back at the meeting in March; had also run well on ground softer than ideal in two big handicap chases at the track during the winter and could yet land a big prize there.

Brain Power (Ire)

5 b g Kalanisi - Blonde Ambition (Old Vic)

Nicky Henderson   Michael Buckley

PLACINGS: 10/121/381185-   RPR **162h**

Starts	1st	2nd	3rd	4th	Win & Pl
11	5	1	1	-	£143,035

12/16	Asct	1m7¹/₂f Cls1 Gd3 125-150 Hdl Hcap gd-sft	£85,425
12/16	Sand	2m Cls1 List 120-144 Hdl Hcap gd-sft	£33,762
3/16	Kemp	2m Cls4 Nov Hdl good	£3,249
11/15	Kemp	2m Cls4 Nov Hdl 4-6yo gd-sft	£3,899
2/15	Newc	2m1¹/₂f Cls6 NHF 4-6yo gd-sft	£1,560

149 (left margin)
142 (left margin)

Very headstrong in his early days and again pulled away his chance in last season's Champion Hurdle but had earlier won big handicaps at Sandown and Ascot; close fifth at Punchestown after that; has more to offer when learning to settle better.

Brelade

5 b g Presenting - Polivalente (Poliglote)

Gordon Elliott (Ir)   D P Sharkey

PLACINGS: 2/42112368-   RPR **145h**

Starts	1st	2nd	3rd	4th	Win & Pl
9	2	3	1	1	£36,678

11/16	Navn	2m Mdn Hdl yld-sft	£6,331
11/16	Naas	2m NHF 4yo good	£4,070

Not far off the best novice hurdlers in Ireland even though only wins came in a bumper and a maiden; twice placed in Grade 1 events and did well when stepping up in trip for the Neptune at Cheltenham, finishing a ten-length sixth.

Brelan D'As (Fr)

6 b g Crillon - Las De La Croix (Grand Tresor)

Paul Nicholls   John P McManus

PLACINGS: 141P/1-   RPR **145+h**

Starts	1st	2nd	3rd	4th	Win & Pl
5	3	-	-	1	£21,817

11/16	Winc	2m4f Cls3 115-135 Hdl Hcap good	£5,848
10/15	Sabl	2m1f Hdl 4yo gd-sft	£8,558
8/15	Gran	1m7f NHF 4-5yo gd-sft	£3,876

130 (left margin)

Exciting French recruit who showed his true colours after a disappointing British debut when running away with a handicap hurdle at Wincanton last season; missed rest of the campaign but back this term and could make a fine novice chaser.

Facebook.com/racingpost   Twitter @RacingPost

Brio Conti (Fr)

6 gr g Dom Alco - Cadoulie Wood (Cadoudal)

Paul Nicholls   The Gi Gi Syndicate

PLACINGS: 3/1F28115-   RPR **145h**

Starts		1st	2nd	3rd	4th	Win & Pl
8		3	1	1	-	£30,677
134	3/17	Kemp	2m5f Cls2 125-137 Hdl Hcap good			£20,645
	1/17	Donc	2m3½f Cls5 Mdn Hdl good			£3,249
	5/16	Strf	2m1½f Cls5 Mdn NHF 4-6yo gd-sft			£2,274

Got better with experience over hurdles last season and impressed when running away with a competitive handicap at Kempton; just came up short in a Grade 1 subsequently when fifth at Aintree but could be up to that level over fences.

Bristol De Mai (Fr)

6 gr g Saddler Maker - La Bole Night (April Night)

Nigel Twiston-Davies   Simon Munir & Isaac Souede

PLACINGS: 323/21211122/221375-   RPR **170+c**

Starts		1st	2nd	3rd	4th	Win & Pl
21		7	7	3	1	£230,184
154	1/17	Hayd	3m Cls1 Gd2 142-162 Ch Hcap soft			£28,475
	2/16	Sand	2m4f Cls1 Nov Gd1 Ch gd-sft			£25,628
	1/16	Hayd	2m4f Cls1 Nov Gd2 Ch heavy			£18,438
	12/15	Leic	2m4f Cls3 Nov Ch soft			£6,330
	11/15	Wwck	2m Cls3 Nov Ch 4-5yo gd-sft			£9,384
	12/14	Chep	2m Cls1 Gd1 Hdl 3yo heavy			£19,933
	9/14	Autl	2m2f Hdl 3yo v soft			£19,200

Looked a Grade 1 performer in the making when running away with last season's Peter Marsh Chase, relishing 3m on soft ground; disappointing subsequently but found to be lame after a tame run at Newbury and twice not ideally suited by good ground in the spring.

Bun Doran (Ire)

6 b g Shantou - Village Queen (King's Theatre)

Tom George   Crossed Fingers Partnership

PLACINGS: 114153/31P63-   RPR **145c**

Starts		1st	2nd	3rd	4th	Win & Pl
10		3	-	3	-	£28,080
134	12/16	Newc	2m4f Cls3 109-135 Ch Hcap soft			£9,747
	1/16	Hayd	2m3f Cls4 Nov Hdl 4-7yo heavy			£3,899
	11/15	Chep	2m Cls6 NHF 4-6yo good			£1,560

Highly promising novice chaser who caught the eye in big handicaps last spring, especially when third in the Red Rum at Aintree (travelled strongly into the lead three out); also sixth in the novice handicap at the Cheltenham Festival despite making mistakes.

Bunk Off Early (Ire)

5 ro g Zebedee - Ctesiphon (Arch)

Willie Mullins (Ir)   Supreme Horse Racing Club

PLACINGS: 1205-   RPR **147+h**

Starts		1st	2nd	3rd	4th	Win & Pl
4		1	1	-	-	£22,203
	12/16	Leop	2m Mdn Hdl 4yo yield			£5,879

Looked a terrific prospect in first two runs last season, winning at Leopardstown and just beaten in the Grade 1 Deloitte Hurdle having travelled particularly strongly; bitterly disappointing at Cheltenham and Punchestown on quicker ground.

Burbank (Ire)

5 b/br g Yeats - Spring Swoon (Highest Honor)

Nicky Henderson   R A Bartlett

PLACINGS: 121242-   RPR **144h**

Starts		1st	2nd	3rd	4th	Win & Pl
6		2	3	-	1	£16,842
	1/17	Hntg	2m Cls4 Mdn Hdl 4-7yo gd-sft			£3,574
	11/16	Newb	2m1½f Cls5 NHF 4-6yo good			£2,599

Often disappointing last season (beaten at 3-10, 6-4 and 7-4 with sole win over hurdles coming at 8-15) but showed his potential when a staying-on fourth in the Neptune at Cheltenham; may prove best in big fields; yet to run on ground worse than good to soft.

ON THE FIGURES

BRISTOL DE MAI Didn't go on as looked likely after bolting up in a valuable Haydock handicap in January, but his official mark has slipped back into the 150s as a result and another valuable handicap looks set to come his way, particularly when the mud is flying. [Steve Mason, Racing Post Ratings]

Burtons Well (Ire)

8 b g Well Chosen - Despute (Be My Native)

Venetia Williams   Trevor Hemmings

PLACINGS: 1F2/214F-   RPR **141+c**

Starts	1st	2nd	3rd	4th	Win & Pl
7	2	2	-	1	£18,030
129	12/16	Uttx	2m4f Cls3 Nov 125-137 Ch Hcap heavy		£8,758
	10/16	NAbb	2m2¹/₂f Cls4 Nov Hdl 4-6yo soft		£5,064

Fell when 8-1 for the novice handicap chase at the Cheltenham Festival; had finished a promising fourth in another novice handicap at the track having won on his second run over fences; very lightly raced and should improve with experience.

Buveur D'Air (Fr)

6 b g Crillon - History (Alesso)

Nicky Henderson   John P McManus

PLACINGS: 1124/1131/11111-   RPR **171+h**

Starts	1st	2nd	3rd	4th	Win & Pl
13	10	1	1	1	£452,139
	4/17	Aint	2m4f Cls1 Gd1 Hdl good		£112,260
	3/17	Chel	2m¹/₂f Cls1 Gd1 Hdl gd-sft		£227,800
	2/17	Sand	2m Cls1 List Hdl heavy		£14,238
	12/16	Wwck	2m Cls4 Nov Ch soft		£5,198
	12/16	Hayd	1m7¹/₂f Cls2 Nov Ch soft		£11,574
	4/16	Aint	2m¹/₂f Cls1 Nov Gd1 Hdl soft		£42,203
	1/16	Hntg	2m Cls4 Nov Hdl gd-sft		£3,249
	11/15	Newb	2m Cls3 Mdn Hdl soft		£6,498
	10/14	Nant	1m4f NHF 3yo gd-sft		£6,250
	8/14	Sjdm	1m5f NHF 3yo		£4,167

Ended last season firmly established as the best hurdler in training despite starting the campaign over fences; easily won the Champion Hurdle and showed he stays further when adding the Aintree Hurdle; again sets the standard in that division.

C'est Jersey (Fr)

5 b g Protektor - Myrtille Jersey (Murmure)

Willie Mullins (Ir)   Simon Munir & Isaac Souede

PLACINGS: 1642/23101-   RPR **142+h**

Starts	1st	2nd	3rd	4th	Win & Pl
9	3	2	1	1	£33,022
	4/17	Punc	2m4f Hdl gd-yld		£13,141
	1/17	Navn	2m4f Mdn Hdl soft		£6,571
	8/15	Breh	1m3¹/₂f NHF 3yo good		£3,876

Needed three attempts to win a maiden hurdle last season and was then outclassed in the Albert Bartlett but showed his potential when winning at Punchestown next time; described as a fine chasing prospect by his trainer and expected to stay 3m.

'He ended last season the best hurdler in training and again sets the standard in that division'

Calett Mad (Fr)

5 b/br g Axxos - Omelia (April Night)

Nigel Twiston-Davies   Simon Munir & Isaac Souede

PLACINGS: 343/1212952-   RPR **150c**

Starts	1st	2nd	3rd	4th	Win & Pl
10	2	3	2	1	£58,789
	1/17	Tntn	2m7f Cls3 128-138 Ch Hcap good		£8,229
130	11/16	Newc	2m7¹/₂f Cls3 Nov 124-135 Ch Hcap soft		£9,986

Progressed well over fences last season, finishing first or second in his four handicaps and beaten just a head on final start at Ayr; struggled in Graded company, although ran well for a long way in the four-miler at Cheltenham before failing to stay.

Calipto (Fr)

7 b g Califet - Peutiot (Valanour)

Venetia Williams   A Brooks

PLACINGS: 21143/24P6/1338/6F-   RPR **144+c**

Starts	1st	2nd	3rd	4th	Win & Pl
15	5	3	3	2	£71,180
	10/15	Font	2m3f Cls4 Ch gd-sft		£6,498
	2/14	Newb	2m¹/₂f Cls3 Nov Hdl heavy		£6,498
	11/13	Newb	2m¹/₂f Cls3 Hdl 3yo gd-sft		£6,498

Lightly raced since being sent off favourite for the 2014 Triumph Hurdle (fourth after rider lost irons) but two runs last term suggested he retains plenty of ability; sixth in the Grand Annual after a long absence and travelling strongly when he fell at Ayr.

Call Me Lord (Fr)

4 b g Slickly - Sosa (Cape Cross)

Nicky Henderson   Simon Munir & Isaac Souede

PLACINGS: 5111-   RPR **141+h**

Starts	1st	2nd	3rd	4th	Win & Pl
4	3	-	-	-	£63,391
135	4/17	Sand	2m Cls2 109-135 Hdl 4yo Hcap good		£31,280
	3/17	Comp	2m2f Hdl 4yo heavy		£19,692
	12/16	Cagn	2m¹/₂f Hdl 3yo soft		£11,294

Dual winner in France (on soft and heavy ground) and added a juvenile handicap on the final day of last season on first run in Britain, handling quicker conditions well; sure to find things tougher after an 8lb rise, especially as trainer felt initial mark was steep.

Campeador (Fr)

5 gr g Gris De Gris - Royale Video (Video Rock)

Gordon Elliott (Ir)   John P McManus

PLACINGS: 2/14F/5F-   RPR **154+h**

Starts	1st	2nd	3rd	4th	Win & Pl
5	1	1	-	1	£17,732
	6/15	Claf	2m1f Hdl 3yo v soft		£12,651

Yet to win for Gordon Elliott but may well have

done so twice but for final-flight falls; had been well in command of a Fairyhouse handicap when departing on his only run last season and remains totally unexposed; likely contender for top 2m handicaps.

Camping Ground (Fr)

7 b g Goldneyev - Camomille (Pennekamp)

Gary Moore					G L Porter
PLACINGS: 23611/14/U1595/2F51-				RPR **168+h**	

Starts		1st	2nd	3rd	4th	Win & Pl
18		7	2	1	1	£190,344
	2/17	Font	2m3f Cls1 Gd2 Hdl gd-sft			£45,560
	1/16	Chel	2m4¹/₂f Cls1 Gd2 Hdl heavy			£22,780
145	2/15	Wwck	2m4¹/₂f Cls2 Ch Hcap soft			£18,768
	3/14	Autl	2m2f Hdl 4yo v soft			£28,000
	11/13	Autl	2m1¹/₂f Ch 3yo heavy			£22,634
	5/13	Chat	2m1f Hdl 3yo soft			£8,585
	5/13	Nant	1m7¹/₂f Hdl 3yo gd-sft			£6,634

Lost his way for Robert Walford after an easy win in the 2016 Relkeel Hurdle but got back on track on his first run for Gary Moore in February, hacking up in the National Spirit Hurdle; seems best at 2m4f and yet to prove he stays 3m; could go back over fences.

Cap Soleil (Fr)

4 b f Kapgarde - Move Again (Noir Et Or)

Fergal O'Brien					Mrs S A Noott
PLACINGS: 111-				RPR **119+b**	

Starts		1st	2nd	3rd	4th	Win & Pl
3		3	-	-		£25,227
	3/17	Sand	2m Cls1 List NHF 4-6yo soft			£11,390
	1/17	Chel	1m6f Cls1 List NHF 4yo soft			£11,888
	12/16	Newb	1m4¹/₂f Cls6 NHF 3yo gd-sft			£1,949

Unbeaten in three bumpers last season, including Listed contests at Cheltenham (beating Daphne Du Clos, a subsequent winner at that level) and Sandown; both those wins came on soft ground and she may well need a bit of cut to show her best form (hits the ground hard according to her trainer).

Capitaine (Fr)

5 gr g Montmartre - Patte De Velour (Mansonnien)

Paul Nicholls				Martin Broughton & Friends	
PLACINGS: 21/12124P1-1				RPR **142+h**	

Starts		1st	2nd	3rd	4th	Win & Pl
10		5	3	-	1	£54,686
	5/17	NAbb	2m¹/₂f Cls3 Ch good			£7,656
	4/17	Winc	1m7¹/₂f Cls4 Nov Hdl gd-fm			£3,899
	12/16	Asct	1m7¹/₂f Cls1 Nov Gd2 Hdl gd-sft			£18,224
	11/16	Winc	1m7¹/₂f Cls3 Nov Hdl 4-6yo good			£6,498
	4/16	Winc	1m7¹/₂f Cls6 NHF 4-6yo gd-sft			£1,625

Won three times over hurdles last season, including a Grade 2 novice hurdle at Ascot; just came up short in stronger company but likely to be aiming high over fences after a winning

debut at Newton Abbot in May; best going right-handed.

Captain Forez (Fr)

5 b g Network - Pourkoipa Du Forez (Robin Des Champs)

Dan Skelton					J Hales
PLACINGS: 2/322-				RPR **150+h**	

Starts		1st	2nd	3rd	4th	Win & Pl
4		-	3	1	-	£37,410

Failed to win last season but shaped with huge promise every time, especially when second in a 2m4f Grade 1 at Aintree last time having appeared to find 2m too short on his previous start; likely to set a tough standard among new crop of novice hurdlers.

Carlingford Lough (Ire)

11 b g King's Theatre - Baden (Furry Glen)

John Kiely (Ir)					John P McManus
PLACINGS: 221U6/1519/4614/144-				RPR **166c**	

Starts		1st	2nd	3rd	4th	Win & Pl
31		10	3	2	5	£534,460
	4/16	Punc	3m1¹/₂f Gd1 Ch gd-yld			£86,765
	2/16	Leop	3m¹/₂f Gd1 Ch heavy			£62,316
	2/15	Leop	3m Gd1 Ch yield			£66,860
	4/14	Punc	3m1f Nov Gd1 Ch good			£46,500
	12/13	Leop	3m Nov Gd1 Ch yld-sft			£39,634
133	7/13	Gway	2m6¹/₂f 133-147 Ch Hcap soft			£97,866
129	8/12	Gway	2m5¹/₂f 114-142 Hdl Hcap sft-hvy			£21,667
119	7/12	Bell	2m4f 116-135 Hdl Hcap soft			£12,729
109	7/11	Gway	2m 95-116 Hdl Hcap good			£8,625
	7/11	Rosc	2m Mdn Hdl 4-5yo good			£4,461

Veteran staying chaser most well known for winning successive runnings of the Irish Gold Cup, while he went on to add the Punchestown Gold Cup in April 2016; ran only once over fences last season when beaten just five lengths going for an Irish Gold Cup hat-trick; would be no surprise to see him win another decent chase in Ireland this season.

Carole's Destrier

9 b g Kayf Tara - Barton May (Midnight Legend)

Neil Mulholland					Mrs C Skipworth
PLACINGS: 710/21P4115/51P0/29-				RPR **159c**	

Starts		1st	2nd	3rd	4th	Win & Pl
22		6	5			£145,059
146	12/15	Sand	3m5f Cls2 122-148 Ch Hcap gd-sft			£25,024
	3/15	Weth	3m1f Cls4 Nov Ch good			£5,198
142	2/15	Asct	3m Cls1 List 132-152 Ch Hcap soft			£25,748
	11/14	Extr	3m Cls2 Nov Ch gd-sft			£12,628
129	3/14	Kemp	2m5f Cls2 121-135 Hdl Hcap gd-sft			£21,896
	1/14	Hntg	2m4¹/₂f Cls5 Mdn Hdl heavy			£1,949

Ran a huge race on his reappearance last season when running Native River to half a length in the Hennessy; form can be patchy and disappointed on his only other run last term in the Welsh National but has a big staying handicap in him on his day.

Carter McKay

6 gr g Martaline - Saxona (Jade Robbery)

Willie Mullins (Ir)   Pearl Bloodstock Ltd

PLACINGS: 21/1106-   RPR **131+b**

Starts	1st	2nd	3rd	4th	Win & Pl
4	2	-	-	-	£10,942

2/17	Naas	2m3f NHF 5-7yo soft	£5,791
12/16	Leop	2m NHF 4-6yo yield	£4,296

Point-to-point winner who added two bumpers last season, including over 2m3f on soft ground at Naas, but twice disappointed in Grade I bumpers in the spring; should benefit from stepping back up in trip over hurdles.

Casse Tete (Fr)

5 b g Poliglote - Ellapampa (Pampabird)

Gary Moore   John Stone

PLACINGS: 528F5/221F431-   RPR **146+c**

Starts	1st	2nd	3rd	4th	Win & Pl
12	2	3	1		£39,548

128	3/17	Sand	2m4f Cls3 Nov 117-128 Ch Hcap gd-sft	£7,798
	10/16	Autl	2m5¹/₂f Ch 4yo v soft	£19,412

Bought from France after winning a chase at Auteuil by ten lengths last October and finally confirmed that potential with a 27-length win in a novice handicap at Sandown in March (had failed to get home in two previous races); should continue to improve.

Cause Of Causes (USA)

9 b g Dynaformer - Angel In My Heart (Rainbow Quest)

Gordon Elliott (Ir)   John P McManus

PLACINGS: 0/7518/0051P/5P0512-   RPR **158c**

Starts	1st	2nd	3rd	4th	Win & Pl
39	8	7	3	1	£563,888

142	3/17	Chel	3m6f Cls2 Ch good	£40,235
	3/16	Chel	3m2f Cls2 134-145 Am Ch Hcap good	£38,974
	3/15	Chel	4m Cls1 Nov List Am Ch gd-sft	£50,966
	1/13	Navn	2m Hdl heavy	£10,569
142	12/12	Asct	1m7¹/₂f Cls1 List 130-155 Hdl Hcap heavy	£84,405
	11/12	Fair	2m Hdl soft	£5,750
	7/12	Dpat	2m2f Hdl good	£5,750
	5/12	Kbgn	2m3f Mdn Hdl 4yo good	£4,313

Pulled off a remarkable Cheltenham Festival hat-trick in three different races when winning last season's Cross Country Chase; often out of form through the winter on softer ground but showed he can excel away from Cheltenham when second in the Grand National.

Cause Toujours (Fr)

5 b g Khalkevi - Viana (Signe Divin)

Dan Skelton   Carl Hinchy

PLACINGS: U/19-   RPR **125+b**

Starts	1st	2nd	3rd	4th	Win & Pl
2	1	-	-	-	£1,624

12/16	Wwck	2m Cls6 NHF 4-6yo soft	£1,625

Sent off favourite for last season's Champion Bumper at Cheltenham after an easy win at Warwick (good time) but disappointed in ninth; trainer had been particularly bullish beforehand and may well prove much better than that over hurdles.

Ch'Tibello (Fr)

6 b g Sageburg - Neicha (Neverneyev)

Dan Skelton   The Can't Say No Partnership

PLACINGS: 1/2231/35132-   RPR **158h**

Starts	1st	2nd	3rd	4th	Win & Pl
10	3	3	3	-	£167,595

11/16	Hayd	2m Cls2 Hdl heavy	£61,900
135	4/16	Ayr	2m Cls1 Gd2 133-147 Hdl Hcap gd-sft	£57,520
4/15	Comp	2m1f Hdl 4yo heavy	£8,186

Developed into a high-class 2m hurdler last season, winning a valuable conditions race at Haydock and placed behind Yanworth in the Christmas and Kingwell Hurdles; missed the Champion Hurdle with a foot infection; has had a wind operation.

Champagne West (Ire)

9 b g Westerner - Wyndham Sweetmarie (Mister Lord)

Henry de Bromhead (Ir)   R S Brookhouse

PLACINGS: 114/112F/2PFP/31194-   RPR **170+c**

Starts	1st	2nd	3rd	4th	Win & Pl
20	7	4	1	2	£157,534

154	1/17	Gowr	3m1f 137-157 Ch Hcap soft	£50,427
	1/17	Tram	2m5f List Ch sft-hvy	£13,566
	12/14	Chel	2m5f Cls2 Nov Ch gd-sft	£13,436
	11/14	Chel	2m4¹/₂f Cls2 Nov Ch soft	£12,512
	1/14	Asct	2m5¹/₂f Cls3 Nov Hdl 4-7yo heavy	£5,630
123	12/13	Winc	2m5¹/₂f Cls2 121-147 Hdl Hcap heavy	£11,711
	12/13	Wwck	2m5f Cls4 Mdn Hdl gd-sft	£3,769

Lost his way when trained by Philip Hobbs but rejuvenated by switch to Ireland last season and produced a terrific performance to win the Thyestes; something to prove at Grade I level after twice disappointing in the spring but may do better back on soft ground.

Facebook.com/racingpost   Twitter @RacingPost

Champers On Ice (Ire)

7 gr g Robin Des Champs - Miss Nova (Ra Nova)

David Pipe			Professor Caroline Tisdall & Bryan Drew

PLACINGS: **U1/121133/126P-** RPR **148c**

Starts	1st	2nd	3rd	4th	Win & Pl
10	4	2	2	-	£53,128

12/16	Uttx	3m Cls3 Nov Ch soft	£6,330
1/16	Chel	2m4¹/₂f Cls3 Nov Hdl heavy	£6,256
11/15	Newb	2m4¹/₂f Cls3 Nov Hdl soft	£6,498
4/15	Punc	2m2f NHF 5-7yo gd-yld	£5,884

Fine third in the Albert Bartlett in 2016 and surely better than he showed in four runs over fences last season; stayed on eyecatchingly on penultimate start over 2m5f at Cheltenham but jumped poorly when pulled up in the National Hunt Chase; acts on any going.

Charbel (Ire)

6 b g Iffraaj - Eoz (Sadler's Wells)

Kim Bailey			Mrs Julie Martin & David R Martin

PLACINGS: **11/412215/512F3-** RPR **158c**

Starts	1st	2nd	3rd	4th	Win & Pl
13	5	3	1	1	£83,497

10/16	Uttx	2m Cls3 Ch good	£9,384
2/16	Muss	1m7¹/₂f Cls2 Nov Hdl gd-sft	£14,389
10/15	Strf	2m3¹/₂f Cls3 Nov Hdl 4-6yo soft	£6,498
3/15	Limk	2m List NHF 4yo heavy	£12,597
2/15	Leop	2m NHF 4yo soft	£5,349

High-class 2m novice chaser last season who was unlucky not to win more than once, running a cracker behind Altior at Sandown and falling two out when still in front in the Arkle; jumping fell apart last time when favourite for a Grade 1 at Aintree.

Charli Parcs (Fr)

4 b g Anabaa Blue - Ella Parcs (Nikos)

Nicky Henderson			John P McManus

PLACINGS: **11F6-** RPR **141+h**

Starts	1st	2nd	3rd	4th	Win & Pl
4	2	-	-	-	£31,834

12/16	Kemp	2m Cls2 Hdl 3yo good	£12,512
11/16	Engh	2m1¹/₂f Hdl 3yo v soft	£17,647

Hugely impressive on his British debut last season when beating Master Blueyes but failed to build on that, falling two out at Kempton (would have struggled to beat Master Blueyes) and finishing sixth in the Triumph; may appreciate a longer trip.

Chase The Spud

9 b g Alflora - Trial Trip (Le Moss)

Fergal O'Brien			Mrs C Banks

PLACINGS: **1244/1PP/2P13/72751-** RPR **144+c**

Starts	1st	2nd	3rd	4th	Win & Pl
19	4	3	2	2	£104,836

130	3/17	Uttx	4m1¹/₂f Cls1 List 129-144 Ch Hcap soft	£70,338
	2/16	Extr	3m Cls2 Ch heavy	£12,820
120	11/14	Extr	3m Cls3 Nov 116-133 Ch Hcap soft	£6,330
	11/13	Hntg	2m3¹/₂f Cls4 Nov Hdl gd-sft	£4,549

Dour stayer who relished stepping up in trip when winning last season's Midlands National on soft ground; still unexposed as a stayer having run beyond 3m2f just twice previously, including when second to a handicap blot at Haydock last term.

Chef D'Oeuvre (Fr)

6 b g Martaline - Kostroma (Lost World)

Warren Greatrex			McNeill Family

PLACINGS: **4/131410/U241F3-** RPR **147+c**

Starts	1st	2nd	3rd	4th	Win & Pl
11	3	1	2	2	£21,143

2/17	Hrfd	3m1f Cls3 Ch heavy	£7,149
2/16	Font	2m5¹/₂f Cls4 Nov Hdl heavy	£3,899
12/15	Ling	2m3¹/₂f Cls4 Nov Hdl heavy	£4,549

Has gained all four wins (including point-to-point) on heavy ground and beaten only once in those conditions behind Yanworth; latest victory came by 30 lengths in a novice chase at Hereford and could make a very useful chaser on that evidence given his ground.

Chesterfield (Ire)

7 ch g Pivotal - Antique (Dubai Millennium)

Seamus Mullins			The Rumble Racing Club

PLACINGS: **1211F/80211-** RPR **149+h**

Starts	1st	2nd	3rd	4th	Win & Pl
10	5	2			£110,052

143	4/17	Ayr	2m Cls1 Gd2 135-155 Hdl Hcap gd-sft	£59,798
132	4/17	Aint	2m¹/₂f Cls2 120-143 Hdl Hcap good	£30,950
123	11/14	Chel	2m1¹/₂f Cls3 Nov 100-130 Hdl Hcap soft	£7,507
	10/14	Hntg	2m Cls4 Nov Hdl good	£3,899
	7/14	Worc	2m Cls4 Nov Hdl good	£3,249

Off the track for nearly two years before returning last season and really found his feet in the spring, romping home at Aintree and defying an 11lb higher mark by a short head in the Scottish Champion Hurdle; going the right way after all his issues.

Cilaos Emery (Fr)

5 b g Califet - Queissa (Saint Preuil)

Willie Mullins (Ir)				Luke McMahon
PLACINGS: 11251-				RPR **153h**

Starts	1st	2nd	3rd	4th	Win & Pl
5	3	1	-	-	£70,812

	4/17	Punc	2m¹/₂f Nov Gd1 Hdl gd-yld	£50,427
	12/16	Navn	2m Mdn Hdl sft-hvy	£6,331
	4/16	Punc	2m NHF 4yo gd-yld	£5,426

Signed off last season with a Grade 1 win at Punchestown, benefiting from a strongly run race to beat stablemate Melon; had been far too keen prior to that when beaten at 4-9 at Punchestown and only fifth in the Supreme; full of potential if learning to settle.

Claimantakinforgan (Fr)

5 b g Great Pretender - Taquine D'Estrees (Take Risks)

Nicky Henderson				Grech & Parkin
PLACINGS: S1/16235-				RPR **127b**

Starts	1st	2nd	3rd	4th	Win & Pl
5	1	1	1	-	£13,445

	11/16	Hayd	1m7¹/₂f Cls4 NHF 4-6yo heavy	£3,249

Beaten favourite twice after making a winning debut under rules at Haydock last season but ran a cracker when third in the Champion Bumper at Cheltenham; not quite at that level at Aintree (still a fair fifth) and should appreciate a greater stamina test over hurdles.

Clan Des Obeaux (Fr)

5 b/br g Kapgarde - Nausicaa Des Obeaux (April Night)

Paul Nicholls		G Mason, Sir A Ferguson & Mr & Mrs P K Barber
PLACINGS: 1/126/412514-		RPR **154+c**

Starts	1st	2nd	3rd	4th	Win & Pl
10	4	2	-	2	£54,573

	3/17	Extr	2m3f Cls3 Nov Ch gd-sft	£7,148
	11/16	Newb	2m4f Cls1 Nov Gd2 Ch gd-sft	£19,933
	12/15	Newb	2m¹/₂f Cls4 Hdl 3yo soft	£3,249
	4/15	Lrsy	1m4f NHF 3yo	£3,899

Hugely impressive when winning a Grade 2 at Newbury by ten lengths on his second run over fences last season and disappointing he couldn't build on that, with only other win coming against two rivals at Exeter; full of ability though and still only five.

Cliffs Of Dover

4 b g Canford Cliffs - Basanti (Galileo)

Paul Nicholls				Mr & Mrs J D Cotton
PLACINGS: 1311111-				RPR **138+h**

Starts	1st	2nd	3rd	4th	Win & Pl
7	6	-	1	-	£56,739

	12/16	Donc	2m¹/₂f Cls1 Gd2 Hdl 3yo good	£22,780
	10/16	Weth	2m Cls1 List Hdl 3yo good	£11,390
129	10/16	Chel	2m¹/₂f Cls3 110-136 Cond Hdl Hcap good	£6,256
	10/16	Kemp	2m Cls3 Hdl 3yo good	£5,525
121	10/16	Winc	1m7¹/₂f Cls3 120-129 Hdl Hcap gd-fm	£5,848
	8/16	Worc	2m Cls4 Mdn Hdl 3yo good	£3,509

Went from strength to strength when winning six juvenile hurdles early last term before missing the end of the season through injury; interesting to see how he fares in good 2m handicaps, although assessor taking few chances with a mark of 145.

Cloudy Dream (Ire)

7 gr g Cloudings - Run Away Dream (Acceglio)

Malcolm Jefferson				Trevor Hemmings
PLACINGS: 31/13112/1122221-				RPR **158+c**

Starts	1st	2nd	3rd	4th	Win & Pl
14	7	5	2	-	£152,031

	4/17	Ayr	2m4¹/₂f Cls1 Nov Gd2 Ch good	£26,283
	11/16	Hayd	2m¹/₂f Cls2 Ch soft	£12,996
	10/16	Carl	2m Cls4 Ch soft	£3,899
122	3/16	MRas	2m2¹/₂f Cls3 115-129 Hdl Hcap soft	£9,384
	11/15	Donc	2m3¹/₂f Cls4 Nov Hdl 4-6yo good	£3,899
	10/15	Carl	2m1f Cls6 NHF 4-6yo good	£1,560
	4/15	Hexm	2m Cls6 NHF 4-5yo good	£1,711

Never finished out of the first two in seven runs over fences last season and thrived when faced with a stiffer stamina test, staying on well for a fine second in the Arkle before two big runs over 2m4f (won a Grade 2 at Ayr); trainer is convinced he'll get further, which will open up options,

Clyne

7 b g Hernando - Lauderdale (Nebos)

Evan Williams				David M Williams
PLACINGS: 135/311/1123-				RPR **152h**

Starts	1st	2nd	3rd	4th	Win & Pl
10	5	1	3		£73,646

140	12/16	Hayd	2m3f Cls2 114-140 Hdl Hcap soft	£12,512
132	11/16	Hayd	1m7¹/₂f Cls3 106-132 Hdl Hcap heavy	£12,996
119	2/16	Wwck	2m Cls4 104-119 Hdl Hcap good	£3,899
115	12/15	Ffos	2m Cls3 107-132 Hdl Hcap heavy	£6,498
	12/14	Ffos	2m Cls4 Nov Hdl soft	£3,119

Has gone from strength to strength during the last two seasons, winning four in a row before finishing second in the Champion Hurdle Trial and third in the Betfair Hurdle; was 4lb well in that day at Newbury so may have missed the chance to win a big one; yet to run on ground quicker than soft.

Cogry

8 b g King's Theatre - Wyldello (Supreme Leader)

Nigel Twiston-Davies   Graham & Alison Jelley

PLACINGS: 16F/4P33/FBUF1P3622-   RPR **142c**

Starts		1st	2nd	3rd	4th	Win & Pl
27		6	3	4	1	£119,314
128	1/17	Chel	3m Cls2 128-143 Hdl Hcap soft			£12,512
	2/15	Wwck	3m2f Cls3 Nov Ch soft			£9,384
128	12/14	Chep	2m7¹/₂f Cls3 Nov 120-137 Ch Hcap heavy			£6,498
	2/14	Wwck	2m3f Cls4 Nov Hdl 4-7yo soft			£3,899
	1/14	Leic	2m4¹/₂f Cls4 Nov Hdl heavy			£3,899
	10/13	Sthl	1m7¹/₂f Cls6 Mdn NHF 4-6yo gd-sft			£1,560

Badly lost his way with four successive non-completions last season but won over hurdles at Cheltenham to restore his confidence and progressed well back over fences; came within a neck of winning the Scottish National and raised just 2lb for that.

Cole Harden (Ire)

8 b g Westerner - Nosie Betty (Alphabatim)

Warren Greatrex   Mrs Jill Eynon & Robin Eynon

PLACINGS: /123412/334/2324P-23   RPR **162h**

Starts		1st	2nd	3rd	4th	Win & Pl
24		7	5	4	4	£329,397
	3/15	Chel	3m Cls1 Gd1 Hdl good			£170,850
	11/14	Weth	3m1¹/₂f Cls1 Gd2 Hdl good			£21,072
	1/14	Newb	2m3f Cls4 Nov Hdl soft			£3,574
	11/13	Font	2m3f Cls4 Mdn Hdl heavy			£3,119
	8/13	Worc	2m Cls6 NHF 4-6yo good			£1,560
	3/13	Sedg	2m1f Cls6 NHF 4-6yo heavy			£1,560

Hasn't won since the 2015 Stayers' Hurdle but has continued to run well in similar races, including when fourth in the last two runnings of that race; seemed to resent a first-time visor when pulled up at Aintree; didn't appear to take to chasing.

Colin's Sister

6 b m Central Park - Dd's Gienalla (Be My Native)

Fergal O'Brien   Mrs Caroline Beresford-Wylie

PLACINGS: 44552/11115-   RPR **142 + h**

Starts		1st	2nd	3rd	4th	Win & Pl
10		4	1	-	2	£43,919
	2/17	Sand	2m4f Cls1 Nov Gd2 Hdl soft			£17,085
	12/16	Hayd	2m3f Cls1 Nov List Hdl soft			£11,390
	11/16	Wwck	2m5f Cls4 Nov Hdl soft			£3,899
	10/16	Chep	2m3¹/₂f Cls4 Nov Hdl soft			£3,899

Won first four races over hurdles last season, including a Grade 2 mares' novice by nine lengths at Sandown under a penalty; finished only fifth at Grade 1 level at Fairyhouse but may have found ground quicker than ideal (last three wins all on soft).

Coney Island (Ire)

6 b g Flemensfirth - Millys Gesture (Milan)

Edward Harty (Ir)   John P McManus

PLACINGS: 32151/2212-   RPR **156c**

Starts		1st	2nd	3rd	4th	Win & Pl
9		3	4	1	-	£99,061
	12/16	Fair	2m4f Nov Gd1 Ch gd-yld			£36,875
130	3/16	Fair	3m Nov 109-131 Hdl Hcap yield			£23,860
	12/15	Leop	2m Mdn Hdl 4yo heavy			£6,953

Missed last season's Cheltenham Festival with a bruised foot but had already proved himself up there with the best novice chasers; won the Drinmore Chase at Fairyhouse and arguably even better when stepped up to 3m to finish a close second to Our Duke; not hard to see him winning valuable races in Ireland during the winter.

Coneygree

10 b g Karinga Bay - Plaid Maid (Executive Perk)

Mark Bradstock   The Max Partnership

PLACINGS: 18/1113/1111/1/23-   RPR **172c**

Starts		1st	2nd	3rd	4th	Win & Pl
13		9	1	2	-	£520,223
	11/15	Sand	3m Cls1 List Ch gd-sft			£17,085
	3/15	Chel	3m2¹/₂f Cls1 Gd1 Ch soft			£313,225
	2/15	Newb	2m7¹/₂f Cls1 Gd2 Ch soft			£28,475
	12/14	Kemp	3m Cls1 Nov Gd1 Ch gd-sft			£42,047
	11/14	Newb	2m4f Cls1 Nov Gd2 Ch soft			£18,184
	12/12	Chel	3m Cls1 Nov Gd2 Hdl heavy			£14,238
	11/12	Chel	2m5f Cls1 Nov Gd2 Hdl soft			£14,238
	11/12	Uttx	2m4f Cls4 Nov Hdl soft			£2,534
	11/11	Uttx	2m Cls6 NHF 4-6yo gd-sft			£1,365

Brilliant winner of the Gold Cup as a novice in 2015; has suffered a string of injury problems since then, running just three times, but suggested he retains all his ability with a close third to Sizing John and Djakadam at Punchestown on ground quicker than ideal; had been due to return in Kerry National at Listowel during September but missed race on account of ground being too testing.

Constantine Bay

6 b g Kayf Tara - Alina Rheinberg (Waky Nao)

Nicky Henderson   Grech & Parkin

PLACINGS: 21/11144-   RPR **147h**

Starts		1st	2nd	3rd	4th	Win & Pl
5		3	-	-	2	£37,995
	1/17	Donc	3m1¹/₂f Cls1 Nov Gd2 Hdl good			£17,085
	1/17	Chep	2m3¹/₂f Cls4 Nov Hdl heavy			£3,574
	11/16	Hayd	2m3f Cls3 Nov Hdl 4-7yo good			£5,393

Smart novice hurdler last season, winning a Grade 2 at Doncaster and finishing fourth in 3m

'He proved himself up there with the best novice chasers last season and it's not hard to see him winning valuable races'

UTTOXETER
RACECOURSE

JUMP TO IT

Home to the Betfred Midlands Grand National, Uttoxeter Racecourse is firmly established as one of the leading National Hunt tracks in the Midlands.

With 25 fixtures per year, the racing calendar runs from January right the way through to 31 December for New Year's Eve Racing.

2017/18 JUMP SEASON FIXTURES

2017

Sunday 24 September	Autumn Family Fun Raceday
Sunday 8 October	Oktoberfest Raceday
Thursday 19 October	1907 Raceday
Friday 3 November	Gentlemen's Day
Saturday 18 November	Beer Festival Raceday
Sunday 26 November	Afternoon Racing
Tuesday 12 December	Money Where Your Mouth Is Raceday
Friday 22 December	Betfred Christmas Party Raceday
Sunday 31 December	New Year's Eve Raceday

2018

Saturday 27 January	Super Saturday
Saturday 10 February	Super Saturday
Saturday 17 March	Betfred Midlands Grand National
Saturday 7 April	Super Saturday

2018/19 Jump Season Championship will be under starters orders on 5 May 2018 with the first professional meeting of the season being held at Uttoxeter Racecourse.

01889 562561 | uttoxeter-racecourse.co.uk

Grade 1 events at Cheltenham and Aintree; all those runs came on good ground but believed by connections to prefer softer (has won on heavy); likely to go novice chasing.

Copain De Classe (Fr)

5 b g Enrique - Toque Rouge (Loup Solitaire)

Paul Nicholls				Kyle, Stewart, Vogt & Wylie

PLACINGS: 1F/31P1-				RPR **135**+h

Starts	1st	2nd	3rd	4th	Win & Pl
6	3	-	1	-	£14,183

	3/17	Winc	1m7¹/₂f Cls4 Nov Hdl gd-sft	£3,899
	11/16	Chep	2m Cls4 Nov Hdl gd-sft	£3,899
	5/15	Vich	1m4f NHF 3yo soft	£5,814

Impressive winner of novice hurdles at Chepstow and Wincanton last season either side of sole disappointment when unsuited by heavy ground; should get 2m4f in time; looks a good prospect for novice chases.

Crack Mome (Fr)

5 ch g Spanish Moon - Peche Mome (April Night)

Willie Mullins (Ir)				Andrea & Graham Wylie

PLACINGS: 1/120-				RPR **142**+h

Starts	1st	2nd	3rd	4th	Win & Pl
4	2	1	-	-	£16,012

	12/16	Clon	2m1f Mdn Hdl soft	£4,522
	5/15	Seno	1m3¹/₂f NHF 3yo heavy	£4,264

French recruit who earned a big reputation at home last season but didn't quite deliver on the track; beaten at 4-11 in a Grade 2 at Fairyhouse and still sent off just 11-1 for the Supreme when tailed off; seems sure to prove better in time.

Cue Card

11 b g King's Theatre - Wicked Crack (King's Ride)

Colin Tizzard				Mrs Jean R Bishop

PLACINGS: 4452/4111F1/43121F2-				RPR **176**+c

Starts	1st	2nd	3rd	4th	Win & Pl
37	16	9	2	5	£1,372,065

	2/17	Asct	2m5f Cls1 Gd1 Ch soft	£85,425
	11/16	Hayd	3m Cls1 Gd1 Ch heavy	£119,689
	4/16	Aint	3m1f Cls1 Gd1 Ch gd-sft	£84,655
	12/15	Kemp	3m Cls1 Gd1 Ch gd-sft	£114,436
	11/15	Hayd	3m Cls1 Gd1 Ch soft	£112,540
	10/15	Weth	3m Cls1 Gd2 Ch soft	£56,950
	11/13	Hayd	3m Cls1 Gd1 Ch soft	£112,637
	3/13	Chel	2m5f Cls1 Gd1 Ch soft	£156,613
	2/13	Asct	2m5f Cls1 Gd1 Ch soft	£84,405
157	11/12	Extr	2m1¹/₂f Cls1 Gd2 140-160 Ch Hcap gd-sft	£35,594
	12/11	Newb	2m2¹/₂f Cls3 Nov Ch soft	£7,323
	10/11	Chep	2m3¹/₂f Cls3 Nov Ch good	£7,148
	11/10	Chel	2m¹/₂f Cls1 Nov Gd2 Hdl good	£14,253
	10/10	Aint	2m4f Cls3 Nov Hdl 4-6yo gd-sft	£4,554
	3/10	Chel	2m¹/₂f Cls1 Gd1 NHF 4-6yo good	£34,206
	1/10	Font	1m5¹/₂f Cls6 NHF 4-6yo soft	£1,431

Evergreen staying chaser who wasn't quite at his brilliant best last season but showed he can still win top races, landing the Betfair and Ascot Chases before going close in the Betway

Bowl; going nowhere when falling three out in the Gold Cup for the second time; reportedly in great shape for his latest campaign and due to kick off in the Charlie Hall before going back to Kempton for the King George in which he finished second last year having won the race the previous season.

Cyrus Darius

8 b g Overbury - Barton Belle (Barathea)

Malcolm Jefferson				Mr & Mrs G Calder & P M Warren

PLACINGS: 4/3111/1/419-				RPR **146**+h

Starts	1st	2nd	3rd	4th	Win & Pl
9	5	-		2	£68,559

	2/17	Kels	2m2f Cls2 Hdl heavy	£16,643
	9/15	Prth	2m4f Cls3 Nov Ch gd-sft	£6,882
	4/15	Aint	2m1¹/₂f Cls1 Nov Gd2 Hdl gd-sft	£33,762
	3/15	Hexm	2m Cls4 Nov Hdl gd-sft	£3,285
	3/15	Newc	2m¹/₂f Cls4 Nov Hdl good	£3,249

Off the track for nearly 18 months before his return last season but looked to retain all his ability when winning the Morebattle Hurdle at Kelso, although out of his depth in the Champion Hurdle; could go back over fences (won only novice chase in 2015).

De Plotting Shed (Ire)

7 b g Beneficial - Lady Willmurt (Mandalus)

Gordon Elliott (Ir)				Ives Ashley Vasey Partnership

PLACINGS: F/214212/9111264224-				RPR **155**h

Starts	1st	2nd	3rd	4th	Win & Pl
16	5	6	-	3	£76,118

	11/16	Naas	2m4f Hdl good	£9,496
	10/16	Thur	2m6¹/₂f Hdl good	£8,140
	9/16	Navn	2m6f Hdl yld-sft	£7,461
	2/16	Clon	2m3f Mdn Hdl heavy	£4,522
	11/15	Fair	2m NHF 5-7yo sft-hvy	£4,814

Won three in a row last autumn and continued to run well in better company, finishing second in three Grade 2 races and far from disgraced behind Vroum Vroum Mag and Unowhatimeanharry at Grade 1 level; has the size and scope to thrive over fences.

Dead Right

5 b g Alflora - April Queen (Midnight Legend)

Neil Mulholland				John P McManus

PLACINGS: 281-				RPR **127**+b

Starts	1st	2nd	3rd	4th	Win & Pl
3	1	1	-	-	£9,976

	4/17	Punc	2m NHF 4-7yo gd-yld	£9,214

Picked up a small injury when only eighth on his hurdling debut last season but showed his true colours when reverting to a bumper at Punchestown, comfortably beating Champion Bumper fourth Next Destination; smart prospect going back over hurdles.

Death Duty (Ire)

6 b g Shantou - Midnight Gift (Presenting)

Gordon Elliott (Ir)   Gigginstown House Stud

PLACINGS: 13/112/1111U3-   RPR **150+h**

Starts	1st	2nd	3rd	4th	Win & Pl
10	6	1	2	-	£120,677
1/17	Naas	2m4f Nov Gd1 Hdl soft			£45,385
12/16	Navn	2m4f Nov Gd2 Hdl sft-hvy			£18,438
11/16	Navn	2m4f Nov Gd3 Hdl yld-sft			£18,438
10/16	Rosc	2m4f Mdn Hdl heavy			£4,522
12/15	Navn	2m List NHF 4-7yo heavy			£12,597
10/15	DRoy	2m NHF 4-7yo yld-sft			£4,814

Won first four races over hurdles last season, including a Grade 1 at Naas; helped by Augusta Kate's fall at the last that day and failed to live up to his billing subsequently, although clearly failed to stay 3m when favourite for the Albert Bartlett.

Debece

6 b g Kayf Tara - Dalamine (Sillery)

Tim Vaughan   Robert Kirkland

PLACINGS: 441/123313-   RPR **148h**

Starts	1st	2nd	3rd	4th	Win & Pl
121	3	1	3	2	£24,277
3/17	Newb	2m4½f Cls4 99-121 Hdl Hcap soft			£4,549
5/16	Kemp	2m Cls4 Nov Hdl good			£3,249
3/16	MRas	2m½f Cls6 Mdn NHF 4-6yo soft			£1,560

Got better as he stepped up in trip last season, running away with a handicap hurdle at Newbury and finishing a half-length third in the Grade 1 Sefton at Aintree on last two starts; half-brother to Don Poli and should come into his own over fences.

Cue Card: marvellous staying chaser who should again prove a force at the top at around 3m

Debuchet (Fr)

4 gr g Smadoun - Luzerne Du Poitou (Royal Charter)

Mags Mullins (Ir)				Force Eight Syndicate
PLACINGS: 2121-				RPR **125+b**

Starts	1st	2nd	3rd	4th	Win & Pl
4	2	2	-		£42,476

4/17	Limk	2m List NHF 4yo soft	£20,171
1/17	Leop	2m NHF 4yo good	£4,731

Ran a huge race for a four-year-old when second in the Champion Bumper at Cheltenham (would have been only the second of that age to win in 20 years after Cue Card); won at Leopardstown and Limerick either side of that and should make a fine novice hurdler.

Defi Du Seuil (left): top-notch juvenile hurdler completed a memorable Cheltenham-Aintree double

Defi Du Seuil (Fr)

4 b g Voix Du Nord - Quarvine Du Seuil (Lavirco)

Philip Hobbs				John P McManus
PLACINGS: 2/11111111-				RPR **150+h**

Starts	1st	2nd	3rd	4th	Win & Pl
9	8	1	-	-	£212,705

4/17	Aint	2m1f Cls1 Gd1 Hdl 4yo good	£56,181
3/17	Chel	2m1f Cls1 Gd1 Hdl 4yo good	£71,188
1/17	Chel	2m1f Cls1 Gd2 Hdl 4yo soft	£17,085
12/16	Chep	2m Cls1 Gd1 Hdl 3yo soft	£28,475
12/16	Chel	2m1f Cls2 Hdl 3yo gd-sft	£12,512
11/16	Chel	2m¹/₂f Cls2 Gd2 Hdl 3yo gd-sft	£17,165
10/16	Ffos	2m Cls5 Mdn Hdl 3yo good	£2,599
4/16	Pari	1m4f NHF 3yo v soft	£5,882

Outstanding juvenile who won all seven races last term, including the Cheltenham-Aintree double; had been seen as a soft-ground horse before the Triumph but proved arguably even better on quicker; looks a future chaser but could be a Champion Hurdle candidate first.

Definitly Red (Ire)

8 ch g Definite Article - The Red Wench (Aahsaylad)

Brian Ellison   P J Martin

PLACINGS: 1211P/2122F1/131U1P-   RPR **162+c**

Starts	1st	2nd	3rd	4th	Win & Pl
20	10	4	1	-	£189,700

149	3/17	Donc	3m2f Cls2 137-161 Ch Hcap soft	£34,408
141	12/16	Weth	3m Cls1 Gd3 131-153 Ch Hcap gd-sft	£22,780
140	10/16	Carl	2m4f Cls2 122-148 Hdl Hcap gd-sft	£12,512
137	4/16	Ayr	2m4¹/₂f Cls1 List 132-148 Ch Hcap soft	£25,628
	1/16	Catt	3m1f Cls4 Nov Ch soft	£7,148
	2/15	Hayd	2m7f Cls1 Nov Gd2 Hdl soft	£15,735
	1/15	Catt	2m3¹/₂f Cls4 Nov Hdl gd-sft	£4,874
	11/14	Chel	2m¹/₂f Cls1 List NHF 4-6yo soft	£11,390
	2/14	Newb	2m¹/₂f Cls1 List NHF 4-6yo heavy	£11,390
	12/13	Uttx	2m Cls6 Mdn NHF 4-6yo heavy	£1,949

Came of age last season when storming to impressive handicap wins in the Rowland Meyrick and the Grimthorpe; pulled up when jockey lost his irons in the Grand National; starts this season 10lb higher on 159 but could still be progressing.

Diakali (Fr)

8 gr g Sinndar - Diasilixa (Linamix)

Willie Mullins (Ir)   Wicklow Bloodstock (Ireland)

PLACINGS: 241/211343/34/10/41-   RPR **164+h**

Starts	1st	2nd	3rd	4th	Win & Pl
17	7	2	3	4	£337,096

4/17	Fair	2m Hdl gd-yld	£11,564
7/15	Tipp	2m Gd3 Hdl good	£31,492
11/13	Naas	2m Gd3 Hdl 4yo yld-sft	£14,533
6/13	Autl	2m3¹/₂f Gd1 Hdl 4yo v soft	£98,780
4/13	Punc	2m Gd1 Hdl 4yo heavy	£40,325
1/13	Punc	2m Gd3 Hdl 4yo heavy	£14,533
11/12	Gowr	2m Mdn Hdl 3yo heavy	£5,750

Very high-class hurdler in his youth and beaten just a head and a nose in the 2014 Aintree Hurdle; missed the following season and then out again for nearly two years until returning last spring but wide-margin win at Fairyhouse suggests he retains his ability.

Diamond King (Ire)

9 b g King's Theatre - Georgia On My Mind (Belmez)

Gordon Elliott (Ir)   Mrs Diana L Whateley

PLACINGS: 131/7P/4211/4154PP-5   RPR **144c**

Starts		1st	2nd	3rd	4th	Win & Pl
18		7	1	1	3	£92,607
	10/16	Gway	2m2f Ch good			£5,879
149	3/16	Chel	2m5f Cls1 Gd3 139-158 Hdl Hcap good			£51,255
	1/16	Punc	2m4f Hdl heavy			£8,118
	1/14	Donc	2m¹/₂f Cls4 Nov Hdl gd-sft			£3,119
	11/13	Weth	2m Cls4 Nov Hdl gd-sft			£3,422
	4/13	Bang	2m¹/₂f Cls6 Am NHF 4-6yo good			£1,643
	2/13	Weth	2m Cls6 NHF 4-5yo soft			£1,643

Won the Coral Cup in 2016 and looked a terrific chasing prospect when scoring on his chasing debut last season (favourite for the Drinmore next time); lost his way, including when again favourite for a Cheltenham Festival repeat, but surely has more to offer.

Diego Du Charmil (Fr)

5 b g Ballingarry - Daramour (Anabaa Blue)

Paul Nicholls   Mrs Johnny De La Hey

PLACINGS: 32214/19010-   RPR **151+h**

Starts		1st	2nd	3rd	4th	Win & Pl
10		3	2	1	1	£104,766
140	2/17	Muss	1m7¹/₂f Cls1 List 117-143 Hdl Hcap good			£28,475
138	10/16	Chep	2m Cls2 120-140 4yo Hcap good			£12,996
133	3/16	Chel	2m¹/₂f Cls1 Gd3 128-142 4yo Hcap good			£42,713

Landed the Fred Winter Hurdle in 2016 on his first run for Paul Nicholls; struggled in top handicaps last season but still won less competitive races at Chepstow and Musselburgh; has gained all three wins in Britain after at least seven weeks off.

Different Gravey (Ire)

7 b g High Chaparral - Newtown Dancer (Danehill Dancer)

Nicky Henderson   Mr & Mrs R Kelvin-Hughes

PLACINGS: 1/1411/15/155P-   RPR **152+c**

Starts		1st	2nd	3rd	4th	Win & Pl
10		5	-	-	1	£70,442
	11/16	Asct	2m3f Cls3 Ch gd-sft			£7,798
149	2/16	Asct	2m3¹/₂f Cls2 126-149 Hdl Hcap soft			£28,152
	4/15	Ayr	2m4¹/₂f Cls3 Nov Hdl good			£6,498
	2/15	Hntg	2m3¹/₂f Cls1 Nov List Hdl soft			£14,266
	11/14	Newb	2m¹/₂f Cls3 Mdn Hdl soft			£6,498

Very lightly raced in recent seasons (six runs in two years) but has shown glimpses of vast

....

'High-class novice chaser last season, but his third place behind Yorkhill in the JLT suggests he may come up short against the very best'

potential, winning a valuable Ascot handicap by 16 lengths and hacking up on his chasing debut last term; lost his way subsequently, including back over hurdles.

Disko (Fr)

6 gr g Martaline - Nikos Royale (Nikos)

Noel Meade (Ir)   Gigginstown House Stud

PLACINGS: 1/221/6133131-   RPR **157c**

Starts		1st	2nd	3rd	4th	Win & Pl
11		5	2	3		£152,220
	4/17	Punc	3m¹/₂f Nov Gd1 Ch gd-yld			£50,427
	2/17	Leop	2m5¹/₂f Nov Gd1 Ch soft			£42,863
	10/16	Punc	2m4f Ch yield			£5,879
	11/15	Naas	2m4f Mdn Hdl soft			£6,686
	2/15	Punc	2m NHF 4yo soft			£4,814

Proved himself a high-class novice chaser last season having too much toe for Our Duke (better over further) and proving equally effective at 3m when gaining second Grade 1 win; third behind Yorkhill in the JLT suggests he may come up short against the very best, however.

Divin Bere (Fr)

4 b g Della Francesca - Mofa Bere (Saumarez)

Nicky Henderson   Chris Giles

PLACINGS: 12/2122-   RPR **146h**

Starts		1st	2nd	3rd	4th	Win & Pl
6		2	4	-	-	£78,298
	1/17	Hntg	2m Cls2 Hdl 4yo gd-sft			£12,512
	3/16	Pari	1m7f Hdl 3yo v soft			£7,059

Ran three big races following switch from France last season, especially when bustling up Defi Du Seuil at Aintree; proved himself in a big field when a neck second in the Fred Winter at Cheltenham and likely to ply his trade in similar 2m handicaps.

Djakadam (Fr)

8 b g Saint Des Saints - Rainbow Crest (Baryshnikov)

Willie Mullins (Ir)   Mrs S Ricci

PLACINGS: 11F/812/21F23/21342-   RPR **173+c**

Starts		1st	2nd	3rd	4th	Win & Pl
22		7	7	2	2	£570,965
	12/16	Punc	2m4f Gd1 Ch yld-sft			£36,875
	12/15	Punc	2m4f Gd1 Ch heavy			£39,535
145	1/15	Gowr	3m1f 117-145 Ch Hcap heavy			£46,512
	1/14	Leop	2m5f Nov Gd2 Ch soft			£21,667
	12/13	Leop	2m3f Ch yld-sft			£7,293
	3/13	Limk	2m Hdl 4yo heavy			£7,293
	2/13	Gowr	2m Mdn Hdl 4yo heavy			£5,890

Top-class staying chaser who has twice finished second in the Gold Cup but failed to win as often as he should, managing just a single victory in each of the last three seasons; won his second John Durkan last season and just touched off by Sizing John at Punchestown.

Doing Fine (Ire)

9 b g Presenting - Howaya Pet (Montelimar)

Neil Mulholland | Ashley Carr

PLACINGS: 1/1U428/03PF/522215-					RPR **143**+c
Starts	1st	2nd	3rd	4th	Win & Pl
18	3	5	2	1	£48,216

I29	4/17	Chel	3m4f Cls3 111-132 Ch Hcap good	£7,507
I26	10/14	Ffos	3m Cls3 Nov 116-135 Ch Hcap soft	£6,498
	11/13	Asct	2m5¹/₂f Cls2 Nov Hdl gd-sft	£10,010

Thorough stayer who won for the first time since his chasing debut when scoring over 3m4f at Cheltenham in April having finished second on three previous runs; missed a good opportunity in the bet365 Gold Cup (8lb well in) but did well to get to within two lengths having jumped poorly.

Dolos (Fr)

4 b g Kapgarde - Redowa (Trempolino)

Paul Nicholls | Mrs Johnny De La Hey

PLACINGS: 313330212-					RPR **132**h
Starts	1st	2nd	3rd	4th	Win & Pl
9	2	2	4	-	£62,947

	4/17	Chep	2m Cls4 Nov Hdl good	£3,899
	10/16	Chep	2m Cls4 Hdl 3yo good	£3,899

Failed to live up to Grade 1 hopes early last season (well beaten twice at that level) but did much better in good juvenile handicaps in the spring, finishing placed at Ascot and Sandown; could be the sort of young chaser with whom his trainer excels.

Disko: won twice in Grade 1 company over fences last season

Don't Touch It (Ire)

7 b g Scorpion - Shandora (Supreme Leader)

Jessica Harrington (Ir) John P McManus

PLACINGS: 42/212213/1331221-54 RPR **151c**

Starts		1st	2nd	3rd	4th	Win & Pl
17		5	6	3	2	£117,647
144	4/17	Punc	2m 117-145 Ch Hcap gd-yld			£32,778
	2/17	Thur	2m Ch soft			£6,318
	4/16	Punc	2m Nov Gd1 Hdl gd-yld			£43,382
	1/16	Leop	2m Mdn Hdl soft			£6,596
	10/15	Punc	2m NHF 5-7yo yield			£4,814

Has come good at the Punchestown Festival in each of the last two seasons, winning a Grade 1 novice hurdle in 2016 and a fiercely competitive handicap chase last season; clearly thrives on better ground, with both wins on soft coming at odds-on.

Double Shuffle (Ire)

7 b g Milan - Fiddlers Bar (Un Desperado)

Tom George Crossed Fingers Partnership

PLACINGS: 3/5611/24135/2P512P- RPR **158+c**

Starts		1st	2nd	3rd	4th	Win & Pl
15		4	3	1	1	£86,431
143	12/16	Kemp	3m Cls2 126-143 Ch Hcap good			£25,024
134	12/15	Ludl	2m4f Cls3 Nov 120-134 Ch Hcap soft			£11,372
	3/15	Newb	2m¹/₂f Cls4 Nov Hdl gd-sft			£3,422
	2/15	Donc	2m¹/₂f Cls4 Nov Hdl 4-7yo good			£3,574

Won well at Kempton last season and has been placed in a couple of bigger handicaps over the

Douvan: powerhouse chaser will again be a major force in the 2m division – and perhaps over further

last two seasons, including back at that course in the BetBright Chase; has clearly improved for the step up to 3m but failed to get home in the Grand National.

Double W's (Ire)

7 ch g Fruits Of Love - Zaffre (Mtoto)

Malcolm Jefferson — Wharton & Wilson

PLACINGS: 39/3232210/2117291P- — RPR **149+c**

Starts	1st	2nd	3rd	4th	Win & Pl
20	5	7	3	-	£86,816

139	4/17	Aint	2m Cls1 Gd3 128-150 Ch Hcap good	£50,643
135	10/16	Weth	1m7f Cls3 Nov 132-139 Ch Hcap good	£6,498
128	10/16	Carl	2m Cls3 Nov 113-132 Ch Hcap good	£6,498
	3/16	Hayd	1m7½f Cls4 Nov Hdl good	£3,899
	10/14	Ayr	2m Cls6 NHF 4-6yo gd-sft	£1,643

Won the Red Rum Chase at Aintree last season, benefiting from the return to 2m having failed to stay in the novice handicap chase at the Cheltenham Festival (led two out); inconsistent otherwise but a smart 2m handicapper on his day.

Douvan (Fr)

7 b g Walk In The Park - Star Face (Saint Des Saints)

Willie Mullins (Ir) — Mrs S Ricci

PLACINGS: 21111/111111/11117- — RPR **178+c**

Starts	1st	2nd	3rd	4th	Win & Pl
16	14	1	-	-	£523,730

2/17	Punc	2m Gd2 Ch soft	£22,692
12/16	Leop	2m1f Gd1 Ch yield	£43,382
12/16	Cork	2m1f Gd2 Ch sft-hvy	£21,691
4/16	Punc	2m Nov Gd1 Ch yield	£49,890
4/16	Aint	2m Cls1 Nov Gd1 Ch gd-sft	£56,270
3/16	Chel	2m Cls1 Gd1 Ch gd-sft	£85,827
1/16	Leop	2m1f Nov Gd1 Ch soft	£39,706
12/15	Leop	2m1f Nov Gd1 Ch heavy	£42,558
11/15	Navn	2m1f Ch soft	£8,558
4/15	Punc	2m Nov Gd1 Hdl gd-yld	£44,186
3/15	Chel	2m½f Cls1 Nov Gd1 Hdl gd-sft	£68,340
1/15	Punc	2m Nov Gd2 Hdl soft	£20,155
11/14	Gowr	2m Nov Hdl 4yo heavy	£7,475
6/14	Comp	2m1f Hdl 4yo v soft	£8,800

Brilliant chaser who had won nine out of nine over fences – as well as his last five over hurdles – before picking up an injury when 2-9 for a third Cheltenham Festival win in the Champion Chase; yet to run beyond 2m1f but seems sure to get further.

Drumacoo (Ire)

8 b g Oscar - My Native (Be My Native)

Ben Pauling — Mrs Robin Birley

PLACINGS: F202/4111/14/F- — RPR **155c**

Starts	1st	2nd	3rd	4th	Win & Pl
9	4	1	-	2	£24,902

1/16	Hntg	2m7½f Cls4 Nov Ch soft	£3,834
11/14	Thur	2m6½f Nov Hdl soft	£6,900
10/14	Punc	2m6f Mdn Hdl good	£5,750
10/14	Dpat	2m2f NHF 4-7yo yield	£4,313

Brilliant winner on his chasing debut two seasons ago but hasn't lived up to that potential yet, albeit in just two starts; too keen when fourth in the Reynoldstown next time and fell early on in his only run last season at Newbury (favourite both times).

Dusky Legend

7 b m Midnight Legend - Tinagoodnight (Sleeping Car)

Alan King — Mr & Mrs R Kelvin-Hughes

PLACINGS: 16222/22/112232- — RPR **142h**

Starts	1st	2nd	3rd	4th	Win & Pl
13	3	8	1	-	£65,245

11/16	Newb	2m½f Cls2 Nov Hdl good	£12,996
5/16	Wwck	2m Cls5 Mdn Hdl good	£2,738
10/14	Font	1m5½f Cls6 NHF 4-6yo gd-sft	£1,643

Placed in both runnings of the mares' novice hurdle at the Cheltenham Festival in each of the last two seasons and has run several other fine races in defeat, finally also winning twice last term; regarded as an exciting chasing prospect by her trainer.

El Bandit (Ire)

6 b/br g Milan - Bonnie Parker (Un Desperado)

Paul Nicholls — Colm Donlon, Barry Fulton & Chris Giles

PLACINGS: 6/831/1111710-1 — RPR **143+c**

Starts	1st	2nd	3rd	4th	Win & Pl
12	7	-	1	-	£69,173

	5/17	Wwck	3m1½f Cls2 Nov Ch good	£13,436
139	2/17	Muss	3m2f Cls2 120-146 Hdl Hcap good	£14,296
	10/16	Chel	2m5f Cls2 Nov Hdl good	£10,635
	10/16	Chep	2m3½f Cls1 Nov Gd2 Hdl good	£19,933
	6/16	Font	2m5½f Cls4 Nov Hdl good	£3,899
112	5/16	Wwck	2m5f Cls4 95-120 Hdl Hcap gd-sft	£3,249
	4/16	Wwck	2m5f Cls4 Mdn Hdl good	£3,249

Prolific hurdler whose sole defeats last season after completing a five-timer came on soft ground (best form all on good) and in the Pertemps Final; made a winning start over fences in May and should prove a useful staying novice on good ground.

Emerging Force (Ire)

7 b g Milan - Danette (Exit To Nowhere)

Harry Whittington — Webb, Holt, Carpenter & Tucker

PLACINGS: 63/3131U/P1145- — RPR **152+c**

Starts	1st	2nd	3rd	4th	Win & Pl
9	4	-	1	1	£35,757

	11/16	Extr	3m Cls2 Nov Ch good	£14,076
	10/16	Hrfd	2m5f Cls4 Ch good	£5,062
128	2/16	Donc	3m½f Cls3 105-130 Hdl Hcap gd-sft	£9,747
	11/15	Font	2m3f Cls4 Mdn Hdl soft	£3,249

Won first two races over fences this season before a fair fourth at Cheltenham; subsequently laid out for Aintree but below par when only a distant fifth in Listed handicap chase; given a light campaign as expected to be better this term; has lots more to offer.

Empire Of Dirt (Ire)
10 b g Westerner - Rose Of Inchiquin (Roselier)

Gordon Elliott (Ir) — Gigginstown House Stud

PLACINGS: /4F32F1F/F2P11/124P- **RPR 169+c**

Starts 25	1st 6	2nd 5	3rd 1	4th 3	Win & Pl £240,220

148	11/16	Navn	3m 125-150 Ch Hcap yld-sft	£43,382
142	3/16	Chel	2m5f Cls1 Gd3 135-157 Ch Hcap good	£56,950
133	1/16	Leop	2m5f 125-153 Ch Hcap soft	£44,118
125	2/15	Naas	2m4f Nov 119-134 Ch Hcap sft-hvy	£25,194
	3/14	Naas	2m Nov List Hdl yld-sft	£13,542
	10/13	Punc	2m Mdn Hdl yld-sft	£5,610

Late developer who has flourished over the last two seasons, winning the Troytown last term to add to his 2016 Cheltenham Festival success; subsequently stepped up to Grade 1 level and seemed best over 3m when second to Sizing John in the Irish Gold Cup.

Fagan
7 ro g Fair Mix - Northwood May (Teenoso)

Gordon Elliott (Ir) — R A Bartlett

PLACINGS: U/234111/111224/P-1 **RPR 147+c**

Starts 9	1st 4	2nd 2	3rd 1	4th 1	Win & Pl £43,692

7/17	Prth	3m Cls4 Nov Ch good	£5,004
12/15	Muss	1m7¹/₂f Cls4 Nov Hdl 4-6yo soft	£3,899
10/15	Ayr	2m Cls6 NHF 4-6yo good	£1,711
9/15	Prth	2m Cls6 NHF 4-6yo gd-sft	£2,053

High-class novice hurdler two seasons ago, winning over 2m and proving even better over 3m when second in the Albert Bartlett behind Unowhatimeanharry; ran only once last term but returned this summer to win over fences at Perth.

Faugheen (Ire)
9 b g Germany - Miss Pickering (Accordion)

Willie Mullins (Ir) — Mrs S Ricci

PLACINGS: 1/111111/1111/1211/ **RPR 177h**

Starts 13	1st 12	2nd 1	3rd -	4th -	Win & Pl £695,657

1/16	Leop	2m Gd1 Hdl soft	£48,529
12/15	Kemp	2m Cls1 Gd1 Hdl gd-sft	£56,950
5/15	Punc	2m Gd1 Hdl gd-yld	£93,023
3/15	Chel	2m¹/₂f Cls1 Gd1 Hdl gd-sft	£227,800
12/14	Kemp	2m Cls1 Gd1 Hdl gd-sft	£57,218
11/14	Asct	2m3¹/₂f Cls1 Hdl soft	£50,643
4/14	Punc	2m Nov Gd1 Hdl gd-yld	£46,500
3/14	Chel	2m5f Cls1 Nov Gd1 Hdl good	£68,340
12/13	Limk	3m Nov Gd3 Hdl heavy	£15,061
12/13	Navn	2m4f Nov Hdl gd-yld	£7,293
11/13	Punc	2m6f Mdn Hdl yield	£7,293
5/13	Punc	2m NHF 5yo yield	£4,488

Superstar hurdler who has been beaten only once in a career that has brought seven wins at Grade 1 level and victories at the Cheltenham Festival in the Neptune and in the 2015 Champion Hurdle; missed last season after a series of setbacks and has not been seen since winning the Irish Champion Hurdle in January 2016; back in work and would be a threat to all in the top 2m hurdles if returning to his best form.

Fayonagh (Ire)
6 b m Kalanisi - Fair Ina (Taipan)

Gordon Elliott (Ir) — Mrs M Gittins

PLACINGS: 81111- **RPR 129+b**

Starts 5	1st 4	2nd -	3rd -	4th -	Win & Pl £117,832

4/17	Punc	2m Gd1 NHF 4-7yo gd-yld	£50,427
3/17	Chel	2m¹/₂f Cls1 Gd1 NHF 4-6yo gd-sft	£42,713
2/17	Fair	2m List NHF 4-7yo sft-hvy	£20,171
11/16	Naas	2m NHF 4-7yo yld-sft	£4,522

Unbeaten in four bumpers last season including a stunning Grade 1 double; made all to score at Punchestown having done remarkably well to overcome a tardy start when forced to come from the rear at Cheltenham; top-class prospect for novice hurdles.

Finian's Oscar (Ire)
5 b g Oscar - Trinity Alley (Taipan)

Colin Tizzard — Alan Potts

PLACINGS: 111112- **RPR 155+h**

Starts 5	1st 4	2nd 1	3rd -	4th -	Win & Pl £114,470

4/17	Aint	2m4f Cls1 Nov Gd1 Hdl good	£56,168
2/17	Extr	2m1f Cls1 Nov List Hdl soft	£12,676
1/17	Sand	2m Cls1 Nov Gd1 Hdl soft	£25,748
12/16	Hrfd	2m5¹/₂f Cls4 Nov Hdl soft	£3,639

Made rapid strides after winning a point-to-point last October, landing the Tolworth Hurdle at Sandown; even better when stepped up in trip on better ground in the spring, winning a second Grade 1 at Aintree and beaten a short head at Punchestown.

Fixe Le Kap (Fr)
5 gr g Kapgarde - Lady Fix (Turgeon)

Nicky Henderson — Simon Munir & Isaac Souede

PLACINGS: 52/41128/2-1 **RPR 144+h**

Starts 9	1st 3	2nd 3	3rd -	4th 1	Win & Pl £78,842

5/17	Comp	2m3f List Hdl v soft	£34,872
1/16	Wwck	2m Cls4 Hdl 4yo soft	£3,899
12/15	Newb	2m¹/₂f Cls3 Hdl 3yo soft	£6,498

Missed much of last season but returned with a terrific second in the Imperial Cup and then won a Listed hurdle in France; needs soft ground according to his trainer (eighth in the 2016 Fred Winter in only race on quicker); set to go novice chasing.

'Would be a threat to all if returning to his best form'

Flintham

8 b g Kayf Tara - Plaid Maid (Executive Perk)

Mark Bradstock				The Rasher Partnership	
PLACINGS: 333/31151P/P010/42P-					RPR **143c**

Starts	1st	2nd	3rd	4th	Win & Pl
17	4	1	4	1	£38,250

	1/16	Wwck	3m2f Cls2 112-138 Hdl Hcap heavy	£11,574
138				
130	3/15	Ffos	2m6f Cls3 108-130 Hdl Hcap heavy	£5,523
115	12/14	Asct	2m7¹/₂f Cls4 Nov 108-120 Hdl Hcap gd-sft	£6,256
109	11/14	Chep	2m3¹/₂f Cls4 Nov 95-109 Hdl Hcap soft	£3,119

Useful staying hurdler who finally delivered at the third attempt over fences when beaten a short head in last season's Reynoldstown; pulled up in the National Hunt Chase but has twice flopped at the Cheltenham Festival and will be better back on soft ground.

Flying Angel (Ire)

6 gr g Arcadio - Gypsy Kelly (Roselier)

Nigel Twiston-Davies				R J Rexton	
PLACINGS: 12353123/1FP161P-					RPR **158+c**

Starts	1st	2nd	3rd	4th	Win & Pl
15	5	2	3	-	£170,039

	4/17	Aint	2m4f Cls1 Nov Gd1 Ch good	£56,130
	2/17	Wwck	2m Cls1 Nov Gd2 Ch heavy	£22,780
	9/16	Prth	2m4f Cls3 Nov Ch soft	£7,611
133	3/16	Sand	2m Cls1 Gd3 123-149 Hdl Hcap soft	£39,865
	10/15	Worc	2m4f Cls4 Nov Hdl good	£3,249

Hit and miss with his jumping last season but proved a very smart novice chaser on his day, gaining his biggest victory in a 2m4f Grade 1 at Aintree when outbattling Cloudy Dream; had been unlucky when badly hampered at Cheltenham; trainer expects him to stay 3m.

Flying Tiger (Ire)

4 bl g Soldier Of Fortune - Ma Preference (American Post)

Nick Williams				The Macaroni Beach Society	
PLACINGS: 1/2P61414-					RPR **135+h**

Starts	1st	2nd	3rd	4th	Win & Pl
8	3	1		2	£68,676

	3/17	Chel	2m¹/₂f Cls1 Gd3 124-139 Hdl 4yo Hcap gd-sft	£45,560
134				
	1/17	Newb	2m¹/₂f Cls4 Hdl 4yo soft	£4,549
	4/16	Comp	2m1f Hdl 3yo v soft	£7,765

Won last season's Fred Winter Hurdle at Cheltenham, doing particularly well having raced keenly early on; unable to get away with similar tendencies in top company and pulled notably hard at Aintree; should have more to offer back in big-field handicaps.

Footpad (Fr)

5 b g Creachadoir - Willamina (Sadler's Wells)

Willie Mullins (Ir)				Simon Munir & Isaac Souede	
PLACINGS: 7213113F/1124243-					RPR **162+h**

Starts	1st	2nd	3rd	4th	Win & Pl
15	5	3	3	2	£317,104

	6/16	Autl	2m3¹/₂f Gd1 Hdl 4yo soft	£89,338
	5/16	Autl	2m3¹/₂f Gd3 Hdl 4yo v soft	£44,669
	2/16	Leop	2m Gd1 Hdl 4yo sft-hvy	£36,875
	1/16	Gowr	2m Hdl 4yo heavy	£10,037
	11/15	Gowr	2m Mdn Hdl 3yo soft	£6,419

Dual Grade 1 winner as a four-year-old and ran well in top 2m hurdles last season, including when fourth in the Champion Hurdle; stepped up to 3m and saw out longer trip well enough when third at Punchestown, suggesting future lies in staying hurdles.

Forest Bihan (Fr)

6 ch g Forestier - Katell Bihan (Funny Baby)

Brian Ellison				P J Martin	
PLACINGS: 731/3642P36/U121152-					RPR **160c**

Starts	1st	2nd	3rd	4th	Win & Pl
18	4	4	3	1	£97,667

	1/17	Donc	2m¹/₂f Cls1 Nov Gd2 Ch good	£20,554
	1/17	Newc	2m¹/₂f Cls4 Nov Ch soft	£4,549
	11/16	Towc	2m Cls3 Nov Ch good	£7,220
	11/14	Engh	2m1¹/₂f Hdl 3yo heavy	£20,000

Won three novice chases last season, including the Lightning at Doncaster, but could manage only a distant fifth in the Arkle; much better back on a flat track when second at Aintree but still slightly disappointing he couldn't capitalise on Politologue's exit.

Fountains Windfall

7 b g Passing Glance - Fountain Crumble (Dr Massini)

Anthony Honeyball				The Fountains Partnership	
PLACINGS: 16432/173111-					RPR **149+h**

Starts	1st	2nd	3rd	4th	Win & Pl
11	5	1	2	1	£58,582

	4/17	Aint	3m¹/₂f Cls1 Gd3 134-151 Hdl Hcap good	£39,389
137				
	3/17	Plum	2m4¹/₂f Cls4 Nov Hdl gd-sft	£3,249
	3/17	Winc	2m5¹/₂f Cls4 Nov Hdl soft	£3,899
	5/16	Font	2m1¹/₂f Cls4 Mdn Hdl good	£3,249
	6/15	Font	2m1¹/₂f Cls6 NHF 4-6yo good	£1,560

Went from strength to strength last spring and completed a hat-trick in a competitive handicap hurdle at Aintree by eight lengths (given plenty of rope in front); likely to stick to hurdles initially off 9lb higher mark but looks a fine chasing prospect.

ON THE CLOCK

FOUNTAINS WINDFALL Routed his rivals to complete a hat-trick at Aintree in April, Anthony Honeyball's seven-year-old may have more to offer at around three miles on good ground.
[Dave Edwards, Topspeed]

Fox Norton (Fr)

7 b g Lando - Natt Musik (Kendor)

Colin Tizzard — Alan Potts

PLACINGS: 381/11233331/112211-   RPR **174+c**

Starts		1st	2nd	3rd	4th	Win & Pl
22		10	4	5	1	£518,351
	4/17	Punc	2m Gd1 Ch gd-yld			£126,068
	4/17	Aint	2m4f Cls1 Gd1 Ch good			£112,310
	11/16	Chel	2m Cls1 Gd2 Ch soft			£42,713
146	10/16	Chel	2m Cls2 131-157 Ch Hcap good			£31,280
	4/16	Chel	2m¹/₂f Cls2 Nov Ch good			£12,512
	10/15	MRas	2m1f Cls3 Nov Ch good			£7,798
	5/15	Hntg	2m¹/₂f Cls4 Nov Ch good			£3,769
140	2/15	Tntn	2m¹/₂f Cls2 129-145 Hdl Hcap soft			£11,078
	12/13	Donc	2m¹/₂f Cls1 Gd2 Hdl 3yo good			£15,876
	4/13	Fntb	2m Hdl 3yo soft			£8,585

Big improver last season and thrived on decent ground in the spring, winning at Aintree and Punchestown after a near miss in the Champion Chase; particularly impressive over 2m4f in the Melling Chase and could step up to 3m for the King George.

Foxrock (Ire)

9 b g Flemensfirth - Midnight Light (Roselier)

Ted Walsh (Ir) — Barry Connell

PLACINGS: 2120/86343/5521111P-   RPR **145+c**

Starts		1st	2nd	3rd	4th	Win & Pl
28		9	4	5	1	£211,080
	3/17	Gowr	3m1f Hunt Ch heavy			£7,897
	2/17	Leop	3m¹/₂f Hunt Ch soft			£8,424
	1/17	Thur	3m Hunt Ch yld-sft			£5,256
	12/16	DRoy	2m4¹/₂f Hunt Ch soft			£4,070
149	1/15	Leop	2m5f Cls3 123-151 Ch Hcap soft			£46,512
	2/14	Navn	3m Nov Gd2 Ch heavy			£20,313
	1/14	Naas	3m Nov Gd2 Ch sft-hvy			£21,667
	11/13	Fair	2m5¹/₂f Ch gd-yld			£6,732
	3/13	Naas	3m Mdn Hdl soft			£5,610

Former Grade 1 performer (second in the Irish Gold Cup and third in the Lexus in 2015) who proved a class apart in four hunter chases last season; should again thrive in that sphere and could go for a big staying handicap (pulled up in the Irish National).

Foxtail Hill (Ire)

8 b g Dr Massini - Flynn's Girl (Mandalus)

Nigel Twiston-Davies — Options O Syndicate

PLACINGS: /163P/64P/F13511F92-   RPR **146+c**

Starts		1st	2nd	3rd	4th	Win & Pl
19		4	1	2	2	£61,489
133	1/17	Chel	2m5f Cls1 Gd3 131-156 Ch Hcap soft			£34,170
124	1/17	Kemp	2m4¹/₂f Cls3 129-136 Ch Hcap gd-sft			£6,279
115	10/16	Worc	2m4¹/₂f Cls4 101-118 Ch Hcap good			£5,064
	10/14	Strf	2m¹/₂f Cls6 Mdn Hdl good			£2,599

Thrived during a busy campaign last season, especially when stepped up to 2m4f with wins around that trip at Kempton and Cheltenham (only subsequent disappointment when dropped in trip at Aintree); second in the Silver Trophy back at Cheltenham last time.

Free Expression (Ire)

8 b g Germany - Create A Storm (Bob Back)

Gordon Elliott (Ir) — John P McManus

PLACINGS: 11/113/233/2-   RPR **135+c**

Starts		1st	2nd	3rd	4th	Win & Pl
8		3	2	3	-	£69,423
	11/14	Navn	2m4f Nov Gd2 Hdl soft			£20,313
	11/14	Naas	2m Mdn Hdl soft			£5,750
	4/14	Fair	2m2f NHF 4-6yo gd-yld			£24,792

Slightly disappointing since winning his first races in bumpers and novice hurdles (up to Grade 2 level) but has mixed it in top company since going chasing and shown smart form in defeat; back from injury after running only once last season.

Frodon (Fr)

5 b g Nickname - Miss Country (Country Reel)

Paul Nicholls — P J Vogt & Ian Fogg

PLACINGS: /3F543185/11101F115-   RPR **150+c**

Starts		1st	2nd	3rd	4th	Win & Pl
18		8	-	2	1	£188,599
	2/17	Kemp	2m4¹/₂f Cls1 Nov Gd2 Ch good			£18,793
	2/17	Muss	2m4f Cls3 Nov Ch good			£7,798
149	12/16	Chel	2m5f Cls1 Gd3 132-158 Ch Hcap soft			£56,950
	11/16	Winc	2m4f Cls1 Nov Gd2 Ch good			£28,486
	9/16	Font	2m5f Cls4 Nov Ch good			£5,198
	9/16	NAbb	2m¹/₂f Cls3 Nov Ch good			£7,181
	2/16	Hayd	1m7¹/₂f Cls2 Hdl 4yo heavy			£9,747
	4/15	Autl	1m7f Hdl 3yo heavy			£20,465

Prolific novice chaser last season who won six times, most notably in a valuable Cheltenham handicap in December; brilliantly placed otherwise (odds-on four times and only finisher once) and twice found out at Grade 1 level, although didn't stay 3m on one occasion

Garde La Victoire (Fr)

8 b g Kapgarde - Next Victory (Akarad)

Philip Hobbs — Mrs Diana L Whateley

PLACINGS: 1/31541/111FF/12318-   RPR **165+c**

Starts		1st	2nd	3rd	4th	Win & Pl
23		12	2	2	2	£196,568
154	1/17	Sand	1m7¹/₂f Cls2 134-154 Ch Hcap soft			£15,640
148	10/16	Ffos	2m Cls2 135-148 Hdl Hcap gd-sft			£18,768
	1/16	Ludl	2m Cls3 Nov Ch heavy			£6,657
	11/15	Chel	2m Cls1 Nov Gd2 Ch gd-sft			£18,224
	10/15	Uttx	2m Cls4 Ch soft			£3,833
	1/15	Sand	2m Cls1 List Hdl soft			£14,238
144	11/14	Chel	2m¹/₂f Cls1 Gd3 121-147 Hdl Hcap soft			£56,950
	4/14	Tntn	2m4¹/₂f Cls2 Nov Hdl good			£10,010
	4/14	Chel	2m3f Cls4 Nov Hdl good			£4,106
	11/13	Wwck	2m Cls4 Nov Hdl gd-sft			£3,899
	10/13	Aint	2m Cls4 Mdn Hdl gd-sft			£4,549
	10/12	Extr	1m5f Cls6 NHF 3yo gd-sft			£1,365

Has won five times over the last two seasons, including a Grade 2 novice chase and a handicap off 154 at Sandown, often looking a star in the making; let down by his jumping on the biggest stage, most recently in the Champion Chase, but still has time.

General Principle: could prove a useful force in staying handicap chases this season

Gardefort (Fr)

8 b/br g Agent Bleu - La Fresnaie (Exit To Nowhere)

Venetia Williams   A Brooks

PLACINGS: 1PF6/13/P132F/U2412-   RPR **149**c

Starts			1st	2nd	3rd	4th	Win & Pl
30			6	7	3	1	£154,365
139	2/17	Winc	1m7½f Cls2 132-148 Ch Hcap soft				£12,558
132	1/16	Weth	1m7f Cls2 129-144 Ch Hcap heavy				£11,711
124	12/14	Ludl	2m Cls3 124-138 Ch Hcap gd-sft				£16,245
	11/13	Autl	2m5½f Ch 4yo heavy				£22,634
	11/13	Pari	2m1f Ch 4yo good				£7,415
	11/12	Engh	2m1½f Hdl 3yo heavy				£20,000

Excellent second in last season's Grand Annual at Cheltenham, doing particularly well given previous best form had come in small fields on soft or heavy ground; starts this season only 3lb higher and may still have plenty of leeway in that mark.

Gayebury
7 b g Overbury - Gaye Sophie (Environment Friend)

Evan Williams				R Abbott & M Stavrou
PLACINGS: 1d13/122101-				RPR **147+h**

Starts	1st	2nd	3rd	4th	Win & Pl
9	4	3	1	-	£39,921

	4/17	Prth	3m Cls1 Nov List Hdl good	£11,390
132	2/17	Chep	2m7⅛f Cls2 127-143 Hdl Hcap soft	£12,512
	11/16	Ffos	2m4f Cls5 Mdn Hdl soft	£3,249
	1/16	Extr	2m1f Cls6 Mdn NHF 4-6yo heavy	£1,625

Smart and progressive staying novice hurdler last season, with sole disappointment coming in the Pertemps Final; put that behind him when winning a Listed novice contest at Perth and had run away with a Chepstow handicap prior to that; acts on any going.

General Principle (Ire)
8 b g Gold Well - How Provincial (Be My Native)

Gordon Elliott (Ir)				Gigginstown House Stud
PLACINGS: 110/126/322F26115-				RPR **142c**

Starts	1st	2nd	3rd	4th	Win & Pl
14	4	4	1	-	£58,227

3/17	Limk	3m Nov Gd3 Ch soft	£21,432
3/17	Gowr	2m4f Ch heavy	£7,897
2/16	Navn	2m Mdn Hdl sft-hvy	£5,426
2/15	Punc	2m NHF 5-7yo soft	£4,814

Took a long time to find his feet over fences

last season but came good in the spring, winning twice and particularly impressive when stepped up to 3m at Limerick; good fifth in the Irish National on his handicap debut on ground perhaps quicker than ideal.

Getabird (Ire)
5 b g Getaway - Fern Bird (Revoque)

Willie Mullins (Ir)				Mrs S Ricci
PLACINGS: 01/11-				RPR **132+b**

Starts	1st	2nd	3rd	4th	Win & Pl
2	2	-	-	-	£10,903

1/17	Gowr	2m NHF 5-7yo soft	£6,833
12/16	Fair	2m NHF 4yo gd-yld	£4,070

Point-to-point winner who won bumpers at Fairyhouse and Gowran before missing the rest of last season through injury; had been favourite for the Champion Bumper at Cheltenham at the time of his setback and may well take high rank as a novice hurdler.

'This point-to-point winner was favourite for the Champion Bumper before a setback and may well take high rank as a novice hurdler'

Gilgamboa (Ire)

9 b g Westerner - Hi Native (Be My Native)

Enda Bolger (Ir)				John P McManus

PLACINGS: 3110/11321/34554/2B- **RPR 157c**

Starts		1st	2nd	3rd	4th	Win & Pl
17		6	2	3	2	£233,061
	4/15	Fair	2m4f Nov Gd1 Ch soft			£46,512
	12/14	Limk	2m3¹/₂f Nov Gd2 Ch sft-hvy			£21,125
	11/14	Navn	2m Ch yld-sft			£8,625
128	1/14	Leop	2m 115-142 Hdl Hcap soft			£50,000
120	12/13	Punc	2m4f 106-128 Hdl Hcap heavy			£8,134
	10/13	Gway	2m Mdn Hdl 5yo heavy			£6,171

Wonderfully versatile chaser who finished fourth in the Grand National in 2016 yet had the speed to finish a short-head second in a 2m Grade 2 during an abbreviated campaign last term; yet to win beyond 2m4f but clearly has the stamina to thrive over further.

Gino Trail (Ire)

10 br g Perugino - Borough Trail (Woodborough)

Kerry Lee				Mrs Jan Smith

PLACINGS: P/1/2/1/3P/P1122216- **RPR 152c**

Starts		1st	2nd	3rd	4th	Win & Pl
12		4	4	1	-	£41,538
	3/17	Ludl	2m Cls3 Nov Ch soft			£8,546
134	12/16	Hayd	1m7¹/₂f Cls3 122-140 Ch Hcap soft			£7,798
129	11/16	Ludl	2m Cls3 Nov 123-129 Ch Hcap good			£6,975
	1/15	Towc	2m Cls4 Nov Hdl soft			£3,249

First or second in six of his last seven races and ran well when sixth in the Red Rum at Aintree on ground quicker than ideal (best form on soft or heavy); very lightly raced for his age having run only four times under rules prior to last season.

Give Me A Copper (Ire)

7 ch g Presenting - Copper Supreme (Supreme Leader)

Paul Nicholls				Done, Ferguson, Kyle, Mason & Wood

PLACINGS: 11/161- **RPR 141+h**

Starts		1st	2nd	3rd	4th	Win & Pl
4		3	-	-	-	£14,444
	4/17	Ayr	2m4¹/₂f Cls3 Nov Hdl gd-sft			£6,498
	12/16	Extr	2m7f Cls4 Mdn Hdl soft			£3,249
	3/16	Cork	2m3f NHF 5-7yo heavy			£4,296

Exciting chasing prospect who won his sole point-to-point and bumper before adding two wins out of three over hurdles; found to be wrong when well beaten in a Grade 2 at Doncaster and got back on track at Ayr in April; should be better over 3m.

God's Own (Ire)

9 b g Oscar - Dantes Term (Phardante)

Tom George				Crossed Fingers Partnership

PLACINGS: 17322F/3241/1233553- **RPR 170c**

Starts		1st	2nd	3rd	4th	Win & Pl
29		7	7	7	2	£483,912
	4/16	Punc	2m Gd1 Ch gd-yld			£86,765
	4/16	Aint	2m4f Cls1 Ch gd-sft			£112,788
155	11/14	Extr	2m1¹/₂f Cls1 Gd2 152-172 Ch Hcap gd-sft			£35,594
	5/14	Punc	2m Nov Gd1 Ch yield			£56,833
129	11/13	Kemp	2m5f Cls2 129-155 Hdl Hcap gd-sft			£11,574
	2/13	Muss	2m3¹/₂f Cls4 Nov Hdl good			£3,899
	11/12	Donc	2m¹/₂f Cls4 Nov Hdl soft			£3,899

Failed to win last season having signed off the previous campaign with Grade 1 victories at Aintree and Punchestown; still ran a string of good races, including when third back at Punchestown and in the Tingle Creek; best on good ground.

Gold Present (Ire)

7 br g Presenting - Ouro Preto (Definite Article)

Nicky Henderson				Mr & Mrs J D Cotton

PLACINGS: 2211/P60/1522F- **RPR 147+c**

Starts		1st	2nd	3rd	4th	Win & Pl
12		3	4	-	-	£44,517
130	11/16	Donc	2m3f Cls3 Nov 120-134 Ch Hcap gd-sft			£12,512
	4/15	MRas	2m2¹/₂f Cls4 Nov Hdl good			£3,899
	3/15	Strf	2m2¹/₂f Cls4 Mdn Hdl gd-sft			£3,249

Lost his way over hurdles two seasons ago but got back on track when switched to fences last term; ran a huge race when second in the novice handicap at the Cheltenham Festival and going well when falling in the Topham; has the scope to improve again.

Golden Birthday (Fr)

6 b g Poliglote - Gold Or Silver (Glint Of Gold)

Harry Fry				G C Stevens

PLACINGS: 233/1261430-1311 **RPR 141+h**

Starts		1st	2nd	3rd	4th	Win & Pl
14		5	2	4	1	£48,202
132	9/17	NAbb	2m5¹/₂f Cls2 123-149 Hdl Hcap good			£22,522
126	7/17	NAbb	2m2¹/₂f Cls3 113-135 Hdl Hcap gd-sft			£6,823
122	5/17	Wwck	2m3f Cls3 122-131 Hdl Hcap good			£6,498
	1/17	Plum	2m Cls4 Nov Hdl soft			£3,899
	5/16	Winc	1m7¹/₂f Cls6 NHF 4-6yo gd-fm			£1,625

Sharply progressive hurdler who went from strength to strength this summer, gaining his third win out of four by ten lengths off 132 at

Newton Abbot having kicked off his winning run from a mark of 122; has won on soft ground but trainer feels he's better on good.

Goodtoknow

9 b g Presenting - Atlantic Jane (Tamure)

Kerry Lee			Burling, Daresbury, Macechern, Nolan & Potter

PLACINGS: F222P7/2P11P/8521P0-   **RPR 150+c**

Starts		1st	2nd	3rd	4th	Win & Pl
31		5	7	3	1	£59,601
137	2/17	Hrfd	3m1f Cls3 124-140 Ch Hcap heavy			£13,051
136	3/16	Tntn	3m4¹/₂f Cls3 125-138 Ch Hcap gd-sft			£8,229
122	2/16	Weth	3m Cls3 110-130 Ch Hcap heavy			£6,498
111	12/13	Bang	3m Cls4 103-125 Ch Hcap heavy			£3,769
	12/12	Towc	2m Cls5 Mdn Hdl heavy			£1,689

Has gained four of his five wins on heavy ground and thrived in testing conditions last winter, winning well at Hereford having chased home Grand National hero One For Arthur at Warwick; could land a big staying prize when the mud is flying.

Great Field (Fr)

6 b g Great Pretender - Eaton Lass (Definite Article)

Willie Mullins (Ir)			John P McManus

PLACINGS: 2/11/1P/1111-   **RPR 160+c**

Starts		1st	2nd	3rd	4th	Win & Pl
9		7	1	-	-	£121,791
	4/17	Punc	2m Nov Gd1 Ch gd-yld			£57,991
	3/17	Thur	2m2f Nov List Ch yld-sft			£15,769
	3/17	Leop	2m1f Nov Ch sft-hvy			£11,038
	1/17	Gowr	2m Ch soft			£7,096
	2/16	Leop	2m2f Hdl soft			£9,496
	11/14	Pari	2m1f Hdl 3yo gd-sft			£8,400
	9/14	Pari	2m1f Hdl 3yo gd-sft			£8,000

Has won five out of his six starts since joining Willie Mullins from France and looked particularly exciting when landing all four outings over fences last season, including a Grade 1 at Punchestown; yet to be seriously tested and could be anything.

Gwencily Berbas (Fr)

6 b g Nickname - Lesorial (Lesotho)

Alan Fleming			Barry Connell

PLACINGS: R3119/136/426-21   **RPR 137+c**

Starts		1st	2nd	3rd	4th	Win & Pl
13		4	2	2	1	£80,318
	6/17	Rosc	3m1f Ch yld-sft			£6,318
	11/15	Naas	2m gd3 Hdl 4yo soft			£16,376
	2/15	Fair	2m gd2 Hdl 4yo soft			£21,163
	10/14	Autl	2m1¹/₂f Hdl 3yo heavy			£19,200

Talented hurdler (finished third in the 2015 Hatton's Grace) who needed time over fences last season but got off the mark at Roscommon in June when stepped up to 3m1f; had been very patiently handled over hurdles and may reward the patience of his connections as a staying chaser.

Hammersly Lake (Fr)

9 b g Kapgarde - Loin De Moi (Loup Solitaire)

Charlie Longsdon			Robert Aplin

PLACINGS: 206/62F/315233P1-122   **RPR 156c**

Starts		1st	2nd	3rd	4th	Win & Pl
25		4	6	7	4	£124,813
138	5/17	Hayd	2m5¹/₂f Cls2 123-139 Ch Hcap good			£18,768
	4/17	Hntg	2m¹/₂f Cls4 Nov Ch good			£3,899
	8/16	MRas	2m3f Cls4 Nov Ch good			£3,899
	4/11	Autl	1m7f Hdl 3yo v soft			£23,172

Took a long time to find his form over fences last season but flourished on better ground, getting off the mark in the final week of the campaign and soon following up; unsuited by the drop in trip when second next time on first run for new yard.

Haymount (Ire)

8 ch g Presenting - Ali's Dipper (Orchestra)

Willie Mullins (Ir)			Mrs C M Hurley

PLACINGS: 1/222314/5124337-P   **RPR 149c**

Starts		1st	2nd	3rd	4th	Win & Pl
15		3	4	3	2	£47,835
	11/16	Punc	2m4f Ch soft			£5,879
	3/16	Gowr	2m Mdn Hdl soft			£5,426
	4/15	Tipp	2m4f NHF 5-7yo good			£4,814

Unable to build on chase debut victory last season but did better when stepped well up in trip, finishing strongly to take third in the National Hunt Chase at Cheltenham; one for marathon handicap chases on that evidence, although finished only seventh when 7-1 for the Irish National.

Henllan Harri (Ire)

9 br g King's Theatre - Told You So (Glacial Storm)

Peter Bowen			Einsley Harries

PLACINGS: 212P0/PP0553251231-4   **RPR 134c**

Starts		1st	2nd	3rd	4th	Win & Pl
29		7	6	5	1	£131,290
126	4/17	Sand	3m5f Cls1 Gd3 126-152 Ch Hcap good			£84,405
118	3/17	Ffos	2m5f Cls4 95-120 Ch Hcap heavy			£5,198
	8/15	NAbb	3m2f Cls3 Nov Ch gd-sft			£6,657
125	5/15	Uttx	2m4f Cls3 108-131 Hdl Hcap good			£5,444
	6/14	Ffos	2m6f Cls4 Nov Hdl gd-sft			£3,119
	5/14	Ffos	2m4f Cls4 Nov Hdl gd-sft			£3,249
	7/13	Prth	2m¹/₂f Cls6 NHF 4-6yo gd-fm			£2,053

Has improved with practice over fences and pulled off a major upset when winning last season's bet365 Gold Cup; went up just 4lb for that success and ran better than bare form when fourth in the Summer Cup (best of those ridden prominently).

'He looked exciting when landing all four outings over fences and could be anything'

Henryville

9 b g Generous - Aquavita (Kalaglow)

Harry Fry		R P B Michaelson & E M Thornton		
PLACINGS: 121/48B4P3981-1305U0			RPR **158c**	

Starts	1st	2nd	3rd	4th	Win & Pl
35	8	7	3	4	£139,764

147	5/17	NAbb	2m5f Cls2 128-147 Ch Hcap good	£13,826
140	4/17	Chel	2m5f Cls1 Gd2 138-158 Ch Hcap good	£28,475
	3/16	Extr	2m3f Cls3 Nov Ch good	£6,498
	10/15	Font	2m5f Cls4 Nov Ch good	£6,725
138	10/14	Font	2m3f Cls2 119-138 Hdl Hcap good	£9,812
130	8/14	NAbb	2m5¹/₂f Cls2 121-147 Hdl Hcap good	£22,378
118	3/14	Font	2m3f Cls4 101-120 Hdl Hcap gd-sft	£3,119
	3/13	Plum	2m4¹/₂f Cls4 Nov Hdl gd-sft	£4,874

Rated 156 over hurdles after a fine fourth under a big weight in the 2015 Pertemps Final but slow to reach a similar level over fences; finally took a big step forward with wins at Cheltenham and Newton Abbot in the spring; best on good ground.

Houblon Des Obeaux (Fr)

10 b g Panoramic - Harkosa (Nikos)

Venetia Williams		Mrs Julian Blackwell		
PLACINGS: /2220F/99841P/34840-			RPR **150c**	

Starts	1st	2nd	3rd	4th	Win & Pl
50	8	8	3	7	£324,557

	2/16	Newb	2m7¹/₂f Cls1 Gd2 Ch soft	£28,978
152	12/13	Asct	3m Cls1 List 132-152 Ch Hcap soft	£24,525
144	11/13	Asct	3m Cls1 Gd3 133-153 Ch Hcap gd-sft	£56,270
	11/12	Winc	2m5f Cls1 Nov Gd2 Ch gd-sft	£14,238
	10/12	Worc	2m7f Cls4 Nov Ch gd-sft	£3,054
135	1/12	Chel	3m Cls2 134-160 Hdl Hcap gd-sft	£12,512
	2/11	Hayd	2m Cls2 Hdl 4yo heavy	£6,895
	5/10	Seno	1m7f Hdl 3yo good	£5,522

Obliterated his handicap mark with a runaway win in the 2016 Denman Chase but slipped a long way down the weights last season despite

Irish Cavalier (grey): last season's talented Charlie Hall winner is a potent force when conditions are in his favour

several good runs, including when third in the Welsh National; has a much more realistic chance in similar races now.

Housesofparliament (Ire)

4 ch g Galileo - Sharp Lisa (Dixieland Band)

Joseph O'Brien (Ir)		John P McManus		
PLACINGS: 27-1			RPR **127+h**	

Starts	1st	2nd	3rd	4th	Win & Pl
3	1	1	-	-	£15,096

	8/17	Gway	2m1¹/₂f Nov Hdl good	£13,141

High-class Flat stayer (third in the 2016 St Leger) who was reportedly slow to adapt when sent hurdling last season, not helped by a cut knee in the Grade 1 Spring Juvenile Hurdle; got off the mark over hurdles at Galway and could yet be a smart novice.

Ibis Du Rheu (Fr)

6 b g Blue Bresil - Dona Du Rheu (Dom Pasquini)

Paul Nicholls		J Hales		
PLACINGS: 21/64/23518/323P-			RPR **150c**	

Starts	1st	2nd	3rd	4th	Win & Pl
13	2	3	3	1	£84,864

139	3/16	Chel	2m4¹/₂f Cls2 135-142 Cond Hdl Hcap good	£37,536
	4/14	Engh	2m¹/₂f Hdl 3yo v soft	£19,200

Without a win since the 2016 Martin Pipe Hurdle but ran promisingly in a couple of novice handicap chases last season; found the Cheltenham Festival too hot when expected to improve for stepping up to 3m1f but worth another chance after only four runs over fences.

Identity Thief (Ire)

7 b g Kayf Tara - Miss Arteea (Flemensfirth)

Henry de Bromhead (Ir)   Gigginstown House Stud

PLACINGS: 11P2/31126/211PU460-   RPR **146+c**

Starts	1st	2nd	3rd	4th	Win & Pl
17	6	3	1	1	£182,649

11/16	Punc	2m Nov Gd2 Ch soft	£19,305
10/16	Punc	2m Ch yield	£5,879
11/15	Newc	2m¹/₂f Cls1 Gd1 Hdl soft	£63,585
10/15	DRoy	2m Gd2 Hdl yld-sft	£23,256
12/14	Leop	2m4f Mdn Hdl 4yo soft	£6,325
11/14	Fair	2m NHF 4yo yield	£4,600

Hugely talented horse who won the Fighting Fifth in 2015 but had a miserable campaign last season; seemed unlucky initially (went lame and then unseated rider early in two runs after victory on chase debut) but failed to sparkle even when sent back over hurdles.

Impulsive Star (Ire)

7 b g Busy Flight - Impulsive Ita (Supreme Leader)

Neil Mulholland   Robert Waley-Cohen

PLACINGS: 11/14110-   RPR **137+h**

Starts	1st	2nd	3rd	4th	Win & Pl
6	4	-	-	1	£24,192

2/17	Extr	2m7f Cls2 122-147 Hdl Hcap soft	£11,574
1/17	Catt	3m1¹/₂f Cls4 Nov Hdl good	£3,249
11/16	Ffos	2m4f Cls5 Mdn Hdl soft	£3,249
3/16	Cork	2m3f NHF 5-6yo heavy	£4,522

Won three out of five over hurdles last season, although tailed off when sent off favourite for the Pertemps Final at Cheltenham; imposing type who won his sole point-to-point by 15 lengths and should make a fine staying chaser.

Invitation Only (Ire)

6 b g Flemensfirth - Norabelle (Alamo Bay)

Willie Mullins (Ir)   Andrea & Graham Wylie

PLACINGS: 1/1/1136-   RPR **141h**

Starts	1st	2nd	3rd	4th	Win & Pl
5	3		1	-	£19,681

11/16	Gowr	2m Mdn Hdl gd-yld	£5,426
4/16	Punc	2m NHF 4-7yo yield	£6,783
3/16	Navn	2m NHF 5-7yo sft-hvy	£4,296

Looked a hugely exciting prospect when winning on his hurdling debut last season to follow two bumper victories but bitterly disappointing when twice beaten at short odds subsequently; no surprise to see him bounce back.

Irish Cavalier (Ire)

8 gr g Aussie Rules - Tracker (Bustino)

Rebecca Curtis   A McIver

PLACINGS: 42155P5F/151P35P03-P   RPR **164c**

Starts	1st	2nd	3rd	4th	Win & Pl
30	8	2	4	2	£233,937

10/16	Weth	3m Cls1 Gd2 Ch good	£56,950
4/16	Punc	2m4f 125-153 Ch Hcap gd-yld	£43,382
10/15	NAbb	2m5f Cls2 Ch gd-sft	£18,838
3/15	Chel	2m4¹/₂f Cls1 Nov List 134-140 Ch Hcap gd-sft	£34,170
3/14	Bang	2m¹/₂f Cls4 Nov Hdl gd-sft	£3,249
10/13	Bang	2m¹/₂f Cls4 Nov Hdl soft	£3,249
10/13	Strf	2m¹/₂f Cls3 Nov Hdl 4-6yo soft	£6,330
5/13	Worc	2m Cls6 NHF 4-6yo good	£1,560

High-class staying chaser on good ground and won last season's Charlie Hall Chase at 16-1 with conditions in his favour; has also come first and third in the same Punchestown Festival handicap for last two seasons having seen mark fall due to form on softer.

Irish Saint (Fr)

8 b/br g Saint Des Saints - Minirose (Mansonnien)

Paul Nicholls   Mrs Johnny De La Hey

PLACINGS: /F0136/1312143/5639-   RPR **149c**

Starts	1st	2nd	3rd	4th	Win & Pl
21	7	2	5	1	£191,334

2/15	Kemp	2m4¹/₂f Cls1 Nov Gd2 Ch soft	£18,224
12/14	Asct	2m5f Cls2 Ch gd-sft	£15,784
11/14	Sand	1m7¹/₂f Cls2 Nov Ch gd-sft	£12,904
1/14	Asct	2m3¹/₂f Cls1 Gd2 125-145 Hdl Hcap heavy	£22,780
2/13	Kemp	2m Cls1 Gd2 Hdl 4yo good	£15,661
12/12	Kemp	2m Cls3 Hdl 3yo heavy	£5,848
9/12	Autl	2m2f List Hdl 3yo v soft	£26,000

Back from long-term injury last season and failed to match strong novice form, although shaped with enough promise to be sent off favourite for the BetBright Chase on final start; has slipped in handicap and may do better dropped back in trip.

Irving

9 b g Singspiel - Indigo Girl (Sternkoenig)

Paul Nicholls				Axom XLIX
PLACINGS: 119/F1P2P/1164/1F36-				RPR **158h**

Starts		1st	2nd	3rd	4th	Win & Pl
18		8	1	1	1	£286,962
	11/16	Newc	2m¹/₂f Cls1 Gd1 Hdl soft			£67,843
	11/15	Hayd	2m Cls2 Hdl soft			£61,900
154	11/15	Winc	1m7¹/₂f Cls1 Gd2 134-154 Hdl Hcap soft			£34,170
	11/14	Newc	2m¹/₂f Cls1 Gd1 Hdl soft			£56,270
	2/14	Kemp	2m Cls1 Nov Gd2 Hdl soft			£15,661
	12/13	Asct	1m7¹/₂f Cls1 Nov Gd2 Hdl soft			£17,387
	11/13	Asct	1m7¹/₂f Cls3 Hdl gd-sft			£6,882
	11/13	Tntn	2m¹/₂f Cls3 Nov Hdl good			£5,848

Has a remarkable record during November, achieving his last four wins during that month including a high-class performance to beat Apple's Jade for his second Fighting Fifth Hurdle last term; has always struggled to maintain that form through the season.

Its'afreebee (Ire)

7 b g Danroad - Aphra Benn (In The Wings)

Dan Skelton				Rebel Jumping
PLACINGS: 3/543121113/15133P7-				RPR **146+c**

Starts		1st	2nd	3rd	4th	Win & Pl
15		6	1	4	1	£63,882
	12/16	Weth	2m3¹/₂f Cls3 Nov Ch gd-sft			£6,410
	10/16	Fknm	2m5f Cls3 Nov Ch good			£7,798
	1/16	Hayd	1m7¹/₂f Cls1 Nov Gd2 Hdl heavy			£17,085
	12/15	Hayd	2m3f Cls4 Nov Hdl 4-7yo heavy			£3,899
	11/15	Bang	2m¹/₂f Cls4 Nov Hdl soft			£3,249
	8/15	Bell	2m1f NHF 4-7yo yld-sft			£5,081

Third behind Yorkhill and Yanworth in the 2016 Neptune Hurdle but disappointing since; lost his way over fences last season after a promising start, although still sent off just 11-1 for the novice handicap at the Cheltenham Festival (pulled up) and on an enticing mark.

Irving: does particularly well during the first part of the season and not hard to see him winning a decent race or two again this autumn

Ivanovich Gorbatov (Ire)

5 b g Montjeu - Northern Gulch (Gulch)

Joseph O'Brien (Ir)				John P McManus
PLACINGS: 1412/3334336-				RPR **153h**

Starts		1st	2nd	3rd	4th	Win & Pl
11		2	1	5	2	£132,620
	3/16	Chel	2m1f Cls1 Gd1 Hdl 4yo good			£68,340
	12/15	Leop	2m Mdn Hdl 3yo heavy			£7,488

Won the Triumph Hurdle in 2016 but came up short in open Grade 1 company last season; produced his best effort back at Cheltenham when a three-length sixth in the County Hurdle; both those runs on good ground and much less effective on softer.

Javert (Ire)

8 b g Kayf Tara - Royalrova (Garde Royale)

Emma Lavelle				Axom LII
PLACINGS: 4/455/1U1U/1-				RPR **153c**

Starts		1st	2nd	3rd	4th	Win & Pl
8		3	-	-	1	£32,239
139	5/16	Hayd	2m5¹/₂f Cls2 127-148 Ch Hcap good			£18,838
130	12/15	Donc	2m3f Cls3 121-137 Ch Hcap soft			£6,498
121	11/15	Chep	2m Cls3 Nov 106-124 Ch Hcap soft			£6,498

Made it three wins in three completed chases when scoring at Haydock in May 2016, although he had been well beaten when unseating his rider in the novice handicap at that year's Cheltenham Festival; back from injury and unexposed.

Jenkins (Ire)
5 b g Azamour - Aladiyna (Indian Danehill)

Nicky Henderson   Pump & Plant Services

PLACINGS: 1/2141-   RPR **131h**

Starts	1st	2nd	3rd	4th	Win & Pl
5	3	1	-	1	£26,888
	4/17	Ffos	2m Cls4 Nov Hdl good		£3,899
	11/16	Newb	2m¹/₂f Cls3 Mdn Hdl soft		£6,498
	4/16	Newb	2m¹/₂f Cls6 NHF 4-6yo soft		£1,689

Looked a potential star when winning on his bumper debut in April 2016 and sent off at odds-on for every run since with mixed results; at least managed to win a couple of novice hurdles last term and has scope with a handicap mark of 137 given his early promise.

Jer's Girl (Ire)
5 b m Jeremy - African Scene (Scenic)

Gavin Cromwell   John P McManus

PLACINGS: 11251/125F-   RPR **141h**

Starts	1st	2nd	3rd	4th	Win & Pl
9	4	2	-	-	£125,497
	4/16	Punc	2m4f Nov Gd1 Hdl yield		£43,382
	3/16	Fair	2m4f Nov Gd1 Hdl yield		£43,382
	12/15	Aint	2m1f Cls1 List Hdl 3yo soft		£12,529
	11/15	Limk	2m Mdn Hdl 3yo soft		£5,349

Won two Grade 1 races as a novice hurdler two seasons ago but had her limitations exposed in top 2m hurdles last term; could still be a force back in mares' races and was going well when falling three out in the Mares' Hurdle at Cheltenham.

Jerrysback (Ire)
5 b g Jeremy - Get A Few Bob Back (Bob Back)

Philip Hobbs   John P McManus

PLACINGS: 42/F111-   RPR **129+h**

Starts	1st	2nd	3rd	4th	Win & Pl
2	2	-	-	-	£6,822
	2/17	Weth	2m3¹/₂f Cls4 Nov Hdl gd-sft		£3,574
	1/17	Plum	2m4¹/₂f Cls4 Nov Hdl heavy		£3,249

Bought off the Irish point-to-point circuit last season and went on to win both novice hurdles at Plumpton and Wetherby on contrasting ground; likely to go straight over fences and looks a fine prospect for staying novice chases.

'Beautifully bred horse finally showed his true colours when winning the Swinton and the Summer Hurdle; could be top-class on good ground'

Jezki (Ire)
9 b g Milan - La Noire (Phardante)

Jessica Harrington (Ir)   John P McManus

PLACINGS: 11241/122341/1/1285-   RPR **152+h**

Starts	1st	2nd	3rd	4th	Win & Pl
25	14	4	2	2	£875,284
	1/17	Navn	2m Hdl yld-sft		£11,038
	4/15	Punc	3m Gd1 Hdl yield		£93,023
	4/15	Aint	2m4f Cls1 Gd1 Hdl gd-sft		£113,072
	5/14	Punc	2m Gd1 Hdl gd-yld		£100,000
	3/14	Chel	2m¹/₂f Cls1 Gd1 Hdl gd-sft		£238,051
	12/13	Fair	2m4f Gd1 Hdl gd-yld		£42,276
	11/13	DRoy	2m Gd2 Hdl gd-yld		£26,423
	4/13	Leop	2m Nov Gd1 Hdl soft		£43,333
	12/12	Leop	2m Nov Gd1 Hdl soft		£40,625
	12/12	Fair	2m Nov Gd1 Hdl soft		£40,625
	11/12	Naas	2m Gd3 Hdl 4yo sft-hvy		£14,896
	10/12	Naas	2m Mdn Hdl 4yo soft		£5,750
	3/12	Leop	2m NHF 4yo good		£5,750
	1/12	Leop	2m NHF 4yo yield		£4,600

Won the Champion Hurdle in 2014 and proved equally good over 3m when winning a Grade 1 at Punchestown the following year; won on his return from a long injury layoff last season but disappointing subsequently, including in the Stayers' Hurdle.

John Constable (Ire)
6 b g Montjeu - Dance Parade (Gone West)

Evan Williams   Walters Plant Hire

PLACINGS: 11/206/47600F-11   RPR **156+h**

Starts		1st	2nd	3rd	4th	Win & Pl
13		4	1	-	1	£75,458
150	7/17	MRas	2m¹/₂f Cls1 List 124-150 Hdl Hcap good		£19,933
134	5/17	Hayd	1m7¹/₂f Cls1 Gd3 130-144 Hdl Hcap good		£34,170
	4/15	Hntg	2m Cls4 Nov Hdl gd-sft		£3,249
	1/15	Ludl	2m Cls5 Mdn Hdl 4yo soft		£2,599

Beautifully bred horse who suffered initially over hurdles from remaining an entire; finally showed his true colours when winning the Swinton and Summer Hurdle, soaring up the handicap from 134 to 156; could be top-class on good ground.

Josses Hill (Ire)
9 b g Winged Love - Credora Storm (Glacial Storm)

Nicky Henderson   A D Spence

PLACINGS: 21/21234/F18/115573-   RPR **165+c**

Starts		1st	2nd	3rd	4th	Win & Pl
20		7	5	2	1	£192,176
	12/16	Hntg	2m4f Cls1 Gd2 Ch gd-sft		£37,018
	11/16	Kemp	2m4¹/₂f Cls2 Ch good		£12,512
	2/16	Kemp	2m4¹/₂f Cls2 Ch soft		£12,996
	1/15	Donc	2m¹/₂f Cls4 Nov Ch good		£3,899
	4/14	Aint	2m¹/₂f Cls1 Nov Gd2 Hdl gd-sft		£34,170
	12/13	Newb	2m¹/₂f Cls4 Mdn Hdl soft		£3,899
	11/13	Asct	1m7¹/₂f Cls5 NHF 4-6yo gd-sft		£2,283

Slow to find his feet over fences and still very inconsistent last season, although he won the Peterborough Chase convincingly at Huntingdon; possible he needs a right-handed track and no further than around 2m4f.

Jury Duty (Ire)

6 b g Well Chosen - Swan Heart (Broken Hearted)

Gordon Elliott (Ir)					Sideways Syndicate
PLACINGS: 63/334413/21236-					RPR **150h**

Starts	1st	2nd	3rd	4th	Win & Pl
11	2	2	4	2	£54,245
126	11/16	Navn	2m6½f 118-146 Hdl Hcap yld-sft		£21,691
111	2/16	Navn	2m4f 88-116 Hdl Hcap sft-hvy		£5,426

Progressive staying hurdler who won a couple of handicaps at Navan in 2016 and was then third in the Pertemps Final after a good prep run at Chepstow (had a midwinter break); only sixth when stepped up to Grade 1 level at Punchestown.

Karalee (Fr)

6 gr m Martaline - Change Partner (Turtle Island)

Willie Mullins (Ir)					Mrs S Ricci
PLACINGS: 2/1/13-					RPR **140h**

Starts	1st	2nd	3rd	4th	Win & Pl
4	2	1	1	-	£25,606
	3/17	Limk	2m3f Hdl soft		£7,897
	5/15	Klny	2m1f Mdn Hdl 4yo gd-yld		£5,616

Missed more than two years through injury after winning her maiden hurdle but returned with another easy win at Limerick in March; fair third when stepped up to Grade 1 level at Punchestown, albeit no match for Apple's Jade; could go novice chasing.

Keeper Hill (Ire)

6 b g Westerner - You Take Care (Definite Article)

Warren Greatrex					McNeill Family
PLACINGS: 13/211176-					RPR **142+h**

Starts	1st	2nd	3rd	4th	Win & Pl
8	4	1	1	1	£28,290
	2/17	Hntg	2m3½f Cls1 Nov List Hdl gd-sft		£17,085
	1/17	Hrfd	2m3½f Cls4 Nov Hdl soft		£3,379
	11/16	Bang	2m3½f Cls4 Nov Hdl soft		£3,899
	11/15	MRas	2m1½f Cls6 NHF 4-6yo gd-sft		£1,643

Smart novice hurdler who won three times last season and ran better than bare form in two runs at Grade 1 level; stayed on into seventh in the Neptune after losing his place with a blunder five out and didn't quite get home when stepped up to 3m at Aintree.

Kilcrea Vale (Ire)

7 b g Beneficial - Inflation (Port Etienne)

Nicky Henderson					A D Spence
PLACINGS: 11/F69/12158-2					RPR **150+c**

Starts	1st	2nd	3rd	4th	Win & Pl
10	3	2	-	-	£41,713
	2/17	Font	2m1½f Cls2 Nov Ch soft		£12,660
	12/16	Ludl	2m4f Cls3 Nov Ch gd-sft		£11,650
	1/15	MRas	2m2½f Cls4 Nov Hdl gd-sft		£3,249

Won novice chases at Ludlow and Fontwell last season and far from disgraced when fifth in the JLT at Cheltenham; good second in a handicap chase at Haydock in May confirmed his level but could find more when stepped up to 3m.

King's Odyssey (Ire)

8 b g King's Theatre - Ma Furie (Balleroy)

Evan Williams					Mr & Mrs William Rucker
PLACINGS: 2/2421/311/3F30-					RPR **133c**

Starts	1st	2nd	3rd	4th	Win & Pl
12	3	3	3	1	£32,872
139	1/16	Chel	2m5f Cls2 Nov 126-152 Ch Hcap heavy		£15,640
	12/15	Winc	2m4f Cls3 Nov Ch soft		£6,657
	3/15	Wwck	2m5f Cls4 Mdn Hdl heavy		£3,249

Smart novice two seasons ago but disappointing last term, twice in small fields and again on ground too quick (two wins on heavy); going well when falling six out in bid for a second big Cheltenham handicap and worth another chance granted optimum conditions.

Knockgraffon (Ire)

7 b g Flemensfirth - Gleaming Spire (Overbury)

Dan Skelton					Mrs Barbara Hester
PLACINGS: 32/21271/3125-					RPR **153c**

Starts	1st	2nd	3rd	4th	Win & Pl
11	3	4	2	1	£30,541
132	11/16	Newb	2m1½f Cls3 Nov 121-140 Ch Hcap gd-sft		£12,512
	3/16	NAbb	2m2½f Cls4 Nov Hdl gd-sft		£4,549
	11/15	Leic	2m4½f Cls4 Nov Hdl gd-sft		£5,198

Missed the end of last season after a below-par run at Warwick but had already proved himself a very useful novice chaser in two 2m novice handicaps at Newbury, including when just beaten off a mark of 144; has also won over 2m4½f as a hurdler.

Kotkikova (Fr)

6 gr m Martaline - Kotkita (Subotica)

Nicky Henderson   John P McManus

PLACINGS: 11213111/111F1/150-   RPR **144h**

Starts		1st	2nd	3rd	4th	Win & Pl
16		11	1	1	-	£544,970
	4/16	Autl	2m2f Hdl v soft			£16,941
	4/16	Autl	2m2f Hdl 5yo v soft			£18,353
	6/15	Autl	2m5¹/₂f Gd3 Ch 4yo soft			£54,070
	5/15	Autl	2m5¹/₂f Gd1 Ch 4yo v soft			£122,093
	4/15	Autl	2m5¹/₂f Gd2 Ch 4yo v soft			£76,744
	3/15	Autl	2m5¹/₂f Gd3 Ch 4yo heavy			£54,070
	11/14	Engh	2m1f List Ch 3yo heavy			£34,000
	11/14	Engh	2m1f Ch 3yo heavy			£22,000
	10/14	Autl	2m2f List Hdl 3yo heavy			£34,000
	6/14	Autl	2m1¹/₂f List Hdl 3yo soft			£46,000
	6/14	Autl	1m7f Hdl 3yo heavy			£19,200

Exciting mare who won multiple races over hurdles and fences in France up to Grade 1 level before being bought for big money; earned rave home reviews last season but twice disappointing on the track before picking up an injury.

L'Ami Serge (Ire)

7 b g King's Theatre - La Zingarella (Phardante)

Nicky Henderson   Simon Munir & Isaac Souede

PLACINGS: 114/11232/2233251-21   RPR **156h**

Starts		1st	2nd	3rd	4th	Win & Pl
24		7	9	5	1	£438,991
	6/17	Autl	3m1¹/₂f Gd1 Hdl v soft			£142,308
	4/17	Sand	2m5¹/₂f Cls1 Gd2 Hdl good			£28,475
	1/16	Weth	2m3¹/₂f Cls4 Nov Ch heavy			£3,899
	1/16	Plum	2m1f Cls3 Nov Ch heavy			£6,498
	1/15	Sand	2m Cls1 Nov Gd1 Hdl soft			£23,491
	12/14	Asct	1m7¹/₂f Cls1 Nov Gd2 Hdl soft			£18,690
132	11/14	Newb	2m7¹/₂f Cls1 List 129-149 Hdl Hcap soft			£22,780

Hugely frustrating at times but underlined vast

talent when winning the French Champion Hurdle in June, coping well with step up to 3m1½f; had also won a Grade 2 at Sandown but threw away other golden opportunities with weak finishes.

La Bague Au Roi (Fr)

6 b m Doctor Dino - Alliance Royale (Turgeon)

Warren Greatrex   Mrs Julien Turner & Andrew Merriam

PLACINGS: 1/117/111761-   RPR **140+h**

Starts		1st	2nd	3rd	4th	Win & Pl
10		7	-	-	-	£42,791
	4/17	Hntg	2m4¹/₂f Cls4 Nov Hdl good			£3,899
	11/16	Newb	2m¹/₂f Cls1 Nov List Hdl gd-sft			£13,968
	11/16	Weth	2m Cls4 Nov Hdl gd-sft			£3,574
	10/16	Uttx	2m Cls4 Mdn Hdl good			£3,379
	12/15	Hntg	2m Cls1 List NHF 4-6yo gd-sft			£11,390
	10/15	Aint	2m1f Cls4 NHF 4-6yo good			£3,249
	4/15	NAbb	2m1f Cls6 NHF 4-6yo good			£1,711

Prolific mare who has won seven of her ten races under rules, including four out of six over hurdles last season, but no better than sixth in three runs at Graded level; has the physique for fences and could do well in mares' chases.

Lalor: surprise Aintree bumper winner has won three of his four starts

Label Des Obeaux (Fr)
6 b g Saddler Maker - La Bessiere (Loup Solitaire)

Alan King | David Sewell & Terry Warner

PLACINGS: F232/321320/2321101- **RPR 156c**

Starts	1st	2nd	3rd	4th	Win & Pl
18	4	6	4	-	£86,670

148	4/17	Ayr	3m¹/₂f Cls2 Nov 126-148 Ch Hcap good	£16,245
141	2/17	Extr	3m Cls3 Nov 119-141 Ch Hcap gd-sft	£9,495
	2/17	Ludl	3m Cls4 Nov Ch soft	£4,660
	12/15	Sand	2m4f Cls1 Nov Gd2 Hdl soft	£17,085

Got better with every run when sent novice chasing last season apart from a blip when well beaten at the Cheltenham Festival; back on track at Ayr next time when gaining third win in four starts and trainer feels he may be better again on a right-handed track.

Lalor (Ger)
5 b g It's Gino - Laviola (Waky Nao)

Richard Woollacott | D G Staddon

PLACINGS: 1211- **RPR 129+b**

Starts	1st	2nd	3rd	4th	Win & Pl
4	3	1	-	-	£29,467

	4/17	Aint	2m1f Cls1 Gd2 NHF 4-6yo good	£25,322
	3/17	Winc	1m7¹/₂f Cls6 Mdn NHF 4-6yo heavy	£1,949
	12/16	Winc	1m7¹/₂f Cls6 NHF 4-6yo soft	£1,625

Pulled off a 33-1 upset in the Grade 2 bumper at Aintree's Grand National meeting, showing much-improved form on better ground; had won on heavy at Wincanton, albeit in a maiden bumper (had finished second on debut before being awarded race later).

Landofhopeandglory (Ire)
4 b g High Chaparral - Wurfklinge (Acatenango)

Joseph O'Brien (Ir) | John P McManus

PLACINGS: 1112352-41F **RPR 143+h**

Starts	1st	2nd	3rd	4th	Win & Pl
10	4	2	1	1	£62,765

	6/17	Kbgn	2m4f Nov Ch soft	£7,897
	12/16	Fair	Cls3 Hdl 3yo gd-yld	£14,697
	11/16	Punc	2m Hdl 3yo soft	£6,783
	11/16	Fair	2m Mdn Hdl 3yo good	£4,522

Not far off the best juvenile hurdlers last season, finishing fifth in the Triumph Hurdle and second in a Grade 1 at Punchestown after sole flop on heavy ground (has won twice on soft but prefers quicker); solid start over fences this summer despite falling at Galway.

Last Goodbye (Ire)
6 b g Millenary - Welsh Ana (Welsh Term)

Elizabeth Doyle (Ir) | Last Goodbye Syndicate

PLACINGS: 81111/026157- **RPR 146+c**

Starts	1st	2nd	3rd	4th	Win & Pl
11	5	1	-	-	£42,137

	12/16	DRoy	2m4f Ch soft	£6,331
130	3/16	Cork	2m3f 107-131 Hdl Hcap heavy	£13,566
	1/16	Navn	2m4f Nov Hdl sft-hvy	£8,118
	10/15	Wxfd	2m Mdn Hdl 4yo soft	£5,616
	9/15	Rosc	2m NHF 4yo good	£4,814

Off the mark at the third attempt over fences last season and ran a stormer in the novice handicap at the Cheltenham Festival, finishing an eight-length fifth despite being very unlucky in running; jumping fell apart at Punchestown next time.

Le Breuil (Fr)
5 ch g Anzillero - Slew Dancer (Fabulous Dancer)

Ben Pauling | Miss Emma Collins

PLACINGS: 1411P- **RPR 140+h**

Starts	1st	2nd	3rd	4th	Win & Pl
5	3	-	-	1	£10,215

	3/17	Newb	2m4¹/₂f Cls4 Nov Hdl soft	£4,549
	11/16	Sedg	2m4f Cls4 Nov Hdl gd-sft	£3,899
	5/16	Wwck	2m Cls6 NHF 4-6yo gd-sft	£1,625

Missed much of last season but won his first two novice hurdles impressively either side of a layoff; pulled up when stepped up to Grade 1 level at Aintree but held in very high regard by his trainer and no surprise if he makes a mark in that grade in time.

Le Prezien (Fr)
6 br g Blue Bresil - Abu Dhabi (Saint Cyrien)

Paul Nicholls | John P McManus

PLACINGS: 83/211212/21138P- **RPR 155+c**

Starts	1st	2nd	3rd	4th	Win & Pl
14	5	4	2	-	£94,150

	12/16	Extr	2m1¹/₂f Cls2 Ch soft	£12,512
	11/16	Chel	2m Cls1 Nov Gd2 Ch soft	£19,078
	3/16	Kels	2m2f Cls1 Nov Gd2 Hdl soft	£21,356
	1/16	Donc	2m¹/₂f Cls4 Nov Hdl soft	£3,249
	12/15	Ludl	2m Cls4 Mdn Hdl soft	£3,899

Big gamble when 7-2 favourite for last season's Grand Annual but could manage only eighth, looking likely to do better over further; had already won at Cheltenham and did well to finish third in the Scilly Isles behind Top Notch despite sketchy jumping.

Let's Dance (Fr)

5 b m Poliglote - Baraka Du Berlais (Bonnet Rouge)

Willie Mullins (Ir)   Mrs S Ricci

PLACINGS: 2/234/21111124-   RPR **146+h**

Starts	1st	2nd	3rd	4th	Win & Pl
12	5	4	1	2	£155,172
	3/17	Chel	2m1f Cls1 Nov Gd2 Hdl good		£45,560
	1/17	Leop	2m4f Nov Gd2 Hdl good		£22,692
	12/16	Leop	2m4f Gd3 Hdl yield		£17,353
	11/16	Punc	2m2f List Hdl soft		£13,566
	5/16	Slig	2m Mdn Hdl 4yo gd-yld		£4,522

Prolific novice hurdler last season, completing a five-timer in the mares' novice at the Cheltenham Festival; 0-5 at Grade 1 level (in the first four every time) but may not have been at her best at end of last season.

Lil Rockerfeller (USA)

6 ch g Hard Spun - Layounne (Mt. Livermore)

Neil King   Davies, Smith, Govier & Brown

PLACINGS: 2411/3312317/322420-   RPR **168h**

Starts	1st	2nd	3rd	4th	Win & Pl
19	4	5	6	2	£274,160
	2/16	Font	2m3f Cls1 Gd2 Hdl gd-sft		£45,560
146	12/15	Sand	2m Cls1 List 125-147 Hdl Hcap soft		£34,170
133	4/15	Sand	2m Cls2 111-137 Hdl 4yo Hcap gd-sft		£31,280
125	3/15	Asct	1m7¹/₂f Cls2 120-142 Hdl 4yo Hcap gd-sft		£25,992

Ran a string of fine races in defeat last season, most notably when a close second in the Stayers' Hurdle; also second in the Long Walk but did better on good ground at Cheltenham; should do well in similar races now connections know his trip.

Limini (Ire)

6 ch m Peintre Celebre - Her Grace (Spectrum)

Willie Mullins (Ir)   Mrs S Ricci

PLACINGS: 1113/213-   RPR **158+h**

Starts	1st	2nd	3rd	4th	Win & Pl
7	4	1	2	-	£116,541
	2/17	Punc	2m4f List Hdl heavy		£17,083
	3/16	Chel	2m1f Cls1 Nov Gd2 Hdl good		£42,713
	1/16	Fair	2m2f Nov Gd3 Hdl heavy		£16,728
	5/15	Punc	2m Mdn Hdl good		£6,419

Very smart mare who has won four of her seven starts since moving from France, including a comprehensive defeat of Apple's Jade last season; third behind that rival at Cheltenham though when a beaten favourite at Grade 1 level for the third time.

Long House Hall (Ire)

9 b g Saddlers' Hall - Brackenvale (Strong Gale)

Dan Skelton   Carl Hinchy

PLACINGS: P1/91026611/1U25/41-   RPR **154c**

Starts	1st	2nd	3rd	4th	Win & Pl
14	5	2	-	1	£82,094
143	7/16	MRas	2m5¹/₂f Cls1 List 131-157 Ch Hcap good		£28,475
	5/15	Bang	2m1¹/₂f Cls4 Nov Ch good		£3,899
125	4/15	Chel	2m4f Cls3 111-135 Hdl Hcap good		£12,512
119	4/15	MRas	2m2¹/₂f Cls3 106-125 Hdl Hcap good		£9,747
	5/14	Kbgn	2m3¹/₂f Mdn Hdl good		£4,600

Won the 2016 Summer Plate on only his fifth run over fences but missed the rest of last season; had also finished second in the Coral Cup that spring and still feasibly handicapped in both spheres.

Mall Dini (Ire)

7 b g Milan - Winsome Breeze (Glacial Storm)

Pat Kelly (Ir)   Philip J Reynolds

PLACINGS: 121/46314331/333235-   RPR **147+c**

Starts	1st	2nd	3rd	4th	Win & Pl
16	3	2	7	2	£76,702
139	3/16	Chel	3m Cls1 List 135-154 Hdl Hcap good		£51,255
	12/15	Thur	2m6³/₄f Mdn Hdl sft-hvy		£6,953
	3/15	Cork	2m NHF 4-7yo heavy		£4,814

Won the Pertemps Final in 2016 and not far off a second Cheltenham Festival victory last season when staying on late into a three-length fifth in the Kim Muir; beaten favourite four times before that over fences and still a novice but has the ability to win good races.

Max Ward (Ire)

8 b g Milan - Made Easy (Rudimentary)

Tom George   N T Griffith & H M Haddock

PLACINGS: 65481/2212/13F214-   RPR **148c**

Starts	1st	2nd	3rd	4th	Win & Pl
15	4	4	1	2	£61,679
134	3/17	Kemp	2m4¹/₂f Cls2 129-137 Ch Hcap good		£25,024
130	11/16	Hntg	2m1¹/₂f Cls3 Nov 124-135 Ch Hcap good		£6,498
124	6/14	Aint	2m1f Cls3 108-134 Hdl Hcap good		£5,848
	4/14	Tntn	2m3f Cls5 Mdn Hdl good		£2,738

Useful novice chaser last season, winning twice on good ground having waited for better conditions in the spring after being a beaten favourite on soft in January; far from disgraced at Grade 1 level at Aintree and should make a good handicapper.

 ON THE FIGURES

MIGHT BITE Hugely talented chaser who had landed Grade 1s at both Cheltenham and Aintree last season having earlier looked set to win another by a very wide margin when falling at Kempton. Could prove hard to beat in the King George. [Steve Mason, Racing Post Ratings]

Mega Fortune (Fr)

4 b g Soldier Of Fortune - Far Across (Common Grounds)

Gordon Elliott (Ir)   C Jones

PLACINGS: F133124-   RPR **144h**

Starts	1st	2nd	3rd	4th	Win & Pl
7	2		2	1	£81,932

	2/17	Leop	2m Gd1 Hdl 4yo soft	£40,342
	11/16	DRoy	2m Hdl 3yo good	£6,331

Just the best of the Irish runners when second in last season's Triumph Hurdle at Cheltenham; had arguably been even better on soft ground when winning a Grade 1 at Leopardstown but below his best at Punchestown; should get further.

Melon

5 ch g Medicean - Night Teeny (Platini)

Willie Mullins (Ir)   Mrs J Donnelly

PLACINGS: 122-   RPR **155h**

Starts	1st	2nd	3rd	4th	Win & Pl
3	1	2	-	-	£49,785

	1/17	Leop	2m Mdn Hdl good	£6,833

Lived up to his huge reputation despite winning only once from three starts last season; went straight to the Supreme after that winning debut and ran a stormer in second before going off too fast when second again at Punchestown; has lots more to offer.

Meri Devie (Fr)

4 ch f Spirit One - Folle Biche (Take Risks)

Willie Mullins (Ir)   Andrea & Graham Wylie

PLACINGS: 143-0   RPR **135+h**

Starts	1st	2nd	3rd	4th	Win & Pl
4	1	-	1	1	£16,758

	12/16	Leop	2m Mdn Hdl 3yo yield	£6,331

Smart juvenile hurdler last season; reported by her trainer to have been left short of work when well beaten in her first Grade 1 last season but much better when a close third to Bapaume at Punchestown; should do well in mares' hurdles.

Mick Jazz (Fr)

6 b g Blue Bresil - Mick Maya (Siam)

Gordon Elliott (Ir)   George P Mahoney

PLACINGS: 6232/P/1231-   RPR **143+h**

Starts	1st	2nd	3rd	4th	Win & Pl
9	2	3	2	-	£42,425

	2/17	Punc	2m Nov List Hdl soft	£17,083
	10/16	Clon	2m¹/₂f Mdn Hdl good	£4,522

Held in such high regard as a youngster that he was sent off favourite for the 2015 Greatwood Hurdle as a novice and finally began to fulfil that potential for a new yard last season, winning twice; strong traveller who may yet land a big handicap.

Midnight Tour

7 b m Midnight Legend - Uppermost (Montjeu)

Alan King   James & Jean Potter

PLACINGS: 1/0315/1215261-   RPR **145+h**

Starts	1st	2nd	3rd	4th	Win & Pl
12	5	2	1	-	£33,556

135	4/17	Chel	2m4¹/₂f Cls5 List 121-145 Hdl Hcap good	£12,529
122	11/16	Hrfd	2m Cls3 98-123 Hdl Hcap soft	£5,651
	5/16	Ludl	2m5f Cls4 Nov Hdl good	£3,899
	3/16	Bang	2m¹/₂f Cls5 Mdn Hdl soft	£3,249
	3/15	Catt	1m7¹/₂f Cls5 Am NHF 4-6yo gd-sft	£1,949

Went from strength to strength after switching from David Loder's yard last season, signing off with a Listed victory at Cheltenham; fine sixth in the Grade 1 Mares' Hurdle there on her previous run; likely contender for more good mares' hurdles.

Might Bite (Ire)

8 b g Scorpion - Knotted Midge (Presenting)

Nicky Henderson   The Knot Again Partnership

PLACINGS: 311/517/21F111-   RPR **170+c**

Starts	1st	2nd	3rd	4th	Win & Pl
12	7	1	1	-	£202,984

	4/17	Aint	3m1f Cls1 Nov Gd1 Ch good	£56,130
	3/17	Chel	3m¹/₂f Cls1 Nov Gd1 Ch gd-sft	£99,663
	2/17	Donc	3m Cls4 Nov Ch gd-sft	£4,758
	12/16	Donc	2m3f Cls4 Nov Ch good	£5,908
138	3/16	Kemp	2m5f Cls2 127-138 Hdl Hcap good	£20,645
	4/15	Chel	2m4¹/₂f Cls5 Nov Hdl soft	£10,102
	3/15	Newb	2m4¹/₂f Cls4 Nov Hdl gd-sft	£3,422

Prodigiously talented staying chaser who produced some of last season's most memorable moments, nearly throwing away the RSA Chase having fallen at the last when clear in a Grade 1 at Kempton; could go right to the top if ironing out his quirks.

Min (Fr)

6 b g Walk In The Park - Phemyka (Saint Estephe)

Willie Mullins (Ir)   Mrs S Ricci

PLACINGS: 43/112/11-   RPR **160+c**

Starts	1st	2nd	3rd	4th	Win & Pl
7	4	1		1	£107,364

	12/16	Leop	2m1f Nov Gd1 Ch yield	£39,044
	11/16	Navn	2m1f Ch yld-sft	£7,235
	1/16	Punc	2m Nov Gd2 Hdl heavy	£18,529
	12/15	Punc	2m2f Mdn Hdl soft	£5,349

Had his bubble burst when beaten into second by Altior in the 2016 Supreme Novices' Hurdle but looked better when winning both chases last season, including a Grade 1 at Leopardstown from Arkle third Ordinary World; missed Cheltenham through injury.

Minella Awards (Ire)

6 b g Oscar - Montys Miss (Presenting)

Harry Fry   Masterson Holdings Limited

PLACINGS: 2/25/211-   RPR **146+h**

Starts		1st	2nd	3rd	4th	Win & Pl
5		2	2	-	-	£70,647
134	4/17	Punc	3m 123-142 Hdl Hcap gd-yld			£30,256
128	3/17	Sand	2m4f Cls1 Nov Gd3 116-132 Hdl 4-7yo Hcap soft			£36,576

Rapidly progressive in just three runs last season and particularly impressive when stepped up to 3m at Punchestown; had needed a stiff 2m4f on soft ground at Sandown to get up to win the EBF Final previously; very lightly raced and should have more to come.

Minella Present (Ire)

8 b g Presenting - Dabaya (In The Wings)

Neil Mulholland   Mrs Jane Gerard-Pearse

PLACINGS: 3313/115P02/3122P/1-   RPR **144c**

Starts		1st	2nd	3rd	4th	Win & Pl
16		5	3	4		£41,525
134	5/16	Uttx	2m4f Cls2 123-146 Ch Hcap good			£16,245
	6/15	Font	2m1¹/₂f Cls4 Nov Ch gd-sft			£3,899
	10/14	Uttx	2m4f Cls4 Nov Hdl gd-sft			£3,249
	10/14	Uttx	2m4f Cls5 Cond Mdn Hdl good			£2,599
	3/14	Chep	2m Cls6 Mdn NHF 4-6yo soft			£1,560

Missed the rest of last season after winning a 2m4f handicap chase at Uttoxeter in May; unexposed around that trip having never run beyond 2m1f over fences previously; won a bumper on soft ground but largely kept away from such conditions since.

Minella Rocco (Ire)

7 b g Shirocco - Petralona (Alleged)

Jonjo O'Neill   John P McManus

PLACINGS: 1/11/3P621/3FU2-   RPR **171+c**

Starts		1st	2nd	3rd	4th	Win & Pl
11		3	2	2		£206,154
	3/16	Chel	4m Cls1 Nov List Am Ch gd-sft			£59,960
	2/15	Newb	2m4¹/₂f Cls4 Nov Hdl soft			£3,249
	2/15	Kemp	2m5f Cls4 Nov Hdl soft			£3,249

Took a long time to find his feet last season but ran a stormer to finish second in the Gold Cup, relishing return to Cheltenham having won 2016 National Hunt Chase; had been ante-post favourite for the Grand National but connections elected to protect him for this season.

Missed Approach (Ire)

7 b g Golan - Polly's Dream (Beau Sher)

Warren Greatrex   Alan & Andrew Turner

PLACINGS: 1113/1P2/413U28-   RPR **149c**

Starts		1st	2nd	3rd	4th	Win & Pl
12		4	2	2	1	£48,008
123	1/17	Ling	2m7¹/₂f Cls4 Nov Ch heavy			£3,899
	11/15	Newb	3m Cls3 120-142 Hdl Hcap soft			£9,384
	11/14	Ffos	2m4f Cls5 Mdn Hdl soft			£1,949
	10/14	Uttx	2m Cls6 NHF 4-6yo good			£1,560

Inconsistent when sent chasing last season but ran a stormer to finish second in the National Hunt Chase; better on soft ground and may have found conditions too quick when eighth in the Scottish National (first run on good since pulled up in the 2016 Pertemps Final).

Missy Tata (Fr)

5 b m Astarabad - Queen Running (Cadoudal)

Gordon Elliott (Ir)   Simon Munir & Isaac Souede

PLACINGS: 53/3124/11111-   RPR **144+h**

Starts		1st	2nd	3rd	4th	Win & Pl
11		6	1	2	1	£86,540
	12/16	Limk	2m List Hdl 4yo sft-hvy			£12,888
	11/16	Naas	2m Gd3 Hdl 4yo gd-sft			£15,827
	10/16	Limk	2m2f Hdl 4yo yield			£9,496
	5/16	Klny	2m1f Hdl good			£7,914
	4/16	Punc	2m Nov Hdl yield			£11,305
	10/15	DRoy	2m Hdl 3yo yld-sft			£7,488

Won five in a row over hurdles last season, most notably in a Grade 3 at Naas, although hasn't been seriously tested in general (sent off bigger than 13-8 just once when fourth in the 2016 Fred Winter); expected by connections to be even better over fences.

Mister Miyagi (Ire)

8 b g Zagreb - Muckle Flugga (Karinga Bay)

Dan Skelton   Ben Turner & Jay Tabb

PLACINGS: 3FF/2311/1161/3260-   RPR **153h**

Starts		1st	2nd	3rd	4th	Win & Pl
12		5	2	2	-	£39,897
	4/16	Chel	2m4¹/₂f Cls2 Nov Hdl gd-sft			£10,010
	11/15	Tntn	2m1¹/₂f Cls4 Nov Hdl gd-sft			£4,549
	10/15	Chel	2m1¹/₂f Cls3 Mdn Hdl good			£6,279
	3/15	Strf	2m1¹/₂f Cls5 NHF 4-6yo good			£2,599
	3/15	Strf	2m1¹/₂f Cls5 Mdn NHF 4-6yo gd-sft			£2,599

Smart novice hurdler two seasons ago when winning three out of four and finishing sixth in a red-hot Supreme; failed to build on that last term.

but looks the type to progress again over fences; well below par on only two runs on ground worse than good to soft.

Mixboy (Fr)

7 gr g Fragrant Mix - Leston Girl (Lesotho)

Keith Dalgleish   Paul & Clare Rooney

PLACINGS: 6/024/122/111PF-   RPR **152+c**

Starts		1st	2nd	3rd	4th	Win & Pl
12		4	3	-	1	£23,870
127	1/17	Muss	2m Cls3 112-128 Ch Hcap good			£7,798
	9/16	Sedg	2m¹/₂f Cls4 Nov Ch good			£4,549
	7/16	Ctml	2m5f Cls4 Ch good			£3,899
115	12/15	Sedg	2m1f Cls4 95-116 Hdl Hcap heavy			£4,029

Made it three out of three over fences with a wide-margin handicap win at Musselburgh in January, all on good ground; pulled up in the novice handicap chase at the Cheltenham Festival but still going well when falling five out at Ayr next time.

Modus

7 ch g Motivator - Alessandra (Generous)

Paul Nicholls   John P McManus

PLACINGS: 180/2/311300/327165-   RPR **157h**

Starts		1st	2nd	3rd	4th	Win & Pl
17		5	2	3		£98,724
145	1/17	Kemp	2m5f Cls1 List 127-153 Hdl Hcap gd-sft			£22,780
	11/15	Newb	2m¹/₂f Cls3 Nov Hdl soft			£6,279
	11/15	Tntn	2m3f Cls3 Nov Hdl good			£5,697
	1/14	Chel	1m6f Cls1 List NHF 4yo soft			£11,888
	10/13	Extr	1m5f Cls6 NHF 3yo gd-sft			£1,560

Placed in a couple of top 2m handicap hurdles

Missed Approach: ran a blinder in the National Hunt Chase and could be a force in staying handicaps

early last season before finding significant improvement when stepped up to 2m5f for the Lanzarote Hurdle; hit hard with an 11lb rise for that, although still ran another cracker when sixth in the Coral Cup.

Monalee (Ire)

6 b g Milan - Tempest Belle (Glacial Storm)

Henry de Bromhead (Ir)				Barry Maloney
PLACINGS: 12/212124-				RPR **150h**

Starts	1st	2nd	3rd	4th	Win & Pl
7	2	4	-	1	£65,045
	2/17	Clon	3m Nov Gd3 Hdl heavy		£19,712
	11/16	Punc	2m6f Mdn Hdl soft		£6,331

Thrived when stepped up to 3m last season, easily winning a Grade 3 at Clonmel on heavy ground and proving equally effective on good when second in the Albert Bartlett; below par at Punchestown next time; thorough stayer who should do well over fences.

Moon Racer (Ire)

8 b g Saffron Walden - Angel's Folly (Wesaam)

David Pipe				Professor Caroline Tisdall & Bryan Drew
PLACINGS: 1/11/211P6-				RPR **140+h**

Starts	1st	2nd	3rd	4th	Win & Pl
8	5	1			£123,509
	11/16	Chel	2m¹/₂f Cls1 Nov Gd2 Hdl soft		£17,085
	9/16	Prth	2m Cls4 Nov Hdl good		£3,249
	3/15	Chel	2m¹/₂f Cls1 Gd1 NHF 4-6yo good		£34,170
	10/14	Chel	2m¹/₂f Cls4 NHF 4-6yo gd-sft		£4,549
	4/14	Fair	2m NHF 4-5yo gd-yld		£49,167

Landed the Champion Bumper in 2015 and won twice over hurdles last season after a long injury absence; gamble of running in the Champion Hurdle as a novice backfired and was below par again at Aintree; will surely prove better than that.

More Of That (Ire)

9 b g Beneficial - Guigone (Esprit Du Nord)

Jonjo O'Neill				John P McManus
PLACINGS: 1/1111/3/113/P36U6P-				RPR **165c**

Starts	1st	2nd	3rd	4th	Win & Pl
15	7		3	-	£277,320
	12/15	Chel	2m5f Cls2 Nov Ch soft		£15,451
	11/15	Chel	2m4¹/₂f Cls2 Nov Ch good		£14,389
	3/14	Chel	3m Cls1 Gd1 Hdl good		£156,613
	12/13	Chel	2m4¹/₂f Cls1 Gd2 Hdl good		£22,780
137	11/13	Hayd	2m3f Cls2 121-147 Hdl Hcap soft		£24,692
130	11/13	Weth	2m4f Cls3 110-131 Hdl Hcap gd-sft		£5,523
	12/12	Folk	2m1¹/₂f Cls5 Mdn Hdl soft		£1,779

2014 World Hurdle winner who won first two starts over fences but hasn't lived up to his promise since then; did better when stepped back up to 3m last season and beaten less than ten lengths in the Gold Cup, although he was pulled up in the Grand National.

Mount Mews (Ire)

6 b g Presenting - Kneeland Lass (Bob Back)

Malcolm Jefferson				Trevor Hemmings
PLACINGS: 1/112112-				RPR **147+h**

Starts	1st	2nd	3rd	4th	Win & Pl
7	5	2	-	-	£58,248
	3/17	Kels	2m2f Cls1 Nov Gd2 Hdl heavy		£24,687
	1/17	Donc	2m¹/₂f Cls4 Nov Hdl good		£3,899
	12/16	Kels	2m Cls4 Nov Hdl gd-sft		£3,249
	5/16	Kels	2m Cls5 NHF 4-6yo good		£2,599
	4/16	MRas	2m¹/₂f Cls6 Mdn NHF 4-6yo soft		£1,560

Won three of his first four races over hurdles last season and ran a solid race up in grade when second to Pingshou at Aintree; not the biggest so set to stay hurdling, with his trainer mentioning the Fighting Fifth, although he may fare better in handicaps.

Movewiththetimes (Ire)

6 ch g Presenting - Dare To Venture (Darazari)

Paul Nicholls				John P McManus
PLACINGS: 1/1512-				RPR **151+h**

Starts	1st	2nd	3rd	4th	Win & Pl
5	3	1	-	-	£43,999
	12/16	Winc	1m7¹/₂f Cls4 Nov Hdl gd-sft		£3,249
	10/16	Font	2m1¹/₂f Cls4 Nov Hdl gd-sft		£5,198
	4/16	Winc	1m7¹/₂f Cls6 NHF 4-6yo gd-sft		£1,625

Terrific second behind handicap snip Ballyandy in last season's Betfair Hurdle, relishing an end-to-end gallop having disappointed off a slow

ON THE CLOCK

MOVEWITHTHETIMES Successful at Fontwell and Wincanton, Paul Nicholls' lightly raced six-year-old ran a blinder to chase home Ballyandy in the Betfair Hurdle at Newbury in February. Suited by ease in the ground, a big pot at around two miles could come his way. [Dave Edwards, Topspeed]

Injured Jockeys Fund

Christmas Gifts for 2017

Visit **www.ijf.org.uk** or Freephone **08080 453 453**

pace when previously stepped up in class at Cheltenham; ruled out of the festival by injury when likely to step up in trip.

Mr Mix (Fr)

6 gr g Al Namix - Royale Surabaya (Turgeon)

Paul Nicholls			Dan Macdonald & Ian Fogg	

PLACINGS: 3/3312F/51PU0-1   RPR **146+h**

Starts		1st	2nd	3rd	4th		Win & Pl
12		3	1	3	-		£35,271
	5/17	Worc	2m7f Cls4 Nov Ch good				£4,127
139	12/16	Winc	2m5¹/₂f Cls2 114-140 Hdl Hcap soft				£11,574
	1/16	Tntn	2m3f Cls4 Nov Hdl 4-7yo heavy				£4,549

Useful hurdler who won a decent handicap at Wincanton off 139 last season; unseated on his chase debut but got off the mark at Worcester in May, albeit by just a head at odds-on; expected to be better in bigger fields and could be one for novice handicaps.

My Tent Or Yours (Ire)

10 b g Desert Prince - Spartan Girl (Ela-Mana-Mou)

Nicky Henderson			John P McManus	

PLACINGS: 121/1123/22/3324222-   RPR **165h**

Starts		1st	2nd	3rd	4th		Win & Pl
22		7	11	3	1		£745,971
	2/14	Kemp	2m Cls3 NHF std-slw				£6,330
	12/13	Kemp	2m Cls1 Gd1 Hdl soft				£56,950
	11/13	Newc	2m1/₂f Cls1 Gd1 Hdl good				£56,270
	4/13	Aint	2m1/₂f Cls1 Nov Gd2 Hdl gd-sft				£34,170
149	2/13	Newb	2m1/₂f Cls1 Gd3 133-159 Hdl Hcap good				£86,849
	1/13	Hntg	2m Cls4 Nov Hdl 4-7yo soft				£3,444
	11/12	Asct	1m7¹/₂f Cls3 Nov Hdl gd-sft				£7,507
	12/11	Ludl	1m6f Cls5 NHF 4-5yo gd-sft				£2,274

Still a top-class hurdler despite missing more than two years through injury at his peak; finished second in the Champion Hurdle last season for the third time and filled the same spot at Aintree and Punchestown but finds it hard to win when given easier opportunities.

Mysteree (Ire)

9 b g Gold Well - Hillside Native (Be My Native)

Michael Scudamore			Mrs Lynne Maclennan	

PLACINGS: /1224310/13148/1P12-   RPR **142c**

Starts		1st	2nd	3rd	4th		Win & Pl
17		6	3	3	2		£120,800
127	2/17	Newc	4m1/₂f Cls2 126-139 Ch Hcap good				£50,048
120	11/16	Hayd	3m4/₂f Cls3 116-134 Ch Hcap heavy				£16,245
119	2/16	Newc	2m7/₂f Cls4 Nov 105-119 Ch Hcap soft				£3,994
117	12/15	Weth	2m3/₂f Cls3 Nov 117-123 Ch Hcap soft				£6,256
120	3/14	Ayr	3m1/₂f Cls3 110-120 Hdl Hcap heavy				£6,657
	9/13	Prth	2m4f Cls4 Nov Hdl good				£3,249

Progressive staying handicapper on soft/heavy ground who took form to a new level last season, winning twice, including the Eider, and finishing second in the Midlands National; had been below par on last two runs for Lucinda Russell, both on good to soft.

Nambour (Ger)

7 b g Sholokhov - Nanouska (Dashing Blade)

Mouse Morris (Ir)			Gigginstown House Stud	

PLACINGS: 1/113222/14-   RPR **141+c**

Starts		1st	2nd	3rd	4th		Win & Pl
8		3	3	1	1		£40,522
	10/16	Gway	2m6¹/₂f Ch yield				£8,140
	11/15	Fair	2m2f Mdn Hdl sft-hvy				£6,419
	5/15	Punc	2m NHF 4-7yo soft				£5,884

Showed plenty of promise in staying novice hurdles two seasons ago (second three times at Grade 2 level) and looked an even better chaser when winning first time out last term; only fourth behind A Toi Phil next time and missed the rest of the season through injury.

Native River (Ire)

7 ch g Indian River - Native Mo (Be My Native)

Colin Tizzard			Brocade Racing	

PLACINGS: 16F19/3113321/21113-   RPR **171c**

Starts		1st	2nd	3rd	4th		Win & Pl
19		9	2	5	-		£446,124
	2/17	Newb	2m7¹/₂f Cls1 Gd2 Ch soft				£28,475
155	12/16	Chep	3m5¹/₂f Cls1 Gd3 139-155 Ch Hcap soft				£85,425
155	11/16	Newb	3m2f Cls1 Gd3 140-166 Ch Hcap gd-sft				£113,900
	4/16	Aint	3m1f Cls1 Nov Gd1 Ch gd-sft				£56,319
	11/15	Newb	2m7¹/₂f Cls1 Nov Gd2 Ch gd-sft				£20,284
	11/15	Extr	3m Cls2 Nov Ch soft				£12,974
	2/15	Extr	2m1f Cls1 Nov List Hdl gd-sft				£11,390
	11/14	Newc	2m5f Cls2 Nov Hdl soft				£11,261
	10/14	Strf	2m6f Cls5 Mdn Hdl good				£2,599

Thorough stayer who improved throughout last season, completing a big handicap double when winning the Hennessy Gold Cup and Welsh Grand National before finishing a fine third in the Gold Cup; effective on any ground but may find things tougher this season off higher mark.

Nichols Canyon

7 b g Authorized - Zam Zoom (Dalakhani)

Willie Mullins (Ir)			Andrea & Graham Wylie	

PLACINGS: 1U131/111333/312F12-   RPR **168+h**

Starts		1st	2nd	3rd	4th		Win & Pl
18		9	2	5	-		£625,093
	3/17	Chel	3m Cls1 Gd1 Hdl good				£170,850
	11/16	Punc	2m Gd1 Hdl soft				£36,875
	12/15	Leop	2m Gd1 Hdl heavy				£46,512
	11/15	Punc	2m Gd1 Hdl soft				£39,535
	5/15	Punc	2m4f Nov Gd1 Hdl gd-yld				£44,186
	4/15	Aint	2m4f Cls1 Nov Gd1 Hdl good				£42,203
	2/15	Leop	2m2f Nov Gd1 Hdl yield				£41,860
	11/14	Fair	2m Nov Gd1 Hdl yield				£40,625
	11/14	Cork	2m Nov Hdl 4yo soft				£5,750

Top-class hurdler from 2m to 3m but took his form to a new level at the longer trip last spring, winning the Stayers' Hurdle at Cheltenham before just being touched off by Unowhatimeanharry at Punchestown; likely to be a major force in all the top staying hurdles.

Nietzsche

4 ch g Poet's Voice - Ganga (Generous)

Brian Ellison   D Gilbert, M Lawrence, A Bruce & G Wills

PLACINGS: 2213113-   RPR **130+h**

Starts	1st	2nd	3rd	4th	Win & Pl
7	3	2	2	-	£30,904

123	1/17	Catt	2m3¹/₂f Cls3 115-137 Hdl Hcap gd-sft £5,848
122	1/17	MRas	2m2¹/₂f Cls4 99-122 Cond Hdl Hcap soft £3,249
	12/16	Catt	1m7¹/₂f Cls4 Hdl 3yo gd-sft £3,249

Tough juvenile hurdler last season who finished the campaign on a sharp upward curve, beating older horses in handicaps at Market Rasen and Catterick before coming within half a length of adding the Fred Winter; could win a big 2m handicap.

No Comment

6 br g Kayf Tara - Dizzy Frizzy (Loup Sauvage)

Philip Hobbs   John P McManus

PLACINGS: 22/1U2111722-   RPR **147+h**

Starts	1st	2nd	3rd	4th	Win & Pl
11	4	5	2	1	£46,726

	1/17	Plum	2m4¹/₂f Cls3 Nov Hdl 4-7yo soft £6,498
	12/16	Plum	2m4¹/₂f Cls4 Nov Hdl gd-sft £3,249
	11/16	MRas	2m2¹/₂f Cls4 Nov Hdl gd-sft £3,249
	4/16	Punc	2m2f NHF 5-7yo yield £5,426

Punchestown bumper winner who added a hat-trick of ordinary novice hurdles last season; much improved when stepping into handicaps in the spring but just came up short at Aintree and Punchestown; suited by big fields and still going the right way.

No Hassle Hoff (Ire)

5 b/br g Craigsteel - Endless Patience (Miner's Lamp)

Dan Skelton   Mrs Jacky Allen

PLACINGS: 2/F13224-   RPR **140h**

Starts	1st	2nd	3rd	4th	Win & Pl
6	1	2	1	1	£22,480

	11/16	Hrfd	3m1¹/₂f Cls5 Mdn Hdl soft £2,729

Won only a maiden hurdle last season but got better with experience and ran several fine races in defeat, including when placed three times at Grade 2 level; fair fourth of 22 on his handicap debut at Aintree when sent off favourite.

Noble Endeavor (Ire)

8 b g Flemensfirth - Old Moon (Old Vic)

Gordon Elliott (Ir)   C Jones

PLACINGS: /22125/2312F/P54136-   RPR **160c**

Starts	1st	2nd	3rd	4th	Win & Pl
21	5	5	2	2	£147,991

143	12/16	Leop	3m¹/₂f 123-150 Ch Hcap yield £76,838
	12/15	DRoy	2m4f Ch heavy £7,488
	1/15	Punc	2m4f Hdl soft £6,953
	2/14	Punc	2m4f Mdn Hdl heavy £6,325
	12/13	Leop	2m NHF 4yo soft £5,049

Landed a big gamble when winning the Paddy Power Chase at Leopardstown last season and ran well in other big staying handicaps, finishing third in the Ultima and fourth in the Troytown; handicapper may just have his measure now.

North Hill Harvey

6 b g Kayf Tara - Ellina (Robellino)

Dan Skelton   Mrs G Widdowson & Mrs R Kelvin-Hughes

PLACINGS: 1/21294/100-   RPR **151h**

Starts	1st	2nd	3rd	4th	Win & Pl
8	2	2	-	1	£75,142

141	11/16	Chel	2m¹/₂f Cls1 Gd3 129-153 Hdl Hcap soft £56,950
	12/15	Chel	2m1f Cls3 Nov Hdl 4-6yo sft £7,507

Terrific winner of last season's Greatwood Hurdle at Cheltenham and form worked out very well; disappointing in the spring when well beaten at Cheltenham and Aintree but perhaps unsuited by quicker ground (best form on soft); likely to go chasing.

O O Seven (Ire)

7 b g Flemensfirth - Kestral Heights (Eagle Eyed)

Nicky Henderson   Triermore Stud

PLACINGS: 120/11218/213154-   RPR **154+c**

Starts	1st	2nd	3rd	4th	Win & Pl
14	6	3	1	1	£85,264

148	1/17	Hntg	2m4f Cls3 Nov 129-148 Ch Hcap gd-sft £6,498
	11/16	Chel	2m4¹/₂f Cls2 Nov Ch good £15,698
	2/16	Muss	3m Cls2 Hdl soft £14,389
	12/15	Sand	2m Cls3 Nov Hdl soft £6,498
	11/15	Hntg	2m Cls5 Mdn Hdl gd-sft £2,599
	12/14	Hntg	2m Cls6 NHF 4-6yo gd-sft £1,560

Very useful novice chaser last season, with both disappointing runs coming when tried over 3m; particularly impressive first time out at

Facebook.com/racingpost   Twitter @RacingPost

Cheltenham and did very well for a novice when fourth in the Topham over the Grand National fences at Aintree.

Old Guard

6 b g Notnowcato - Dolma (Marchand De Sable)

Paul Nicholls | The Brooks, Stewart Families & J Kyle

PLACINGS: P293/1114/P14347747- RPR **154h**

Starts		1st	2nd	3rd	4th	Win & Pl
18		5	1	2	4	£193,257
	10/16	Extr	2m1¹/₂f Cls4 Ch good			£6,498
	12/15	Chel	2m1f Cls1 Gd2 Hdl soft			£74,035
145	11/15	Chel	2m¹/₂f Cls1 Gd3 128-147 Hdl Hcap gd-sft			£56,950
137	10/15	Chel	2m¹/₂f Cls3 116-139 Cond Hdl Hcap good			£6,256
	11/14	Newb	2m¹/₂f Cls3 Hdl 3yo soft			£6,498

Won the Greatwood and International Hurdles in 2015 but struggled to match that form last season, although not beaten far under big weights in the Lanzarote Hurdle and Coral Cup; could go back over fences (unimpressive in winning a beginners' chase last autumn).

Oldgrangewood

6 b g Central Park - Top Of The Class (Rudimentary)

Dan Skelton | Chris Giles & Sandra Giles

PLACINGS: 1/2413/31B11P3- RPR **150c**

Starts		1st	2nd	3rd	4th	Win & Pl
11		4	1	3	1	£33,992
134	2/17	Weth	2m3¹/₂f Cls2 143-143 Ch Hcap soft			£11,574
130	12/16	Weth	2m3¹/₂f Cls3 Nov 125-137 Ch Hcap gd-sft			£6,498
120	11/16	Kemp	2m2f Cls4 Nov 108-120 Ch Hcap good			£4,660
	2/16	Ayr	2m Cls5 Mdn Hdl soft			£2,599

Progressive novice chaser last season, winning three handicaps and coping well with a step up in grade when third at Ayr on his final start; pulled up when favourite for the Greatwood Gold Cup but likely to be a contender again for similar big handicaps.

One For Arthur (Ire)

8 b g Milan - Nonnetia (Trempolino)

Lucinda Russell | Two Golf Widows

PLACINGS: 33111P/1335243/1511- RPR **160+c**

Starts		1st	2nd	3rd	4th	Win & Pl
19		7	3	5	1	£638,938
148	4/17	Aint	4m2¹/₂f Cls1 Gd3 143-161 Ch Hcap gd-sft			£561,300
137	1/17	Wwck	3m5f Cls1 Gd3 129-152 Ch Hcap soft			£34,170
127	10/16	Kels	3m2f Cls3 109-135 Ch Hcap gd-sft			£11,047
	10/15	Kels	2m7¹/₂f Cls4 Nov Ch good			£4,549
	3/15	Ayr	3m¹/₂f Cls4 Nov Hdl soft			£3,899
120	2/15	Ayr	3m¹/₂f Cls4 Nov 94-120 Hdl Hcap soft			£3,574
	1/15	Hayd	2m3f Cls4 Nov Hdl 4-7yo heavy			£3,899

Brilliant winner of last season's Grand National, doing remarkably well to make up a huge amount of ground in final mile when the leaders weren't stopping; it would be no surprise to see him run well in that race again but could even be a Grade 1 performer given his rate of progress.

One Track Mind (Ire)

7 b g Flemensfirth - Lady Petit (Beneficial)

Warren Greatrex | Andy Weller

PLACINGS: 1/1U41/512/1535-9 RPR **148h**

Starts		1st	2nd	3rd	4th	Win & Pl
13		5	1	1	1	£123,763
	4/16	Punc	3m Gd1 Hdl yield			£86,765
140	12/15	Newb	2m4¹/₂f Cls2 125-140 Hdl Hcap soft			£11,574
	2/15	Weth	2m3¹/₂f Cls4 Nov Hdl good			£3,119
	11/14	Weth	2m3¹/₂f Cls4 Nov Hdl soft			£3,422
	4/14	Weth	2m Cls6 NHF 4-6yo gd-sft			£1,643

Won a Grade 1 at Punchestown in 2016 (weak race for the grade) but bitterly disappointing since then, failing to sparkle in two runs over fences last season and doing little better back over hurdles; may be best trying his luck as a novice chaser again.

Ordinary World (Ire)

7 br g Milan - Saucy Present (Presenting)

Henry de Bromhead (Ir)   C Jones

PLACINGS: 342/51848F/012232-   RPR **149c**

Starts	1st	2nd	3rd	4th	Win & Pl
15	2	4	2	2	£69,336
	10/16 Fair	2m Ch good			£4,974
	10/15 Tipp	2m Mdn Hdl gd-yld			£5,349

Ran well in the face of some seemingly impossible tasks last season, finishing second behind Min and Great Field either side of his third in the Racing Post Arkle; sights likely to be lowered now out of novice company and should win races.

Otago Trail (Ire)

9 b g Heron Island - Cool Chic (Roselier)

Venetia Williams   Mrs Marie Shone

PLACINGS: 12/1132/2113P3/1P21-   RPR **162+c**

Starts	1st	2nd	3rd	4th	Win & Pl
17	7	4	4	-	£146,111
151	2/17 Sand	3m Cls2 133-151 Ch Hcap soft			£31,152
146	11/16 Newc	2m7¹/₂f Cls1 List 132-155 Ch Hcap soft			£45,560
141	1/16 Chep	2m3¹/₂f Cls2 123-141 Ch Hcap heavy			£19,166
133	12/15 Extr	2m3f Cls3 119-133 Ch Hcap heavy			£15,698
	1/15 Winc	1m7¹/₂f Cls3 Nov Hdl heavy			£5,523
	11/14 Carl	2m4f Cls4 Nov Hdl soft			£3,249
	2/14 Font	2m1¹/₂f Cls6 NHF 4-6yo heavy			£1,560

Did well last season, winning good handicap chases at Newcastle and Sandown as well as finishing second in the Peter Marsh; has gained all seven wins on soft or heavy ground and is 0-5 on quicker; could spring a surprise in a big race if mud is flying.

Our Duke (Ire)

7 b g Oscar - Good Thyne Jenny (Good Thyne)

Jessica Harrington (Ir)   Cooper Family Syndicate

PLACINGS: 121P3/1121-   RPR **172+c**

Starts	1st	2nd	3rd	4th	Win & Pl
9	5	2	1	-	£305,622
153	4/17 Fair	3m5f 136-156 Ch Hcap gd-yld			£230,769
	12/16 Leop	3m Nov Gd1 Ch yield			£36,875
	12/16 Navn	2m4f Ch yld-sft			£6,105
	1/16 Leop	2m4f Mdn Hdl soft			£6,596
	11/15 Punc	2m NHF 5-7yo soft			£4,814

Produced an outstanding performance to win last season's Irish Grand National by 14 lengths, becoming first horse to win the race with more than 11st since 2000; had also won a Grade 1 novice chase over 3m and looks a leading Gold Cup contender.

Our Duke: Irish Grand National winner could be a leading Gold Cup contender

Our Kaempfer (Ire)

8 b g Oscar - Gra-Bri (Rashar)

Charlie Longsdon   Swanee River Partnership

PLACINGS: /43113/42B5/223U1PP-   RPR **152+c**

Starts		1st	2nd	3rd	4th	Win & Pl
20		4	3	4	2	£55,232
138	1/17	Kemp	3m Cls2 125-150 Ch Hcap gd-sft			£11,574
	3/15	Kemp	2m5f Cls4 Nov Hdl good			£3,899
	2/15	MRas	2m4¹/₂f Cls4 Nov Hdl gd-sft			£3,249
	10/13	Worc	2m Cls6 NHF 4-6yo good			£1,560

Below his best in the spring (pulled up at Cheltenham and Aintree) but had been progressing well as a novice chaser prior to that, easily winning a good handicap at Kempton; open to further improvement after only seven runs over fences.

Outlander (Ire)

9 b g Stowaway - Western Whisper (Supreme Leader)

Gordon Elliott (Ir)   Gigginstown House Stud

PLACINGS: 2162/3111F2/22F210P-   RPR **170+c**

Starts		1st	2nd	3rd	4th	Win & Pl
22		9	6	1	-	£239,638
	12/16	Leop	3m Gd1 Ch yield			£65,074
	2/16	Leop	2m5¹/₂f Nov Gd1 Ch sft-hvy			£36,875
	12/15	Limk	2m3¹/₂f Nov Gd2 Ch heavy			£21,163
	11/15	Punc	2m4f Ch soft			£6,953
	1/15	Leop	2m4f Nov Gd2 Hdl yield			£19,903
	11/14	Fair	2m Mdn Hdl sft-hvy			£4,600
	2/13	Naas	2m NHF 4-7yo sft-hvy			£7,573
	12/12	Leop	2m NHF 4-7yo soft			£6,325
	12/12	Fair	2m NHF 4yo soft			£4,888

Has generally tended to come up short against the very best but looked to improve for the step up to 3m when winning the Lexus Chase last season; lost his way in the spring when tailed off in the Gold Cup and pulled up at Punchestown.

Overland Flyer (Ire)

6 b g Westerner - Love Train (Sadler's Wells)

Paul Nicholls   Colm Donlon

PLACINGS: 211/14-   RPR **142+h**

Starts		1st	2nd	3rd	4th	Win & Pl
2		1	-	-	1	£4,311
	1/17	Tntn	3m Cls5 Mdn Hdl good			£3,249

Dual point-to-point winner who made a big impression on his first run under rules last season, winning a maiden hurdle at Taunton by 22 lengths; beaten at odds-on next time but still a fine prospect, especially when sent chasing.

Overtown Express (Ire)

9 br g Overbury - Black Secret (Gildoran)

Harry Fry   Mrs Lorna Squire & Richard Metherell

PLACINGS: 6U1/F1153/3416-   RPR **148+c**

Starts		1st	2nd	3rd	4th	Win & Pl
9		3	-	2	1	£19,871
132	1/17	Wwck	2m Cls3 120-137 Ch Hcap soft			£7,798
	3/16	Ling	2m Cls4 Nov Hdl heavy			£4,660
	2/16	Extr	2m2¹/₂f Cls4 Nov Hdl heavy			£3,249

Has gained all three wins on soft or heavy ground and improved massively when getting those conditions for the first time over fences, winning a 2m handicap chase at Wetherby; didn't run his race when up in class at Warwick next time.

Pacha Du Polder (Fr)

10 b g Muhtathir - Ambri Piotta (Caerwent)

Paul Nicholls   The Stewart Family

PLACINGS: 6/212/32U156/334114-   RPR **145c**

Starts		1st	2nd	3rd	4th	Win & Pl
30		9	4	3	2	£149,672
	3/17	Chel	3m2¹/₂f Cls2 Am Hunt Ch good			£26,982
	2/17	Bang	2m4¹/₂f Cls6 Am Hunt Ch soft			£1,317
	3/16	Winc	2m4f Cls6 Am Hunt Ch soft			£1,248
	3/15	Ludl	2m4f Cls5 Am Hunt Ch good			£2,496
145	3/13	Newb	2m4f Cls1 Gd3 130-154 Ch Hcap gd-sft			£28,475
	4/12	Ayr	2m4f Cls1 Nov Gd2 Ch good			£17,832
	1/12	Wwck	2m4¹/₂f Cls3 Nov Ch gd-sft			£5,653
	11/11	Sand	1m7¹/₂f Cls4 Ch gd-sft			£3,899
	3/11	Engh	2m2f Hdl 4yo v soft			£21,517

Famous for carrying Victoria Pendleton to fifth place in the 2016 Foxhunters' Chase and built on the promise of that run by winning the same race last season; close fourth next time at Aintree; likely to be a leading contender for top hunter chases again.

Pendra (Ire)

9 ch g Old Vic - Mariah Rollins (Over The River)

Charlie Longsdon   John P McManus

PLACINGS: 1120/11730/45/150/2-   RPR **150c**

Starts		1st	2nd	3rd	4th	Win & Pl
16		6	2	1	1	£107,494
140	10/15	Asct	3m Cls1 Gd3 137-159 Ch Hcap good			£56,950
	11/13	Ling	2m Cls4 Nov Ch heavy			£3,769
	10/13	Carl	2m Cls4 Ch gd-sft			£4,549
	12/12	Plum	2m Cls4 Nov Hdl soft			£4,106
	11/12	Plum	2m Cls5 Mdn Hdl soft			£2,053
	3/12	Hntg	2m Cls6 NHF 4-6yo good			£1,365

Restricted to just one run last season but did

remarkably well to finish second in the Kim Muir, just tying up close home; raised just 3lb for that third top-five finish at the Cheltenham Festival; had won a valuable Ascot handicap the previous season.

Penhill

6 b g Mount Nelson - Serrenia (High Chaparral)

Willie Mullins (Ir)   Tony Bloom

PLACINGS: 161114112-   RPR **155+h**

Starts	1st	2nd	3rd	4th	Win & Pl
9	6	2	1	-	1	£149,704

3/17	Chel	3m Cls1 Nov Gd1 Hdl good	£71,188
12/16	Limk	3m Nov Gd2 Hdl sft-hvy	£19,305
10/16	Tipp	2m Nov Gd3 Hdl soft	£14,697
9/16	List	2m Nov Hdl yield	£9,949
7/16	Gway	2m¹/₂f Nov Hdl gd-yld	£11,305
5/16	Tram	2m Mdn Hdl good	£4,522

Useful middle-distance horse on the Flat but found his niche as a staying hurdler last season, gaining his biggest win in the Albert Bartlett at Cheltenham (second run over 3m); just got going too late when second at Punchestown; acts on any ground.

Peregrine Run (Ire)

7 b g King's Theatre - Masriyna's Article (Definite Article)

Peter Fahey (Ir)   V Byrne

PLACINGS: 10007/00111130-21131   RPR **146+h**

Starts	1st	2nd	3rd	4th	Win & Pl
21	8	2	4	-	£83,113

8/17	Klny	2m4¹/₂f Nov Ch good	£7,634
7/17	Wxfd	2m Nov Ch good	£7,897
6/17	Wxfd	2m Ch good	£6,581
11/16	Chel	2m5f Cls1 Nov Gd2 Hdl good	£17,085
10/16	Limk	2m5f Nov List Hdl yield	£15,375
119	9/16	Gowr	2m4f 105-127 Hdl Hcap good	£7,235
8/16	DRoy	2m4f Mdn Hdl good	£4,522
8/15	Klny	2m1f NHF 4-7yo good	£4,814

Won a red-hot Grade 2 novice hurdle at Cheltenham last season (beat Wholestone and West Approach) and added a couple of novice chases this summer; fine prospect on that good-ground form but has failed to run to form on softer.

Perfect Candidate (Ire)

10 b g Winged Love - Dansana (Insan)

Fergal O'Brien   ISL Recruitment

PLACINGS: 1715150/25101/02P1P-   RPR **164+c**

Starts	1st	2nd	3rd	4th	Win & Pl
26	6	3	1	3	£80,792

150	2/17	Extr	3m Cls2 124-150 Ch Hcap soft	£18,768
142	4/16	Chel	3m2f Cls2 122-148 Ch Hcap good	£12,512
134	1/16	Chel	3m2¹/₂f Cls2 119-139 Ch Hcap heavy	£12,512
124	1/15	Leic	2m6¹/₂f Cls3 Nov 117-132 Ch Hcap gd-sft	£6,330
115	11/14	Bang	2m4¹/₂f Cls4 97-120 Ch Hcap soft	£3,994
5/14	Weth	3m1¹/₂f Cls4 Nov Hdl soft	£3,119

Has a particularly good record at Cheltenham, having won two handicap chases at the track

and twice finished second over the last two seasons (beaten a nose at last season's December meeting); now in veteran stage of his career, but produced a career-best effort at Exeter in February and could be winning more races.

Peter The Mayo Man (Ire)

7 ch g Dylan Thomas - Mommkin (Royal Academy)

Paul Nicholls   Masterson Holdings

PLACINGS: 561/44/111236-   RPR **142h**

Starts	1st	2nd	3rd	4th	Win & Pl
11	4	1	1	2	£29,841

130	11/16	Newb	2m¹/₂f Cls3 115-135 Hdl Hcap good	£9,097
9/16	Wwck	2m Cls4 Nov Hdl good	£3,574
9/16	Worc	2m Cls4 Nov Hdl good	£3,379
4/15	Fair	2m NHF 4-7yo good	£4,814

Hugely impressive when winning at Newbury on his handicap debut to complete a hat-trick but forced into tougher company by a 12lb rise and just came up short; still showed smart form (beaten six lengths in the Dovecote) and slipped back down handicap; has since left Neil Mulholland.

Petit Mouchoir (Fr)

6 gr g Al Namix - Arnette (Denham Red)

Henry de Bromhead (Ir)   Gigginstown House Stud

PLACINGS: 1/113482/23F113-   RPR **165+h**

Starts	1st	2nd	3rd	4th	Win & Pl
12	4	2	3	1	£234,494

1/17	Leop	2m Gd1 Hdl good	£55,470
12/16	Leop	2m Gd1 Hdl yield	£43,382
11/15	Thur	2m Mdn Hdl 4yo soft	£5,349
4/15	Punc	2m NHF 4-5yo gd-yld	£45,736

Developed into probably the leading 2m hurdler in Ireland last season with other big guns injured, winning two Grade 1s including the Irish Champion Hurdle; far from disgraced when third in the Champion Hurdle but perhaps better on a flat track.

Pilgrims Bay (Ire)

7 b g Turtle Island - Lady Ariadna (Supreme Leader)

Neil Mulholland   Clifford, Gosden & House

PLACINGS: 3/4367512325/1F2310-   RPR **141+c**

Starts	1st	2nd	3rd	4th	Win & Pl
17	3	3	4	1	£80,243

130	2/17	Kemp	3m Cls1 Gd3 130-154 Ch Hcap good	£56,950
124	12/16	Sand	2m4f Cls3 Nov 106-125 Ch Hcap good	£7,535
110	1/16	Winc	2m5¹/₂f Cls3 101-123 Hdl Hcap soft	£5,523

Often let down by his jumping last season but won the BetBright Chase at Kempton despite again making several minor errors; starts this season 7lb higher than at Kempton but capable of better if ironing out jumping problems.

Pingshou (Ire)

7 b g Definite Article - Quest Of Passion (Saumarez)

| Colin Tizzard | | | | Alan Potts |

| PLACINGS: 8/414013- | | | | RPR **149+h** |

Starts	1st	2nd	3rd	4th	Win & Pl
7	2	-	1	2	£73,162
	4/17	Aint	2m¹/₂f Cls1 Nov Gd1 Hdl good	£56,130
	12/16	Chel	2m1f Cls3 Nov Hdl good	£7,798

Surprise 16-1 winner of a Grade 1 novice hurdle at Aintree last season having flopped in the Supreme and backed that up with another solid effort at Punchestown; had looked a non-stayer on only run over 2m4f but should make a fine 2m novice chaser.

Pistol Park (Fr)

6 b g Poliglote - Pistolera (Monsun)

| Brian Ellison | | | | Brian's Mates |

| PLACINGS: 5P41432/63/31412212- | | | | RPR **145c** |

Starts	1st	2nd	3rd	4th	Win & Pl
17	4	4	3	3	£74,050
131	2/17	Newc	2m¹/₂f Cls3 124-131 Ch Hcap heavy	£7,148
122	11/16	Newc	2m¹/₂f Cls3 Nov 122-135 Ch Hcap gd-sft	£7,473
	6/16	Hexm	1m7¹/₂f Cls4 Nov Ch gd-sft	£5,198
	1/15	Pau	2m1¹/₂f Hdl 4yo heavy	£11,907

Progressive novice chaser last season, winning three times including a handicap at Newcastle by eight lengths; would have gone close next time but for stumbling (rider briefly lost iron) two out; best form on heavy ground but has won twice on good to soft.

Plaisir D'Amour (Fr)

5 b m Linngari - Analfabeta (Anabaa)

| Venetia Williams | | | | Kate & Andrew Brooks |

| PLACINGS: 3261214/P11315- | | | | RPR **145+c** |

Starts	1st	2nd	3rd	4th	Win & Pl
13	5	2	2	1	£67,017
132	4/17	Chel	2m5f Cls1 Nov List 122-146 Ch Hcap good	£22,774
127	3/17	Newb	2m5/₂f Cls1 109-127 Ch Hcap soft	£6,498
120	2/17	Weth	1m7f Cls4 106-120 Ch Hcap gd-sft	£4,549
	4/16	Mars	2m3f Hdl 4yo good	£7,765
	2/16	Mars	2m1¹/₂f Hdl 4yo heavy	£7,412

Ex-French mare who won three times last season, looking best when improving for better ground and a step up to 2m5f in a Listed mares' handicap chase at Cheltenham; good effort when beaten less than four lengths back against geldings at Sandown.

Pleasant Company (Ire)

9 b g Presenting - Katie Flame (Alderbrook)

| Willie Mullins (Ir) | | | | Malcolm C Denmark |

| PLACINGS: /1134/43/3413P/1419- | | | | RPR **150c** |

Starts	1st	2nd	3rd	4th	Win & Pl
14	4	-	4	4	£76,807
	2/17	Fair	3m1f Gd3 Ch heavy	£22,692
139	4/16	Punc	3m1f 120-145 Ch Hcap yield	£26,029
	12/15	Punc	3m1f Ch heavy	£6,953
	11/13	Asct	1m7¹/₂f Cls4 NHF 4-6yo gd-sft	£3,128

Laid out for last season's Grand National (sent off just 11-1 after winning the Bobbyjo Chase at Fairyhouse on his prep run) but could manage only ninth; lack of experience perhaps a factor on only his seventh run over fences and may fulfil his potential in time.

Pobbles Bay (Ire)

7 b g Oscar - Rose De Beaufai (Solon)

| Evan Williams | | | | David M Williams |

| PLACINGS: 33/5124/115- | | | | RPR **147+c** |

Starts	1st	2nd	3rd	4th	Win & Pl
9	3	1	2	1	£33,628
139	12/16	Chep	2m7¹/₂f Cls3 Nov 127-146 Ch Hcap gd-sft	£12,996
125	11/16	Uttx	2m4f Cls3 Nov 116-135 Ch Hcap soft	£9,384
113	12/15	Ffos	2m4f Cls3 104-122 Hdl Hcap heavy	£5,848

Big improver when sent chasing last season, winning novice handicaps at Uttoxeter and Chepstow; came up short when stepped up in grade at Warwick but open to further progress after just three runs over fences; stays further than 3m.

Politologue (Fr)

6 gr g Poliglote - Scarlet Row (Turgeon)

| Paul Nicholls | | | | J Hales |

| PLACINGS: 21U210/11214F- | | | | RPR **160+c** |

Starts	1st	2nd	3rd	4th	Win & Pl
12	5	3	-	1	£104,521
	2/17	Kemp	2m4¹/₂f Cls2 Ch gd-sft	£12,512
	12/16	Asct	2m5f Cls1 Nov Gd2 Ch gd-sft	£18,224
	11/16	Hayd	2m5¹/₂f Cls2 Nov Ch soft	£16,245
	2/16	Extr	2m1f Cls1 Nov List Hdl heavy	£11,524
	6/15	Autl	2m2f Hdl 4yo soft	£17,860

Smart novice chaser last season; spent much of his time racing at around 2m4f, including when fourth in the JLT at Cheltenham, but looked happier back at 2m when a desperately unlucky loser at Aintree (clipped his own heel when landing in front over the last).

Potters Legend

7 b g Midnight Legend - Loose Morals (Luso)

Lucy Wadham   Mrs J May

PLACINGS: 1221223/1124244-   RPR **147+c**

Starts		1st	2nd	3rd	4th	Win & Pl
14		4	6	1	3	£67,352
	11/16	Bang	2m4¹/₂f Cls3 Nov Ch soft			£6,498
	11/16	Kemp	3m Cls3 Nov Ch good			£6,498
	1/16	Hntg	2m Cls5 Mdn Hdl soft			£2,274
	10/15	Fknm	2m Cls6 Am NHF 4-6yo gd-sft			£2,053

Smart staying hurdler who took well to fences last season, winning twice and running several good races in defeat; seemed to improve for the step up to 3m2f when staying on for a close fourth in the Kim Muir.

Pougne Bobbi (Fr)

6 b/br g Protektor - Amicus (Xaar)

Nicky Henderson   Juergen Meyer

PLACINGS: 312/5157-   RPR **148+c**

Starts		1st	2nd	3rd	4th	Win & Pl
7		2	1	1	-	£18,470
128	2/17	Ludl	2m4f Cls3 109-131 Ch Hcap soft			£12,512
	2/16	Chep	2m Cls4 Nov Hdl 4-7yo heavy			£3,899

Impressive winner of a 2m4f handicap chase at Ludlow; later got outpaced over 2m and then failed to stay 3m; should resume progress back over a more suitable distance.

Premier Bond

7 b g Kayf Tara - Celtic Native (Be My Native)

Nicky Henderson   Middleham Park Racing XI

PLACINGS: 331/2147/2113P-   RPR **144+c**

Starts		1st	2nd	3rd	4th	Win & Pl
12		4	2	3	1	£26,279
	1/17	Donc	3m Cls4 Nov Ch good			£4,549
	1/17	Catt	3m1f Cls4 Nov Ch gd-sft			£5,198
	12/15	Newb	2m¹/₂f Cls4 Hdl soft			£3,128
	4/15	Ffos	2m Cls6 NHF 4-5yo gd-sft			£1,643

Very useful staying novice chaser last season when beaten only by Might Bite in first three runs and then a strong-finishing length-and-a-half third in the Kim Muir; well below his best in the Scottish National but could be a force in similar races.

Present Man (Ire)

7 b g Presenting - Glen's Gale (Strong Gale)

Paul Nicholls   Woodhouse & Sutton

PLACINGS: /10/226242/21U1141P-   RPR **152+c**

Starts		1st	2nd	3rd	4th	Win & Pl
16		5	5	-	2	£64,992
	4/17	Asct	2m5f Cls3 Nov Ch good			£9,747
	12/16	Donc	3m Cls1 Nov Gd2 Ch good			£19,933
132	11/16	Asct	2m5f Cls3 114-138 Ch Hcap gd-sft			£16,245
125	10/16	Winc	2m4f Cls3 119-127 Ch Hcap gd-fm			£6,498
	11/14	Winc	1m7¹/₂f Cls6 NHF 4-6yo gd-sft			£1,625

Flourished when sent chasing last season, winning four times including a 3m Grade 2 at Doncaster

and twice over 2m5f at Ascot; looked a non-stayer when pulled up in the bet365 Gold Cup; could win more good races if dropped in trip.

Presenting Percy

6 b g Sir Percy - Hunca Munca (Presenting)

Pat Kelly (Ir)   Philip J Reynolds

PLACINGS: 21/741154116-   RPR **156+h**

Starts		1st	2nd	3rd	4th	Win & Pl
11		5	1	-	2	£88,632
146	3/17	Chel	3m Cls1 List 137-147 Hdl Hcap good			£54,103
130	2/17	Fair	2m4f 108-138 Hdl Hcap heavy			£13,667
115	11/16	Punc	2m Nov 90-121 Hdl Hcap soft			£7,235
	10/16	Gway	2m Mdn Hdl 4-5yo yield			£5,879
	4/16	Baln	2m1f NHF 4-7yo heavy			£4,296

Subject of a handicapping controversy at last season's Cheltenham Festival but proved he was still ahead of the assessor by running away with the Pertemps Final; only sixth at Grade 1 level subsequently on a trip to Punchestown, but looks an exciting chasing prospect.

Prince Of Scars (Ire)

7 b g Flemensfirth - Spirit Leader (Supreme Leader)

Gordon Elliott (Ir)   Gigginstown House Stud

PLACINGS: 5/125/81113/236P3-   RPR **139+c**

Starts		1st	2nd	3rd	4th	Win & Pl
13		4	2	3	-	£95,869
	12/15	Leop	3m Gd1 Hdl heavy			£39,535
139	11/15	Navn	2m7f 111-139 Hdl Hcap soft			£15,116
130	11/15	Clon	3m 109-136 Hdl Hcap heavy			£12,093
	1/15	Leop	2m Mdn Hdl yield			£3,624

Quickly developed into a leading staying hurdler two seasons ago, winning a Grade 1 on heavy ground at Leopardstown; fell well short of expectations over fences last season but retains novice status and starts on an enticing mark.

Ptit Zig (Fr)

8 b g Great Pretender - Red Rym (Denham Red)

Paul Nicholls   Chris Giles & B Fulton

PLACINGS: 1F5/12FU21/4134862-8   RPR **160h**

Starts		1st	2nd	3rd	4th	Win & Pl
32		10	7	2	4	£571,755
	6/16	Autl	3m1¹/₂f Gd1 Hdl soft			£122,426
	4/16	Sand	2m4¹/₂f Cls1 List Hdl good			£28,475
	10/15	DRoy	2m4f Gd2 Ch yld-sft			£23,256
	1/15	Chel	2m5f Cls1 Nov Gd2 Ch soft			£18,310
	12/14	Asct	2m3f Cls1 Nov Gd2 Ch soft			£17,162
	11/14	Wwck	2m Cls3 Nov Ch 4-5yo soft			£9,384
	11/14	Extr	2m1¹/₂f Cls4 Ch soft			£4,660
	11/13	Autl	2m3¹/₂f Gd1 Hdl 4yo heavy			£98,780
134	4/13	Sand	2m Cls2 112-134 Hdl 4yo Hcap good			£15,640
	2/13	Ludl	2m Cls4 Mdn Hdl soft			£3,249

Lost confidence over fences after winning three Grade 2 contests in 2014-15 but reverted to hurdles with plenty of success in 2016, most notably landing the French Champion Hurdle;

largely disappointing since, although finished a good second at Sandown in April and with the right trainer to see a return to winning form.

Rashaan (Ire)
5 ch g Manduro - Rayyana (Rainbow Quest)

Colin Kidd (Ir)				Mrs T J Kidd & Mrs R Treacy
PLACINGS: 111562/70521359-1711				RPR **154+h**

Starts	1st	2nd	3rd	4th	Win & Pl
18	7	2	1	-	£102,559
	9/17	DRoy	3m¹/₂f Hdl yield.................................£10,530
	7/17	Cork	2m4f Hdl good £11,038
	6/17	DRoy	2m4f Hdl good £9,214
	11/16	DRoy	2m Gd2 Hdl good £21,691
	11/15	Fair	2m Gd3 Hdl 3yo soft £15,116
	9/15	List	2m Hdl 3yo soft...............................£10,078
	8/15	Rosc	2m Mdn Hdl 3yo gd-yld....................£5,616

Hit hard by the British handicapper for making most of race fitness to beat Apple's Jade and Petit Mouchoir at Down Royal last season and missed big spring targets as a result; did well this summer but connections will now be hoping for more leniency from the assessor.

Rather Be (Ire)
6 b g Oscar - Irish Wedding (Bob Back)

Nicky Henderson				Matt & Lauren Morgan
PLACINGS: U129/112U18-				RPR **143h**

Starts	1st	2nd	3rd	4th	Win & Pl
10	4	2	-	-	£52,916
136	4/17	Aint	2m4f Cls1 Gd3 130-146 Hdl Hcap good............£39,389
	12/16	Hntg	2m3¹/₂f Cls4 Nov Hdl gd-sft......................£3,249
	10/16	Hrfd	2m Cls4 Nov Hdl 4-6yo good.....................£3,899
	12/15	Ludl	1m6f Cls4 NHF 4-5yo soft...........................£3,899

Progressive novice hurdler last season, landing a third win in a competitive handicap at Aintree; didn't run his race when stepped up to Grade 2 level at Sandown, fading tamely; acts on any ground and versatile in terms of trip having won over hurdles from 2m to 2m4f.

Rathnure Rebel (Ire)
7 b g Beneficial - Euro Magic (Eurobus)

Noel Meade (Ir)				Gigginstown House Stud
PLACINGS: 1/671145-				RPR **144+h**

Starts	1st	2nd	3rd	4th	Win & Pl
6	2			1	£23,495
	12/16	Cork	3m Nov Gd3 Hdl sft-hvy £15,827
	11/16	Clon	2m3¹/₂f Mdn Hdl yield.............................£5,879

Signed off for last season with a couple of disappointing efforts but had previously looked a very smart staying novice hurdler, especially on heavy ground when running away with a Grade

3 at Cork; could easily bounce back in similar conditions.

Rathvinden (Ire)
9 b g Heron Island - Peggy Cullen (Presenting)

Willie Mullins (Ir)				R A Bartlett
PLACINGS: F111F23/P-2113				RPR **143+c**

Starts	1st	2nd	3rd	4th	Win & Pl
11	5	2	2	-	£69,359
	8/17	Gway	2m2f Nov Gd3 Ch yield.........................£25,214
	7/17	Wxfd	3m1f Ch good £6,581
	12/13	Cork	2m Mdn Hdl soft £5,610
	11/13	Cork	2m NHF 4-7yo sft-hvy £5,610
	6/13	Dpat	2m2f NHF 4-7yo gd-fm...........................£3,927

Had run only once in more than three years before returning in May but has been making up for lost time, winning his second chase in a Grade 3 at Galway; third to Faugheen in the 2014 Neptune before his problems and clearly retains plenty of ability.

Red Jack (Ire)
4 b g Mahler - Hollygrove Bonnie (Lord America)

Noel Meade (Ir)				John P McManus
PLACINGS: 11-				RPR **119+b**

Starts	1st	2nd	3rd	4th	Win & Pl
2	2	-	-	-	£55,425
	4/17	Fair	2m NHF 4-5yo gd-yld...........................£50,427
	1/17	Naas	2m NHF 4yo soft.....................................£4,998

Snapped up by JP McManus after making a winning debut at Naas (runner-up Debuchet second in the Champion Bumper at Cheltenham) and followed up in a big sales bumper at Fairyhouse; pedigree full of stamina and should be a good staying novice hurdler.

Regal Encore (Ire)
9 b g King's Theatre - Go On Eileen (Bob Back)

Anthony Honeyball				John P McManus
PLACINGS: 0174/53F1PPP/2PP1P8-				RPR **153+c**

Starts	1st	2nd	3rd	4th	Win & Pl
25	5	4	1	3	£117,128
144	12/16	Asct	3m Cls1 List 134-155 Ch Hcap gd-sft.................£56,950
	12/15	Plum	2m1f Cls3 Nov Ch soft...............................£6,498
129	2/15	Extr	2m7f Cls2 127-153 Hdl Hcap gd-sft.........£12,512
	11/13	Plum	2m Cls4 Nov Hdl gd-sft.............................£3,249
	10/12	Chep	2m Cls6 NHF 4-6yo gd-sft..........................£1,754
	2/12	Sthl	2m Cls6 NHF 4-6yo std-slw..........................£1,437

Failed to fulfil his potential since finishing second in the 2013 Champion Bumper but went some way to putting that right when winning last season's Silver Cup at Ascot; pulled up in six of last ten races but first or second in three of the other four.

'Signed off for last season with a couple of disappointing efforts but had previously looked very smart and could easily bounce back'

Centre of Excellence for Training in the Horseracing world

THE BRITISH
RACING SCHOOL

Training for racing

Trainers Courses	Point to Point Pre-season
Level 3 Diploma	Introduction to Management
Assistant Trainers Courses	Management Academy
Jockey Courses	The Racing Industry Course
Yard Managers Courses	Yard Based Training
Health and Safety	Racing Secretaries
Transport	SAGE and Bookkeeping

For more information

T: 01638 665103   E: enquiries@brs.org.uk   W: www.brs.org.uk

THE BRITISH RACING SCHOOL

Renneti (Fr)

8 b g Irish Wells - Caprice Meill (French Glory)

Willie Mullins (Ir)   Mrs S Ricci

PLACINGS: 12FR/143/23816-   RPR **159+h**

Starts	1st	2nd	3rd	4th	Win & Pl
12	3	2	2	1	£87,151

4/17	Fair	2m4f Gd2 Hdl Hcap gd-yld	£35,299
8/15	Slig	2m Hdl heavy	£6,953
10/13	Dpat	2m2f Mdn Hdl 4yo yield	£4,207

Quirky but talented horse who finally began to find more consistent form last spring, easily winning a Grade 2 at Fairyhouse in between good efforts at Cheltenham and Punchestown; has since thrived on the Flat and could still have a big handicap in him over hurdles.

River Frost

5 b g Silver Frost - River Test (Beat Hollow)

Alan King   John P McManus

PLACINGS: 311F19-   RPR **144h**

Starts	1st	2nd	3rd	4th	Win & Pl
6	3	-	1	-	£15,830

133	2/17	Kemp	2m5f Cls3 123-135 Hdl Hcap good	£5,848
123	1/17	Kemp	2m Cls3 115-138 Hdl Hcap gd-sft	£6,256
	11/16	Plum	2m Cls4 Nov Hdl gd-sft	£3,249

Won three times over hurdles last season including two handicaps at Kempton, looking most impressive when stepped up to 2m5f on his penultimate start; 10lb rise looked just too much when only ninth in the Coral Cup but should progress after just six runs.

River Wylde (Ire)

6 b g Oscar - Clarin River (Mandalus)

Nicky Henderson   Grech & Parkin

PLACINGS: 23/1011135-   RPR **148h**

Starts	1st	2nd	3rd	4th	Win & Pl
8	4	-	2	-	£43,190

2/17	Kemp	2m Cls1 Nov Gd2 Hdl good	£17,085
1/17	Ludl	2m Cls4 Nov Hdl soft	£3,899
12/16	Ludl	2m Cls4 Mdn Hdl gd-sft	£3,899
5/16	Wwck	2m Cls6 NHF 4-6yo gd-sft	£1,949

Good winner of a Grade 2 novice hurdle at Kempton last season and ran a huge race when third in the Supreme having been keen early; seemingly over the top when only fifth at Aintree; has won on soft ground (at 3-10) but needs it quicker according to his trainer.

Road To Respect (Ire)

6 ch g Gamut - Lora Lady (Lord Americo)

Noel Meade (Ir)   Gigginstown House Stud

PLACINGS: 1/223135/01432211-   RPR **162c**

Starts	1st	2nd	3rd	4th	Win & Pl
14	4	4	3	1	£147,150

	4/17	Fair	2m4f Nov Gd1 Ch gd-yld	£50,427
145	3/17	Chel	2m5f Cls1 Gd3 133-158 Ch Hcap good	£59,798
	11/16	Naas	2m3f Ch yld-sft	£6,105
	2/16	Thur	2m6¹/₂f Mdn Hdl heavy	£4,522

Much improved last spring, winning a red-hot

Rock The World: could figure in big spring handicaps

handicap chase at the Cheltenham Festival and making the most of Yorkhill's waywardness in the Ryanair Gold Cup at Fairyhouse; yet to prove as effective on softer ground but won a point-to-point and maiden hurdle on heavy.

Road To Riches (Ire)

10 b g Gamut - Bellora (Over The River)

Noel Meade (Ir)					Gigginstown House Stud
PLACINGS: 212113/31232/FP285-0					RPR **156+c**

Starts		1st	2nd	3rd	4th	Win & Pl
27		9	5	4	1	£484,802
	11/15	Clon	2m4f Gd2 Ch sft-hvy			£23,934
	12/14	Leop	3m Gd1 Ch sft-hvy			£75,000
	11/14	DRoy	3m Gd1 Ch yield			£70,000
149	7/14	Gway	2m6½f 134-155 Ch Hcap good			£100,313
	4/14	Fair	2m1f Nov Ch gd-yld			£9,488
	11/13	Naas	2m3f Ch yld-sft			£6,732
	12/12	Cork	3m Nov Gd3 Hdl soft			£14,896
	11/12	Punc	2m4f Mdn Hdl heavy			£7,763
	10/12	Naas	2m3f Hdl 4-7yo heavy			£5,750

Top-class chaser at his best, finishing third in the 2015 Gold Cup having won a couple of Grade 1 chases earlier that season; lightly raced due to injury last season but has soon plummeted in the handicap and may still be good enough to take advantage.

Robinsfirth (Ire)

8 b g Flemensfirth - Phardester (Phardante)

Colin Tizzard					Christine Knowles & Wendy Carter
PLACINGS: 1/4/124/21U-					RPR **149+c**

Starts		1st	2nd	3rd	4th	Win & Pl
8		3	2	-	2	£19,297
	1/17	Extr	2m3f Cls3 Ch soft			£7,798
	12/14	Extr	2m1f Cls4 Nov Hdl 4-6yo gd-sft			£3,574
	4/13	Winc	1m7½f Cls6 NHF 4-6yo good			£1,625

Rated better than Thistlecrack as a novice hurdler by his trainer but subsequently missed nearly two years through injury; showed fair form over fences last season, winning at Exeter and still in contention when departing two out last time; still very lightly raced and open to any amount of improvement.

Rock The Kasbah (Ire)

7 ch g Shirocco - Impudent (In The Wings)

Philip Hobbs					Mrs Diana L Whateley
PLACINGS: 1321P/21100/1324126-					RPR **148c**

Starts		1st	2nd	3rd	4th	Win & Pl
19		7	5	2	1	£122,274
	2/17	Chep	2m7½f Cls3 Nov Ch soft			£6,498
	10/16	Chep	2m3½f Cls2 Nov Ch good			£19,494
144	1/16	Asct	2m3½f Cls1 Gd3 125-151 Hdl Hcap soft			£28,475
136	11/15	Hayd	2m3f Cls2 121-139 Hdl Hcap soft			£25,024
	3/15	Newb	2m3f Cls2 Nov Hdl gd-sft			£5,848
	11/14	Font	2m3f Cls4 Nov Cond Hdl soft			£3,119
	10/14	Ffos	2m Cls6 Mdn NHF 4-7yo soft			£1,643

Didn't quite live up to promise of chase debut

Rock The World (Ire)

9 b g Orpen - Sue N Win (Beneficial)

Jessica Harrington (Ir)					John P McManus
PLACINGS: 512212137/208014-250					RPR **163c**

Starts		1st	2nd	3rd	4th	Win & Pl
147		6	10	2	2	£168,049
	3/17	Chel	2m¼f Cls1 Gd3 135-154 Ch Hcap good			£59,798
	10/15	Chel	2m Cls2 Nov Ch good			£12,512
	9/15	Gway	2m2f Nov Gd3 Ch good			£15,116
	5/15	Baln	2m1f Ch good			£5,884
	12/14	Punc	2m Nov Hdl gd-yld			£8,625
	11/14	DRoy	2m Mdn Hdl 4-6yo yield			£8,050

Won the Grand Annual at Cheltenham at the second attempt last season having finished a well-backed third 12 months earlier; acquitted himself well at Grade 1 level when fourth at Punchestown; best on good ground and may not be seen much until the spring.

Rogue Angel (Ire)

9 b g Presenting - Carrigeen Kohleria (Luso)

Mouse Morris (Ir)					Gigginstown House Stud
PLACINGS: P541216P41/080095PP-					RPR **136c**

Starts		1st	2nd	3rd	4th	Win & Pl
40		5	5	4	5	£254,139
137	3/16	Fair	3m5f 124-150 Ch Hcap yld-sft			£111,765
133	9/15	List	3m 130-147 Ch Hcap heavy			£81,589
127	7/15	Gway	2m6f 114-135 Ch Hcap yield			£13,353
	12/13	Punc	3m Ch heavy			£6,732
	10/12	Gway	2m Mdn Hdl 4yo yld-sft			£6,325

Capped a terrific campaign two seasons ago by winning the Irish National; struggled last season but really caught the eye in the Grand National (jumped boldly in front before paying price for going too fast) and slipping down the handicap.

Roi Des Francs (Fr)

8 b g Poliglote - Grande Souveraine (Sillery)

Gordon Elliott (Ir)					Gigginstown House Stud
PLACINGS: 13P/621166/3205410P-					RPR **157c**

Starts		1st	2nd	3rd	4th	Win & Pl
22		6	3	3	1	£80,587
	3/17	DRoy	3m2f Ch yld-sft			£10,530
	1/16	Naas	3m Nov Gd2 Ch sft-hvy			£18,750
	12/15	Fair	3m Ch heavy			£5,884
	2/15	Clon	2m6f Nov Gd3 Hdl yld-sft			£15,872
	1/15	Thur	2m6f Mdn Hdl sft-hvy			£4,279
	1/14	Tipp	2m4f NHF 5-7yo good			£4,313

Not far off the best novice chasers two seasons ago and began to fulfil that potential last spring when winning well at Down Royal in first-time blinkers; ran well for a long way in the Grand

National and found Irish National coming too soon the following week.

Romain De Senam (Fr)

5 b g Saint Des Saints - Salvatrixe (Housamix)

Paul Nicholls				Dan Macdonald & Chris Giles

PLACINGS: 621/132525/2315752-				RPR **141**c

Starts	1st	2nd	3rd	4th	Win & Pl
16	3	5	2	-	£73,874
	1/17	Leic	2m Cls3 Nov Ch good..£7,596		
	10/15	Winc	1m7¹/₂f Cls4 Hdl 3yo good...................................£5,198		
	4/15	Engh	2m1¹/₂f Hdl 3yo v soft.......................................£17,860		

Beaten a head in the 2016 Fred Winter and picked out by his trainer as a leading hope for a handicap chase at last season's Cheltenham Festival only to miss the cut; looked in need of further when running well in subsequent good 2m handicaps.

Royal Regatta (Ire)

9 b g King's Theatre - Friendly Craic (Mister Lord)

Philip Hobbs				Mrs Lesley Field & Mrs Eileen Murphy

PLACINGS: 313152P/65123/51P3P-				RPR **161**+c

Starts		1st	2nd	3rd	4th	Win & Pl
23		7	2	4	-	£150,984
	11/16	Asct	2m5f Cls1 Gd2 Ch gd-sft...................................£39,865			
	12/15	Asct	2m5f Cls2 Ch gd-sft...£15,857			
138	1/15	Donc	2m¹/₂f Cls2 127-143 Ch Hcap gd-sft...............£11,886			
130	11/14	Newb	2m7¹/₂f Cls3 Nov 128-139 Ch Hcap soft..........£10,948			
	12/13	Leic	2m4f Cls4 Nov Hdl 4-6yo good............................£4,549			
	10/13	Aint	2m4f Cls4 Nov Hdl gd-sft.....................................£5,198			
	3/13	Hayd	1m7¹/₂f Cls5 NHF 4-5yo gd-sft...........................£1,949			

Gutsy all-the-way winner of a Grade 2 at Ascot last November; better than the bare form of subsequent Ascot Chase third to Cue Card (finished very tired having gone hard up front) and seemed to resent switch to hold-up tactics at Aintree.

Royal Vacation (Ire)

7 b g King's Theatre - Summer Break (Foxhound)

Colin Tizzard				Mrs Jean R Bishop

PLACINGS: 232/146110/221311PP-				RPR **155**+c

Starts		1st	2nd	3rd	4th	Win & Pl
19		6	4	2	2	£93,725
143	1/17	Chel	2m5f Cls2 Nov 120-146 Ch Hcap soft...............£15,640			
	12/16	Kemp	3m Cls1 Nov Gd1 Ch good..................................£40,569			
129	11/16	Ling	2m7¹/₂f Cls3 112-129 Ch Hcap heavy..................£8,578			
	3/16	Plum	2m Cls4 Nov Hdl good...£3,899			
125	2/16	Tntn	2m¹/₂f Cls3 115-136 Hdl Hcap heavy.................£11,574			
	10/15	Weth	2m3¹/₂f Cls4 Nov Hdl gd-sft..............................£3,249			

Lucky to exploit Might Bite's final-fence fall when winning a Grade 1 at Kempton but proved a smart horse in his own right when adding a novice handicap at Cheltenham; perhaps helped by soft ground that day and twice pulled up on quicker in the spring.

Samcro (Ire)

5 ch g Germany - Dun Dun (Saddlers' Hall)

Gordon Elliott (Ir)				Gigginstown House Stud

PLACINGS: 1/111-				RPR **136**+b

Starts	1st	2nd	3rd	4th	Win & Pl
3	3	-	-	-	£25,381
	4/17	Fair	2m NHF 4-7yo gd-yld...£8,424		
	12/16	Navn	2m List NHF 4-7yo sft-hvy................................£12,436		
	11/16	Punc	2m NHF 4yo soft...£4,522		

Unbeaten in three bumpers last season; got the job done narrowly in testing conditions in a Listed race and far more impressive on quicker ground when quickening up smartly for a 17-length win at Fairyhouse; should be a high-class novice hurdler.

San Benedeto (Fr)

6 ch g Layman - Cinco Baidy (Lure)

Paul Nicholls				P J Vogt

PLACINGS: 523365/11423U311113-				RPR **163**c

Starts		1st	2nd	3rd	4th	Win & Pl
25		9	4	6	1	£200,670
150	4/17	Aint	2m Cls1 Nov Gd1 Ch good.................................£56,793			
145	4/17	Asct	2m1f Cls2 Nov 124-150 Ch Hcap good...............£29,675			
140	3/17	Donc	2m¹/₂f Cls2 128-145 Ch Hcap soft.....................£18,768			
	2/17	Muss	2m Cls3 127-141 Ch Hcap good..........................£14,296			
	6/16	Worc	2m4f Cls4 Nov Ch good.......................................£4,549			
	5/16	Sedg	2m3¹/₂f Cls4 Nov Ch gd-fm................................£4,029			
130	11/15	Winc	2m4f Cls3 114-134 Hdl Hcap heavy.....................£7,596			
	5/15	Strf	2m¹/₂f Cls4 Nov Hdl good.....................................£3,249			
	3/15	Winc	1m7¹/₂f Cls4 Nov Hdl good..................................£3,249			

Very busy last season but flourished into the spring, completing a four-timer in a Grade 1 novice chase at Aintree; lucky to capitalise on late exit of Politologue though, and put firmly in his place by top 2m chasers at Sandown last time so may be hard to place.

Saphir Du Rheu (Fr)

8 gr g Al Namix - Dona Du Rheu (Dom Pasquini)

Paul Nicholls				The Stewart Family

PLACINGS: 1F121/155665/3F215F-				RPR **168**c

Starts		1st	2nd	3rd	4th	Win & Pl
28		9	2	3	2	£334,498
	2/17	Kels	2m7¹/₂f Cls2 Ch heavy..£16,245			
	11/15	Carl	2m4f Cls1 List Ch gd-sft...................................£15,661			
	4/15	Aint	3m1f Cls1 Nov Gd1 Ch good..............................£50,793			
	1/15	Chel	3m Cls1 Gd2 Hdl soft...£34,170			
	12/14	Extr	2m3f Cls2 Ch gd-sft...£12,512			
158	2/14	Ffos	2m4f Cls2 130-158 Hdl Hcap heavy....................£31,280			
145	12/13	Kemp	2m5f Cls1 List 121-145 Hdl Hcap soft...............£25,628			
130	12/13	Sand	2m6f Cls2 120-142 Hdl Hcap gd-sft..................£12,512			
	1/13	Tntn	2m1¹/₂f Cls4 Nov Hdl heavy.................................£4,106			

Lost his way after finishing second in the World Hurdle and winning a Grade 1 novice chase at Aintree in 2015 but was coaxed back to form last season and beaten little over six lengths when fifth in the Gold Cup; has more to offer at the top level on that evidence.

Saturnas (Fr)
6 b g Davidoff - Sayuri (Acatenango)

Willie Mullins (Ir)   Wicklow Bloodstock (Ireland)

PLACINGS: 1210-   **RPR 147+h**

Starts	1st	2nd	3rd	4th	Win & Pl
4	2	1	-	-	£54,176

12/16	Leop	2m Nov Gd1 Hdl yield	£36,875
11/16	Naas	2m Mdn Hdl yld-sft	£5,426

Proved himself among last season's leading novice hurdlers when winning a Grade 1 at Leopardstown over Christmas; last when favourite for the Deloitte and subsequently missed Cheltenham through injury; should get further than 2m.

Sceau Royal (Fr)
5 b g Doctor Dino - Sandside (Marchand De Sable)

Alan King   Simon Munir & Isaac Souede

PLACINGS: 71/1d211106/114369-   **RPR 157h**

Starts	1st	2nd	3rd	4th	Win & Pl
15	6	2	1	1	£119,326

149	11/16	Winc	1m7¹/₂f Cls1 Gd2 133-149 Hdl Hcap good	£35,772
	10/16	Chel	2m¹/₂f Cls2 Hdl 4yo good	£21,977
	1/16	Hntg	2m Cls2 Hdl 4yo soft	£12,512
	12/15	Chel	2m1f Cls2 Hdl 3yo soft	£12,628
	11/15	Wwck	2m Cls4 Hdl 3yo gd-sft	£3,249
	3/15	Bord	2m¹/₂f Hdl 3yo v soft	£7,814

Flourished early last season when winning at Cheltenham and Wincanton but just found out in better races subsequently, including when sixth in the Champion Hurdle; set to go novice chasing and trainer rates him a very exciting prospect over fences.

Seldom Inn
9 ch g Double Trigger - Portland Row (Zaffaran)

Sandy Thomson   Seldom Inn Partnership

PLACINGS: /1135/223485/12F12P-   **RPR 155+c**

Starts	1st	2nd	3rd	4th	Win & Pl
19	5	4	3	1	£47,984

	3/17	Kels	2m7¹/₂f Cls1 List Ch heavy	£19,015
	10/16	Kels	2m7¹/₂f Cls4 Nov Ch gd-sft	£4,549
	11/14	Newc	2m¹/₂f Cls4 Nov Hdl gd-sft	£3,249
	10/14	Kels	2m Cls4 Mdn Hdl good	£3,249
	12/13	Newc	2m¹/₂f Cls6 NHF 4-6yo good	£1,560

Lightly raced for his age and a big improver last season, gaining a couple of wide-margin wins at Kelso including in the Listed Premier Chase; fair second behind Yala Enki next time but lost all chance with an early blunder in the Scottish National.

Shaneshill (Ire)
8 b g King's Theatre - Darabaka (Doyoun)

Willie Mullins (Ir)   Andrea & Graham Wylie

PLACINGS: 311422/F233F1P0-1322   **RPR 157c**

Starts	1st	2nd	3rd	4th	Win & Pl
26	9	8	4	1	£427,223

	5/17	Autl	2m5¹/₂f Gd2 Hdl v soft	£67,308
	1/17	Gowr	3m Gd2 Hdl soft	£22,692
	1/16	Naas	2m Nov Gd2 Ch heavy	£10,037
	11/15	Thur	2m2f Ch soft	£5,884
	4/15	Fair	2m4f Nov Gd2 Hdl soft	£21,415
	11/14	Fair	2m4f Mdn Hdl sft-hvy	£4,600
	4/14	Punc	2m Gd1 NHF 4-7yo gd-yld	£48,750
	11/13	Fair	2m NHF 4-7yo gd-yld	£5,610
	11/13	Naas	2m NHF 4yo yld-sft	£4,488

Runner-up three times at the Cheltenham Festival, most recently in the 2016 RSA Chase; did well reverting to hurdles last season, although he just comes up short against the best; second in the Galway Plate back over fences and could win a big handicap.

Shantou Bob (Ire)
9 b g Shantou - Bobset Leader (Bob Back)

Warren Greatrex   Fallon, Shipp & Bolingbroke

PLACINGS: 1/111236/P/215-   **RPR 144h**

Starts	1st	2nd	3rd	4th	Win & Pl
10	4	2	1		£38,324

137	12/16	Chep	2m7¹/₂f Cls2 117-138 Hdl Hcap soft	£15,825
	11/14	Ling	2m3¹/₂f Cls4 Nov Hdl 4-6yo soft	£3,444
	10/14	Ffos	2m4f Cls5 Mdn Hdl gd-sft	£1,949
	5/14	Ffos	2m Cls6 NHF 4-6yo soft	£1,711

Resumed progress after a 12-month layoff last season having once been a promising novice hurdler (sixth in the Albert Bartlett after being placed twice at Grade 2 level); won a handicap off top weight at Chepstow before a fine fifth in the Cleeve Hurdle.

Shantou Rock (Ire)
5 b g Shantou - Cool Cool (Anabaa)

Dan Skelton   Mr & Mrs Gordon Pink

PLACINGS: 42/2721211F-   **RPR 140+h**

Starts	1st	2nd	3rd	4th	Win & Pl
8	3	3	-	-	£20,520

125	4/17	Ludl	2m Cls3 122-133 Hdl Hcap gd-sft	£7,798
	3/17	Ludl	2m Cls4 Nov Hdl soft	£5,198
	2/17	Ludl	2m Cls4 Mdn Hdl soft	£3,899

Won three times over hurdles last season, albeit when kept to modest company (sent off no bigger than 1-2 and also beaten at 1-3); unlucky

not to add a fourth win when falling at the last (in command) at Exeter; likely to go novice chasing.

Shantou Village (Ire)

7 b g Shantou - Village Queen (King's Theatre)

Neil Mulholland · Mrs Jane Gerard-Pearse

PLACINGS: 11/112P/11F11- · RPR **154+c**

Starts	1st	2nd	3rd	4th	Win & Pl
10	7	1	-	-	£68,294

146	4/17	Sand	2m4f Cls2 Nov 128-152 Ch Hcap good	£18,768
	4/17	Font	2m5f Cls4 Nov Ch good	£3,899
	10/16	Chel	2m4f Cls2 Nov Ch good	£12,512
	8/16	Font	2m5f Cls4 Nov Ch good	£4,660
	11/15	Chel	2m5f Cls1 Nov Gd2 Hdl good	£17,085
	10/15	Carl	2m4f Cls4 Nov Hdl good	£3,249
	3/15	Weth	2m Cls6 NHF 4-6yo good	£1,711

Won four out of five over fences last season, culminating in a good novice handicap at Sandown; raised just 2lb so still well handicapped and could even step back up to Grade 1 level (was favourite for the Albert Bartlett in 2016 when struck into and pulled up).

Shattered Love (Ire)

6 b m Yeats - Tracker (Bustino)

Gordon Elliott (Ir) · Gigginstown House Stud

PLACINGS: 1/13/1221107- · RPR **141h**

Starts	1st	2nd	3rd	4th	Win & Pl
9	4	2	1		£56,593

	2/17	Fair	2m2f Nov Gd3 Hdl sft-hvy	£18,397
	12/16	Thur	2m Nov List Hdl soft	£15,827
	10/16	Tipp	2m Mdn Hdl yld-sft	£4,522
	3/16	Naas	2m NHF 4-7yo sft-hvy	£4,522

Twice disappointing in Grade 1 novice hurdles in the spring but had been sent off just 8-1 for the Neptune after showing strong form in the winter on softer ground; won Grade 3 and Listed hurdles after a good second behind Let's Dance (pair clear).

Shelford (Ire)

8 b g Galileo - Lyrical (Shirley Heights)

Dan Skelton · Carl Hodgson

PLACINGS: 114F5/11/2586122-223 · RPR **140h**

Starts	1st	2nd	3rd	4th	Win & Pl
19	5	7	1	1	£143,940

	3/17	Towc	3m¹/₂f Cls4 Ch soft	£4,883
	4/16	Engh	2m3f List Hdl v soft	£30,000
	3/16	Engh	2m3f Hdl v soft	£21,176
127	10/14	Chep	2m3¹/₂f Cls1 Gd3 123-149 Hdl Hcap soft	£22,780
	10/14	Chep	2m3¹/₂f Cls4 Nov Hdl gd-sft	£3,899

Came up short at top level over hurdles last season and took a while to get the hang of fences but did better in top handicaps over the summer; may have more to come back over 3m after a never-nearer third when favourite for the Summer Plate.

Silsol (Ger)

8 b g Soldier Hollow - Silveria (Groom Dancer)

Paul Nicholls · Michelle & Dan Macdonald

PLACINGS: 1/1512/611243132/81- · RPR **157+h**

Starts	1st	2nd	3rd	4th	Win & Pl
20	8	5	2	2	£166,771

	10/16	Weth	3m Cls1 Gd2 Hdl good	£22,887
152	4/16	Kels	3m2f Cls2 133-152 Hdl Hcap gd-sft	£12,996
	11/15	Hayd	2m5¹/₂f Cls2 Nov Ch soft	£16,245
	11/15	Carl	2m4f Cls3 Nov Ch heavy	£6,498
151	1/15	Ffos	2m4f Cls2 131-151 Hdl Hcap heavy	£31,280
144	11/14	Newb	2m3f Cls2 124-144 Hdl Hcap soft	£19,494
	4/14	NAbb	2m5¹/₂f Cls4 Nov Hdl gd-sft	£3,509
124	4/14	Ayr	2m4f Cls3 102-128 Hdl Hcap gd-sft	£7,798

Back from injury having missed much of last

season after his win in the West Yorkshire Hurdle at Wetherby; had been switched back to hurdles after proving far from natural over fences and likely to be aimed at the World Hurdle.

Singlefarmpayment

7 b g Milan - Crevamoy (Shardari)

Tom George · N T Griffith & H M Haddock

PLACINGS: /6F2244/2211P/321B2- · RPR **150c**

Starts 16	1st 3	2nd 6	3rd 1	4th 2	Win & Pl £63,292
	12/16	Chel	3m1¹/²f Cls2 Nov Ch good		£15,640
125	1/16	Chel	3m Cls2 125-144 Hdl Hcap heavy		£12,512
	12/15	Sthl	3m Cls4 Nov Hdl soft		£3,899

Won a novice chase at Cheltenham last season and perhaps unlucky not to add a bigger success, getting brought down when going well there in January and beaten a short head at the festival; should be a player in more top handicaps.

Sir Note (Fr)

7 gr g Victory Note - Niangara (Baby Turk)

James Eustace · G F Chesneaux

PLACINGS: /87PU/141P11/131121- · RPR **142+c**

Starts 17	1st 8	2nd 1	3rd 2	4th 1	Win & Pl £54,155
133	4/17	Hntg	2m4f Cls3 128-135 Ch Hcap good		£9,731
130	2/17	Kemp	2m4¹/²f Cls3 111-130 Ch Hcap good		£8,163
120	12/16	Leic	2m Cls3 97-123 Ch Hcap gd-fm		£6,498
108	5/16	MRas	2m1f Cls4 104-120 Ch Hcap good		£4,289
107	3/16	MRas	2m1f Cls4 Nov 103-118 Ch Hcap soft		£5,326
95	1/16	Hntg	2m¹/²f Cls4 Nov 95-105 Ch Hcap soft		£3,994
86	6/15	Uttx	2m Cls5 Nov 74-100 Hdl Hcap good		£2,339
79	5/15	Worc	2m Cls5 74-100 Hdl Hcap gd-sft		£2,599

Massive improver since going chasing in January 2016, winning six out of eight and climbing 42lb up the handicap; still going the right way judging by good win at Huntingdon on final start; has won from 2m to 2m4f and trainer expects him to get further.

Sir Valentino (4): could find life tough from a mark of 160

Sir Valentino (Fr)

8 b g Early March - Valentine (Double Bed)

Tom George · Doone Hulse, Susie Saunders & Lady Cobham

PLACINGS: F/58111525/14815236- · RPR **168+c**

Starts 28	1st 7	2nd 6	3rd 3	4th 1	Win & Pl £177,620
147	11/16	Extr	2m1¹/²f Cls1 Gd2 139-163 Ch Hcap good		£35,594
141	5/16	MRas	2m3f Cls2 129-143 Ch Hcap good		£15,640
139	12/15	Ludl	2m Cls2 128-139 Ch Hcap soft		£17,870
132	12/15	Ludl	2m Cls3 112-135 Ch Hcap soft		£9,747
122	11/15	Leic	1m7¹/²f Cls3 108-122 Hdl Hcap gd-sft		£6,498
124	1/15	Ludl	2m Cls3 Nov 124-130 Ch Hcap soft		£6,498
	4/14	Sthl	1m7¹/²f Cls5 Mdn Hdl good		£1,949

Rapidly progressive last season, winning a handicap chase off 141 first time out and going on to finish third in the Champion Chase; no fluke about that run having also pushed Special Tiara close conceding 7lb at Kempton but may find this season tougher starting on a mark of 160.

Sire De Grugy (Fr)

11 ch g My Risk - Hirlish (Passing Sale)

Gary Moore · The Preston Family & Friends

PLACINGS: 11/U14F/512284/712U- · RPR **170+c**

Starts 38	1st 17	2nd 7	3rd 2	4th 4	Win & Pl £880,644
160	11/16	Asct	2m1f Cls2 139-160 Ch Hcap gd-sft		£62,560
	12/15	Sand	1m7¹/²f Cls1 Gd1 Ch gd-sft		£85,425
172	2/15	Chep	2m Cls2 146-172 Ch Hcap soft		£15,825
	4/14	Sand	1m7¹/²f Cls1 Gd1 Ch gd-sft		£71,188
	3/14	Chel	2m Cls1 Gd1 Ch good		£199,325
	1/14	Asct	1m7¹/²f Cls1 Gd1 Ch heavy		£59,199
	12/13	Kemp	2m Cls1 Gd2 Ch soft		£45,774
	12/13	Sand	1m7¹/²f Cls1 Gd1 Ch good		£76,883
161	10/13	Chep	2m Cls2 135-161 Ch Hcap soft		£16,245
	4/13	Sand	1m7¹/²f Cls1 Gd2 Ch good		£56,950
	4/13	Strf	2m Cls4 Nov Ch good		£4,549
	11/12	Ling	2m Cls4 Nov Ch heavy		£3,217
	10/12	Kemp	2m Cls4 Ch good		£3,899
141	2/12	Tntn	2m¹/²f Cls2 121-147 Hdl Hcap gd-sft		£12,660
	2/12	Kemp	2m Cls1 Nov Gd2 Hdl gd-sft		£12,086
	2/11	Folk	2m1f Cls4 Nov Hdl soft		£1,918
	1/11	Fknm	2m Cls5 Mdn Hdl soft		£1,713

More than three years since he won the 2014 Champion Chase and missed the second half of last season due to disappointing work at home; has bounced back from poor form in the past though, notably when winning a big Ascot handicap last season.

Sizing Codelco (Ire)

8 b g Flemensfirth - La Zingarella (Phardante)

Colin Tizzard   Alan Potts

PLACINGS: 2523/51U2U/38P24011-   RPR **160+c**

Starts	1st	2nd	3rd	4th	Win & Pl
22	4	4	4	1	£108,245

150	4/17	Punc	3m¹/₂f 127-150 Ch Hcap gd-yld	£30,256
139	4/17	Aint	3m1f Cls1 List 131-148 Ch Hcap good	£39,423
	9/15	List	2m1f Ch yld-sft	£8,023
	1/14	Fair	2m Mdn Hdl sft-hvy	£4,600

Took giant steps forward at the end of last season when easily winning 3m handicap chases at Aintree and Punchestown; starts this season 21lb higher than for the first of those wins but totally unexposed as a stayer having been running over shorter before that.

Sizing Granite (Ire)

9 br g Milan - Hazel's Tisrara (Mandalus)

Colin Tizzard   Alan Potts

PLACINGS: 1/91U111/25P2/P5P51-   RPR **162+c**

Starts	1st	2nd	3rd	4th	Win & Pl
18	6	3	1	-	£161,353

146	4/17	Punc	2m4f 127-155 Ch Hcap gd-yld	£50,427
	4/15	Aint	2m Cls1 Nov Gd1 Ch good	£61,897
	2/15	Leop	2m1f Nov Ch soft	£10,581
	1/15	Naas	2m Nov Ch soft	£10,078
	11/14	Naas	2m Ch yield	£8,050
	3/14	Gowr	2m Mdn Hdl soft	£5,750

Out of sorts for much of last season following move to Colin Tizzard but came good when running away with a competitive 2m4f handicap chase at Punchestown in April; had won a Grade 1 novice chase in 2015 so could have more to give now back on track.

Sizing John

7 b g Midnight Legend - La Perrotine (Northern Crystal)

Jessica Harrington (Ir)   Alan Potts

PLACINGS: 41213/211223/321111-   RPR **174+c**

Starts	1st	2nd	3rd	4th	Win & Pl
18	8	5	3	1	£733,942

	4/17	Punc	3m¹/₂f Gd1 Ch gd-yld	£126,068
	3/17	Chel	3m2¹/₂f Cls1 Gd1 Ch good	£327,463
	2/17	Leop	3m¹/₂f Gd1 Ch soft	£72,436
	1/17	Thur	2m4f Gd3 Ch yld-sft	£22,692
	11/15	Punc	2m Nov Gd2 Ch sft-hvy	£21,163
	10/15	Punc	2m Ch yield	£7,488
	12/14	Leop	2m Nov Gd1 Hdl heavy	£43,333
	11/14	Naas	2m Mdn Hdl 4yo yield	£5,750

Flourished when stepped up in trip last season, most notably when winning the Cheltenham Gold Cup; also won Grade 1s at Leopardstown

and Punchestown either side of that, proving effectiveness on different ground; still unexposed and could improve again.

Slowmotion (Fr)

5 b/br m Soldier Of Fortune - Second Emotion (Medaaly)

Joseph O'Brien (Ir)   John P McManus

PLACINGS: 121/52F211212-3   RPR **145c**

Starts	1st	2nd	3rd	4th	Win & Pl
13	5	5	1	-	£139,295

	4/17	Fair	2m4f Gd3 Ch gd-yld	£20,171
	2/17	Naas	2m List Ch soft	£17,083
	1/17	Naas	2m Ch soft	£8,410
	3/16	Naas	2m Gd2 Hdl 4yo yld-sft	£19,522
	10/15	Autl	2m2f Hdl 3yo v soft	£20,465

Sharply progressive chaser who won for the third time in four races in a mares' Grade 3 at Fairyhouse in April; may well have won again at Punchestown on her handicap debut but for a mistake two out and ran a big race when third in the Galway Plate.

Smad Place (Fr)

10 gr g Smadoun - Bienna Star (Village Star)

Alan King   Mrs Peter Andrews

PLACINGS: 12/5284/11416/47383-   RPR **168c**

Starts	1st	2nd	3rd	4th	Win & Pl
32	8	5	7	3	£450,579

155	1/16	Chel	3m1¹/₂f Cls1 Gd2 Ch heavy	£57,218
	11/15	Newb	3m2f Cls1 Gd3 139-163 Ch Hcap soft	£113,900
	11/15	Kemp	2m4¹/₂f Cls2 Ch good	£12,996
	2/14	Newb	2m7¹/₂f Cls3 Nov Ch heavy	£7,798
	11/13	Extr	3m Cls3 Nov Ch gd-sft	£6,330
144	1/12	Asct	2m3¹/₂f Cls1 Gd2 125-145 Nov Hcap gd-sft	£22,780
	2/11	Winc	1m7¹/₂f Cls4 Nov Hdl gd-sft	£2,439
	11/10	Newb	2m¹/₂f Cls3 Hdl 3yo gd-sft	£6,505

Won the Hennessy Gold Cup in 2015 but has generally struggled since, just coming up short in Grade 1 company; kept his form well last season though, finishing with a fair third in the Betway Bowl; starts this season back on a more realistic mark.

Smart Talk (Ire)

7 b m Hubbly Bubbly - Belon Breeze (Strong Gale)

Brian Ellison   Mrs J A Martin

PLACINGS: 41/22113110/   RPR **145h**

Starts	1st	2nd	3rd	4th	Win & Pl
8	4	2	1	-	£50,215

	1/16	Donc	2m1¹/₂f Cls1 Gd2 Hdl good	£28,475
	12/15	Hayd	2m3f Cls1 Nov List Hdl heavy	£11,551
	11/15	Sedg	2m4f Cls4 Nov Hdl gd-sft	£3,769
	10/15	Worc	2m Cls4 Nov Hdl gd-sft	£3,899

Won four times over hurdles two seasons ago, most notably in a Grade 2 at Doncaster, but disappointed at the Cheltenham Festival and missed last season through injury; big mare who could well make a chaser; didn't appear to stay on only run beyond 2m4f.

Snow Falcon (Ire)

7 b g Presenting - Flocon De Neige (Kahyasi)

Noel Meade (Ir)   Mrs Patricia Hunt

PLACINGS: 2156/315F1/11F32538-   RPR **159+h**

Starts	1st	2nd	3rd	4th	Win & Pl
21	6	5	3	-	£128,899
	11/16	Navn	2m4f Gd2 Hdl yld-sft		£18,438
	8/16	Rosc	3m¹/₂f Hdl good		£8,366
	2/16	Navn	2m5f Gd2 Hdl heavy		£19,522
	11/15	Naas	2m4f Hdl yield		£10,078
	1/15	Navn	2m7f Mdn Hdl soft		£5,349
	10/14	Fair	2m NHF 4-7yo good		£4,313

Developed into a very smart staying hurdler last season, beaten less than two lengths in the Stayers' Hurdle at Aintree and the Galmoy Hurdle at Gowran; often just outstayed and has won his last two races at around 2m4f, albeit in weaker company.

Snow Leopardess

5 gr m Martaline - Queen Soraya (Persian Bold)

Charlie Longsdon   Mrs O Fox-Pitt

PLACINGS: 15/13131-   RPR **134+h**

Starts	1st	2nd	3rd	4th	Win & Pl
7	4	-	2		£47,519
123	3/17	Newb	2m4¹/₂f Cls1 Nov Gd2 116-132 Hdl Hcap gd-sft	£22,780
	11/16	Donc	2m3¹/₂f Cls4 Nov Hdl good	£4,549
	9/16	Gowr	2m List NHF 4-7yo good	£14,697
	2/16	Donc	2m¹/₂f Cls6 NHF 4-6yo good	£1,994

Listed bumper winner who progressed well over hurdles last season, signing off with a terrific four-length winner in the EBF Mares' Final at Newbury on her handicap debut; has the scope to progress further, especially when switched to fences.

So Celebre (Ger)

4 ch g Peintre Celebre - Saldennahe (Next Desert)

Ian Williams   Miss Jekaterina Melnika

PLACINGS: 33115-   RPR **126+h**

Starts	1st	2nd	3rd	4th	Win & Pl
5	2	-	2	-	£31,530
125	4/17	Asct	1m7¹/₂f Cls2 107-133 Hdl 4yo Hcap good	£25,024
	3/17	Hntg	2m Cls5 Mdn Hdl gd-sft	£2,924

Progressive juvenile hurdler last season and won at Huntingdon and Ascot in the spring, the latter in a competitive juvenile handicap; favourite against older horses at Aintree just six days later but perhaps found race coming too soon, finishing fifth.

Some Plan (Ire)

9 b g Winged Love - Lough Hyne (Classic Cliche)

Henry de Bromhead (Ir)   R S Brookhouse

PLACINGS: 4/1210/5404/01F1166-   RPR **153+c**

Starts	1st	2nd	3rd	4th	Win & Pl
17	5	2	-	3	£99,663
	1/17	Leop	2m1f Nov Gd1 Ch good	£45,385
	1/17	Naas	2m Nov Ch soft	£11,038
	10/16	Punc	2m Ch good	£6,105
	2/15	Muss	1m7¹/₂f Cls2 Nov Hdl good	£12,512
	11/14	Sthl	1m7¹/₂f Cls4 Nov Hdl gd-sft	£3,119

Won three of first four completed starts over fences last season but fortunate to gain his biggest win in the Irish Arkle when Royal Caviar fell at the last; twice outclassed in Grade 1 company subsequently, although probably didn't stay when stepped up to 2m4f.

Southfield Royale

7 b g Presenting - Chamoss Royale (Garde Royale)

Neil Mulholland   Mrs Angela Yeoman

PLACINGS: 112201/21124/70F0-   RPR **125c**

Starts	1st	2nd	3rd	4th	Win & Pl
15	5	4	-	1	£56,085
	12/15	Donc	3m Cls1 Nov Gd2 Ch heavy	£19,221
	10/15	Weth	3m Cls4 Nov Ch soft	£3,861
	3/15	Hntg	2m3¹/₂f Cls4 Nov Hdl gd-sft	£3,899
	11/14	Font	2m3f Cls4 Nov Hdl heavy	£3,899
	6/14	MRas	2m¹/₂f Cls6 NHF 4-6yo good	£1,560

Very smart novice chaser two seasons ago, finishing second in a Grade 1 at Kempton and fourth in the National Hunt Chase (bad blunder two out); showed little in three runs last season but down to a very good mark on his novice form.

Southfield Theatre (Ire)

9 b g King's Theatre - Chamoss Royale (Garde Royale)

Paul Nicholls   Mrs Angela Yeoman

PLACINGS: 34321/11212/34B4/F8-   RPR **157c**

Starts	1st	2nd	3rd	4th	Win & Pl
23	8	3	5	4	£157,921
	2/15	Extr	2m3f Cls3 Nov Ch gd-sft	£6,498
	11/14	Winc	2m4f Cls1 Nov Gd2 Ch gd-sft	£17,655
	10/14	Chep	2m3¹/₂f Cls2 Nov Ch gd-sft	£12,996
	4/14	Sand	2m6f Cls1 List Hdl gd-sft	£28,475
	10/13	Winc	2m5¹/₂f Cls4 Nov Hdl good	£3,249
	4/13	Winc	2m4f Cls4 Nov Hdl soft	£3,249
	3/13	Extr	2m7f Cls4 Nov Hdl good	£3,249
	10/12	Chel	2m¹/₂f Cls4 NHF 4-6yo gd-sft	£4,549

Yet to hit the heights expected of him following a terrific novice campaign three seasons ago (won three times and second in the RSA Chase); lightly raced since then and showed much promise in his unlucky defeat in last season's Badger Ales Trophy (fell when leading at the last); could well pick up a decent handicap or two this season.

Special Tiara
10 b g Kayf Tara - Special Choice (Bob Back)

Henry de Bromhead (Ir)   Mrs S Rowley-Williams

PLACINGS: 3/534131/423/631512-   RPR **170c**

Starts	1st	2nd	3rd	4th	Win & Pl
28	7	5	7	3	£632,012

3/17	Chel	2m Cls1 Gd1 Ch gd-sft	£208,300
12/16	Kemp	2m Cls1 Gd2 Ch good	£46,981
4/15	Sand	1m7¹/₂f Cls1 Gd1 Ch good	£71,188
12/14	Kemp	2m Cls1 Gd2 Ch soft	£46,096
4/13	Aint	2m Cls1 Nov Gd1 Ch good	£62,190
9/12	Baln	2m1f Ch yld-sft	£4,600
7/12	Kbgn	2m Mdn Hdl 4-5yo yield	£4,313

Won the Champion Chase at the fourth attempt last season, although he probably didn't have to improve on his previous placed efforts in the race with Douvan injured and Fox Norton better over further; well beaten by Altior subsequently.

Speredek (Fr)
6 b/br g Kapgarde - Sendamagic (Sendawar)

Nigel Hawke   Kapinhand

PLACINGS: 31/446P126/PP111-   RPR **141+c**

Starts	1st	2nd	3rd	4th	Win & Pl
14	5	1	1	2	£32,251

129	3/17	Ludl	2m Cls2 129-142 Ch Hcap soft	£12,512
122	2/17	Sand	1m7¹/₂f Cls3 113-135 Ch Hcap soft	£7,507
115	2/17	Tntn	2m2f Cls4 Nov 106-120 Ch Hcap soft	£5,697
107	3/16	Extr	2m7f Cls4 93-114 Hdl Hcap gd-sft	£3,249
	3/15	Carl	2m1f Cls6 NHF 4-6yo soft	£1,560

Only a modest hurdler and pulled up on first two runs over fences last season yet flourished when dropped to 2m, winning three successive handicaps; best when able to dominate but survived being taken on last time despite making several errors.

Squouateur (Fr)
6 gr g Martaline - Samansonnienne (Mansonnien)

Gordon Elliott (Ir)   John P McManus

PLACINGS: 4/121176/578P2U-   RPR **135c**

Starts	1st	2nd	3rd	4th	Win & Pl
13	3	2	-	1	£36,893

128	2/16	Fair	2m4f 120-136 Hdl Hcap heavy	£10,853
120	12/15	Leop	2m4f Nov 109-128 Hdl Hcap heavy	£13,605
	11/15	Fair	2m Mdn Hdl 4yo yield	£5,349

Held in extremely high regard at home – sent off favourite at two Cheltenham Festivals – but yet to fully deliver on the track and unseated his rider in last season's Kim Muir; still a novice over fences and likely to do better in time.

Starchitect (Ire)
6 b g Sea The Stars - Humilis (Sadler's Wells)

David Pipe   Paul & Clare Rooney

PLACINGS: 11224F/253/1331535-   RPR **147+c**

Starts	1st	2nd	3rd	4th	Win & Pl
16	4	3	4	1	£94,746

	1/17	Ayr	1m7¹/₂f Cls4 Nov Ch heavy	£4,029
143	5/16	NAbb	2m5¹/₂f Cls2 117-143 Hdl Hcap gd-fm	£12,512
	10/14	Aint	2m1f Cls4 Hdl 3yo good	£5,198
	10/14	Bang	2m¹/₂f Cls4 Hdl 3yo good	£3,249

Well fancied for several big spring chases last season and shaped better than bare form (unlucky in running in the Festival Plate, didn't quite stay 3m1f at Aintree and easily forgiven below-par fifth just 11 days later); starts season 10lb lower over fences than hurdles.

Stowaway Magic (Ire)
6 b g Stowaway - Irish Mystics (Ali-Royal)

Nicky Henderson   Grech & Parkin

PLACINGS: 1/14/121512-   RPR **141h**

Starts	1st	2nd	3rd	4th	Win & Pl
8	4	2		1	£22,054

130	4/17	Kemp	2m5f Cls3 107-133 Hdl Hcap good	£6,498
	1/17	Donc	2m¹/₂f Cls4 Nov Hdl gd-sft	£3,249
	5/16	Wwck	2m3f Cls4 Nov Hdl good	£3,249
	2/16	Kemp	2m Cls5 Mdn NHF 4-6yo good	£2,274

Won a couple of novice hurdles last season before adding a third success in good style on his handicap debut at Kempton; improved again when second off 9lb higher at Sandown; progressive type who should do well over fences.

Sub Lieutenant (Ire)
8 b g Brian Boru - Satellite Dancer (Satco)

Henry de Bromhead (Ir)   Gigginstown House Stud

PLACINGS: 14/4342341P/3113222-   RPR **166c**

Starts	1st	2nd	3rd	4th	Win & Pl
27	6	8	4	4	£234,992

11/16	DRoy	2m3¹/₂f Gd2 Ch good	£21,691
10/16	Limk	2m3¹/₂f Ch yield	£11,305
3/16	Naas	2m4f Nov Gd3 Ch heavy	£14,697
2/15	Thur	2m4f Nov Gd2 Hdl heavy	£20,155
11/14	Fair	2m4f Mdn Hdl yld-sft	£5,750
10/14	Thur	2m NHF 4-7yo good	£4,313

Progressed well last season and ran well in several top chases, including when second in the Ryanair and Melling Chases; often tried over 3m earlier in his career (even ran in 2016 Irish Grand National) but yet to win beyond 2m4f.

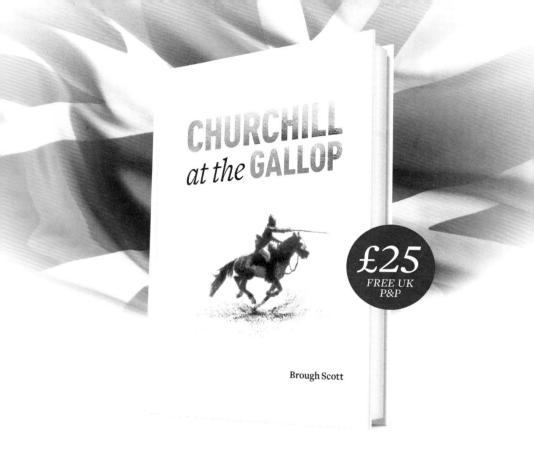

"Please let me go on with my riding ...
I enjoy it more than anything else"

WINSTON S CHURCHILL

Essential reading about one of the most important leaders of the twentieth century, his love for horses and how they played an integral part in his life

ORDER NOW
RACING POST.com/shop
ORDERLINE 01933 304858

Supasundae

7 b g Galileo - Distinctive Look (Danehill)

| Jessica Harrington (Ir) | | | | Alan Potts |

PLACINGS: 1/16/9317/4812412- RPR **159+h**

Starts		1st	2nd	3rd	4th	Win & Pl
14		5	2	1	2	£124,463
148	3/17	Chel	2m5f Cls1 Gd3 136-156 Hdl Hcap gd-sft............£54,103
	12/16	Punc	2m4f Hdl soft...£9,044
	12/15	Leop	2m Mdn Hdl heavy.....................................£7,488
	12/14	Asct	1m7¹/₂f Cls1 List NHF 4-6yo soft..................£11,390
	3/14	Weth	2m Cls6 NHF 4-6yo good.............................£1,711

Flourished on good ground last spring, winning the Coral Cup at Cheltenham and finishing second to Yanworth in the Stayers' Hurdle at Aintree when coping well with longer trip and step up in class; Flat-bred but likely to try his luck over fences.

Superb Story (Ire)

6 b g Duke Of Marmalade - Yes My Love (Anabaa)

| Dan Skelton | | | A Holt, J Robinson, A Taylor & S Miller |

PLACINGS: 1444/121/P1- RPR **150h**

Starts		1st	2nd	3rd	4th	Win & Pl
9		4	1	-	3	£115,768
145	1/17	Muss	1m7¹/₂f Cls2 119-145 Hdl Hcap good............£25,992
138	3/16	Chel	2m1f Cls1 Gd3 138-152 Hdl Hcap good..........£51,255
120	10/15	Weth	2m Cls3 119-133 Hdl Hcap good.....................£5,523
	1/15	Muss	1m7¹/₂f Cls3 Hdl 4yo gd-sft...........................£9,747

Smart performer who has done well in handicaps, most notably when winning the 2016 County Hurdle; suffered a tendon injury when being prepared for last season's Champion Hurdle but back in training and could belatedly step up to the top level.

Sutton Place (Ire)

6 b g Mahler - Glebe Beauty (Good Thyne)

| Gordon Elliott (Ir) | | | | John P McManus |

PLACINGS: 3111/11P- RPR **162+h**

Starts		1st	2nd	3rd	4th	Win & Pl
7		5	-	1	-	£77,059
	2/17	Navn	2m5f Gd2 Hdl sft-hvy...............................£22,692
	1/17	Naas	2m3f Hdl yld-sft......................................£17,083
	3/16	Fair	2m Nov Gd2 Hdl yld-sft.............................£19,522
	3/16	Naas	2m Nov List Hdl sft-hvy.............................£12,436
	1/16	Fair	2m NHF 5-7yo heavy..................................£4,566

Lightly raced hurdler who took winning sequence to five with a couple of impressive wins last season, thriving when stepped up to 2m5f to win the Boyne Hurdle at Navan; lame when pulled up at Punchestown next time; should make a fine novice chaser.

Taquin Du Seuil (Fr)

10 b/br g Voix Du Nord - Sweet Laly (Marchand De Sable)

| Jonjo O'Neill | | | Martin Broughton & Friends |

PLACINGS: 11/32P49/165/615424- RPR **166c**

Starts		1st	2nd	3rd	4th	Win & Pl
25		9	4	2	3	£334,685
156	11/16	Chel	2m4¹/₂f Cls1 Gd3 131-157 Ch Hcap gd-sft....£91,120
152	2/16	Wwck	2m4f Cls2 130-152 Ch Hcap soft....................£18,768
	3/14	Chel	2m4f Cls1 Nov Gd2 Ch good........................£68,340
	1/14	Hayd	2m4f Cls1 Nov Gd2 Ch heavy........................£17,912
	11/13	Chel	2m4¹/₂f Cls2 Nov Ch good............................£12,512
	10/13	Ffos	2m Cls4 Nov Ch heavy.................................£4,549
	12/12	Newb	2m4¹/₂f Cls1 Nov Gd1 Hdl heavy...................£17,165
	12/12	Sand	2m4f Cls1 Nov Gd2 Hdl heavy......................£12,676
	10/12	Uttx	2m Cls5 Mdn Hdl gd-sft................................£2,144

Generally struggled since winning a Grade 1 novice chase in 2014 (0-7 at the top level since) but still dangerous when back in handicaps; won the BetVictor Gold Cup last season and ran a stormer reverting to hurdles when second in the Coral Cup.

Tea For Two

8 b g Kayf Tara - One For Me (Tragic Role)

| Nick Williams | | | Mrs Jane Williams & Len Jakeman |

PLACINGS: 13112P/67113/5241U1- RPR **172c**

Starts		1st	2nd	3rd	4th	Win & Pl
21		9	4	2	1	£239,386
	4/17	Aint	3m1f Cls1 Gd1 Ch good..............................£84,365
	2/17	Extr	3m Cls2 Ch soft.......................................£13,898
	12/15	Kemp	3m Cls1 Nov Gd1 Ch gd-sft.........................£39,865
	2/15	Extr	2m3f Cls2 Nov Ch heavy.............................£12,686
134	1/15	Kemp	2m5f Cls1 List 129-155 Hdl Hcap soft...........£25,628
	12/14	Towc	2m Cls4 Nov Hdl 4-6yo gd-sft........................£3,249
	10/14	Kemp	2m5f Cls4 Nov Hdl gd-sft.............................£3,899
	4/14	Extr	2m1f Cls6 NHF 4-6yo good...........................£1,625
	4/13	Winc	1m7¹/₂f Cls6 NHF 4-6yo good.........................£1,625

Dual Grade 1 winner over fences and gained biggest win when beating Cue Card by a neck in the Betway Bowl in April; suspicion that was a modest race for the grade but hadn't been beaten far in the King George and should run well in more top 3m chases.

Tell Us More (Ire)

8 b g Scorpion - Zara's Victory (Old Vic)

| Gordon Elliott (Ir) | | | Gigginstown House Stud |

PLACINGS: 11/126/31F2/410- RPR **152c**

Starts		1st	2nd	3rd	4th	Win & Pl
11		4	2	1	1	£52,057
	11/16	Naas	2m Gd3 Ch good......................................£14,697
	1/16	Gowr	2m2f Ch heavy..£6,849
	11/14	Gowr	2m Mdn Hdl heavy.....................................£5,750
	3/14	Gowr	2m2f NHF 4-7yo soft...................................£4,600

Sent off odds-on for a Grade 1 in younger days (finished second) but has had issues since and

'Lightly raced hurdler took winning sequence to five with a couple of impressive wins last season; pulled up lame at Punchestown on his final start, but should make a fine novice chaser'

ran only three times last season; still promised much when winning a Grade 3 chase easily but tailed off when trying to exploit lower hurdles mark in the County Hurdle.

Tenor Nivernais (Fr)
10 b g Shaanmer - Hosanna II (Marasali)

Venetia Williams | | Boultbee Brooks

PLACINGS: 44694/1322P5/343120-   RPR **166+c**

Starts			1st	2nd	3rd	4th	Win & Pl
38			8	3	6	5	£164,234
152	2/17	Asct	3m Cls1 List 135-155 Ch Hcap soft				£25,748
132	11/15	Asct	2m5f Cls3 114-133 Ch Hcap soft				£16,245
132	11/14	Kemp	2m4¹/₂f Cls3 109-135 Ch Hcap soft				£9,747
	12/12	Bang	2m1¹/₂f Cls4 Nov Ch soft				£3,054
130	2/12	Carl	2m4f Cls3 104-130 Hdl Hcap soft				£5,523
118	12/11	Hayd	2m Cls3 102-120 Hdl Hcap heavy				£8,123
	8/10	Vich	2m1¹/₂f Hdl 3yo soft				£9,345
	8/10	Vich	2m1¹/₂f Hdl 3yo good				£7,221

Consistent in top handicap chases, although often handicapped just too high; seemed to improve hugely when stepped up to 3m at Ascot in February and still on a fair mark if that form taken literally (starts this season just 5lb higher).

The Druids Nephew (Ire)
10 b g King's Theatre - Gifted (Shareef Dancer)

Neil Mulholland | | The Stonehenge Druids

PLACINGS: 2P/12751F/662P5/978-   RPR **149c**

Starts			1st	2nd	3rd	4th	Win & Pl
27			4	4	2	1	£108,934
146	3/15	Chel	3m1f Cls1 Gd3 133-155 Ch Hcap gd-sft				£51,255
132	10/14	Hntg	2m7¹/₂f Cls3 122-132 Ch Hcap soft				£6,657
	1/13	Winc	2m5f Cls3 Nov Ch soft				£6,975
	1/12	Kemp	2m5f Cls3 Nov Hdl good				£5,848

Hit hard by the handicapper for winning at the 2015 Cheltenham Festival and has largely struggled since; slipped back down the weights last term, though, and confirmed he's still a force when beaten less than three lengths in the bet365 Gold Cup.

The Last Samuri (Ire)
9 ch g Flemensfirth - Howaboutthis (Oscar)

Kim Bailey | | Paul & Clare Rooney

PLACINGS: 19/211U12/3112/5320-   RPR **166c**

Starts			1st	2nd	3rd	4th	Win & Pl
19			8	5	2		£352,035
149	3/16	Donc	3m2f Cls2 132-155 Ch Hcap soft				£34,536
140	12/15	Kemp	3m Cls2 127-145 Ch Hcap gd-sft				£25,992
132	3/15	Kels	3m2f Cls2 125-150 Ch Hcap gd-sft				£16,245
	1/15	Ayr	3m1¹/₂f Cls4 Nov Ch soft				£4,029
	11/14	Bang	3m Cls3 Nov Ch soft				£8,406
	1/14	Catt	3m1¹/₂f Cls4 Nov Hdl soft				£3,249
	11/13	Bang	2m3¹/₂f Cls4 Nov Hdl soft				£3,249
	11/13	Kels	2m6³/₄f Cls4 Nov Hdl gd-sft				£3,899

Ran a mighty race to finish second in the 2016 Grand National on ground softer than ideal; suspicion that was his big chance given he was 10lb well in and not quite as good last season

(well-beaten favourite in the Grimthorpe and tailed off in the National).

The New One (Ire)
9 b g King's Theatre - Thuringe (Turgeon)

Nigel Twiston-Davies | | S Such & CG Paletta

PLACINGS: /11115/1214F/121534-   RPR **163h**

Starts			1st	2nd	3rd	4th	Win & Pl
31			18	5	2	2	£918,630
	1/17	Hayd	1m7¹/₂f Cls1 Gd2 Hdl soft				£43,215
	12/16	Chel	2m1f Cls1 Gd2 Hdl soft				£74,035
	1/16	Hayd	1m7¹/₂f Cls1 Gd2 Hdl heavy				£42,713
	10/15	Kemp	2m Cls1 List Hdl good				£17,085
	1/15	Hayd	2m Cls1 Gd2 Hdl heavy				£42,713
	12/14	Chel	2m1f Cls1 Gd2 Hdl gd-sft				£74,035
	11/14	Hayd	2m Cls1 Gd2 Hdl soft				£61,900
	10/14	Kemp	2m Cls1 List Hdl gd-sft				£14,238
	4/14	Aint	2m4f Cls1 Gd1 Hdl good				£112,540
	12/13	Chel	2m1f Cls1 Gd2 Hdl soft				£74,035
	10/13	Kemp	2m Cls1 List Hdl gd-sft				£14,238
	3/13	Chel	2m5f Cls1 Nov Gd1 Hdl gd-sft				£68,340
	1/13	Wwck	2m5f Cls1 Nov Gd2 Hdl soft				£15,735
	10/12	Chel	2m5f Cls2 Nov Hdl gd-sft				£10,635
	10/12	NAbb	2m2¹/₂f Cls4 Nov Hdl soft				£2,924
	4/12	Aint	2m1f Cls1 Gd2 NHF 4-6yo good				£14,238
	1/12	Chel	1m6f Cls1 List NHF 4-6yo gd-sft				£7,133
	11/11	Wwck	1m6f Cls6 NHF 3yo soft				£2,053

Wonderfully prolific at around 2m and won his third International Hurdle at Cheltenham and Champion Hurdle Trial at Haydock last season; tends to get outpaced against the very best and may need to step up in trip to stay competitive at the top level.

The Nipper (Ire)
6 b m Scorpion - Sharp Single (Supreme Leader)

Warren Greatrex | | Smith, Ratcliffe & Bowring

PLACINGS: 111/OF1116-   RPR **134+h**

Starts			1st	2nd	3rd	4th	Win & Pl
9			6	-	-	-	£28,749
	3/17	Hayd	2m3f Cls4 Nov Hdl heavy				£4,874
	2/17	Newc	2m1¹/₂f Cls4 Nov Hdl heavy				£3,249
	1/17	Ling	2m Cls4 Nov Hdl heavy				£3,249
	3/16	Bang	2m Cls1 List NHF 4-7yo soft				£11,390
	11/15	Bang	2m1¹/₂f Cls6 NHF 4-6yo heavy				£2,053
	5/15	Bang	2m1¹/₂f Cls5 NHF 4-6yo good				£3,080

Beaten only once when completing, although also looked held when falling at Wetherby last season on good to soft ground; gained three subsequent wins on heavy going and again seemed to find quicker conditions too lively when well beaten at Punchestown.

The Storyteller (Ire)
6 ch g Shantou - Bally Bolshoi (Bob Back)

Gordon Elliott (Ir) | | Mrs P Sloan

PLACINGS: 24/21F211-   RPR **148+h**

Starts			1st	2nd	3rd	4th	Win & Pl
8			3	3		1	£22,784
	1/17	Thur	2m6¹/₂f Nov Hdl yld-sft				£7,622
	12/16	DRoy	2m3¹/₂f Mdn Hdl soft				£5,879
	5/16	Dpat	2m2f NHF 4-7yo good				£4,070

Long-time favourite for last season's Martin Pipe

Hurdle at Cheltenham before being ruled out by injury; had won the last two of his four races over hurdles and should have lots more to offer, especially when stepped up to 3m.

The Unit (Ire)

6 b g Gold Well - Sovana (Kadounor)

Alan King   International Plywood (Importers)

PLACINGS: 31/722/4311213-   RPR **142h**

Starts	1st	2nd	3rd	4th	Win & Pl
12	4	3	3	1	£69,946
131	3/17	Tntn	2m3f Cls3 121-137 Hdl Hcap good		£6,330
	12/16	Tntn	2m3f Cls4 Nov Hdl good		£6,330
	11/16	Donc	2m5f Cls4 Nov Hdl gd-sft		£5,198
	3/15	Newb	2m¹/₂f Cls2 NHF 4-5yo good		£36,911

Progressive novice hurdler last season, taking a big step forward when winning for the third time with victory at Taunton and backing up that success with a fine effort when third in a Grade 1 at Aintree behind Pingshou; set to go novice chasing; effective from 2m to 2m4f.

The Worlds End (Ire)

6 b g Stowaway - Bright Sprite (Beneficial)

Tom George   McNeill Family

PLACINGS: F1/3111F1-   RPR **150+h**

Starts	1st	2nd	3rd	4th	Win & Pl
7	5	-	1	-	£85,286
	4/17	Aint	3m¹/₂f Cls1 Nov Gd1 Hdl good		£56,141
	2/17	Hayd	2m7f Cls1 Nov Gd2 Hdl gd-sft		£16,972
	1/17	Chep	2m3¹/₂f Cls4 Nov Hdl soft		£3,249
	12/16	Chep	2m3¹/₂f Cls3 Mdn Hdl gd-sft		£6,498
	4/16	Chep	2m Cls6 NHF 4-6yo soft		£1,949

Top staying novice hurdler last season who may even have won the Albert Bartlett but for falling two out; got back on track with a Grade 1 strike at Aintree and better than bare form (mistake at the last); looks a future chaser but trainer is keen to see how far he can go over hurdles first.

The Young Master

8 b g Echo Of Light - Fine Frenzy (Great Commotion)

Neil Mulholland   Mike Burbidge & The Old Masters

PLACINGS: /111d17/2U4631/F06F9-   RPR **148c**

Starts	1st	2nd	3rd	4th	Win & Pl
28	7	2	2	1	£186,356
148	4/16	Sand	3m5f Cls1 Gd3 144-159 Ch Hcap good		£84,405
144	12/14	Asct	3m Cls1 List 135-161 Ch Hcap gd-sft		£56,270
121	10/14	Chel	3m1f Cls3 107-125 Am Ch Hcap good		£7,195
	9/14	Worc	2m7f Cls4 Ch good		£4,327
110	1/14	Sedg	3m Cls4 100-112 Hdl Hcap heavy		£3,899
103	1/14	Fknm	2m7¹/₂f Cls4 102-108 Hdl Hcap heavy		£3,249
94	11/13	Font	2m5¹/₂f Cls5 Nov 69-95 Hdl Hcap heavy		£1,949

Suffered last season as a result of being trained for the Grand National, falling in the big race having done the same in the Becher; had won major handicaps in each of the previous two seasons (Silver Cup at Ascot and bet365 Gold Cup) and down to a good mark.

Theatre Guide (Ire)

10 b g King's Theatre - Erintante (Denel)

Colin Tizzard   Mrs Jean R Bishop

PLACINGS: 640R/3231F8/2817383-   RPR **160c**

Starts	1st	2nd	3rd	4th	Win & Pl
33	7	4	7	2	£263,849
149	12/16	Chel	3m2f Cls1 Gd3 134-157 Ch Hcap good		£25,628
139	2/16	Kemp	3m Cls1 Gd3 133-159 Ch Hcap gd-sft		£56,950
	11/14	Kemp	2m4¹/₂f Cls2 Ch soft		£8,412
	4/13	NAbb	2m5f Cls3 Nov Ch gd-sft		£8,578
	11/12	Extr	2m1¹/₂f Cls2 Nov Ch gd-sft		£9,902
	2/12	Winc	1m7¹/₂f Cls4 Nov Hdl soft		£3,249
	4/11	Chep	2m Cls6 NHF 4-6yo gd-sft		£1,821

Evergreen staying chaser who has been placed in two Hennessy Gold Cups and was better than ever last season despite getting little respite from the handicapper; won a big one at Cheltenham in December and signed off with a close third in the bet365 Gold Cup.

Theinval (Fr)

7 b g Smadoun - Kinevees (Hard Leaf)

Nicky Henderson   Mr & Mrs Sandy Orr

PLACINGS: 11/3P09/31334132227-   RPR **154c**

Starts	1st	2nd	3rd	4th	Win & Pl
31	5	7	5	4	£158,191
	12/16	Plum	2m1f Cls3 Nov Ch gd-sft		£6,498
	5/16	Uttx	2m4f Cls4 Ch good		£4,431
144	4/15	Aint	2m4f Cls1 Gd3 127-149 Hdl Hcap gd-sft		£28,135
134	3/15	Kemp	2m5f Cls2 115-135 Hdl Hcap good		£22,743
119	11/14	Kemp	2m Cls3 105-129 Cond Hdl Hcap soft		£5,393

Remarkably busy at the end of last season and kept up a high level of form when second three times in just over two weeks (including twice in two days at Ayr) in top handicaps from 2m-2m4f and a Grade 2 novice chase; still on a decent mark and deserves a big win.

Thistlecrack

9 b g Kayf Tara - Ardstown (Ardross)

Colin Tizzard   John & Heather Snook

PLACINGS: 517151/211111/11112-   RPR **176+c**

Starts	1st	2nd	3rd	4th	Win & Pl
19	13	2	1	-	£644,653
	12/16	Kemp	3m Cls1 Gd1 Ch good		£119,026
	11/16	Newb	2m7¹/₂f Cls1 Nov Gd2 Ch gd-sft		£20,167
	11/16	Chel	3m¹/₂f Cls2 Nov Ch gd-sft		£16,025
	10/16	Chep	3m¹/₂f Cls3 Nov Ch gd-sft		£7,798
	4/16	Aint	3m¹/₂f Cls1 Gd1 Hdl soft		£84,405
	3/16	Chel	3m Cls1 Gd1 Hdl good		£170,850
	1/16	Chel	3m Cls1 Gd2 Hdl heavy		£34,170
	12/15	Asct	3m¹/₂f Cls1 Gd1 Hdl gd-sft		£56,950
	11/15	Newb	3m Cls1 Gd2 Hdl soft		£25,628
	4/15	Aint	3m¹/₂f Cls1 Nov Gd1 Hdl gd-sft		£56,437

Won the World Hurdle in 2016 and then pulled off an astonishing feat when landing the King George as a novice on only his fourth run over fences last season; far from disgraced when second to Many Clouds next time before getting injured; leading Gold Cup contender.

Thomas Brown

8 b g Sir Harry Lewis - Tentsmuir (Arctic Lord)

Harry Fry					The Corse Lawners

PLACINGS: 1/121P6/121U74/1870-   **RPR 147+c**

Starts	1st	2nd	3rd	4th	Win & Pl
19	7	2	-	2	£68,773

137	11/16	Aint	2m4f Cls2 127-150 Ch Hcap gd-sft	£24,817
	1/16	Donc	3m Cls4 Nov Ch gd-sft	£5,326
	11/15	Asct	2m3f Cls3 Ch soft	£7,798
	1/15	Chel	2m4¹/₂f Cls3 Nov Hdl soft	£6,256
	11/14	Extr	2m5¹/₂f Cls3 Nov Hdl gd-sft	£5,523
	3/14	Bang	2m1¹/₂f Cls5 NHF 4-6yo gd-sft	£2,053
	11/13	Newb	2m1¹/₂f Cls4 NHF 4-6yo gd-sft	£3,249

Very talented chaser but has been let down by inability to produce his best in big-field handicaps, disappointing several times; still to be feared in smaller fields (1211211 in single-figure contests over jumps) and back down to a good mark.

Thomas Hobson

7 b g Halling - La Spezia (Danehill Dancer)

Willie Mullins (Ir)					Mrs S Ricci

PLACINGS: F1211P/39P017-   **RPR 158h**

Starts	1st	2nd	3rd	4th	Win & Pl
12	4	1	2	1	£93,291

143	4/17	Fair	2m 125-143 Hdl Hcap gd-yld	£50,427
	1/16	Wwck	2m5f Cls1 Nov Gd2 Hdl heavy	£17,165
	12/15	Punc	2m4f Hdl soft	£6,686
	7/15	Gway	2m Mdn Hdl good	£7,756

Out of sorts for much of last season but came good to win a 2m handicap hurdle at Fairyhouse in style despite connections seeing him as better over further; has since done well on the Flat (six-length winner at Royal Ascot).

Three Faces West (Ire)

9 b g Dr Massini - Ardnataggle (Aristocracy)

Philip Hobbs					Paul & Clare Rooney

PLACINGS: 1/4111/3221/P11-   **RPR 160+c**

Starts	1st	2nd	3rd	4th	Win & Pl
11	6	2	1	1	£59,154

135	12/16	Newb	2m7¹/₂f Cls2 Ch gd-sft	£12,021
129	11/16	Hayd	3m Cls2 126-141 Ch Hcap heavy	£18,768
	3/16	Extr	3m Cls2 127-148 Ch Hcap good	£11,574
	3/15	Hayd	2m3f Cls4 Nov Hdl gd-sft	£3,899
	2/15	Carl	2m3¹/₂f Cls4 Nov Hdl soft	£3,249
	1/15	Ayr	2m Cls4 Nov Hdl soft	£3,249

Impressive when winning his last two chases last season, albeit in small fields when able to dominate; being trained for the Grand National when ruled out by a suspensory injury; still lightly raced and should have more to offer.

Three Musketeers (Ire)

7 b g Flemensfirth - Friendly Craic (Mister Lord)

Dan Skelton			Mrs G Widdowson & Mrs R Kelvin-Hughes

PLACINGS: 2113/3154/6U167-   **RPR 159+c**

Starts	1st	2nd	3rd	4th	Win & Pl
12	4	-	2	1	£71,860

	1/17	MRas	2m5¹/₂f Cls2 Ch soft	£12,660
	11/15	Newb	2m4f Cls1 Nov Gd2 Ch soft	£20,026
	1/15	Wwck	2m5f Cls1 Nov Gd2 Hdl soft	£15,946
	12/14	Weth	2m5¹/₂f Cls4 Nov Hdl soft	£3,249

Well short of expectations last season given he was sent off at 7-4 to win the Old Roan Chase first time out after a promising novice campaign; at least won a graduation chase at Market Rasen and beaten only six lengths in the BetBright Chase.

Tiger Roll (Ire)

7 b g Authorized - Swiss Roll (Entrepreneur)

Gordon Elliott (Ir)					Gigginstown House Stud

PLACINGS: 30/40/P114U2221331P-   **RPR 157+c**

Starts	1st	2nd	3rd	4th	Win & Pl
25	7	4	3	3	£254,748

138	3/17	Chel	4m Cls1 Nov Gd2 Am Ch gd-sft	£71,952
	10/16	Limk	3m 131-144 Ch Hcap yield	£43,382
	6/16	Kbgn	2m4f Nov Ch good	£6,331
	5/16	Baln	2m1f Ch good	£5,200
	10/14	Chel	2m1¹/₂f Cls2 Hdl 4yo gd-sft	£18,768
	3/14	Chel	2m1f Cls1 Gd1 Hdl 4yo good	£68,340
	11/13	MRas	2m1¹/₂f Cls4 Hdl 3yo soft	£3,899

Disappointing after winning the 2014 Triumph Hurdle until stepped up in distance over fences last season, winning the Munster National and the National Hunt Chase over 4m; should continue to be a force in top staying handicaps.

Tigris River (Ire)

6 b g Montjeu - Hula Angel (Woodman)

Joseph O'Brien (Ir)					John P McManus

PLACINGS: 3112144/45-711   **RPR 150+h**

Starts	1st	2nd	3rd	4th	Win & Pl
12	5	1	1	3	£199,897

140	8/17	Gway	2m 132-155 Hdl Hcap yield	£151,282
	7/17	Bell	2m4f Hdl good	£6,844
	10/15	Limk	2m2f Hdl 4yo yield	£10,581
	8/15	Cork	2m Hdl 4-5yo good	£8,023
	8/15	Gway	2m Mdn Hdl yield	£6,419

Pulled off a year-long plan when winning the Galway Hurdle this summer having been an unlucky fifth in the race 12 months earlier; strong stayer at that 2m trip and had previously won over 2m4f; acts on softer ground.

 Facebook.com/racingpost    Twitter @RacingPost

Tin Soldier (Fr)
6 b g Soldier Of Fortune - Everlast (Anabaa)

Willie Mullins (Ir)				Philip J Reynolds

PLACINGS: 0/23557452/84/1183-				RPR **150h**

Starts	1st	2nd	3rd	4th	Win & Pl
15	2	2	2	2	£97,521

	2/17	Thur	2m4¹/₂f Nov Gd3 Hdl heavy	£22,692
	1/17	Fair	3m¹/₂f Mdn Hdl yld-sft	£5,256

Only eighth when the subject of a gamble for last season's Coral Cup having won his only two outings for Willie Mullins following a move from France but proved his ability when third in a Grade 1 at Punchestown next time; more to come.

Tobefair
7 b/br g Central Park - Nan (Buckley)

Debra Hamer				Down The Quay Club

PLACINGS: 265406/111/11110-				RPR **145+h**

Starts	1st	2nd	3rd	4th	Win & Pl
14	7	1		1	£47,211

134	2/17	Newb	3m Cls2 115-139 Hdl Hcap soft	£12,512
126	1/17	Wwck	3m2f Cls2 115-138 Hdl Hcap soft	£12,512
120	12/16	Chep	2m7¹/₂f Cls3 110-129 Hdl Hcap good	£6,498
116	11/16	Ffos	3m Cls3 115-132 Hdl Hcap good	£6,498
109	9/15	Chep	2m7¹/₂f Cls4 93-120 Hdl Hcap good	£3,249
95	7/15	Worc	2m7f Cls5 Nov 74-100 Hdl Hcap gd-fm	£2,599
81	6/15	Worc	2m7f Cls5 Nov 73-99 Hdl Hcap gd-fm	£2,599

One of last season's great success stories, climbing 62lb in the handicap; failed to run his race in the Pertemps Final at Cheltenham; thorough stayer (3m2f winner on soft ground) and should make a fine novice chaser.

Tombstone (Ire)
7 ch g Robin Des Champs - Connaught Hall (Un Desperado)

Gordon Elliott (Ir)				Gigginstown House Stud

PLACINGS: 31/11224/31038-				RPR **153h**

Starts	1st	2nd	3rd	4th	Win & Pl
12	4	2	3	1	£79,299

	2/17	Gowr	2m Gd3 Hdl heavy	£22,692
	11/15	Fair	2m2f Mdn Hdl sft-hvy	£6,419
	10/15	DRoy	2m NHF 4-7yo yld-sft	£6,953
	1/15	Naas	2m3f NHF 5-7yo soft	£4,279

Won a Grade 2 at Gowran last season but disappointing in the spring, including when tailed off as a well-backed favourite for the Coral Cup; may well stamp his authority on the novice chase division.

Tommy Silver (Fr)
5 b g Silver Cross - Sainte Mante (Saint Des Saints)

Paul Nicholls				Done, Ferguson, Mason & Wood

PLACINGS: 2173/571016-				RPR **147+h**

Starts	1st	2nd	3rd	4th	Win & Pl
10	3	1	1		£59,263

137	4/17	Plum	2m Cls3 122-137 Hdl Hcap gd-fm	£21,977
134	2/17	Tntn	2m¹/₂f Cls2 112-137 Hdl Hcap good	£11,574
	2/16	Muss	1m7¹/₂f Cls1 Hdl 4yo soft	£17,085

Won a couple of fair handicap hurdles last

season, most notably the Sussex Champion Hurdle at Plumpton by nine lengths; strong stayer over 2m but didn't get home when stepped up in trip for the Martin Pipe at Cheltenham.

Top Gamble (Ire)
9 ch g Presenting - Zeferina (Sadler's Wells)

Kerry Lee				Walters Plant Hire & James & Jean Potter

PLACINGS: /111251/P3311/53346-				RPR **165c**

Starts	1st	2nd	3rd	4th	Win & Pl
22	8	2	4	1	£155,859

	3/16	Fair	2m1f Gd2 Ch yield	£18,438
	2/16	Newb	2m¹/₂f Cls1 Gd2 Ch soft	£28,475
	4/15	Ayr	2m4¹/₂f Cls1 Nov Gd2 Ch good	£27,197
143	1/15	Newb	2m¹/₂f Cls3 Nov 125-144 Ch Hcap soft	£6,498
135	12/14	Wwck	2m Cls3 Nov 124-135 Ch Hcap good	£6,498
	11/14	Weth	1m7f Cls4 Nov Ch soft	£4,106
	2/13	Ffos	2m Cls4 Nov Hdl heavy	£3,899
	12/12	Ffos	2m Cls6 Mdn NHF 4-6yo heavy	£1,430

Won a pair of Grade 2 chases at around 2m in 2016 and ran to a similar level last season, including when fourth in the Champion Chase; gets further and has also finished third under big weights in good 2m5f handicap chases at Cheltenham.

Top Notch (Fr)
6 b g Poliglote - Topira (Pistolet Bleu)

Nicky Henderson				Simon Munir & Isaac Souede

PLACINGS: /1112/22515/3111123-				RPR **163+c**

Starts	1st	2nd	3rd	4th	Win & Pl
18	10	4	2	-	£252,757

	2/17	Sand	2m4f Cls1 Nov Gd1 Ch soft	£28,475
	12/16	Asct	2m5f Cls2 Ch gd-sft	£15,640
	11/16	Plum	2m1f Cls3 Nov Ch gd-sft	£6,498
	11/16	Wwck	2m Cls3 Nov Ch 4-5yo soft	£9,384
	2/16	Kels	2m2f Cls2 Hdl heavy	£16,245
	2/15	Hayd	1m7¹/₂f Cls2 Hdl 4yo soft	£9,747
	1/15	Asct	1m7¹/₂f Cls3 Hdl 4yo soft	£6,498
	12/14	Newb	2m¹/₂f Cls3 Hdl 3yo gd-sft	£6,498
	4/14	Engh	2m¹/₂f Hdl 3yo v soft	£19,200
	3/14	Bord	2m¹/₂f Hdl 3yo heavy	£8,400

Very smart hurdler who finished second in the 2015 Triumph Hurdle and proved equally good over fences last season, winning four times before getting closest to Yorkhill in the JLT; below his best when only third at Aintree last time.

Traffic Fluide (Fr)
7 b g Astarabad - Petale Rouge (Bonnet Rouge)

Gary Moore				Galloping On The South Downs Partnership

PLACINGS: P37142113/3/46632-				RPR **164c**

Starts	1st	2nd	3rd	4th	Win & Pl
15	3	2	4	2	£96,456

137	3/15	Sand	1m7¹/₂f Cls3 Nov 122-140 Ch Hcap good	£6,498
129	2/15	Plum	2m1f Cls3 Nov 129-145 Ch Hcap gd-sft	£7,988
	10/14	Stra	2m4f Ch 4yo heavy	£8,800

Third in the 2016 Clarence House Chase on first

run outside novice company but then missed more than a year through injury and was generally below that level last spring, although still beaten less than eight lengths in the Champion Chase; may do better over further.

Tully East (Ire)

7 b g Shantou - Ghillie's Bay (King's Ride)

Alan Fleming					Barry Connell

PLACINGS: 3d22/16164/1621P-   RPR **149+c**

Starts		1st	2nd	3rd	4th	Win & Pl
13		4	3	-		£73,404
138	3/17	Chel	2m4¹/₂f Cls1 Nov List 137-142 Ch Hcap gd-sft...... £39,865
	12/16	Thur	2m2f Ch yield £4,974
120	11/15	Punc	2m Nov 96-120 Hdl Hcap soft £8,558
	9/15	List	2m Mdn Hdl 5yo heavy... £6,953

Well-backed winner of the novice handicap chase at last season's Cheltenham Festival, confirming the rich promise of his fourth in the Martin Pipe (went for home too soon) at the meeting in 2016; likely contender for big handicaps at the track again.

Two Taffs (Ire)

7 b g Flemensfirth - Richs Mermaid (Saddlers' Hall)

Dan Skelton				Walters Plant Hire & James & Jean Potter

PLACINGS: 1/32341/1722331-   RPR **152+c**

Starts		1st	2nd	3rd	4th	Win & Pl
13		4	3	4	1	£70,141
142	4/17	Ayr	2m4¹/₂f Cls1 List 130-148 Ch Hcap gd-sft........... £28,475
	10/16	Carl	2m4f Cls4 Nov Hdl gd-sft £3,249
129	4/16	Ayr	2m5¹/₂f Cls2 124-150 Hdl Hcap gd-sft £12,996
	3/15	MRas	2m¹/₂f Cls6 Mdn NHF 4-6yo good....................... £1,560

Found his feet last spring after patchy initial form over fences (beaten at 1-6 at Catterick); finished a fine third in the novice handicap at the Cheltenham Festival before winning a Listed contest at Ayr; type to get better with age and will get 3m.

Ucello Conti (Fr)

9 b g Martaline - Gazelle Lulu (Altayan)

Gordon Elliott (Ir)				Simon Munir & Isaac Souede

PLACINGS: P/69/1P/6236/74724U-   RPR **156c**

Starts		1st	2nd	3rd	4th	Win & Pl
31		8	6	2	3	£331,700
	6/14	Rost	2m5f Ch gd-fm... £6,000
	8/12	Roya	1m6¹/₂f NHF.. £6,667
	2/12	Ange	2m1f Hdl 4yo gd-sft £10,400
	11/11	Engh	2m1f List Hdl 4yo gd-sft............................ £35,172
	9/11	Autl	2m1¹/₂f Ch 3yo v soft.................................. £23,172
	7/11	Sabl	1m5¹/₂f NHF 3yo gd-sft................................ £6,034
	7/11	Claf	2m1f Hdl 3yo soft...................................... £13,241
	5/11	Nanc	2m1f Hdl 3yo gd-fm.................................... £8,276

Went close in several top staying handicaps last season, including when beaten less than three lengths in the Becher Chase at Aintree; unseated his rider when going well back there in the Grand National and looks a likely type for that race again.

Ultragold (Fr)

9 b/br g Kapgarde - Hot D'Or (Shafoun)

Colin Tizzard				Brocade Racing, JP Romans & Terry Warner

PLACINGS: 46/F481512/651B6791-   RPR **143c**

Starts		1st	2nd	3rd	4th	Win & Pl
34		7	2	2	6	£183,019
136	4/17	Aint	2m5f Cls3 Gd3 131-157 Ch Hcap good £67,356
136	11/16	Newb	2m¹/₂f Cls2 125-145 Ch Hcap gd-sft £21,896
129	4/16	Newb	2m¹/₂f Cls3 112-129 Ch Hcap good £67,356
120	2/16	Winc	1m7¹/₂f Cls2 120-141 Ch Hcap soft £12,628
119	12/14	Extr	2m3f Cls3 119-137 Ch Hcap gd-sft............ £15,640
	4/13	Autl	2m6f Ch 5yo v soft £21,463
	3/13	Sbri	2m2f Ch 5yo heavy £6,634

Shock 50-1 winner of last season's Topham Chase at Aintree, producing a terrific effort over the National fences; career-high mark will require more but could have rediscovered true calling as a stayer having been running over 2m previously (had started out over 3m as a youngster).

Un De Sceaux (Fr)

9 b g Denham Red - Hotesse De Sceaux (April Night)

Willie Mullins (Ir)					Edward O'Connell

PLACINGS: 1/F111/1F122/161112-   RPR **174+c**

Starts		1st	2nd	3rd	4th	Win & Pl
24		18	3	-	-	£940,926
	3/17	Chel	2m5f Cls1 Gd1 Ch good £170,850
	1/17	Chel	2m1f Cls1 Gd1 Ch soft £40,053
	12/16	Sand	1m7¹/₂f Cls1 Gd1 Ch gd-sft........................ £84,405
	5/16	Autl	2m5¹/₂f Gd2 Hdl v soft.............................. £57,904
	1/16	Asct	2m1f Cls1 Gd1 Ch soft £71,188
	4/15	Punc	2m Nov Gd1 Ch yield................................ £53,488
	3/15	Chel	2m Cls1 Gd1 Ch gd-sft.............................. £85,425
	1/15	Leop	2m1f Nov Gd1 Ch yld-sft........................... £37,209
	12/14	Fair	2m Ch soft... £6,900
	4/14	Autl	2m3¹/₂f Gd2 Hdl heavy £65,625
	3/14	Autl	2m3¹/₂f Gd3 Hdl v soft.............................. £50,625
	2/14	Gowr	2m Gd2 Hdl heavy.................................... £21,667
	1/14	Navn	2m Hdl soft.. £10,833
	12/13	Thur	2m Hdl soft... £8,695
	4/13	Punc	2m Nov Hdl heavy £11,890
	2/13	Punc	2m Mdn Hdl sft-hvy................................... £4,207
	10/12	Sbri	1m4f NHF 4yo v soft.................................. £4,167
	2/12	Mchl	1m4f NHF 4yo gd-sft.................................. £4,167

Won a hat-trick of Grade 1 chases last season to take tally at the top level to seven; most impressive when winning the Ryanair Chase at

---

> ### 'Well-backed winner of the novice handicap chase at last season's Cheltenham Festival and looks a likely contender for big handicaps at the track again'

Cheltenham over 2m5f and probably needs that sort of trip on good ground, although still a force over 2m on soft.

Un Temps Pour Tout (Ire)

8 b g Robin Des Champs - Rougedespoir (Bonnet Rouge)

David Pipe   Professor Caroline Tisdall & Bryan Drew

PLACINGS: 1/3363/122414/10361-   RPR **163c**

Starts		1st	2nd	3rd	4th	Win & Pl
26		8	3	10	2	£498,350
155	3/17	Chel	3m1f Cls1 Gd3 134-155 Ch Hcap gd-sft			£59,798
	11/16	Aint	2m4f Cls2 Hdl gd-sft			£19,230
148	3/16	Chel	3m1f Cls1 Gd3 131-153 Ch Hcap gd-sft			£56,950
	6/15	Autl	3m1½f Gd1 v soft			£129,010
	2/14	Asct	2m3½f Cls2 Nov Hdl heavy			£15,640
	9/13	Autl	2m2f Gd3 Hdl 4yo v soft			£49,390
0	5/13	Autl	2m3½f List Hdl 4yo Hcap heavy			£34,756
	5/13	Bord	2m2½f Hdl 4yo gd-sft			£8,585

Has won the Ultima Handicap Chase at Cheltenham for the last two seasons, although probably not required to improve on his 2016 win as a novice to follow up off top weight in a weaker renewal last term; has struggled to match that form before the spring.

Unowhatimeanharry

9 b g Sir Harry Lewis - Red Nose Lady (Teenoso)

Harry Fry   John P McManus

PLACINGS: /34237P/11111/11131-   RPR **168h**

Starts		1st	2nd	3rd	4th	Win & Pl
23		10	1	9	2	£397,494
	4/17	Punc	3m Gd1 Hdl gd-yld			£126,068
	1/17	Chel	3m Cls1 Gd2 Hdl soft			£34,170
	12/16	Asct	3m1½f Cls1 Gd1 Hdl gd-sft			£56,950
	11/16	Newb	3m Cls1 Gd2 Hdl soft			£28,475
	3/16	Chel	3m Cls1 Nov Gd1 Hdl good			£68,340
138	2/16	Extr	2m7f Cls2 124-139 Hdl Hcap heavy			£11,617
	12/15	Chel	3m Cls1 Nov Gd2 Hdl soft			£17,165
123	11/15	Newb	2m4½f Cls4 Nov 109-123 Hdl Hcap soft			£6,498
123	11/15	Chel	2m5f Cls3 118-125 Cond Hdl Hcap gd-sft			£7,507
	2/13	Font	2m1½f Cls6 NHF 4-6yo soft			£1,625

Has gone from strength to strength over the last two seasons, winning nine out of ten races with sole defeat coming when third in the Stayers' Hurdle; made amends for that when beating Nichols Canyon at Punchestown, taking Grade 1 tally to three.

Val De Ferbet (Fr)

8 b/br g Voix Du Nord - Intrigue Deferbet (Lights Out)

Andrew McNamara (Ir)   Andrew Heffernan

PLACINGS: 151/P2P22/244212011-   RPR **147+c**

Starts		1st	2nd	3rd	4th	Win & Pl
22		6	7	-	4	£118,351
	4/17	Cork	3m Gd3 Ch gd-yld			£17,083
	3/17	Clon	2m4f Ch sft-hvy			£9,214
	12/16	Limk	2m4f Hdl heavy			£7,009
	3/15	Limk	3m Nov Gd2 Ch soft			£20,155
	2/14	Fair	3m Ch soft			£5,175
	12/13	Pau	2m1½f Hdl 4yo soft			£12,488

Took a long time to fulfil early promise over

fences for Willie Mullins but flourished for his new trainer last spring, producing dominant front-running performances at Clonmel and Cork; also won over hurdles so should find plenty of opportunities.

Valseur Lido (Fr)

8 b g Anzillero - Libido Rock (Video Rock)

Henry de Bromhead (Ir)   Gigginstown House Stud

PLACINGS: 01/211236/12FU22/14-   RPR **169+c**

Starts		1st	2nd	3rd	4th	Win & Pl
20		8	5	1	1	£334,511
	11/16	DRoy	3m Gd1 Ch good			£60,735
	4/15	Punc	3m1f Nov Gd1 Ch gd-yld			£44,186
	11/14	Fair	2m4f Nov Gd1 Ch yld-sft			£40,625
	11/14	Punc	2m4f Ch yield			£6,900
	4/14	Fair	2m Nov Gd2 Hdl soft			£21,667
	12/13	Navn	2m Nov Hdl sft-hvy			£7,293
	11/13	Cork	2m Mdn Hdl 4yo sft-hvy			£5,610
	11/12	Pari	1m4f NHF 3yo v soft			£12,500

Began last season with a runaway Grade 1 win at Down Royal, although that was a weak race for the grade and he was only fourth next time in the Lexus before picking up an injury; not the first time he's been outstayed but just lacks the pace for top 2m4f races.

Value At Risk

8 b g Kayf Tara - Miss Orchestra (Orchestra)

Dan Skelton   D M Huglin

PLACINGS: 110/3125/FF921/4175-   RPR **142+c**

Starts		1st	2nd	3rd	4th	Win & Pl
17		5	3	1	1	£69,022
	10/16	Bang	2m4½f Cls4 Nov Ch good			£5,198
	3/16	Fair	2m4f Gd2 Hdl yld-sft			£26,029
	12/14	Newb	2m4f Cls4 Nov Hdl 4-6yo soft			£3,899
	12/13	Leop	2m NHF 4-7yo soft			£6,171
	12/13	Fair	2m NHF 4yo gd-yld			£4,768

Smart hurdler who was widely expected to prove even better over fences but has found it hard work; fell twice when first tried as a chaser and disappointed again in the spring having got off the mark in a four-runner race at Bangor; still a good prospect.

Vaniteux (Fr)

8 br g Voix Du Nord - Expoville (Video Rock)

David Pipe

PLACINGS: /22285/121U3/331814-   RPR **165+c**

Starts		1st	2nd	3rd	4th	Win & Pl
20		4	4	2	2	£181,593
153	4/17	Ayr	1m7½f Cls1 List 131-157 Ch Hcap good			£22,780
	1/17	Kemp	2m4½f Cls1 List Ch gd-sft			£19,490
	1/16	Donc	2m1½f Cls1 Nov Gd2 Ch good			£19,933
	11/15	Kemp	2m Cls4 Nov Ch gd-sft			£4,660
	2/14	Donc	2m3½f Cls4 Nov Hdl 4-7yo gd-sft			£3,574
	12/13	Sand	2m Cls3 Nov Hdl gd-sft			£6,498

Bought by David Pipe for £125,000 out of Nicky Henderson's yard in May; had come up short at the top level for Henderson but still managed to win a Listed chase at Kempton and a good handicap at Ayr last season; effective from 2m to 2m4f.

Verni (Fr)
8 ch g Sabrehill - Nobless D'Aron (Ragmar)

Philip Hobbs   Paul & Clare Rooney

PLACINGS: 342/31/1212-   RPR **139h**

Starts	1st	2nd	3rd	4th	Win & Pl
9	3	3	2	1	£37,462
125	2/17	Tntn	2m3f Cls3 125-138 Hdl Hcap soft		£9,495
120	10/16	NAbb	2m1f Cls3 Nov 107-125 Hdl Hcap good		£6,173
	4/16	NAbb	2m2½f Cls4 Mdn Hdl soft		£4,549

Progressive over hurdles last season and has won three of his last five races and finished second in the Martin Pipe Hurdle at the Cheltenham Festival; bumped into a subsequent Grade 1 winner that day and may still have a big handicap in him.

Vicente (Fr)
8 b g Dom Alco - Ireland (Kadalko)

Paul Nicholls   Trevor Hemmings

PLACINGS: 12F0/1131451/F669F1-   RPR **158c**

Starts	1st	2nd	3rd	4th	Win & Pl
24	7	3	3	2	£311,255
146	4/17	Ayr	4m Cls1 Gd3 127-148 Ch Hcap good		£122,443
146	4/16	Ayr	4m Cls1 Gd3 135-155 Ch Hcap gd-sft		£119,595
	11/15	Chel	3m1½f Cls2 Nov Ch gd-sft		£14,588
	5/15	Winc	3m1f Cls4 Nov Ch gd-fm		£3,994
	4/15	NAbb	2m5f Cls4 Ch gd-fm		£4,328
	10/14	Chel	2m5f Cls2 Nov Hdl good		£10,635
126	3/14	Winc	2m4f Cls3 113-129 Cond Hdl Hcap gd-sft		£6,330

Has won the last two runnings of the Scottish Grand National, both times off a mark of 146 having struggled over shorter trips and on softer ground in between, and starts this season only 4lb higher; fell at the first in last season's Grand National.

Viconte Du Noyer (Fr)
8 gr g Martaline - Zouk Wood (Woodman)

Colin Tizzard   Alan Potts

PLACINGS: /33F/0311333/310PP2-   RPR **156c**

Starts	1st	2nd	3rd	4th	Win & Pl
25	4	1	8	-	£112,673
148	11/16	Chel	3m3½f Cls1 Gd3 132-158 Ch Hcap gd-sft		£28,475
	8/15	Klny	2m4½f Nov Ch good		£7,756
	7/15	Klny	2m1f Ch gd-yld		£6,151
	4/12	Autl	1m7f Hdl 3yo heavy		£24,000

Produced his two best runs following move to Colin Tizzard last season, winning at Cheltenham over 3m3½f and finishing second at Punchestown over 2m4f; showed nothing in three runs in between but clearly capable on his day and versatile regarding trip.

Vieux Lion Rouge (Fr)
8 ch g Sabiango - Indecise (Cyborg)

David Pipe   Prof Caroline Tisdall & John Gent

PLACINGS: 103/390/111U267/116-   RPR **160+c**

Starts	1st	2nd	3rd	4th	Win & Pl
22	11	1	2	-	£204,872
146	2/17	Hayd	3m4½f Cls1 Gd3 132-152 Ch Hcap gd-sft		£42,713
142	12/16	Aint	3m2f Cls1 Gd3 133-159 Ch Hcap gd-sft		£78,582
139	11/15	Hayd	3m Cls2 128-145 Ch Hcap soft		£21,896
	6/15	MRas	2m3f Cls4 Nov Ch good		£3,861
	5/15	Towc	2m5½f Cls4 Nov Ch gd-sft		£3,769
	2/14	Sedg	2m1f Cls4 Nov Hdl heavy		£3,379
	1/14	Winc	1m7½f Cls3 Nov Hdl heavy		£5,523
	1/14	Winc	1m7½f Cls4 Nov Hdl heavy		£3,899
	2/13	Extr	2m4f Cls6 NHF 4yo heavy		£1,625
	1/13	Newb	1m4½f Cls6 NHF 4yo soft		£1,643
12/12		Ffos	2m Cls6 NHF 3-5yo heavy		£1,430

Has failed to stay when sixth and seventh in the Grand National for the last two years but has a fine record in other top staying handicaps, winning the Becher Chase and Haydock's Grand National Trial last season; should be a force in similar races again.

Village Vic (Ire)
10 b g Old Vic - Etoile Margot (Garde Royale)

Philip Hobbs   Alan Peterson

PLACINGS: /3412P/111190/2320P-   RPR **164c**

Starts	1st	2nd	3rd	4th	Win & Pl
27	9	5	2	2	£188,915
144	1/16	Chel	2m5f Cls1 Gd3 136-160 Ch Hcap heavy		£34,170
136	12/15	Chel	2m5f Cls1 Gd3 136-162 Ch Hcap soft		£56,950
129	11/15	Muss	2m4f Cls3 109-135 Ch Hcap good		£11,696
125	10/15	Weth	2m3½f Cls3 110-134 Ch Hcap good		£6,256
120	2/15	Newb	2m1½f Cls3 109-125 Ch Hcap gd-sft		£6,498
	9/13	Worc	2m4f Cls5 Mdn Hdl good		£1,949
	12/11	Chep	2m Cls6 NHF 4-6yo heavy		£1,365

Standing dish in big 2m4f handicap chases at Cheltenham in recent seasons, managing a second course win on New Year's Day 2016 and placed three times there last term; twice disappointing subsequently, though, and needs help from the handicapper.

Vintage Clouds (Ire)

7 gr g Cloudings - Rare Vintage (Germany)

Sue Smith   Trevor Hemmings

PLACINGS: 3215/21222P/222F3F7-   RPR **140+c**

Starts		1st	2nd	3rd	4th	Win & Pl
17		2	8	2	-	£35,649
	11/15	Hayd	2m3f Cls3 Nov Hdl 4-7yo soft			£6,498
	1/15	Weth	2m Cls6 NHF 4-6yo soft			£1,643

Coped well when quickly thrust into big handicap chases last season, finishing third in the Grand National Trial at Haydock and only four lengths down when falling two out in the Ultima at Cheltenham; open to further progress after only seven runs over fences.

Virgilio (Fr)

8 b g Denham Red - Liesse De Marbeuf (Cyborg)

Dan Skelton   C J Edwards, D Futter & A H Rushworth

PLACINGS: 5144/111P5/11P223-1   RPR **155+c**

Starts		1st	2nd	3rd	4th	Win & Pl
16		7	2	1	2	£121,420
142	5/17	Aint	3m1f Cls2 121-146 Ch Hcap good			£13,928
	10/16	NAbb	2m5f Cls2 Ch good			£21,270
	5/16	Wwck	2m4f Cls4 Nov Hdl gd-sft			£3,899
138	12/15	Aint	2m4f Cls2 125-144 Hdl Hcap soft			£13,763
125	5/15	Aint	2m4f Cls2 125-146 Hdl Hcap soft			£11,574
118	5/15	Wwck	2m3f Cls3 118-133 Hdl Hcap soft			£6,498
	10/13	Sabl	2m1f Hdl 4yo v soft			£9,756

Came up short in top company after winning his first two chases last season but got back on track when winning a good handicap at Aintree in May (jockey reported Virgilio had issues with his wind); could progress again if over problems.

Vroum Vroum Mag (Fr)

8 b m Voix Du Nord - Naiade Mag (Kadalko)

Willie Mullins (Ir)   Mrs S Ricci

PLACINGS: 2/11111/1111/121127-   RPR **157+h**

Starts		1st	2nd	3rd	4th	Win & Pl
21		14	5	1	-	£426,040
	1/17	Donc	2m1/2f Cls1 Gd2 Hdl good			£28,475
	12/16	Leop	3m Gd1 Hdl yield			£36,875
	4/16	Punc	2m Gd1 Hdl yield			£86,765
	3/16	Chel	2m4f Cls1 Gd1 Hdl gd-sft			£58,802
	1/16	Asct	2m7½f Cls1 Gd2 Hdl soft			£28,475

Lost her aura of invincibility last season but still has a sensational record, winning 12 of her last 15 races; beaten by Apple's Jade twice when outstayed both times over 2m4f and may be best at 2m, although has won over 3m; went lame when well beaten at Punchestown.

Vyta Du Roc (Fr)

8 gr g Lion Noir - Dolce Vyta (Grand Tresor)

Nicky Henderson   Simon Munir & Isaac Souede

PLACINGS: 1111242/12155/36P52-   RPR **147c**

Starts		1st	2nd	3rd	4th	Win & Pl
19		6	4	2	1	£159,891
	2/16	Asct	3m Cls1 Nov Gd2 Ch soft			£22,887
	12/15	Bang	2m1½f Cls4 Nov Ch heavy			£4,660
	12/14	Sand	2m4f Cls1 Nov Gd2 Hdl soft			£17,085
	11/14	Chel	2m1/2f Cls1 Nov Gd2 Hdl soft			£17,085
	6/14	Hexm	2m Cls3 Nov Hdl good			£5,817
	5/14	Uttx	2m Cls5 Mdn Hdl good			£2,339

Has been slightly disappointing given early promise (rated 150 as a novice hurdler and then won the 2016 Reynoldstown) but has gradually dropped to a competitive mark; came within a head of winning last season's bet365 Gold Cup and looks a thorough stayer.

Wait For Me (Fr)

7 b g Saint Des Saints - Aulne River (River Mist)

Philip Hobbs   Andrew L Cohen

PLACINGS: 13/2114/865091-2   RPR **143+h**

Starts		1st	2nd	3rd	4th	Win & Pl
135		4	2	1	1	£49,824
	4/17	Sand	2m4f Cls2 118-140 Hdl Hcap good			£18,768
	1/16	Kemp	2m Cls4 Nov Hdl soft			£3,249
	12/15	Newb	2m1/2f Cls4 Mdn Hdl soft			£3,249
	2/15	Asct	1m7½f Cls4 NHF 4-6yo soft			£4,549

Former Champion Bumper third who took an age to fulfil potential over hurdles but finally clicked when stepped up to 2m4f at Sandown in April having been a beaten favourite in four big handicaps since his last win; could go novice chasing.

Waiting Patiently (Ire)

6 b g Flemensfirth - Rossavon (Beneficial)

Malcolm Jefferson   Richard Collins

PLACINGS: 221/111-   RPR **158+c**

Starts		1st	2nd	3rd	4th	Win & Pl
6		4	2	-	-	£37,382
	1/17	Hayd	2m4f Cls1 Nov Gd2 Ch soft			£18,546
	12/16	Newc	2m1/2f Cls3 Nov Ch soft			£6,498
123	11/16	Sedg	2m1/2f Cls3 Nov 115-130 Ch Hcap soft			£6,498
	1/16	Sedg	2m4f Cls4 Nov Hdl gd-sft			£3,798

Won three out of three when sent chasing last season, including a Grade 2 at Haydock when outstaying Politologue; gained all his wins on soft ground and missed Cheltenham due to quicker conditions, although had run well on good ground over hurdles.

The Racing Post app.
Home to racing's top information.
Home to racing's top bookies.

Why continually flit between apps when racing's best information and top bookies are sitting side by side in one app? Better yet, you can remain logged in to all four bookies at once and simply switch account to bet with the best odds. Home sweet home, as they say.

When You Bet on Racing, You Can Bet on Racing Post.

Warriors Tale
8 b g Midnight Legend - Samandara (Kris)

Paul Nicholls — Michelle & Dan Macdonald

PLACINGS: 7112/2P205/13253115-   RPR **146+c**

Starts		1st	2nd	3rd	4th	Win & Pl
21		5	5	2	1	£50,988
137	3/17	Newb	2m4f Cls2 125-143 Ch Hcap gd-sft			£12,660
130	3/17	Newb	2m4f Cls3 Nov 130-143 Ch Hcap soft			£6,498
	5/16	Prth	3m Cls4 Nov Ch gd-fm			£4,328
110	2/15	Kels	2m6¹/₂f Cls3 110-125 Hdl Hcap gd-sft			£6,498
	1/15	Ayr	2m4¹/₂f Cls5 Mdn Hdl soft			£2,469

Won over 3m on chase debut last season but did better when dropped in trip in the spring, winning twice at Newbury, although disappointed when up in grade at Ayr; win on soft ground came in a three-runner race and prefers quicker conditions.

West Approach
7 b g Westerner - Ardstown (Ardross)

Colin Tizzard — John & Heather Snook

PLACINGS: 14/93520/1235U3PP-   RPR **156h**

Starts		1st	2nd	3rd	4th	Win & Pl
15		2	2	3	1	£31,147
	5/16	NAbb	2m1f Cls2 Nov Hdl good			£9,495
	1/15	Newb	2m¹/₂f Cls5 NHF 4-6yo heavy			£2,053

Boldly campaigned as a novice last season and produced by far his two best runs in top company, including when third to Unowhatimeanharry in the Cleeve Hurdle; had failed to show that form in more winnable races, with sole success at Newton Abbot.

Western Ryder (Ire)
5 b g Westerner - Seesea (Dr Massini)

Warren Greatrex — The Albatross Club

PLACINGS: 121253-   RPR **126b**

Starts		1st	2nd	3rd	4th	Win & Pl
6		2	2	1	-	£31,869
	12/16	Asct	1m7¹/₂f Cls1 List NHF 4-6yo gd-sft			£17,085
	5/16	Ffos	2m Cls4 NHF 4-6yo good			£3,249

Won a Listed race at Ascot last season and remained hugely consistent in top bumpers; second to Daphne Du Clos (received 21lb) at Newbury before finishing fifth at Cheltenham and third at Aintree; should make a good novice hurdler.

....

'He was found to be sick after the Greatwood and raced too keenly in the Scottish Champion Hurdle. He could yet land a big handicap'

Whisper (Fr)
9 b g Astarabad - Belle Yepa (Mansonnien)

Nicky Henderson — Walters Plant Hire

PLACINGS: 331211/251/5P8/1122-   RPR **165c**

Starts		1st	2nd	3rd	4th	Win & Pl
22		10	4	2	2	£330,823
	1/17	Chel	2m5f Cls1 Nov Ch soft			£18,224
	12/16	Chel	2m5f Cls2 Nov Ch gd-sft			£15,698
	4/15	Aint	3m1¹/₂f Cls1 Gd1 Hdl good			£67,582
	4/14	Aint	3m1¹/₂f Cls1 Gd1 Hdl gd-sft			£67,524
153	3/14	Chel	2m5f Cls1 Gd3 135-154 Hdl Hcap good			£45,560
140	12/13	Newb	2m4¹/₂f Cls2 134-144 Hdl Hcap heavy			£11,574
	4/13	Chel	2m4¹/₂f Cls2 Nov Hdl gd-sft			£10,010
	2/13	Ffos	2m4f Cls4 Nov Hdl 4-7yo heavy			£3,574
	12/12	Ffos	2m4f Cls4 Nov Hdl heavy			£2,599
	4/12	Ffos	2m Cls6 NHF 4-5yo good			£1,848

Reportedly took a long time to get to grips with fences at home but made up for lost time last season, winning twice at Cheltenham and twice finishing second to Might Bite; flattered to get so close to the winner both times though and might be hard to place.

Wholestone (Ire)
6 br g Craigsteel - Last Theatre (King's Theatre)

Nigel Twiston-Davies — Simon Munir & Isaac Souede

PLACINGS: 13F/112113-   RPR **147h**

Starts		1st	2nd	3rd	4th	Win & Pl
9		5	1	2	-	£65,792
	1/17	Chel	2m4¹/₂f Cls1 Nov Gd2 Hdl good			£17,085
	12/16	Chel	3m Cls1 Nov Gd2 Hdl soft			£17,085
	10/16	Chel	3m Cls3 Nov Hdl good			£6,256
	9/16	Wwck	2m5f Cls4 Mdn Hdl good			£3,574
	9/15	Worc	2m Cls6 NHF 4-6yo good			£1,625

Broke his duck over hurdles at Warwick last season and subsequently did all his racing at Cheltenham, winning three times more and finishing third in the Albert Bartlett; likely to go novice chasing and love of Cheltenham bodes well if taking to new challenge.

Wicklow Brave
8 b g Beat Hollow - Moraine (Rainbow Quest)

Willie Mullins (Ir) — Wicklow Bloodstock (Ireland)

PLACINGS: 11166/F580P1/033/71-   RPR **165h**

Starts		1st	2nd	3rd	4th	Win & Pl
20		7	1	2	-	£232,856
	4/17	Punc	2m Gd1 Hdl gd-yld			£126,068
138	3/15	Chel	2m1f Cls1 Gd3 134-146 Hdl Hcap soft			£45,560
	2/14	Punc	2m Nov List Hdl heavy			£16,250
	1/14	Cork	2m Mdn Hdl 4-5yo heavy			£6,038
	10/13	Tipp	2m NHF 4-7yo good			£6,030
	9/13	List	2m NHF 4-7yo soft			£7,854
	7/13	Gway	2m NHF 4-7yo good			£4,488

Rarely sighted over hurdles since coming up short at the top level at the end of 2015 but has progressed on the Flat and translated that improvement back over hurdles last spring, winning well at Punchestown; possible he was given too much rope in front previously and might benefit from different tactics.

Wild West Wind (Ire)

8 b g Westerner - Mhuire Na Gale (Norwich)

| Tom George | | | | Simon W Clarke |

PLACINGS: 1/2F3122/113-   RPR **145+c**

Starts		1st	2nd	3rd	4th	Win & Pl
9		3	3	2	-	£23,831
135	2/17	Hrfd	3m1f Cls3 Nov 119-135 Ch Hcap heavy			£6,498
123	1/17	Winc	2m4f Cls3 Nov 112-132 Ch Hcap soft			£7,988
	2/16	Chep	2m7¹/₂f Cls4 Nov Hdl heavy			£3,899

Won two out of three when sent chasing last season, with sole defeat a fair third behind Label Des Obeaux on ground quicker than ideal; has gained all his wins on soft or heavy ground and could still be on a fair mark given those conditions.

William Henry (Ire)

7 b g King's Theatre - Cincuenta (Bob Back)

| Nicky Henderson | | | | Walters Plant Hire |

PLACINGS: 411/2121-   RPR **143+h**

Starts		1st	2nd	3rd	4th	Win & Pl
7		4	2	-	1	£32,475
	4/17	Chel	2m4¹/₂f Cls2 Nov Hdl good			£10,010
	12/16	Newb	2m1¹/₂f Cls4 Hdl gd-sft			£4,549
	4/15	Ayr	2m Cls3 NHF 4-6yo good			£6,498
	3/15	Kemp	2m Cls5 Mdn NHF 4-6yo soft			£2,599

Quickly developed into a useful novice hurdler last season despite a long layoff (missed previous season through injury); finished off with a smooth win at Cheltenham after missing the Neptune with sore shins; likely to go novice chasing.

Willoughby Court (Ire)

6 br g Court Cave - Willoughby Sue (Dabali)

| Ben Pauling | | | | Paul & Clare Rooney |

PLACINGS: 3/115/2111-   RPR **152+h**

Starts		1st	2nd	3rd	4th	Win & Pl
8		5	1	1		£100,239
	3/17	Chel	2m5f Cls1 Nov Gd1 Hdl gd-sft			£71,188
	1/17	Wwck	2m5f Cls1 Nov Gd2 Hdl soft			£19,933
	12/16	Wwck	2m5f Cls4 Mdn Hdl gd-sft			£3,574
	12/15	Wwck	2m Cls6 NHF 4-6yo soft			£1,625
	11/15	Sthl	1m7¹/₂f Cls6 NHF 4-6yo soft			£1,949

Game winner of last season's Neptune Hurdle at Cheltenham, beating Neon Wolf to complete a hat-trick after two wins at Warwick; proved effectiveness on quicker ground having seemed to thrive on soft previously; should make a fine chaser.

Winter Escape (Ire)

6 b g Robin Des Pres - Saddleeruppat (Saddlers' Hall)

| Alan King | | | | John P McManus |

PLACINGS: 111/050-   RPR **142h**

Starts		1st	2nd	3rd	4th	Win & Pl
6		3	-	-	-	£26,453
	2/16	Kemp	2m Cls1 Nov Gd2 Hdl gd-sft			£17,085
	2/16	Muss	2m¹/₂f Cls4 Nov Hdl gd-sft			£3,899
	12/15	Donc	2m7¹/₂f Cls5 Mdn Hdl gd-sft			£2,924

Unbeaten in three novice hurdles two seasons ago but had little go right last term; found to be sick after the Greatwood and raced too keenly in the Scottish Champion Hurdle (favourite both times); finished a good fifth in the County Hurdle at Cheltenham in between and could yet land a big handicap.

Wonderful Charm (Fr)

9 b g Poliglote - Victoria Royale (Garde Royale)

| Paul Nicholls | | | | RJH Geffen, Sir J Ritblat & R Waley-Cohen |

PLACINGS: 3/123783P/2P7/1120-3   RPR **144+c**

Starts		1st	2nd	3rd	4th	Win & Pl
29		8	6	4	2	£224,563
	2/17	Hayd	3m Cls3 Am Hunt Ch gd-sft			£6,239
	2/17	Muss	3m2¹/₂f Cls3 Am Hunt Ch good			£5,996
	10/14	NAbb	2m5f Cls2 Ch gd-sft			£18,941
	11/13	Newb	2m4f Cls1 Nov Gd2 Ch gd-sft			£17,912
	11/13	Winc	2m5f Cls1 Nov Gd2 Ch gd-sft			£17,912
	10/13	Fknm	2m5f Cls3 Nov Ch good			£6,990
	10/12	Chep	2m3¹/₂f Cls1 Nov Gd2 Hdl gd-sft			£12,073
	3/12	Autl	2m2f Hdl 4yo v soft			£28,000

Not the force of old but still showed much of his old zest in hunter chases last season, finishing second in the Foxhunter at Cheltenham after a couple of soft wins; also dropped 15lb through the season (back to a mark 21lb below peak).

Woodland Opera (Ire)

7 br g Robin Des Champs - Opera Hat (Strong Gale)

Jessica Harrington (Ir)

Mrs T K Cooper, Miss Diana Cooper & Mrs C A Water

PLACINGS: 1/193/154311-F   RPR **153+c**

Starts		1st	2nd	3rd	4th	Win & Pl
11		5	-	2	1	£86,273
142	4/17	Punc	2m5f Nov 125-146 Ch Hcap gd-yld			£50,427
	4/17	Fair	2m1f Ch sft-hvy			£7,897
	4/16	Punc	2m4f Hdl gd-yld			£11,305
	11/15	Navn	2m Mdn Hdl soft			£7,488
	1/15	Leop	2m NHF 5-7yo yield			£4,279

Much improved for a breathing operation after

Christmas last season and won twice in the spring, most notably in a 2m5f novice handicap chase at Punchestown; struggles to get that trip on soft ground and beaten when falling two out (odds-on) in a Grade 3 at Killarney.

ON THE FIGURES

YANWORTH Cheltenham Festival runs apart, he is unbeaten in the past two seasons and if he can match his hurdles RPR of 165 when chasing he should take high rank in the novice division. [Steve Mason, Racing Post Ratings]

Work In Progress (Ire)

7 b g Westerner - Parsons Term (The Parson)

Dan Skelton   Donlon & Doyle

PLACINGS: F8/12618/6240P-15111   RPR **155+c**

Starts		1st	2nd	3rd	4th	Win & Pl
19		6	3	-	2	£40,762
	7/17	Uttx	2m4f Cls3 Nov Ch soft			£6,330
	7/17	MRas	2m3f Cls4 Nov Ch good			£4,549
	6/17	MRas	2m3f Cls4 Nov Ch good			£3,899
124	5/17	Font	2m3f Cls3 113-124 Hdl Hcap gd-fm			£7,862
	2/16	Fknm	2m4f Cls3 Nov Hdl 4-7yo gd-sft			£6,498
	10/15	Kemp	2m5f Cls4 Nov Hdl good			£3,899

Reverted to hurdles after failing to get off the mark over fences last season but did much better when given another crack at chasing this summer, completing a quickfire hat-trick at Uttoxeter in July; seems best on good ground.

Yanworth: top-notch hurdler who should be a force over fences this season

Yala Enki (Fr)
7 b/br g Nickname - Cadiane (Cadoudal)

Venetia Williams   Hills Of Ledbury (Aga)

PLACINGS: /2232/15131P5/31441-   RPR **157+c**

Starts 24	1st 7	2nd 5	3rd 3	4th 4	Win & Pl £169,162
146	3/17	Kels	3m2f Cls2 125-147 Ch Hcap heavy		...£17,545
139	12/16	Hayd	2m7f Cls2 120-139 Ch Hcap soft		...£15,640
	2/16	Asct	2m3¹/₂f Cls2 Nov Hdl soft		...£15,640
130	1/16	Kemp	2m5f Cls1 List 127-153 Hdl Hcap soft		...£22,780
	11/15	Extr	2m5¹/₂f Cls3 Nov Hdl gd-sft		...£5,523
	2/14	Fntb	2m2f Ch 4yo v soft		...£9,600
	10/13	Pari	2m1f Ch 3yo gd-sft		...£7,415

Won twice over fences in France before joining Venetia Williams and flourished when switched back to chasing last season, running away with good handicaps at Haydock and Kelso; had also done well over hurdles and could do well in each discipline.

Yanworth
7 ch g Norse Dancer - Yota (Galetto)

Alan King   John P McManus

PLACINGS: 1124/11112/111dis1-   RPR **165+h**

Starts 14	1st 10	2nd 2	3rd -	4th 1	Win & Pl £312,343
	4/17	Aint	3m¹/₂f Cls1 Gd1 Hdl good		...£84,251
	2/17	Winc	1m7¹/₂f Cls1 Gd2 Hdl soft		...£34,170
	12/16	Kemp	2m Cls1 Gd1 Hdl good		...£56,950
	11/16	Asct	2m3¹/₂f Cls1 Gd2 Hdl gd-sft		...£56,950
	1/16	Chel	2m Cls1 Nov Gd2 Hdl heavy		...£17,085
	12/15	Asct	1m7¹/₂f Cls1 Nov Gd2 Hdl soft		...£17,085
	11/15	Wwck	2m Cls4 Nov Hdl gd-sft		...£3,899
	11/15	Extr	2m1f Cls3 Nov Hdl soft		...£5,523
	11/14	Newb	2m Cls6 NHF 4-6yo soft		...£1,689
	5/14	Winc	1m7¹/₂f Cls6 NHF 4-6yo gd-sft		...£1,625

Sent off favourite for last season's Champion Hurdle after beating lesser opposition over 2m but seemed to find trip too short when only seventh and subsequently disqualified for failing a post-race test; looked better suited to 3m when winning at Aintree next time; goes novice chasing and it would be no surprise to see him do well.

Yorkhill (Ire)
7 ch g Presenting - Lightning Breeze (Saddlers' Hall)

Willie Mullins (Ir)   Andrea & Graham Wylie

PLACINGS: U11/11111/41112-   RPR **165+c**

Starts 11	1st 9	2nd 1	3rd	4th 1	Win & Pl £288,919
	3/17	Chel	2m4f Cls1 Nov Gd1 Ch good		...£89,275
	1/17	Leop	2m3f Nov Gd3 Ch good		...£22,692
	12/16	Fair	2m Ch sft-hvy		...£6,331
	4/16	Aint	2m4f Cls1 Nov Gd1 Hdl soft		...£42,402
	3/16	Chel	2m5f Cls1 Nov Gd1 Hdl good		...£68,340
	1/16	Sand	2m Cls1 Nov Gd1 Hdl heavy		...£23,048
	12/15	Punc	2m4f Mdn Hdl heavy		...£6,419
	4/15	Punc	2m NHF 4-7yo yield		...£6,419
	3/15	Gowr	2m2f NHF 4-7yo soft		...£4,814

Hugely talented but quirky performer who won his first three chases last season but threw away victory in the Ryanair Gold Cup at Fairyhouse on

his final start by jumping violently left and handing the race to Road To Respect; can also pull hard on occasions but loves the Cheltenham Festival having won there for the last two seasons – the JLT Novices' Chase last term and the Neptune Hurdle in 2016.

Zabana (Ire)
8 ch g Halling - Gandia (Danehill)

Andrew Lynch (Ir)   C Jones

PLACINGS: 1015/0312/314U/1417-   RPR **158+c**

Starts 18	1st 7	2nd 1	3rd 3	4th 2	Win & Pl £127,910
	11/16	Gowr	2m4f Ch yld-sft		...£7,688
	4/16	Punc	3m1f Nov Gd1 Ch gd-yld		...£43,382
	12/15	Leop	2m3f Ch heavy		...£7,488
	1/15	Navn	2m Hdl soft		...£10,078
119	1/14	Leop	2m4f 102-128 Hdl Hcap soft		...£8,625
	6/13	Gowr	2m Hdl 4yo gd-fm		...£7,293
	5/13	Slig	2m Mdn Hdl 4-5yo sft-hvy		...£4,628

Won a Grade 1 novice chase at Punchestown two seasons ago but had a frustrating time last term, winning only an ordinary contest at Gowran Park and missing the spring after a setback; should have more to offer after only seven runs over fences.

Zamdy Man
8 b g Authorized - Lauderdale (Nebos)

Venetia Williams   John P McManus

PLACINGS: 8/111/25/3409/12110-   RPR **149+c**

Starts 19	1st 6	2nd 4	3rd 1	4th 1	Win & Pl £92,522
	2/17	Newc	2m1¹/₂f Cls2 Nov Ch soft		...£11,711
	1/17	Hrfd	2m Cls4 Nov Ch soft		...£4,159
	4/16	Uttx	2m Cls3 Ch soft		...£6,330
	1/14	Hayd	1m7¹/₂f Cls1 Nov Gd2 Hdl heavy		...£15,661
	11/13	Hayd	1m7¹/₂f Cls1 Nov List Hdl soft		...£11,888
	11/13	Asct	1m7¹/₂f Cls3 Nov Hdl gd-sft		...£7,507

Won three novice chases last season and easily forgiven distant tenth in the novice handicap chase at the Cheltenham Festival (ground too quick and 2m4f trip perhaps too far); can win more races on softer ground.

Zubayr (Ire)
5 b g Authorized - Zaziyra (Dalakhani)

Paul Nicholls   P J Vogt

PLACINGS: 101/3F5062-5   RPR **147+h**

Starts 10	1st 2	2nd 1	3rd 1	4th -	Win & Pl £59,811
	4/16	Winc	1m7¹/₂f Cls4 Nov Hdl gd-sft		...£3,249
	2/16	Kemp	2m Cls1 Gd2 Hdl 4yo gd-sft		...£17,085

Without a win since landing the Adonis Hurdle in 2016 on his British debut; ran in a string of fiercely competitive 2m handicaps last season though and came within a short head of winning the Scottish Champion Hurdle; still on a reasonable mark.

THIS SEASON'S KEY HORSES LISTED BY TRAINER

Kim Bailey
Charbel (Ire)
The Last Samuri (Ire)

Enda Bolger
Gilgamboa (Ire)

Peter Bowen
Henllan Harri (Ire)

Mark Bradstock
Coneygree
Flintham

Gavin Cromwell
Jer's Girl (Ire)

Rebecca Curtis
Bigbadjohn (Ire)
Binge Drinker (Ire)
Irish Cavalier (Ire)

Keith Dalgleish
Mixboy (Fr)

Henry de Bromhead
Alisier D'Irlande (Fr)
Balko Des Flos (Fr)
Champagne West (Ire)
Identity Thief (Ire)
Monalee (Ire)
Ordinary World (Ire)
Petit Mouchoir (Fr)
Some Plan (Ire)
Special Tiara
Sub Lieutenant (Ire)
Valseur Lido (Fr)

Miss Elizabeth Doyle
Last Goodbye (Ire)

Gordon Elliott
A Toi Phil (Fr)
Apple's Jade (Fr)
Ball D'Arc (Fr)
Blood Crazed Tiger (Ire)
Blow By Blow (Ire)
Brelade
Campeador (Fr)
Cause Of Causes (USA)
De Plotting Shed (Ire)
Death Duty (Ire)
Diamond King (Ire)
Empire Of Dirt (Ire)
Fagan
Fayonagh (Ire)
Free Expression (Ire)
General Principle (Ire)
Jury Duty (Ire)
Mega Fortune (Fr)
Mick Jazz (Fr)
Missy Tata (Fr)
Noble Endeavor (Ire)
Outlander (Ire)
Prince Of Scars (Ire)
Roi Des Francs (Fr)
Samcro (Ire)
Shattered Love (Ire)

Squouateur (Fr)
Sutton Place (Ire)
Tell Us More (Ire)
The Storyteller (Ire)
Tiger Roll (Ire)
Tombstone (Ire)
Ucello Conti (Fr)

Brian Ellison
Definitly Red (Ire)
Forest Bihan (Fr)
Nietzsche
Pistol Park (Fr)
Smart Talk (Ire)

James Eustace
Sir Note (Fr)

Peter Fahey
Peregrine Run (Ire)

Alan Fleming
Gwencily Berbas (Fr)
Tully East (Ire)

Harry Fry
Air Horse One
American (Fr)
Golden Birthday (Fr)
Henryville
Minella Awards (Ire)
Overtown Express (Ire)
Thomas Brown
Unowhatimeanharry

Tom George
Black Op (Ire)
Bun Doran (Ire)
Double Shuffle (Ire)
God's Own (Ire)
Max Ward (Ire)
Singlefarmpayment
Sir Valentino (Fr)
The Worlds End (Ire)
Wild West Wind (Ire)

Warren Greatrex
Chef D'Oeuvre (Fr)
Cole Harden (Ire)
Keeper Hill (Ire)
La Bague Au Roi (Fr)
Missed Approach (Ire)
One Track Mind (Ire)
Shantou Bob (Ire)
The Nipper (Ire)
Western Ryder (Ire)

Debra Hamer
Tobefair

Jessica Harrington
Don't Touch It (Ire)
Jezki (Ire)
Our Duke (Ire)
Rock The World (Ire)
Sizing John
Supasundae
Woodland Opera (Ire)

Eddie Harty
Coney Island (Ire)

Nigel Hawke
Speredek (Fr)

Nicky Henderson
Altior (Ire)
Beat That (Ire)
Beware The Bear (Ire)
Beyond Conceit (Ire)
Brain Power (Ire)
Burbank (Ire)
Buveur D'Air (Fr)
Call Me Lord (Fr)
Charli Parcs (Fr)
Claimantakinforgan (Fr)
Constantine Bay
Different Gravey (Ire)
Divin Bere (Fr)
Fixe Le Kap (Fr)
Gold Present (Ire)
Jenkins (Ire)
Josses Hill (Ire)
Kilcrea Vale (Ire)
Kotkikova (Fr)
L'Ami Serge (Ire)
Might Bite (Ire)
My Tent Or Yours (Ire)
O O Seven (Ire)
Pougne Bobbi (Fr)
Premier Bond
Rather Be (Ire)
River Wylde (Ire)
Stowaway Magic (Ire)
Theinval (Fr)
Top Notch (Fr)
Vaniteux (Fr)
Vyta Du Roc (Fr)
Whisper (Fr)
William Henry (Ire)

Philip Hobbs
Defi Du Seuil (Fr)
Garde La Victoire (Fr)
Jerrysback (Ire)
No Comment
Rock The Kasbah (Ire)
Royal Regatta (Ire)
Three Faces West (Ire)
Verni (Fr)
Village Vic (Ire)
Wait For Me (Fr)

Ellmarie Holden
Abolitionist (Ire)

Anthony Honeyball
Fountains Windfall
Regal Encore (Ire)

Sandra Hughes
Acapella Bourgeois (Fr)

Malcolm Jefferson
Cloudy Dream (Ire)

Cyrus Darius
Double W's (Ire)
Mount Mews (Ire)
Waiting Patiently (Ire)

Patrick Kelly
Mall Dini (Ire)
Presenting Percy

Colin Kidd
Rashaan (Ire)

John Kiely
Carlingford Lough (Ire)

Alan King
Dusky Legend
Label Des Obeaux (Fr)
Midnight Tour
River Frost
Sceau Royal (Fr)
Smad Place (Fr)
The Unit (Ire)
Winter Escape (Ire)
Yanworth

Neil King
Lil Rockerfeller (USA)

Emma Lavelle
Javert (Ire)

Kerry Lee
Bishops Road (Ire)
Gino Trail (Ire)
Goodtoknow
Top Gamble (Ire)

Charlie Longsdon
Hammersly Lake (Ire)
Our Kaempfer (Ire)
Pendra (Ire)
Snow Leopardess

Andrew Lynch
Zabana (Ire)

Tony Martin
Anibale Fly (Fr)

Andrew McNamara
Val De Ferbet (Fr)

Graeme McPherson
Ami Desbois (Fr)

Noel Meade
A Genie In Abottle (Ire)
Bonny Kate (Ire)
Disko (Fr)
Rathnure Rebel (Ire)
Red Jack (Ire)
Road To Respect (Ire)
Road To Riches (Ire)
Snow Falcon (Ire)

Gary Moore
Ar Mad (Fr)
Baron Alco (Fr)
Benatar (Ire)
Camping Ground (Fr)

Casse Tete (Fr)
Sire De Grugy (Fr)
Traffic Fluide (Fr)

Mouse Morris
Alpha Des Obeaux (Fr)
Nambour (Ger)
Rogue Angel (Ire)

Neil Mulholland
Carole's Destrier
Dead Right
Doing Fine (Ire)
Impulsive Star (Ire)
Minella Present (Ire)
Peter The Mayo Man (Ire)
Pilgrims Bay (Ire)
Shantou Village (Ire)
Southfield Royale
The Druids Nephew (Ire)
The Young Master

Margaret Mullins
Debuchet (Fr)

Seamus Mullins
Chesterfield (Ire)

Willie Mullins
Al Boum Photo (Fr)
American Tom (Fr)
Arbre De Vie (Fr)
Arctic Fire (Ger)
Augusta Kate
Bacardys (Fr)
Ballycasey (Ire)
Bapaume (Fr)
Battleford
Bellshill (Ire)
Benie Des Dieux (Fr)
Black Hercules (Ire)
Blazer (Fr)
Bleu Berry (Fr)
Bleu Et Rouge (Fr)
Bunk Off Early (Ire)
C'est Jersey (Fr)
Carter McKay
Cilaos Emery (Fr)
Crack Mome (Fr)
Diakali (Fr)
Djakadam (Fr)
Douvan (Fr)
Faugheen (Ire)
Footpad (Fr)
Getabird (Ire)
Great Field (Fr)
Haymount (Ire)
Invitation Only (Ire)
Karalee (Fr)
Let's Dance (Fr)
Limini (Ire)
Melon
Meri Devie (Fr)
Min (Fr)

Nichols Canyon
Penhill
Pleasant Company (Ire)
Rathvinden (Ire)
Renneti (Fr)
Saturnas (Fr)
Shaneshill (Ire)
Thomas Hobson
Tin Soldier (Fr)
Un De Sceaux (Fr)
Vroum Vroum Mag (Fr)
Wicklow Brave
Yorkhill (Ire)

Paul Nicholls
Alcala (Fr)
Antartica De Thaix (Fr)
Aux Ptits Soins (Fr)
Bouvreuil (Fr)
Brelan D'As (Fr)
Brio Conti (Fr)
Capitaine (Fr)
Clan Des Obeaux (Fr)
Cliffs Of Dover
Copain De Classe (Fr)
Diego Du Charmil (Fr)
Dolos (Fr)
El Bandit (Ire)
Frodon (Fr)
Give Me A Copper (Ire)
Ibis Du Rheu (Fr)
Irish Saint (Fr)
Irving
Le Prezien (Fr)
Modus
Movewiththetimes (Ire)
Mr Mix (Fr)
Old Guard
Overland Flyer (Ire)
Pacha Du Polder (Fr)
Politologue (Fr)
Present Man (Ire)
Ptit Zig (Fr)
Romain De Senam (Fr)
San Benedeto (Fr)
Saphir Du Rheu (Fr)
Silsol (Ger)
Southfield Theatre (Ire)
Tommy Silver (Fr)
Vicente (Fr)
Warriors Tale
Wonderful Charm (Fr)
Zubayr (Ire)

Fergal O'Brien
Barney Dwan (Ire)
Cap Soleil (Fr)
Chase The Spud
Colin's Sister
Perfect Candidate (Ire)

Joseph O'Brien
Housesofparliament (Ire)
Ivanovich Gorbatov (Ire)

Landofhopeandglory (Ire)
Slowmotion (Fr)
Tigris River (Ire)

Jonjo O'Neill
Minella Rocco (Ire)
More Of That (Ire)
Taquin Du Seuil (Fr)

Ross O'Sullivan
Baie Des Iles (Fr)

Ben Pauling
Barters Hill (Ire)
Drumacoo (Ire)
Le Breuil (Fr)
Willoughby Court (Ire)

David Pipe
Champers On Ice (Ire)
Moon Racer (Ire)
Starchitect (Ire)
Un Temps Pour Tout (Ire)
Vieux Lion Rouge (Fr)

Nicky Richards
Baywing (Ire)

Lucinda Russell
Big River (Ire)
One For Arthur (Ire)

Michael Scudamore
Mysteree (Ire)

Dan Skelton
Bedrock
Captain Forez (Fr)
Cause Toujours (Fr)
Ch'Tibello (Fr)
Its'afreebee (Ire)
Knockgraffon (Ire)
Long House Hall (Ire)
Mister Miyagi (Ire)
No Hassle Hoff (Ire)
North Hill Harvey
Oldgrangewood
Shantou Rock (Ire)
Shelford (Ire)
Superb Story (Ire)
Three Musketeers (Ire)
Two Taffs (Ire)
Value At Risk
Virgilio (Fr)
Work In Progress (Ire)

Sue Smith
Vintage Clouds (Ire)

Sandy Thomson
Seldom Inn

Colin Tizzard
Alary (Fr)
Cue Card
Finian's Oscar (Ire)
Fox Norton (Fr)
Native River (Ire)
Pingshou (Ire)

Robinsfirth (Ire)
Royal Vacation (Ire)
Sizing Codelco (Ire)
Sizing Granite (Ire)
Theatre Guide (Ire)
Thistlecrack
Ultragold (Ire)
Viconte Du Noyer (Fr)
West Approach

Nigel Twiston-Davies
Ballyandy
Ballybolley (Ire)
Ballyoptic (Ire)
Blaklion
Bristol De Mai (Fr)
Calett Mad (Fr)
Cogry
Flying Angel (Ire)
Foxtail Hill (Ire)
The New One (Ire)
Wholestone (Ire)

Tim Vaughan
Debece

Lucy Wadham
Potters Legend

Robert Walford
Astre De La Cour (Fr)

Ted Walsh
Second Now (Ire)
Foxrock (Ire)

Harry Whittington
Emerging Force (Ire)

Evan Williams
Clyne
Gayebury
John Constable (Ire)
King's Odyssey (Ire)
Pobbles Bay (Ire)

Ian Williams
So Celebre (Ger)

Nick Williams
Agrapart (Fr)
Flying Tiger (Ire)
Tea For Two

Venetia Williams
Aso (Fr)
Belami Des Pictons (Fr)
Burtons Well (Ire)
Calipto (Fr)
Gardefort (Fr)
Houblon Des Obeaux (Fr)
Otago Trail (Ire)
Plaisir D'Amour (Fr)
Tenor Nivernais (Fr)
Yala Enki (Fr)
Zamdy Man

Richard Woollacott
Lalor (Ger)

LAST SEASON'S LEADING JUMPS JOCKEYS IN BRITAIN

Jockey	Wins-runs	Wins (%)	2nd	3rd	4th	Win prize	Total prize	Profit/loss (£)
Richard Johnson	189-1026	18	192	139	108	£1,539,130	£2,334,380	-167.62
Brian Hughes	144-866	17	164	128	106	£857,238	£1,430,502	-233.69
Sam Twiston-Davies	137-673	20	103	91	63	£1,122,396	£1,707,545	-109.75
Aidan Coleman	122-761	16	97	90	104	£1,027,740	£1,723,257	-64.26
Noel Fehily	118-547	22	93	60	66	£1,433,079	£2,188,954	-39.71
Harry Skelton	101-531	19	103	75	48	£697,771	£1,106,938	-154.60
Tom Scudamore	100-754	13	100	86	118	£859,915	£1,302,740	-272.28
Paddy Brennan	95-454	21	66	62	47	£899,764	£1,282,654	+135.02
Daryl Jacob	88-407	22	63	53	43	£759,630	£1,290,541	+45.30
Tom O'Brien	81-583	14	65	65	79	£659,041	£966,388	-130.67
Sean Bowen	79-432	18	75	42	43	£677,841	£958,532	+21.81
Wayne Hutchinson	74-385	19	72	68	41	£452,560	£778,860	-94.93
Harry Cobden	63-326	19	44	37	24	£579,788	£762,307	+27.75
Will Kennedy	63-463	14	61	69	41	£302,849	£471,600	-96.42
Nico de Boinville	59-299	20	40	37	24	£653,213	£855,364	-90.88
Gavin Sheehan	56-372	15	49	42	39	£275,100	£461,493	-47.75
Adrian Heskin	54-297	18	39	43	18	£494,745	£813,905	+10.71
Danny Cook	51-279	18	47	35	37	£301,615	£473,081	-20.10
Henry Brooke	48-388	12	48	46	31	£261,825	£411,933	-25.04
Jamie Moore	47-429	11	62	52	40	£357,114	£627,419	-73.30
Alan Johns	45-301	15	40	28	34	£219,712	£343,146	-2.39
David Bass	45-324	14	46	40	40	£293,846	£469,269	+28.65
Nick Scholfield	44-397	11	45	51	38	£378,695	£574,103	-115.18
Jeremiah McGrath	43-267	16	40	30	25	£258,447	£495,546	-63.56
Barry Geraghty	41-153	27	19	15	9	£859,266	£1,063,396	+9.09
Leighton Aspell	40-382	10	58	58	40	£306,099	£495,540	-163.88
Sean Quinlan	38-343	11	32	36	36	£199,155	£301,443	-123.69
Tom Cannon	36-344	10	34	50	36	£178,016	£301,746	-108.10
David Noonan	36-378	10	37	44	42	£225,004	£340,856	-138.00
Brian Harding	34-252	13	34	27	26	£138,450	£239,657	-37.55
Paul Moloney	34-319	11	27	44	39	£153,821	£332,591	-134.41
Harry Bannister	31-161	19	26	18	18	£167,299	£249,830	-9.00
Stan Sheppard	29-182	16	15	19	22	£152,498	£211,028	+6.48
Jamie Bargary	29-275	11	33	36	25	£234,008	£419,533	-78.67
Craig Nichol	29-307	9	26	30	41	£156,067	£240,716	-102.66
Brendan Powell	29-317	9	33	31	30	£129,950	£223,277	-108.38
Trevor Whelan	29-327	9	32	26	43	£141,629	£320,710	-80.26
Richie McLernon	29-424	7	39	41	44	£150,113	£260,352	-156.70
Jake Greenall	27-243	11	23	26	27	£120,936	£210,096	-20.15
Kielan Woods	27-247	11	37	33	28	£117,867	£239,479	-32.58
Adam Wedge	27-303	9	37	39	46	£170,264	£389,376	-149.30
Jonathan Moore	26-154	17	10	23	17	£249,584	£326,728	+18.16
Charlie Deutsch	25-154	16	22	15	28	£185,418	£362,858	-30.36
Tom Bellamy	25-212	12	19	30	17	£178,003	£247,087	-29.27
Robert Dunne	25-239	10	18	31	25	£173,766	£302,317	-11.00
James Best	24-364	7	30	28	53	£208,659	£308,176	-162.75
Adam Nicol	23-209	11	19	21	20	£92,695	£139,631	-53.88
Jack Quinlan	23-217	11	16	29	23	£140,983	£191,289	-12.58
Liam Treadwell	22-178	12	16	19	11	£213,078	£286,203	-49.10
Thomas Dowson	22-206	11	27	20	24	£90,650	£142,100	-45.92

LAST SEASON'S LEADING JUMPS TRAINERS IN BRITAIN

Jockey	Wins-runs	Wins (%)	2nd	3rd	4th	Win prize	Total prize	Profit/loss (£)
Nicky Henderson	154-618	25	100	70	57	£1,883,035	£2,846,487	-113.50
Paul Nicholls	171-673	25	92	80	65	£1,733,594	£2,529,250	-78.39
Colin Tizzard	57-405	14	64	56	39	£1,449,147	£2,041,055	+8.75
Nigel Twiston-Davies	95-586	16	97	84	57	£950,480	£1,582,656	-122.54
Philip Hobbs	111-593	19	93	66	66	£1,004,400	£1,502,991	-92.03
Alan King	104-490	21	91	79	43	£937,375	£1,373,270	-77.18
Dan Skelton	118-698	17	134	101	66	£789,125	£1,329,107	-259.57
Tom George	71-342	21	50	53	29	£600,294	£1,095,737	+49.84
Jonjo O'Neill	78-689	11	84	76	74	£533,688	£1,013,159	-214.33
Willie Mullins	9-52	17	2	4	4	£754,757	£941,892	+9.58
Lucinda Russell	43-411	10	41	53	51	£800,213	£926,414	-73.25
Gordon Elliott	30-170	18	38	26	19	£454,054	£901,405	-16.17
Harry Fry	67-286	23	43	33	33	£648,881	£886,752	+1.52
Neil Mulholland	108-556	19	76	59	58	£602,408	£849,444	+12.93
David Pipe	59-487	12	47	42	72	£538,975	£778,983	-194.09
Venetia Williams	46-312	15	39	34	42	£449,363	£764,603	-83.55
Charlie Longsdon	51-412	12	66	53	40	£493,577	£723,415	-105.30
Fergal O'Brien	60-327	18	36	48	41	£433,222	£611,366	+55.43
Evan Williams	51-461	11	57	55	70	£279,448	£598,389	-157.01
Donald McCain	80-573	14	89	96	68	£351,310	£578,934	-126.20
Gary Moore	40-339	12	47	42	36	£334,052	£577,504	-110.79
Henry de Bromhead	3-34	9	6	4	1	£267,967	£523,388	-13.27
Warren Greatrex	58-320	18	48	53	31	£298,120	£518,501	-80.47
Malcolm Jefferson	40-202	20	49	21	24	£313,171	£504,073	-60.38
Tim Vaughan	71-536	13	49	53	58	£319,098	£478,013	-133.08
Jessica Harrington	3-14	21	1	0	3	£441,363	£477,948	+22.00
Peter Bowen	40-299	13	51	25	35	£319,607	£476,683	-60.11
Ian Williams	46-252	18	28	23	31	£320,788	£450,398	-10.87
Brian Ellison	45-230	20	33	34	30	£274,837	£432,337	-65.17
Rebecca Curtis	30-212	14	16	29	22	£301,181	£428,332	-10.09
Kim Bailey	43-325	13	58	43	35	£207,457	£411,619	-72.29
Sue Smith	41-280	15	33	36	41	£222,258	£373,889	-31.52
Emma Lavelle	35-185	19	25	25	18	£211,474	£373,745	+28.10
Nick Williams	19-147	13	18	20	23	£241,073	£369,928	-18.35
Nicky Richards	44-238	18	35	12	28	£223,254	£344,722	-7.15
Kerry Lee	22-160	14	31	19	20	£124,390	£307,344	-16.84
Ben Pauling	32-199	16	20	23	17	£224,682	£294,864	-8.42
Oliver Sherwood	22-196	11	28	27	19	£195,477	£294,188	-71.77
Richard Newland	35-167	21	23	21	15	£181,180	£291,037	-38.85
Anthony Honeyball	32-143	22	19	23	16	£213,711	£289,483	+13.24
Seamus Mullins	17-241	7	28	36	35	£165,506	£285,284	-43.38
Neil King	17-180	9	34	18	23	£78,961	£276,737	-89.51
Nigel Hawke	28-227	12	24	27	21	£201,705	£252,736	-55.68
Michael Scudamore	26-131	20	12	14	15	£188,745	£249,055	+19.42
David Dennis	20-267	7	38	37	32	£133,327	£233,757	-105.80
Chris Gordon	24-174	14	20	27	21	£133,244	£206,139	-20.24
Jeremy Scott	24-193	12	24	19	18	£114,144	£196,632	-62.00
Graeme McPherson	28-176	16	24	28	23	£113,192	£194,604	+69.08
Jennie Candlish	23-175	13	22	17	17	£129,871	£190,412	-65.79
Jamie Snowden	25-206	12	37	22	31	£107,713	£188,782	-67.48

2017 BRITISH JUMPS FIXTURES

OCTOBER

2	Mon	Newton Abbot, Stratford
3	Tue	Sedgefield, Southwell
4	Wed	Bangor
5	Thu	Huntingdon, Warwick
6	Fri	Fontwell, Hexham
7	Sat	Fontwell
8	Sun	Kelso, Uttoxeter, Limerick
11	Wed	Ludlow, Towcester
12	Thu	Exeter, Worcester
13	Fri	Newton Abbot
14	Sat	Chepstow, Hexham
15	Sun	Chepstow
17	Tue	Hereford, Huntingdon
18	Wed	Wetherby
19	Thu	Carlisle, Uttoxeter
20	Fri	Fakenham, Wincanton
21	Sat	Ffos Las, Market Rasen, Stratford
22	Sun	Kempton
23	Mon	Plumpton
24	Tue	Exeter
25	Wed	Sedgefield, Worcester
26	Thu	Carlisle, Ludlow, Southwell
27	Fri	Cheltenham
28	Sat	Cheltenham, Kelso
29	Sun	Aintree, Wincanton
30	Mon	Ayr
31	Tue	Bangor, Chepstow

NOVEMBER

1	Wed	Fakenham, Taunton
2	Thu	Sedgefield, Stratford
3	Fri	Uttoxeter, Wetherby
4	Sat	Ascot, Ayr, Wetherby
5	Sun	Carlisle, Huntingdon
6	Mon	Plumpton, Southwell
7	Tue	Exeter
8	Wed	Chepstow, Musselburgh
9	Thu	Ludlow, Market Rasen, Newbury
10	Fri	Fontwell, Hexham, Warwick
11	Sat	Aintree, Kelso, Wincanton
12	Sun	Ffos Las, Sandown
13	Mon	Carlisle, Kempton
14	Tue	Hereford, Huntingdon, Lingfield
15	Wed	Ayr, Bangor, Exeter
16	Thu	Ludlow, Taunton
17	Fri	Cheltenham, Newcastle
18	Sat	Cheltenham, Uttoxeter, Wetherby
19	Sun	Cheltenham, Fontwell
20	Mon	Leicester, Plumpton
21	Tue	Fakenham, Southwell
22	Wed	Chepstow, Hexham, Warwick
23	Thu	Market Rasen, Wincanton
24	Fri	Ascot, Catterick, Ffos Las
25	Sat	Ascot, Haydock, Huntingdon
26	Sun	Exeter, Uttoxeter
27	Mon	Ayr, Kempton, Ludlow
28	Tue	Lingfield, Sedgefield
29	Wed	Hereford, Wetherby
30	Thu	Musselburgh, Taunton, Towcester

DECEMBER

1	Fri	Doncaster, Newbury
2	Sat	Bangor, Doncaster, Newbury Newcastle
3	Sun	Carlisle, Leicester
4	Mon	Fakenham, Plumpton
5	Tue	Lingfield, Southwell
6	Wed	Haydock, Ludlow
7	Thu	Leicester, Market Rasen, Wincanton
8	Fri	Exeter, Sandown, Sedgefield
9	Sat	Aintree, Chepstow, Sandown Wetherby
10	Sun	Huntingdon, Kelso
11	Mon	Fontwell, Musselburgh
12	Tue	Ayr, Uttoxeter
13	Wed	Hexham, Leicester
14	Thu	Newcastle, Taunton, Warwick
15	Fri	Bangor, Cheltenham, Doncaster
16	Sat	Cheltenham, Doncaster, Hereford
17	Sun	Carlisle, Southwel
18	Mon	Ffos Las, Plumpton
19	Tue	Catterick, Fakenham
20	Wed	Ludlow, Newbury
21	Thu	Exeter, Towcester
22	Fri	Ascot, Uttoxeter
23	Sat	Ascot, Haydock, Newcastle
26	Tue	Fontwell, Huntingdon, Kempton Market Rasen, Sedgefield, Wetherby, Wincanton,
27	Wed	Chepstow, Kempton, Wetherby
28	Thu	Catterick, Leicester
29	Fri	Doncaster, Kelso
30	Sat	Haydock, Newbury, Taunton
31	Sun	Uttoxeter, Warwick

INDEX OF HORSES

INDEX OF HORSES

INDEX OF HORSES